100

QUESTIONS
EVERY FIRST-TIME
HOME BUYER
SHOULD ASK

ALSO BY ILYCE R. GLINK

*50 Simple Steps You Can Take to Sell Your Home Faster
and for More Money in Any Market*

*50 Simple Steps You Can Take to
Disaster-Proof Your Finances*

*50 Simple Steps You Can Take to
Improve Your Personal Finances*

*100 Questions You Should Ask
About Your Personal Finances*

*10 Steps to Homeownership:
A Workbook for First-Time Buyers*

100 Questions Every Home Seller Should Ask

100

QUESTIONS EVERY FIRST-TIME HOME BUYER SHOULD ASK

With Answers from Top Brokers
from Around the Country

Third Edition

ILYCE R. GLINK

THREE RIVERS PRESS

NEW YORK

This book is intended as a general guide to the topics discussed and does not deliver accounting, personal finance, or legal advice. It is not intended, and should not be used, as a substitute for professional advice (legal or otherwise). You should consult a competent attorney and/or other professional with specific issues, problems, or questions you may have.

Company names, logos, and trademarks used in the book belong to the companies that own them. There is no attempt to appropriate these names, logos, and trademarks, and none should be construed. Also, there is no endorsement, implied or otherwise, of the companies listed in this book. They are used to illustrate the types of places, software, or information centers where readers can find more information. Finally, company names, phone numbers, addresses, and websites may have changed since the publication of this book.

For an up-to-date list of websites, or to contact Ilyce Glink, please visit her website, www.thinkglink.com.

Published in the United States by Three Rivers Press, an imprint of the Crown Publishing Group, a division of Random House, Inc., New York.
www.crownpublishing.com

THREE RIVERS PRESS and the Tugboat design are registered trademarks of Random House, Inc.

Library of Congress Cataloging-in-Publication Data

Glink, Ilyce R., 1964–
100 questions every first-time home buyer should ask : with answers from top brokers from around the country / Ilyce R. Glink.—3rd ed.
Includes index.
1. House buying. 2. Residential real estate—Purchasing. 3. House buying—United States. 4. Residential real estate—Purchasing—United States. I. Title: One hundred questions every first-time home buyer should ask. II. Title.
HD1379.G58 2005
643'.12—dc22   2004020973

ISBN 1-4000-8197-1

Printed in the United States of America

Design by Sarah Gubkin

10 9 8 7 6 5

Third Edition

For my mother, Susanne,
who is the kind of real estate agent
every home buyer dreams of;

for Sam, Alex, and Michael,
without whom my home would be just a house;

and in memory of Harry, Maddie, and Lexi Bull:
may their sunny smiles and happy hearts live on in us always.

Contents

x

Preface

Whether you're a first-time buyer or purchasing your first investment property, your first newly constructed house or your first house in 30 years, you've come to the right place.

This book is a book for first-time buyers and anyone who feels even a bit unsure about the process of buying a house. Others who might find this book helpful include buyers who bought homes within the past few years but had trouble with their agents, the negotiation process, the inspection, the closing, or any of the pieces that go into the complex game called real estate.

But first-time buyers are a breed apart. Brokers say the moment first-time buyers walk into the house of their dreams and realize it is affordable, a glow of complete satisfaction settles on their faces; it is the thrill of finally achieving the American Dream.

The idea for this book came to me as I was writing an article for the "Your Place" section of the *Chicago Tribune* at the start of my career as a real estate and money journalist many years ago. The article was supposed to be about the questions first-time buyers ask. The brokers I interviewed told me all first-time buyers ask the same questions—over and over again. I easily culled a dozen questions from my interviews with brokers. And then another dozen. Over the years, I've added to, and refined, the questions on that list. In this third edition, there are perhaps a dozen new questions, and many more that have been completely rewritten. Because the real estate industry has continued to undergo a remarkable revolution since the last edition of this book was published, almost every *answer* contains changes as well.

One thing remains loud and clear: Home buying is complicated and becomes more so every time the government tries to simplify the process. First-time home buyers often don't know what questions to ask. Even seasoned home buyers don't remember to ask every question they should. In real estate deals, those unasked, unanswered questions are often the ones that cause the most trouble.

This new edition of *100 Questions Every First-Time Home Buyer Should Ask* leads you through the maze of purchasing property by answering questions that pop up at different checkpoints along the way. You'll find plenty of information about shopping for a home and a loan on the World Wide Web, moving across state lines, and buying a brand-new home. The appendixes include a list of things you can do to save money on your home purchase, as well as an updated state-by-state guide that tells you where to file complaints against your mortgage lender and real estate agent or broker, an enhanced General Resources section, and a listing of all the websites used in this book. After this book goes to press, I'll continue to update those lists and add new information as it becomes available, on my website, www.thinkglink.com.

I've tried to phrase these 100 questions in a way that you would think about them and ask them. And I've tried to explain the answers in a way you would understand and recognize. There are two ways to use this book. You can read it cover to cover, starting with the introduction. Or you can pick it up when you have a question, find your question, and read the answer. I recommend you do both.

Good luck. And happy house hunting!

ILYCE R. GLINK
Autumn, 2004

P.S.: Buying a home is an extraordinary experience. If you'd like to share your stories, or if you have questions or comments, please write to me at P.O. Box 366, Glencoe, Illinois 60022. My e-mail address is Ilyce@thinkglink.com and my website is www.thinkglink.com. If you'd like to hear from me regularly, please sign up for my free web newsletter.

100

QUESTIONS EVERY FIRST-TIME HOME BUYER SHOULD ASK

Introduction

So you want to buy your first home. Well, you're not alone; according to a recent report, more than 2 million first-time home buyers purchase property each year. More than 21 million first-time-buyer families purchased a home in the past decade. Many of those sold their homes a few short years later, pocketed fat profits, and traded up to a home that was a bit closer to the house of their dreams.

In many areas of the country, first-time home buyers account for more than half of all home buyers. In some years, in some parts of the country, first-time home buyers accounted for two-thirds of all home buyers. First-time home buyers are expected to remain a large percentage of all home buyers throughout this decade. One reason is that interest rates are historically low. (How low? Anything below 8 percent is considered very low. In the past 15 years, interest rates stayed below that mark except for a few months, here and there.)

The baby boomers have also helped prop up the first-time buyer market. They've had kids, and those members of the "boomlet" (as it is often called) are going to need a place to live. The formation of new households has been strong as well, thanks to more people getting divorced and an influx of immigrants. Harvard University's Joint Center for Housing Studies said immigrants accounted for 27 percent of the households in 2003 and will contribute at least two-thirds of net household growth in the coming decades.

Hispanics (including those who were born in the United States and those who have immigrated to this country) are the fastest-growing minority group in the United States. In states like California, Hispanics make up a sizable amount of all first-time buyers.

1

Single women (and single mothers) are also a fast-growing component of the current housing boom, which is amazing, considering the institutionalized sexism that was once rife in the banking world. Less than a generation ago, many lenders viewed unmarried women who bought property as suspect. I'm happy to report that these lenders have been enlightened.

Finally, most first-time home buyers are working couples who are free to purchase a home the moment they have saved enough money for the down payment; they, unlike the rest of the home-buying population, are not already tied down to a property. They do not have to sell before they buy.

I'm often asked if the real estate market is going to continue to be as strong going forward as it has been since 1988, when I started my journalism career. Although I often joke that my crystal ball is cracked, I do believe that the continuing influx of immigrants, the formation of new households, and our own need to upgrade our standard of living will remain strong. Economists agree. Some believe housing growth will be at least 10 percent higher between 2005 and 2015 than previously projected, with perhaps 13 million new households. All of those people will need a place to live. And perhaps someday, one of them will make an offer for the house you're about to buy.

If you're nervous about taking your first steps toward homeownership, take heart. My grandfather used to say that there was no line too long, as long as there was someone standing in line behind you. Plenty of first-time buyers have walked this path before you, and millions more will walk it long after you close on your first home. There is some comfort in that. This year, you and 2 million other first-time-buyer families will embark on the same voyage. Like you, they will also be learning the language of real estate, with an entirely new vocabulary. You will learn to be selective in choosing a new home, smart in negotiating for that home, careful in inspecting it, and adept at piecing together the details for closing on it.

Real estate agents and brokers say first-time buyers have a naïveté that is genuine and enjoyable. One broker from Florida says working with first-time buyers is like taking your children to Walt Disney World for the first time. Their excitement is contagious. It's easy for a broker to get excited about working with someone who's excited about the prospects of homeownership. Once you've bought and sold your fourth, fifth, or tenth house, looking for a home can become commonplace or even a chore: It isn't necessarily fun for you and it isn't fun for your broker. First-time buyers, for all their questions, for all the hand-holding brokers do, reinvigorate the process of purchasing real estate.

Who Are You?

For years, Chicago Title & Trust conducted a useful survey called "Who's Buying Houses in America." The survey was based on the hundreds of thousands of closings the company and its affiliates conducted each year for home buyers and sellers. It identified the fact that more minority, singles, and never-married first-time buyers were purchasing homes. Over the years, it recognized that first-time buyers were getting older (their average age is over 32 years) and estimated that more time was required to save enough cash for a down payment.

Unfortunately, since the last update of this book, Chicago Title & Trust no longer conducts the study, and I have not yet been able to find a worthy replacement in terms of statistics. But I have pieced together a little bit of information about first-time buyers from other sources, including the U.S. Census, Fannie Mae, and the National Association of Realtors (NAR).

Typically, first-time buyers put down less than 15 percent in cash on their home, and that number has been falling in recent years as more zero-down and super-low-down-payment-options have become available. A new trend is to see first-time buyers use much more creative financing techniques, like interest-only mortgages, and to be increasingly proactive in refinancing their property. A newly identified segment of first-time buyers are 21 to 25 years of age, and some first-timers have begun to purchase their first house as an investment. They never even live in it.

According to the Department of Housing and Urban Development, the average first-time buyer looks at more than 10 homes over a period of about six months. Here's a confession: When my husband, Sam, and I were looking for a house to buy, we looked at more than 100 homes, over four years, and in 10 neighborhoods, before we found the 1880s farmhouse we bought in 1994. So don't feel bad if you end up looking at more homes than the "average" first-time buyer.

Increasingly, first-time buyers are purchasing more expensive homes. In 2004, for example, the median price of a home was $170,800, which was up from $160,400 the previous year. A family of four had a median income of $62,228, which would normally mean that homeownership would have been out of reach, except for historically low interest rates. First-time buyers are also purchasing more newly constructed homes than ever before. One reason for this is because most first-time buyers spend almost everything they have to buy their first homes, and they don't have any left over to fix up the property once they've closed; therefore, they opt for buying new construction rather than an older home that may need renovation or repairs.

Since this book was first published, the sophistication of first-time buyers has grown tremendously. With the advent of the Internet, more information is available than ever before (perhaps even more than is necessary to successfully complete your purchase). Many home buyers are using the Internet to gain market, demographic, and sales information about neighborhoods in which they're interested. They check out interest rates online, read real estate news feeds, and investigate companies with which they'd like to do business. More than 70 percent of all home buyers start their search for a home on the Internet.

As more quality information becomes more readily available, I believe the sophistication of home buyers, particularly first-time buyers, will continue to grow. Although some real estate agents and lenders are wary of home buyers who possess knowledge about the process and about what they want, most are glad to work with buyers who understand what's supposed to happen and how to get from showings to the closing. Those agents and lenders who fail to encourage the understanding of first-time buyers will ultimately see their business dry up.

Jim, a longtime Chicago broker, has worked with hundreds of first-time buyers in his years of brokerage. "First-time buyers are sophisticated, motivated people with money to spend," he says. "But they're sophisticated enough to know they need education and guidance. They know that while they're nervous about making the biggest purchase of their life, education is an antidote to fear."

Are You Ready to Buy a Home?

Think about that question for a moment. Are you really ready to make the commitment required by homeownership?

The answer is more complicated than you might imagine. There is a chasm of difference between a homeowner and a renter. Renters are free to pick up and move at a moment's notice, provided their lease is up or they find someone to sublet their rental apartment or house. Homeowners, while able to list their property for sale, are more vulnerable to the changing tides of the marketplace and must usually wait for their property to sell before moving on.

People rent for many reasons, including:

- They haven't saved up enough money for the down payment.
- They are in a job that may require them to move from location to location.
- They are unsure about where they want to live.
- They believe they can make more money in investments other than a home.
- They don't want to be tied down.
- They think they can't afford what they really want.
- Their personal life is unsettled.
- They are unmarried and believe they shouldn't buy a home until they have found their soul mate.
- They are uneducated about the benefits of homeownership.

If you ask home buyers why they bought, they might tell you:

- It's part of the American Dream.
- Their parents told them it's the single best investment they can make.
- They've saved up enough money for a down payment.
- They see it as an enforced savings plan (since a portion of every mortgage payment is principal and contributes to the equity you have in the home).
- They're tired of "throwing money away" on a rented apartment.
- They don't want to deal with landlords.
- They just want a place to call home.

The Psychology of Homeownership

Clearly, there is a strong psychological barrier between owning and renting.

Frank and Julie have rented an apartment in Chicago for more than 40 years. Sue, a residential real estate broker and Julie's friend, asked her why she still rents, when, in the past 40 years, she could have bought a house or condo and completely paid off the mortgage. Instead, 40 years later, all Frank and Julie have to show for their $624,000 (40 years × $1,300 per month average rent × 12 months per year) are rent payment receipts. Julie said she and Frank never could agree on where to live. He wanted to be downtown near his work, and she thought they'd eventually move to the suburbs. They liked their apartment building and thought if it went condo, they'd buy then. It didn't, and there was always another excuse not to buy a place to live.

My mother, on the other hand, recently sold the home she lived in for nearly 40 years. It was her first home and she bought it for around $35,000 when I was just a couple of years old. She sold it for around 20 times more than she paid. Not everyone will earn that kind of appreciation on their property, but it's a good lesson in how steady appreciation year after year can add up to a whole lot of cash.

Are you psychologically ready for the responsibilities that come with buying and owning a home?

Buying a home means more than simply making a monthly mortgage payment. It also means paying taxes, maintenance costs, and insurance premiums. If you buy a condo, town house, or co-op, you're also taking on the added responsibility of monthly assessments for maintenance of the commonly held areas of the property, like the garage or party room. If you're a homeowner, you shoulder the burden of home maintenance yourself. If the roof leaks, you have to fix it. If the boiler breaks, you must replace it. There is no landlord to call.

As a homeowner, you also shoulder the burden of real estate taxes. You become one of those homeowners who support the local school system, fire and police departments, and city government. Buying a home means you're also buying into your local community. And if someone wants to put a trash dump next door to your house, you'd better be out there fighting against it to protect your property's value.

(After we moved into our 1880s farmhouse, we discovered that the village had a plan in place to widen our street. We spent the first five years we lived in the home fighting the village. The road was completed just before the second edition of this book was published. Not only was the road not widened, parts of it were narrowed. Narrowing, resurfacing, and redoing the landscape on this road will undoubtedly increase the value of our home—and those of our neighbors—over time. As I was completing the third edition of this book, I received a letter from the village proposing, on its own, to narrow the rest of the street. Although these are the same people who once suggested that a wider, four-lane road was safer (for cars, not necessarily people), they now recognize that a smaller, two-lane road with a middle turning lane is the best and safest way to go.

Being a home buyer means you are somewhat subject to the ebb and flow of the market. Although the first-time buyer market is hot now, that could change. If it does, that two-bedroom condo you bought in a bidding war three years ago could sit for 60 to 120 days before you receive a single offer. Renters, on the other hand, can leave at the end of their lease, or they can sublet their unit. Homeowners must either rent out their homes or sell. Neither is an attractive option under pressure.

But homeownership has lots of benefits that compensate nicely for most hardships. In addition to having a place to call your own, you receive support in the form of tax breaks from the federal government. You may deduct the interest you pay on your mortgage, plus any points paid to obtain your loan. You may also take a deduction for your real estate property taxes. If you work out of your home, there are a number of tax benefits, including a deduction for the costs associated with owning and maintaining the portion of the home you use exclusively for business. When you sell the home, current tax law allows you to take the first $250,000 (up to $500,000 if you're married) in capital gains profits tax-free. That's right, the profit is completely tax-free, as long as you've lived in your home for two of the last five years. And you don't even have to tell Uncle Sam about it unless your profit exceeds this amount.

Perhaps the best reason to own a home is that, traditionally, homeownership has been an excellent financial investment. While real estate has often been used to hedge against inflation, during the 1990s, real estate prices increased anywhere from 10 to 100 percent per year in many neighborhoods across the country. For many people, real estate far outperformed the stock market!

Although those kinds of gains can't be counted on every year, real estate appreciation does tend to outpace inflation. In addition, paying down a mortgage offers homeowners an enforced savings plan. Every mortgage payment is part interest and part principal. That little bit of principal is called home equity, and it adds up over time. When you sell, it becomes cash in your pocket.

Over time, studies have shown that the younger you are when you purchase a home, the wealthier you'll be later in life. The main reason for this is you build up your equity mortgage payment by mortgage payment. But perhaps it is also because homeowners tend to spend a fair bit of time thinking about their finances. When you have financial obligations, like a regular mortgage payment due each month, you better know where the cash is going to come from to pay that bill.

If you've already decided you're "in the market" to buy a home, then this book ought to help. It will tell you what questions to ask and then answer those questions in easy-to-understand English. There are no stupid questions in the complex game of real estate. There are only those questions that never seem to get answered.

Women and Real Estate

I'm often asked what changes I see taking place in the real estate industry. A major change in the past generation is that more women are purchasing real estate by themselves. There are more single mothers, divorced mothers, and single women who have good jobs and who have become aware of the financial benefits of homeownership. They, too, want to buy their piece of the American Dream.

But women often face special challenges when purchasing property alone. The decision to buy seems fraught with peril, and the fears that couples have about their purchase seem heavier when sitting on only one pair of shoulders. The financial responsibility is, of course, borne by one, not two. Not all of the female members of the current generation of first-time buyers (who are typically in their twenties and thirties) have been taught that they *can* purchase and maintain property by themselves. These fears and insecurities are often reinforced by naïve or prejudiced brokers who sometimes forget that they must see beyond the curves; the person they are showing around is first and foremost a first-time buyer. Not a man or woman. Not a person of color. Simply, a first-time buyer.

The good news is that since this book was first published, many more women are feeling strong enough to make a purchase on their own. Some are keeping these homes after they marry as investments. It's a good, strong start to a successful financial future.

Malka's Story

There's an old joke in real estate: If you want to get married, buy a studio apartment.

That's what happened to Malka. She rented for years in New York City but finally decided (after helping me publish the first edition of this book) enough was enough. She was no longer going to wait to meet the "man of her dreams" before she acquired real estate. So after much searching, she bought a one-bedroom, co-op apartment.

Sure enough, within six months, she met Mr. Wonderful. It turned out that her apartment was located in the same building that his son and ex-wife lived in! Talk about close quarters.

After Malka got married, she continued to live in her apartment, while Mr. Wonderful lived in his. Within six months of taking their vows, they got rid of both homes and moved in together.

Today, women have more opportunities for involvement with real estate than ever before. In earlier, less enlightened times, women had little opportunity to purchase real estate for themselves and, in fact, were prohibited from owning or inheriting real estate in most of the world. Unfortunately, this kind of rampant discrimination continues to flourish in places such as England, where daughters may still not inherit their fathers' titles of nobility, though now the eldest child of the monarch, whether male or female, can inherit the crown. (Apparently, this will start with Prince William's children, so Princess Anne is out of luck!)

In numerous instances, women have encountered severe and disheartening discrimination and prejudice when trying to buy or sell real estate. When my husband, Sam, and I were shopping for a loan, we went first to the bank where my family has had numerous accounts for more than 50 years. The loan officer (a woman!) looked first at my husband's robust lawyer's salary and then at my smaller freelance-writer's income. With a withering look, she said, "Your income doesn't matter. Only your husband's counts." And she continued the meeting addressing him only.

I was humiliated and ashamed. And at that moment, as I think happens with anyone who experiences hateful prejudice, bias, or bigotry, a little bit of me withered up and died.

Unfortunately, this sort of thing happens all the time. Recently, a professional woman who makes an excellent six-figure salary complained that when she took over the bidding process after her fiancé left town, their broker didn't believe she had "really been given the authority to make an offer and counteroffer." This successful first-time buyer was insulted, and rightly so. There are thousands of these cases. I'd like to be able to say that the discrimination is occurring with less frequency, and perhaps it is. Certainly, I have an equal number of stories where women purchased homes successfully. And more women are purchasing property on their own, so lenders are getting more used to the idea. It's a little more than ironic, however, that the discrimination persists since many women are employed within the real estate industry as brokers, agents, loan officers, and appraisers.

Minority Discrimination

Any discrimination is deplorable. That said, it's best to acknowledge that we live in an imperfect world. We must do what we can to surmount obstacles others have put in our path and strive to achieve our goals.

During the 1990s, a large influx of immigrant home-buying families helped boost homeownership to record levels. Studies showed that an immigrant family's desire to purchase a home far exceeds that of an ordinary American household. Everywhere I traveled, including New York, Boston, Atlanta, Texas, California, and of course in my hometown of Chicago, I met immigrant families who were buying homes only one to three years after arriving in this country. They worked two or three jobs, in some cases making enormous personal sacrifices, all in the name of homeownership. Some of the stories were truly awe-inspiring.

The number of Hispanic and Asian first-time home buyers skyrocketed in the 1990s, and shows no sign of slowing down in this new millennium. Studies show that Spanish-speaking buyers will soon account (if they don't already) for the majority of first-time home buyers in California.

Unfortunately, minorities, particularly African Americans and Hispanics, receive the brunt of the worst kind of discrimination. Study after study has documented that African Americans seem to be rejected for home loans twice as often as Caucasians.

So far, no one has been able to pinpoint the exact reasons, but there are some good guesses. Some say loan officers "redline" a specific neighborhood or town, meaning they don't make loans in certain areas because there is a high rate of default. Others say loan officers simply don't like to make loans to minorities.

Whatever the reason, if you're a member of a minority group or a woman, you'll have to work twice as hard to get your loan. Just remember, homeownership is well worth it. However, if you feel you have a legitimate beef, contact your local office of the Department of Housing and Urban Development (HUD) to file a complaint.

It All Comes Down to You

Your home-buying experience will ultimately be whatever you make of it. As I see it, your job is to remove any obstacle that stands in the way of your ability to purchase property.

Let your broker know that you have the authority and financial wherewithal to make an offer and follow through on it (but don't tell too much about your finances). Don't be afraid to admit what you don't know, but don't appear too weak and indecisive, either.

Take control of the process. Take advantage of the huge amount of information and resources available through the Internet. Keep asking questions until you get answers you understand. Don't let the broker take advantage of your time or good nature. Be confident about asserting yourself. Don't allow the broker to force you to make a decision before you're ready. Remember, you have the money. You're doing the buying. You've got all the cards.

Of course, if you find yourself talked down to, or treated badly, don't hesitate to confront the managing broker about the situation and ask for help. You can also switch brokerage firms if you feel your needs aren't being met. There are hundreds of real estate agents and brokers who will be delighted to help you feel good about the process, and about yourself, and will just as happily collect their share of the commission once you close on your first home.

And that's what it's all about: closing on your first home. Allow me to be your tour guide, with this book as a road map—and with the closing as your final destination.

Let's get going.

1

How Do I Know
What I Want?

**You can't always get what you want. But if you try sometimes,
well you just might find you get what you need.**

Rolling Stones

The difference between being a wannabe and a successful home buyer
may boil down to nothing more than knowing the difference between
what you want in a home and what you can't live without.

It sounds simple, but that difference requires an ability to recognize
what's really important to you and compromise on the rest. Unfortunately, our ability to compromise is often lost between two spouses or
partners who forget that they can't afford to satisfy their every whim.

It might make you feel better to know that an inability to compromise
isn't limited to first-time buyers. Each time we buy a home, we feel
that this is the time we're going to get—or should get—everything
we want. We work hard and deserve it, right? But life doesn't work
that way, and neither does home buying. The next few questions are
designed to give you some insight into what's really important to you
and your family.

20/20

hindsight

13

QUESTION 1

SHOULD I MAKE A WISH LIST?
WHAT ABOUT A REALITY CHECK?

First, let's talk about what exactly constitutes a wish list. A wish list is nothing more than a list of everything you've ever dreamed of having in your house: granite or slate kitchen countertops (or perhaps inlaid, stained concrete), a wood-burning fireplace, three-car garage, four-person whirlpool, the best school district in your state, a five-minute walk to work, four bedrooms, a master suite with his and her closets, and vaulted ceilings. You get the picture.

The best real estate agents and brokers will ask their first-time buyers to create a wish list detailing everything they'd love to have in a home, including:

1. **Location.** Think about where you like to shop, where your children will attend school, where you work, where you worship, and where your friends and family live.

2. **Size.** Think about the number of bedrooms you want, the garden size, the extra room you may need for expansion or family flexibility, where you'll do the laundry, what kind of storage space you need, and if you need a home office.

3. **Amenities.** Think about the garage, kitchen and bathroom appliances, swimming pool, fireplace, air-conditioning, electrical wiring, furnace, and hardwood floors.

4. **Condition.** Do you want a home in move-in condition? Or are you willing to put in some "sweat equity," to borrow a *This Old House* phrase, to build in value?

At first glance, many of these items may seem to be in conflict with each other: You want to be close to a transportation network so it's easy to get around, and yet you want a quiet and peaceful neighborhood. You might want to walk to work, but when you come home, you want your home to be silent and secure. You want a wide variety of shopping, and yet you also need to be close enough to your health club to use it on a regular basis. You want to take advantage of the city, and yet live in the suburbs.

But that's what a wish list is all about. If you're honest about what you want, the inconsistencies and conflicts will come out. Most first-time buyers are confused by all their choices. First-time buyers take on that "kid in a candy store" mentality: Many have difficulty choosing

14

between different styles of homes. One broker says she always has a few first-time buyers each year who need to see at least one of everything in the area: a California ranch, an old Victorian, an in-town condo, and several new subdivisions. It takes a tremendous amount of time, which is wasted if the buyer decides ultimately to go with a loft.

Some agents and brokers also use a tool to help their clients define their needs as well as their wants. They call this a reality check.

Joanne, a real estate sales associate in New Jersey, says she asks her first-time buyers very specific questions about what they need to survive in their first home. "I just know their pocketbook will not allow them to have everything they want. I tell them they'll begin to get what they want with their second home. Not the first."

Here are some of the questions Joanne might ask:

- How many bedrooms do you need?
- How many children do you have or are you planning to have while you live in this home?
- Is a garage absolutely necessary?
- Why do you need a home with a basement or an attic?
- Do you use public transportation on a daily basis?
- How close to work do you need to be?
- Does driving on a major expressway or in traffic make you crazy?
- Do you want to care for a garden or would you prefer a maintenance-free home?

By asking specific questions about your daily lifestyle, Joanne and other brokers can center in on the best location, home size, and amenities for your budget. They can read between the lines on your wish list.

Wish lists and reality checks have another use. By prioritizing the items on these lists, a good real estate agent can tell which items you might be willing to trade off. For example, if the first wish on your list is to have a four-bedroom, two-bath house, and the 38th item is a wood-burning fireplace, then the broker knows you'd probably prefer a four-bedroom, two-bath house without a fireplace to a three-bedroom, two-bath home with a fireplace.

The bottom line is this: Unless you win the lottery or are independently wealthy, you're probably going to have to make some trade-offs when buying your first home.

And sometimes you're going to make a mistake.

The general rule about new construction these days is that you'll get a brand-new place with new appliances, new windows, and the rest, but you'll likely have to make some trade-offs to swing it. If the average existing home costs $170,000 in a major market, the average price of new construction typically tops $225,000. So if you can only spend $170,000, the trade-offs will generally include the overall size of the home and where it's located. Also don't be fooled by the list price of a unit. The typical new construction buyer spends 10 to 15 percent above the "list" price in upgrades, so factor that into your budgeting.

Ilyce and Sam's Story

When Sam and I bought our first place together (a vintage Chicago co-op built in the 1920s), we didn't own a car. Since we lived in the city, overlooking Lake Michigan, and had easy access to public transportation, we couldn't even envision that one day we might change our minds and purchase a car. Our wish list included a parking place, but it was low on the list, maybe around the 20th item.

On the other hand, a wood-burning fireplace was pretty high on the list, about number five. You can guess what happened. When we were given a car a few years later, and began hunting and pecking for parking spaces on the street, we were sorry (particularly on cold, snowy, below-zero Chicago nights) that we didn't have a space in which to park the car. But not as sorry as when we went to sell our unit and discovered that most home buyers in that area won't even consider a building that doesn't have parking. Fewer people cared about the fireplace, although we loved it.

You can bet that a two-car garage was right near the top of our list for the next home we purchased.

Brokers say the best wish list should include everything you want in a home, such as location, schools, shopping, and distance to work. If your initial list says "nice house, four bedrooms," try asking yourself these questions to stimulate your true desires.

- How often do I go to the city? Suburbs? Country? Where would I rather be?
- How long do I want to spend driving to work each day?

- Do I have frequent guests? Do I need a separate guest room?
- Do I work from home? Does my spouse or partner? Do we need separate office space?
- Do I want a special play area for my children?
- Will my children take a bus to school or walk, or will I have to drive them?
- How far away is my house of worship?
- Do I want a big garden?
- Must I have a garage? For two cars? Three cars? Do I need a dedicated parking space?
- How far away is the airport? Grocery store? Dry cleaner? Gym?
- What is my favorite form of recreation and how far away is it?
- Where does my family live? Where do my friends live? How far away from them do I want to be?
- Do I want a home that is in mint condition (also called "blue ribbon" condition by some people in various parts of the country)? Or do I want to buy a small house on a large lot and fix it up or even add onto it over time?

Questions of lifestyle are crucial components of a wish list. Do you and your spouse like to stay in on Saturday nights? Or do you prefer to be "close to the action." And will that change over the years? Are you a single woman or married with children? Are you a single parent? Gay couple? Do you travel frequently? Do you own a car? Do you own, or are you contemplating purchasing, a boat in the near future? Will you want to be within 15 minutes of the marina?

You can see how personal preferences feed into the list. Each spouse or partner has to create his or her own wish list. Then, together, you negotiate the wishes via a reality check. Use the worksheets that follow.

Once you get the information down on paper, try to organize it into a concrete sentence: "I want a four-bedroom, three-bath home with a large garden, fairly new kitchen, loads of closet space, a wood-burning fireplace, and a two-car garage, within a 15-minute commute to the office and church, down the street from the high school, in such-and-such location."

That's a start. Now, prioritize the items in your wish list and think about which items you'd trade off for others. For example, would you give up a wood-burning fireplace if it meant having a two-car garage?

You and your spouse or partner should each create your own wish lists and reality checks (see next worksheet for how to create a reality check). After you're done, sit together and work through each item. Since you'll only be able to afford one home, create one wish list and one reality check from which to start your search.

Your Wish List

Item	You	Spouse/Partner
1.	_____	_____
2.	_____	_____
3.	_____	_____
4.	_____	_____
5.	_____	_____
6.	_____	_____
7.	_____	_____
8.	_____	_____
9.	_____	_____
10.	_____	_____
11.	_____	_____
12.	_____	_____
13.	_____	_____
14.	_____	_____
15.	_____	_____
16.	_____	_____
17.	_____	_____
18.	_____	_____
19.	_____	_____
20.	_____	_____

Note: If your list exceeds 20 items, continue on a blank sheet of paper until everything is in writing. Be as specific and detailed as possible. Being specific will make it easier for your agent to assist you in finding the right home.

Each spouse or partner does his or her own reality check. Afterward, you again sit together and work through each item. You'll be able to afford only one home, so you should end up with one list of basic needs.

Your Reality Check

Item	You	Spouse/Partner
1.	_____	_____
2.	_____	_____
3.	_____	_____
4.	_____	_____
5.	_____	_____
6.	_____	_____
7.	_____	_____
8.	_____	_____
9.	_____	_____
10.	_____	_____
11.	_____	_____
12.	_____	_____
13.	_____	_____
14.	_____	_____
15.	_____	_____
16.	_____	_____
17.	_____	_____
18.	_____	_____
19.	_____	_____
20.	_____	_____

Could you get by with a smaller house if it meant you'd be in a better school district? Would you prefer to be closer to work even though it means giving up a large garden? What if you had to live in a condo but could walk to work?

Again, if a wish list is everything you want in a home, a reality check is everything you can't live without. For example, you may want a four-bedroom home, but you absolutely need three bedrooms. You may want a large garden, but you really need a place to hang out outside and grill "dogs" and burgers for your friends. Your reality check may include many of the same items as your wish list, but perhaps in a pared-down version. This is the place where you want to be completely honest about the minimum you need to be comfortable in your home.

No two people are alike. No matter how compatible you and your spouse or partner are, you are two individuals and you're going to end up with two different (sometimes completely different) lists. But rather than denigrate each other's wish list or reality check items, try to view the lists as a statement of each person's priorities. Some of each person's priorities should make their way into your final wish list and reality check. If either list is too one-sided, you're headed for home-buying trouble.

From your reality check, create a single sentence that represents your basic needs for a home. If you're a single woman, your reality check might include: "I need two bedrooms (mostly for resale purposes), two bathrooms, a dedicated parking space or attached garage, some sort of outdoor living space, security in the building, and a 20-minute drive to work or less."

These details give your broker something to work with. He or she can take your wish list and begin to match it to homes listed in your local multiple-listing service. Are the wish list and reality check worth the time and effort? Brokers say they are. Even though a good broker will spend an hour or two divining the same information, writing up a wish list and reality check will help focus your mind on what you really want and what you can't live without.

An honest wish list is a road map to finding the house of your dreams.

How long you plan to stay in your home is critical to making all kinds of successful decisions when it comes to buying a home. How long you stay will affect everything from where you buy and what you buy to how to finance your home. Although you may have one time line in mind when you create your wish list and reality check ("We won't move until our youngest finishes high school" or ". . . until our home-based business requires larger office space"), later years may bring surprises. I'll talk about time-based planning throughout this book. For now, think carefully about your time line and how long you plan to live in your home when creating your wish list and reality check.

HOW DO I FIGURE OUT WHERE I WANT TO LIVE?

QUESTION 2

Finding the right location is a problem for many buyers, not just first-timers. In part, the answer will be decided in the spot where your bank account meets your wish list. Neighborhoods being what they are, you can almost certainly find something in your price range in an area in which you'd want to live.

In a story I once did for WGN-TV, I took at look at what was available for $220,000 in several different parts of the Chicago metropolitan area. What I found is that you could buy something in almost every location, from the fanciest suburbs to a more modest city neighborhood. What you'd have to do, however, is trade size or amenities for price. For example, when I did that story, $220,000 bought you a tiny one-bedroom apartment with an okay view just off of Michigan Avenue. Or you could spend the same amount of money and buy a three-bedroom ranch-style home in Hainesville, a far northwest suburban town, with a lovely garden, fireplace, sunken tub in the master bath, and a fully finished basement.

The same thing is true in almost every other urban area. For example, I'm sure you could find a relatively affordable one-bedroom condo in a suburb that also includes million-dollar homes. Buildings in Manhattan that contain apartments costing $10 million or more are right next to buildings in which the apartments go for a tiny fraction of that amount. But if you must have three bedrooms, that expensive suburb or building will most likely be out of your price range.

The point is, you can find something affordable in nearly every neighborhood. Whether it meets your needs is another story.

The first thing to do is to find a suburb or neighborhood that offers homes that meet your needs, at a price you can afford. Sometimes the easiest way to find what you're looking for is to cross out options that don't work for one reason or another. Start by asking your broker to cross-match your price range with your reality list. That should instantly narrow your choices to maybe several suburbs or neighborhoods. Now, take a close look at these areas, and apply some of the features of your wish list: Is one in a better school district? Is another closer to work? Does one have more character or better shopping? Is one located on a golf course? Is one nearer (or farther away from) your parents or in-laws?

Once you've narrowed down your choice of areas to two or three suburbs, neighborhoods, or even streets, take an extensive driving tour of these areas. Get out and walk around. Sit on a bench and watch the people go by. After all, these might be your future neighbors. Next, start looking at some of the houses in the neighborhood, perhaps during a Sunday open-house tour. If you begin to see homes you like in an acceptable, affordable neighborhood, you're on the right track.

web resources

The Internet has made shopping for a community a much easier task, particularly for out-of-state home buyers. There are websites for most major metropolitan areas, and many brokerage sites (both national and local) contain a fair amount of community information. You can shop for a home by going to a site and simply keying in some of the items on your reality checklist. For example, you can request all listing information for homes that match a particular description (say, four bedrooms, two baths, under $300,000) within a certain location. If nothing comes up that meets your needs, at the price you can afford, it may mean (1) the neighborhood is too expensive for your price range, (2) the type of housing in which you're interested doesn't exist, or (3) you need to try another website.

QUESTION 3

WHAT DOES "LOCATION, LOCATION, LOCATION" REALLY MEAN?

Among real estate industry professionals, "location, location, location" is called the broker's maxim. It's the credo that all real estate agents live by, and during the days, weeks, and months when your broker helps you search for a home, you're likely to hear this phrase more than once. What does it really mean?

Brokers say that successful buying and selling is linked to the location of the home. You can usually change everything about a home *except* its location. Think about it: You can paint, decorate, gut the interior of the house, replace the asphalt shingles with slate, put on new siding, add a deck, repave the driveway, and plant flowers. The only thing you can't do is move the home to a different location.

(Of course, some houses can be literally picked up and moved. People do buy houses that are slated to be torn down and move them to new locations. And there are mobile homes or manufactured homes that come prebuilt from a factory and are placed on a lot. That's not what we're talking about here. You're not going to move an apartment from midtown Manhattan to New Jersey. And no one takes a 150-year-old brick town house from Boston's North End and move it to Newburyport, Massachusetts.)

If the house of your dreams is located next to a railroad yard, you should probably just go back to sleep. A poor location will severely limit the property's ability to appreciate in value and will hamper your ability to sell the property quickly in the future. Look for the reasons why a house is priced very low or has been for sale for a long time.

Ed's Story

Ed, a real estate attorney, bought and sold several homes before he bought the one that backed up to Chicago's famous elevated train tracks, known as the "El." It was an 1880s brick two-story house with a nice yard that desperately needed some TLC.

But it backed up to the El. Trains run by there every 10 to 15 minutes, faster in rush hour. The whole house shakes. Ed stood for a while inside the house before he made an offer. He didn't seem to think it would be a problem. "You get used to it; I hardly even hear it." So he bought the house.

He proceeded to completely renovate it and even put in a sauna. When he decided to move to Texas, he put the house on the market. Two years later, it was still for sale, waiting for someone who wanted to spend several hundred thousand dollars buying an overimproved house in a good neighborhood, but in a very poor location.

What is a poor location? Defining *poor* is often a matter of taste. To brokers, a poor location means a home may be difficult to sell because it is located:

- Next to a railroad yard or railroad tracks.
- Near a toxic waste or municipal garbage dump.
- On top of, or next to, a freeway, expressway, or interstate highway.
- In the center of nightlife activity.
- Near a busy intersection, or on the busiest street in town, even if that street is a comparatively quiet rural lane.
- Next to a school.
- In the midst of gang territory or an otherwise high-crime area.
- On a run-down block or in a deteriorating neighborhood.
- In a city, town, or suburb having significant budget problems, poor public schools, or a lousy local economy.
- Backing up to, or next to, a type of housing that is different from the rest of the neighborhood. For example, if you're looking at a single-family house and all of the other single-family homes back up to other single-family homes, but the one you like backs up to an apartment complex, that could be a geographical problem.

Of course, plenty of people can spin what might normally be called a poor location into a positive selling point. If you buy a home in a run-down neighborhood that is surrounded by yuppie housing, you might be able to turn a nice profit as the neighborhood improves over the years. Being located next to a noisy high school may mean you can keep an eye on your children throughout the day.

20/20 hindsight

Location doesn't just refer to the particular suburb or neighborhood in which you live. It also refers to the block on which your home is located, and even to your home's placement on that block. If corner lots are more valuable in your neighborhood, and you live in the middle of the block, that's a geographic factor you're not going to be able to change. Since you can't change this factor, always think about how easy or difficult this home may be to sell *before* you make an offer to purchase.

A good location, on the other hand, is one that allows the owner to thoroughly enjoy every aspect of his or her home. It will be located close, but not too close, to shopping, restaurants, work, transportation, good schools, and so on. A good location is one that you can easily sell to someone else, giving you additional flexibility (not to mention peace of mind). If, when you're looking for homes, you're faced with the choice between a beautiful home in a lousy location, or a slightly smaller, less beautiful home in an excellent location, which one will you choose?

When you buy in a new development, you are often looking at a large, vacant cornfield with perhaps a spec house or two (houses the developer builds and furnishes to show you what the other homes in the development will be like). From that, you're supposed to extrapolate what the neighborhood will look like. When it comes to new construction, location is even more important. Certain lots will be deemed "premier," and the developer will charge a higher fee for them. For example, on a golf course development, lots that face the golf course might be two to three times as costly as lots that face the outside street. But they might also appreciate in value at twice the rate of a nonview lot. Should you buy the most expensive lot? Brokers say it depends what you want, and what you can afford. If you want to live on a golf course, and a golf course view is important to you, and you can afford it, then buy the view. If your choice is to buy a nonview lot or live outside the community, you might want to compromise the view just to get inside the gates. When you look at the developer's master plan for the area, think through which lots are most and least expensive and try to understand the developer's reasoning behind his or her pricing strategy. That could be important information when it comes time to sell.

HOW LONG DO I PLAN TO LIVE IN MY FUTURE HOME?

This may be the single most important question for you to answer in the book. Why? Because the answer directly affects the size and type of home you buy, where it's located, as well as the type of mortgage you use to finance your purchase.

Times have changed since our parents bought their homes. Chances are, unless they've retired or are in professions where they are required to relocate to different parts of the country from time to

time, your parents are still living in the home in which you grew up. My mother, Susanne, lived in the same co-op apartment building for nearly 40 years. It was the first (and only) apartment she and my father purchased. After more than 20 years as a top-selling real estate agent, she began to look around for a new place to buy. She finally found a brand-new building going up just a block and a half west of Michigan Avenue, on Chicago's near north side. At the end of 2003, the building was finally completed, and she moved into her new apartment. A few months later, she finally sold the co-op in which I was raised.

My mother's experience with homeownership is pretty typical of her generation. But it will likely be quite different from yours. Statistics from the National Association of Realtors (NAR), a national trade association based in Washington, DC, reveal that today, on average, people live in their homes only about 5 to 7 years. That's it. Then, they move. This number includes renters and homeowners. If you separate out the homeowner statistics, the number rises to between 7 and 10 years. To be sure, plenty of homeowners stay in one place for 10 or even 20 years. But there are also plenty who sell after 2 or 3 years.

Andy and Katie's Story

Andy and Katie met when he returned from years of working in Europe, and she was recently divorced with two young boys. They decided to get married and move from the Chicago suburb in which she lived to one five miles away that would be closer to where Andy worked.

But it didn't work out. The schools weren't right for Katie's boys, and they started to fail in their classes. So she signed them up for private school. She and Andy had their first baby together and got pregnant with a second right away. Suddenly, Katie thought about how much money she would be spending to send four children to private schools.

Instead, they sold their new home and moved back to the suburb where she and her children had been so happy for so many years. The compromise will be Andy's commute, which he is willing to make for the sake of their children.

How are you supposed to know how long you're going to live in your home? I suppose there's no way to know for sure—unless you're hiding a crystal ball from me. Here are some general guidelines, which I like to refer to as the Cycle of Life.

Cycle of Life

If you buy a home when you're young and single, but you are interested in having a long-term relationship or getting married, it's likely that what you can afford as a single person won't be quite enough space for two. Within five to seven years you'll probably find that long-term partner or spouse and will trade your one-bedroom or two-bedroom home for something larger.

If you're a newly married couple and want to have children, you'll probably start a family within a few years of your marriage. Within five to seven years, you'll need additional space as your family starts to grow (and their stuff multiplies exponentially).

If you get divorced or separated, that's another move. At that point, in your second or third home, with young children in school, you'll probably settle down for a while. You might even find a house in a good school district and decide to stay there for 10 to 15 years, until your children are through with school. If you remarry, you may need to move again.

Once your children are grown and out of the house for good, you might decide to sell your big house, take your profits (up to $250,000 for qualified single homeowners and up to $500,000 for married homeowners, tax-free) and move to a smaller condo somewhere warm or perhaps cold, if you like skiing.

A new trend in homeownership is "re-retirement," which basically means that seniors are picking up and moving several times during retirement, frequently crossing state lines to find a different place to call home.

And finally, it's possible that you'll purchase a second (or third) home, to which you may actually end up retiring. The most popular age to buy a second home is 55 to 65, followed by 45 to 55, followed by 65 to 75, which means the baby boomers are just beginning to enter their prime second-home-buying years. Statistics show if you buy one second home, you might likely buy two or three over your lifetime.

Moving as a National Pastime

National statistics tell us that the average family will move five to seven times during their lifetime. In addition to accommodating fluctuating family sizes (including grown-up children, grandchildren, and aging parents), buying and selling homes is one of the best ways to accumulate wealth. By purchasing a home, fixing it up, and selling it every five to seven years, you should be able to increase the size of your equity (the cash you have in your home) significantly over the course of your lifetime.

Ted and Susan's Story

Ted and Susan decided they were going to make money by buying fixer-upper properties, putting the time, effort, and cash into making them beautiful, and then selling them for a profit.

It's a good plan, and one that countless home buyers have made use of. But Ted and Susan were so successful that they ended up making hundreds of thousands of dollars in profit from the sale of each home. In one case, they bought a 6,000-square-foot apartment that had been foreclosed on. They gutted it and sold it for more than $2 million. They put that money into a house in a nearby suburb that cost $2.8 million. Over the next 15 months, they gutted it and put it on the market for $9.5 million.

Since the second edition of this book was published, the house was sold and Susan and Ted made millions on that property. The Tax Reform Act of 1997, which allows an individual to keep up to $250,000 (up to $500,000 for married couples) in profits tax-free, provided you've lived in your home at least two of the last five years, helps homeowners cash in on fixer-upper deals. You might not make millions from the sale of a home you've fixed up, but you'll get to keep a far larger portion of the profits today than was possible under earlier tax regulations.

But Wait! There's More . . .

Knowing how long you plan to live in your house is also crucial to choosing the correct mortgage. If you're only going to live in your home for five years, why would you choose a 30-year fixed-rate mortgage? The mortgage market has changed drastically since the early 1990s, and today there are excellent, flexible options that provide you with the stability of a fixed-rate loan (for as long as you'll need it) at a less-expensive interest rate. By choosing an alternative mortgage, such as a two-step mortgage, you might save yourself thousands of dollars over the life of the loan.

If you're going to stay in your home for 10 to 15 years, you might want a 15-year fixed-rate mortgage; when you sell the house, you'll own it free and clear and have a sizable amount of cash for your next purchase. Or you might get a 30-year fixed-rate loan and simply add a little extra to your monthly mortgage payment. (It's called *prepaying*, and it can be an excellent way for you to cut down the term of your mortgage and save yourself thousands of dollars in interest.)

If you have questions on mortgages, turn to the financing section of this book, beginning with Question 56).

Look Before You Leap

Before you start to look for a home, think about where you are in the Cycle of Life, and where you'll be (or hope to be) in five to seven years.

- Is marriage, a life partnership, or living with someone else a possibility within five to seven years?
- How many children do you plan to have during the next five to seven years?
- Are your children near or at school age? Have you chosen the school district you want for them?
- Is it likely you'll be transferred for your job within the next five to seven years?
- Do you have an aging parent in another part of the country who may require your close supervision or attention?
- Do you have an aging parent or post-college-age children who might be moving back home with you? Will you need flexible living space that your current home can't provide?

WHAT ARE THE DIFFERENT TYPES OF HOMES?

QUESTION 5

Your home is supposed to be your castle. But unless your name is Windsor, it's unlikely you'll end up living in one.

Several basic types of homes are commonly available in all parts of the country. They may, however, be called different names. For example, a "two-flat" in Chicago might be called a "two-family" in Boston or a "duplex" on the West Coast.

If you decide to buy a home, you'll end up choosing from a condominium, town house, cooperative apartment, or a single-family home. Or you might get a hybrid or a variation on one of these housing types. Each of these home types has numerous differences, from the rights of ownership to the way the property is maintained. As the saying goes, it's all in the details; knowing the differences between these types of homes is key to making a successful choice.

> If you don't know exactly what you're looking for, or what it is called, don't be shy about asking. Most good real estate agents or brokers would rather work with a knowledgeable buyer, even if they have to fill in the buyer's intelligence gaps along the way. If you plunge ahead, you may think you look smarter, but in the end, you'll just end up wasting a lot of your valuable time.

Condominium

Usually found in urban centers or densely populated suburbs, condos (as they are commonly referred to) became popular in the 1970s when state legislatures passed laws allowing their existence. An apartment building is converted to a condominium by means of a *condominium declaration* (often called a "condo dec"). New construction condominiums must also have a condo dec.

This declaration divvies up the percentage of ownership, defines which areas are commonly held by all owners, determines who is responsible for the maintenance of the property, and states the condo rules.

One of the most important things to remember about a condo is that you don't actually own the unit in which you live. Instead, you own the airspace inside the walls, ceiling, and floor of the unit, possibly the plumbing within your unit, and perhaps a parking space. (With new construction condos, you sometimes have to buy your parking space separately.) With your neighbors, you also jointly own what's known as the *common elements* of the property, which may include the roof, plumbing, common walls, lobby, laundry room, garden area, garden, or garage.

Condos don't always look like tall buildings. Condo developments can take the form of town houses (see page 34), duplexes (condos stacked two-by-two), or four-plexes (condos stacked four-by-four, also known as *quads*). You might get a two-family (or two-flat) house that's been turned into a condo. Or you can have a single-family, maintenance-free community in which the houses are actually condominiums. Suburban condos tend to stretch out (longer than higher). City condos tend to be in mid- or high-rise buildings.

New Construction   Developers building new condos, or renovating an old apartment building to turn it into condos, may keep control of the newly formed condo board or homeowners' association, until a certain percentage of the condos have been sold. This can present some difficulty, especially if there is a physical problem with the units (such as a leak) and the homeowners decide to sue the developer. Another issue to think about is that financing new construction can be tricky. Usually, the developer hooks up with a lender to fund the loans. But the national secondary mortgage market leaders (Fannie Mae and Freddie Mac) require that 70 percent of the units be occupied by homeowners before they will fund a loan. So if you decide to refinance before 70 percent of the units are occupied, you may have some trouble. Similarly, if 31 percent of owners decide to rent their units, you may also have trouble financing or refinancing your unit.

Maintenance   A condo association raises money for maintenance of the common elements through monthly assessments. The building's expenses (including the portion of your monthly payment that goes into the building's emergency reserve account) are tallied, then divided by the percentage of ownership, and then divided by 12. So if your annual share of the building maintenance cost is $2,400, you will pay $200 per month in assessments in addition to the costs of your mortgage and real estate taxes.

If you choose to buy a condo or a co-op (see below), you must understand that the lender will take into account the extra monthly payment you'll have to make and will readjust the amount it is willing to lend you. For example, the lender might tell you that you can purchase a $160,000 house or a $130,000 condo.

The condo declaration will divide up the ownership of the property. You, as a condo owner, will own a certain percentage. Typically, the tax assessor will levy a property tax on your entire condo building. Your share of the tax is typically equal to your percentage share of the building. That's why condo owners sometimes have a tougher time protesting their property taxes.

Cooperative Apartment

Before there were condos, homeowners owned their units by purchasing shares in a corporation that owned the building in which that unit was located. As my friend David puts it, if you own a condo, you own real estate that you can use to secure a mortgage. If you own a co-op, you own shares in a corporation that owns the real estate in which your apartment is located. The shares give you the right to lease your unit from the corporation. You pay a monthly assessment (often called a lease payment or rent) based on the number of shares you own in the corporation.

One sticky issue with co-ops is control. For many years, co-op boards used their power to reject potential buyers at will to keep a firm grip on who moved into the building. Unfortunately, a little of that unpleasantness continues to this day, particularly in swanky neighborhoods and in buildings whose owners have, shall we say, certain "attitudes" about people of color, certain religions, and single parents. In addition, co-op rules often require a higher cash down payment (between 30 and 50 percent is not uncommon) and sometimes refuse to allow purchases financed with a mortgage. Fortunately, many co-ops have relaxed this restriction in recent years. If you're looking for an abundance of co-op units, try New York City and Chicago, although a fair number are spread out over the rest of the United States.

Janice's Story

After looking for a home for nearly a year, Janice came upon a co-op conversion, located in the town in which she was living. The co-op was asking for a 50 percent down payment and wanted to see her finances.

"Literally, they asked me to sign a piece of paper that allowed them to do a full credit and financial background check on me. They wanted past addresses, names of references they could call, my current and past jobs, bank account statements, and my social security number," Janice said.

Although Janice had a good amount of cash saved up for her down payment, 50 percent was pushing it just a bit. She decided that the financial obligations with this particular co-op were too onerous, and she ultimately declined to make a purchase offer.

In the best light, all of this screening should hopefully make for a better neighbor, right? But co-op boards sometimes make mistakes, too. In one New York co-op, the board voted in a family that had impeccable credentials. On paper, they had it all: the best schools, best awards, terrific family history, and glowing letters from the board of the building in which the owners previously lived. Later, after several incidences with these particular owners in which the police had to be called, board members discovered that the former building was only too glad to rid itself of these individuals and wrote the letters hoping to get rid of a problem that had caused tremendous upheaval and unrest.

If you don't "pass the board," as it is commonly called, don't feel bad. Famous celebrities and politicians are often voted down for various reasons. Although it's illegal for a co-op board to reject you because of your race, religion, or sex, more often than not, you'll be told you simply don't have enough money, or it's a "personality" issue. It's hard not to take the rejection personally, but you have to ask yourself if this is really the kind of place that's right for you.

Aside from New York City brokers who are intimately familiar with co-ops, many agents and brokers, especially those new to the business, have trouble understanding the concept of co-ops. They may try to tell you that co-ops aren't a good investment, or try to steer you away for some other reason. Like any type of home, a co-op can be an excellent investment. Sometimes co-op prices are below that of a comparable condominium apartment, partly because brokers may not understand them and partly because co-ops typically require a larger down payment, which makes them unaffordable or impractical for many first-time buyers. On the other hand, if you own a co-op, it may take you longer to sell, on average, than a condo. Also, if agents don't understand how co-op ownership works, and how the costs are broken down, it may seem to be a much more expensive home. The big difference between a co-op and a condo is how you pay your real estate taxes. With a condo they're billed to you individually, once or twice a year (however is common in your area). But in a co-op, the property pays one real estate tax bill. You pay your share monthly as part of your assessment. When comparing a condo assessment to a co-op assessment, subtract out the cost of the real estate taxes to get a better understanding of how the actual operating costs compare between both units.

New Construction   It's rare that a co-op is built from the ground up these days, although it does happen in New York from time to time. More commonly, you'll see an existing rental building converted into a co-op.

Maintenance   Like a condo, your monthly assessments cover the general maintenance of the property. But because the corporation pays the real estate taxes as a whole, your share of the taxes is normally included in your monthly assessment. That means your assessment is going to look pretty steep when compared with a condo building assessment notice. For a fair comparison, you'll have to break out the costs. When looking at a co-op listing sheet, remember that the assessment generally includes property taxes.

Town House

A town house development can take several different forms, but it usually looks like a group of slender houses attached in a long row. Generally, you share a wall in common with each of your neighbors.

The difference is in the way the property is held. Most row houses built in the first half of the twentieth century are held "fee simple," meaning you hold legal title to your home and the land on which it sits. You are also responsible for the property's real estate taxes, even though you share a common wall with your neighbors. Today, many newly built town homes are constructed as condominiums, complete with a homeowners' association.

New Construction   A popular trend in the construction of town houses is a *maintenance-free community*. Essentially, this means that while you own your own property, the homeowners' association manages the exterior of the property, as well as the common elements, and takes care of it for you. So if the town houses need painting, there's no need for you to do anything. The homeowners' association will take care of it. On the other hand, they'll typically choose the color without consulting you.

Maintenance   Even if you hold your property fee simple (the way you'd normally own a single-family house), you may have to join a homeowners' association. Your monthly maintenance costs would cover the common areas not immediately on your property, such as a garage, playground, laundry room, party facilities, workout area, or swimming pool.

Mobile Homes and Manufactured Housing

Once the poor stepchildren of the real estate industry, mobile homes and manufactured housing have become a way for first-time buyers with few resources to purchase a home and stop paying rent. You might not choose to purchase a mobile home if you can afford a regular home, but you might do so if your only other option is renting.

First, let's talk about what is a mobile home. A mobile home is designed to be transported (hence the term "mobile") in one piece to a plot of land, often within a mobile home park. These parks might contain hundreds, if not thousands, of mobile homes. The home comes with bedrooms, bathrooms, a living room, and a kitchen and might be of standard width (approximately 12 to 15 feet wide) or even a double-wide width (approximately 30 feet wide). Typically, you purchase the mobile home and rent the land.

Mobile homes weren't built too well in the past, which is why they have such a shabby reputation today. They didn't last long, and they didn't hold up too well. However, several big companies have gotten into the game and started using technology and improved building materials to construct prefabricated homes or manufactured homes. They're still mobile and can be transported, completely built, to the site. But they're of much better quality and could last a lot longer than mobile homes of the past.

Some mobile home parks have very strict rules, to help increase the value of the homes located there. If the mobile home park in which you're interested has these sorts of rules, it's a good thing.

Marta's Story

A Guatemala native who became an American citizen more than a dozen years ago, Marta finally decided to stop renting and buy a home. She bought a used mobile home for $12,000 and rented a spot for it in the only mobile home park near a tony suburb outside of Chicago. But the rent for her space kept going up and up. After living there for nearly a decade, she decided to sell her mobile home and buy a real home.

Like many Hispanics, Marta saved prodigiously throughout the years. When she found the house she wanted to buy, a two-bedroom, one-bath home near the Wisconsin border, it cost around $120,000. She took out a $40,000 mortgage and paid the rest in cash (and still had cash left in her bank account). In the first two years of homeownership, she was able to pay down her loan by $10,000. Her house has also increased in value by about $15,000.

> The best part (to Marta) about the transaction was how much money she was able to get for her mobile home. When she sold it, she received $14,000, a profit of $2,000.

Manufactured housing is a different but fast-growing part of the new construction industry. The process of building a manufactured home is fascinating. Homes are built in sections, called "modules," and are put together on airplane wheels. The sections are wheeled through various parts of an enormous factory as the walls, floors, wiring, plumbing, drywall, cabinets, doors, hardware, windows, trim, and exterior siding are installed and finished. Most manufactured houses consist of four to eight modules and are completely built in about a week. (I was lucky enough to visit a manufactured housing plant in central Wisconsin for a story I was working on for WGN-TV. It was a fascinating, if dusty, day. You can read the script for the story, called "House in a Day" on my website, thinkglink.com.)

The completed sections are then loaded onto flatbed trucks and driven to their permanent location. The modules are lifted up by crane and delicately put into place. The entire house will generally be installed in a day on a permanent concrete foundation. Once the house has its mechanicals connected, and the exterior work and landscaping are finished, you'd be hard-pressed to tell the difference between a manufactured house and a stick-built home.

Manufacturers say that because the homes are built under controlled conditions (inside a factory where the building conditions are not at all affected by weather), are built to withstand the delivery (which could be up to several hundred miles), and are watched so closely, they tend to have fewer problems than regular stick-built new construction.

Another reason to consider a manufactured home is the price. Most new homes cost developers anywhere from $80 to $125 per square foot to build. In major metropolitan areas, the average might run from $100 to more than $400 per square foot for a top-of-the-line home. Manufactured homes cost between $50 and $100 per square foot, or about half of what it costs to build a comparable stick-built home. If you're watching your pennies, this may be an option you'll want to explore.

New Construction   A newly built mobile or manufactured home will last a lot longer than an old one, thanks to certain regulations builders must follow. Still, even brand-new mobile homes can be upended by tornados. Because manufactured homes are connected to permanently installed foundations, they should be able to withstand nature's fury as well as a stick-built home.

Maintenance   Even if you're renting the land underneath your mobile home, you're typically responsible for the hookups to cable, water, sewer, and garbage pickup. At the same time, you're a homeowner, and as such, you'll need to keep your home looking nice so that you'll be able to sell it when you're financially ready to move up into your next home.

Although their quality is improving and mobile homes are becoming more acceptable, we haven't quite seen the day where a mobile home will appreciate faster than a single-family home, or even a condo or co-op. If you're going to purchase a mobile home, or a manufactured home in a mobile home park, make sure you study the values closely, and make sure you're getting what you think you're paying for.

Single-Family House

Far and away, the most common form of home is the detached, single-family house. The most common feature among single-family homes, which are available in all shapes, sizes, and prices, is that the house sits by itself, on its own piece of property.

New Construction   In some developments, you may have homes clustered together while a large portion of the development sits as open land—a golf course, nature preserve, or man-made lake. Again, you'd own your own plot and house fee simple, but you may have to join a homeowners' association and pay monthly dues for the maintenance and insurance of the common areas.

Maintenance   Single-family homes can be wonderful! But they can also be a lot of work. And you, the homeowners, are responsible for all of the expenses associated with ownership and maintenance, including real estate taxes, garbage removal, water, and sewage.

first time
buyer tip

I'm often asked which appreciates fastest: a single-family home or a condominium or co-op? The truth is, any of these can appreciate quickly. It depends on how much you pay for the home, and what happens to homes in your surrounding neighborhood. Generally speaking, single-family homes appreciate faster than condos or co-ops. That said, if you buy a condo that has been foreclosed on and then fix it up, you may realize a gain of 100 percent or more in a short period of time. Or if you buy a home as a pioneer, in an area that hasn't developed yet, you may realize an enormous gain if your neighborhood suddenly becomes "hot." Although it's seductive to think about buying a home and making a fortune on it, you have to think about whether or not you'll be comfortable living there, day in and day out. We'll talk more about this later in the book.

QUESTION
6

SHOULD I BUY A NEW HOME OR AN EXISTING HOME?

In any given year, approximately one of every six home buyers will purchase a newly constructed home. Buying new homes is tempting because, well, everything is new. No one has ever used the toilet, refrigerator, closet, stove, or sink before. When you move in, everything is as pristine and polished as possible.

The problem with buying a new home is that it becomes an "existing" or "newer" home the day after you move in. The difference is that, unlike buying a new car that loses a third of its value the moment you drive it off the lot, new homes can be an excellent investment. In some areas, newly constructed homes (often referred to as "new construction") appreciate faster than existing homes.

Should you buy a new home or an existing home? I'm asked this question frequently. It's difficult to answer because where you want to live and what your housing options are factor into the decision. I have outlined a few things for you to think about before you make your decision.

1. New construction generally costs more than existing housing. Typically, you'll pay more for a four-bedroom newly built house than for a similarly sized home that was built 5, 10, 20, or even 50 years ago. That premium can be partly explained because new houses

Five Simple Things You Can Do to Make the Home-Buying Process Easier

Buying a home is tough enough. But whether you're buying your first home, or fifth, there are some simple things you can do to make it go a little easier:

1. Get preapproved for your loan. Getting preapproved is the only way to ensure that you're searching in the right price bracket. Too often, people search for homes in a price range they can't afford, either because they don't understand how the numbers work, or because they imagine that they're going to negotiate the seller down to a more affordable number. Not knowing the true costs involved or holding out false hope of a negotiation miracle is a haphazard way to spend several hundred thousand dollars. Instead, spend the time it takes, either online or in person, with a mortgage lender to get preapproved for your loan. Make sure your lender commits in writing to funding your loan (provided the property appraises out in value).

2. Work with a great buyer broker. Would you invest $100,000 in a stock just because you got a hot tip on a cold call? Of course not. But people go out every day and spend hundreds of thousands of dollars on a home without consulting a licensed buyer broker. This is foolish, particularly when consulting a buyer broker typically won't cost you anything out of your own pocket. You need someone who can advise you on the neighborhood, demographics, and sales history of other homes similar to yours in the neighborhood of your choice.

3. Know the neighborhood before you make an offer. You don't just live in the house, you live in the neighborhood. Spend time walking around the area at all times of the day and night *before* you make your offer. Chat with your prospective neighbors about their experiences in the neighborhood. Pay a visit to the local dry cleaners, supermarket, or coffee shop. Stop in at the local police headquarters and inquire about the local crime rate. Pay a visit to the local schools and observe. No matter how much information is on the Internet, learning firsthand about your future neighborhood is something you have to do in person—it will pay off in spades.

4. Protect yourself. Make sure your contract has the right contingencies, and the right language, so that you're protected. If attorneys typically represent buyers and sellers in the state in which you are purchasing a home, then use one. If attorneys aren't used, consider hiring one anyway, so that you have an adviser who doesn't have a vested interest in seeing the deal close. Buy enough homeowner's insurance, and make sure to increase it as the value of your home—and its contents—increases. Stay on top of your purchase so that there are no unpleasant surprises.

5. Have reasonable expectations. If you buy an older home, understand before you close that it's not going to be in perfect condition. There's no way everything will be perfect even if the seller has recently gutted and renovated the whole property. But when home buyers pay list (or over list) prices, it's understandable that they might expect something nearing perfection. However, as a home inspector friend of mine likes to say: "All homes have problems, but older homes have older problems." If you expect perfection in an existing home, you're likely to end up disappointed.

Five Mistakes People Make When Buying New Construction

When you build a new house, or buy new construction, it's easy to get caught up in the excitement of creating something out of nothing. Your new house starts its life as a big hole in the ground. Six months to a year later, it's finished and laden with all the amenities you've chosen.

More home buyers are purchasing newly constructed homes than ever before. According to the National Association of Home Builders (NAHB), new home sales reached 1.25 million for the first time in 2004 and were expected to continue trending upward through the rest of the decade. New home prices swell as demand rises. According to the NAHB, you can expect to pay more than $40,000 to buy the average new home than to purchase the average existing home.

What goes into the average new house? To start, it's about 2,200 square feet. A builder would typically use 3,103 square feet of asphalt shingles and other roofing materials, one fireplace, 8,385 square feet of drywall on the ceiling and walls, 13,837 linear feet of framing lumber, three bathroom sinks, three toilets, two bathtubs, one shower stall, two garage doors, and 19 windows. And that list doesn't even include paint.

The typical kitchen has about 15 cabinets, 5 other cabinets, and 23 linear feet of countertops. Half of new homes have stainless steel sinks. Ten percent of all homes are built with a central vacuum cleaner, and nearly 80 percent have a garbage disposal.

If you could open up the walls of the average new home, you'd see that 40 percent of homes are built with some sort of security system, contain a programmable thermostat, and are wired for multiline phone systems. Seven percent of homes are wired with whole-house audio systems, and 4.6 percent have in-home theater systems. NAHB data indicate that the number of homes with high-end entertainment and security systems is rising.

The average newly constructed house has all sorts of amenities new home buyers in the 1950s could not have even imagined. For example, in 1950, the average new home had 963 square feet, with two bedrooms, and one or one and a half baths. More than half of all new homes built today have more than 2,000 square feet, and 90 percent have three or more bedrooms. Eighty-three percent of homes built today have at least a two-car garage, and nearly 90 percent have central air.

In the 1950s, new home buyers were happy to have a garden. Today, new home buyers are as interested in outdoor living environments as they are in interior space. Outside a newly built home you might find a Jacuzzi, a full kitchen (complete with a grill, cooktop, and refrigerator), a fireplace, and various other outdoor rooms and amenities.

Choosing which amenities you want is easy. It's a lot harder to make it work on your budget. Blowing your new construction budget is one of the common mistakes new home buyers make. I've identified four other common mistakes for you, to help you avoid them and make your dream house a reality.

1. Blowing Your Budget. Wouldn't it be great to put everything you've seen in the model home on your blueprint? Unfortunately, new construction costs a whole lot more than buying an existing home. Adding all the goodies just increases the total cost. The average new home buyer spends another 10 percent of the purchase price on options and upgrades. If you're already looking at the top of your price range, adding 10 percent onto the price can quickly blow your budget. Start your search by deciding how much you really can afford to spend on a home, and then find a way to keep costs under control.

2. Not Checking Out the Builder. Dave the Builder says he can build a great house. He might even have a slick brochure and fancy blueprints. But has he ever built a house? Have you ever talked to anyone who bought from him? If so, have you asked the homeowner if the home has held up physically and if Dave showed up promptly to fix punch-list items? The only way you'll know if your builder is a good one is to spend a lot of time visiting other homeowners who have purchased newly constructed houses from him or her in the past. Knock on doors in other communities where the builder has finished homes and ask homeowners to talk to you about their experiences in the house and with the builder. If you're not getting answers like, "He's fabulous. I'd buy another house from him in a minute," save yourself the heartache and find another builder now. If you get great feedback from homeowners, check out the builder with the state commission that licenses contractors and builders to make sure the builder is in compliance, carries the right amount of insurance, and has had no complaints filed against him. Ask your attorney if he or she has had any experiences with the developer (good or bad). Your final stop is a website like the Better Business Bureau (BBBonline.org). Anyone can get fooled, but if you follow these steps, at least you'll know you tried to find out everything you could ahead of time.

3. Choosing Options and Upgrades That Won't Increase the Value of Your Home. If you can afford it, add on all the options and upgrades the builder offers. But if you want your options and upgrades to help increase the value of your home, and your budget is limited, you'll need to be smart about what you choose. Here are some smart moves: Pay to add on more space, like a fourth bedroom, home office, extra bath, or third garage bay, or to turn a crawl space into a basement. While you're at it, pay the extra few thousand dollars to have the basement dug deep enough to enjoy a nine-foot (or higher) ceiling when finished, and make sure the basement is full size underneath the whole first floor and not a partial basement. Upgraded appliances and countertops in the kitchen will always pay off in the long run. Choose upgraded ceramic tile to dress up a bathroom or the kitchen, and lay the tiles in a creative design to make the room even nicer. Building out closets or the pantry is a good move, and try to add in more closet or storage space wherever you can. Finally, landscaping can add dramatically to your home's value, so consider beefing up the landscaping budget. If you can't afford everything now, consider delaying nonessentials like molding and even hardwood floors in the living room. You can always add the finishing touches, like replacing a pedestal sink with a marble-topped vanity, down the line, when you have rebuilt your savings account.

4. Changing Your Mind. If you change your mind about what you want in your new home, it's going to cost you—time, money, or both. Each change requires the builder to do something differently, and when you give a *change order,* the builder will tell you how much longer the house will take to build and how much more it will cost. In general, once you commit to buying new construction, you commit to a production schedule. Certain things have to happen at certain times, or the house won't be completed on time. (The house may not be delivered to you on time even if you don't put in any change orders, but that's another book.) If you decide you want a particular tile and that tile is ordered but you don't like it when it comes in, and you decide to choose something else, you could set back your project by weeks or months. If you suddenly decide you want all the doors in the house to be eight feet, rather than the standard six feet, eight inches, and the house is already built, the builder might have to do a lot of extra work—and order new doors—to meet your expectations. The time to make changes is when you're still in the blueprint stage. When a design is on a computer or on paper, it's a whole lot easier (and less expensive) to make changes than when the house is three weeks away from completion. The best thing you can do is to make your decisions and then, if at all possible, stick with them. (And don't forget to put all change orders in writing.)

5. Not Putting It in Writing. A handshake is fine when it comes to friendships or business acquaintances, but it has no place when dealing with contractors or builders. When building or buying a newly constructed home, write down everything, including the contract and amendments; specifics regarding appliances, tile, carpet, and other upgrades; and any change orders. Once the contract is signed, both you and the builder will have to live up to the terms. Make sure you understand the terms of the contract and the rights you and the builder each have with respect to the work, delivery date, terms, and payment. Too often, important details are left out of the contract—details that can cost you dearly at closing.

APPENDIX IV

Contracts

Most sellers will expect your *offer to purchase* (also known as a *sales contract*) to be accompanied by the "standard package" of contingencies, including attorney approval (if this applies in your state), financing or mortgage, and inspection. Because these three contingencies are so common these days, I've included samples here. I've also included copies of several other contracts, including the California Transfer Disclosure Statement, which is California's version of a seller disclosure form. These forms are copyrighted by the California Association of Realtors (CAR), and I've reprinted them here with its permission.

Please note: You may find it useful to examine these contracts, disclosures, and addendums, but they may not include the exact language that will protect you in your state. Ask your real estate attorney, agent, title company, or escrow closing company for the correct forms for your state.

CALIFORNIA ASSOCIATION OF REALTORS®

BUYER'S INSPECTION ADVISORY

(C.A.R. Form BIA, Revised 10/02)

Property Address: _____ ("Property").

A. IMPORTANCE OF PROPERTY INVESTIGATION: The physical condition of the land and improvements being purchased is not guaranteed by either Seller or Brokers. For this reason, you should conduct thorough investigations of the Property personally and with professionals who should provide written reports of their investigations. A general physical inspection typically does not cover all aspects of the Property nor items affecting the Property that are not physically located on the Property. If the professionals recommend further investigations, including a recommendation by a pest control operator to inspect inaccessible areas of the Property, you should contact qualified experts to conduct such additional investigations.

B. BUYER RIGHTS AND DUTIES: You have an affirmative duty to exercise reasonable care to protect yourself, including discovery of the legal, practical and technical implications of disclosed facts, and the investigation and verification of information and facts that you know or that are within your diligent attention and observation. The purchase agreement gives you the right to investigate the Property. If you exercise this right, and you should, you must do so in accordance with the terms of that agreement. This is the best way for you to protect yourself. It is extremely important for you to read all written reports provided by professionals and to discuss the results of inspections with the professional who conducted the inspection. You have the right to request that Seller make repairs, corrections or take other action based upon items discovered in your investigations or disclosed by Seller. If Seller is unwilling or unable to satisfy your requests, or you do not want to purchase the Property in its disclosed and discovered condition, you have the right to cancel the agreement if you act within specific time periods. If you do not cancel the agreement in a timely and proper manner, you may be in breach of contract.

C. SELLER RIGHTS AND DUTIES: Seller is required to disclose to you material facts known to him/her that affect the value or desirability of the Property. However, Seller may not be aware of some Property defects or conditions. Seller does not have an obligation to inspect the Property for your benefit nor is Seller obligated to repair, correct or otherwise cure known defects that are disclosed to you or previously unknown defects that are discovered by you or your inspectors during escrow. The purchase agreement obligates Seller to make the Property available to you for investigations.

D. BROKER OBLIGATIONS: Brokers do not have expertise in all areas and therefore cannot advise you on many items, such as soil stability, geologic or environmental conditions, hazardous or illegal controlled substances, structural conditions of the foundation or other improvements, or the condition of the roof, plumbing, heating, air conditioning, electrical, sewer, septic, waste disposal, or other system. The only way to accurately determine the condition of the Property is through an inspection by an appropriate professional selected by you. If Broker gives you referrals to such professionals, Broker does not guarantee their performance. You may select any professional of your choosing. In sales involving residential dwellings with no more than four units, Brokers have a duty to make a diligent visual inspection of the accessible areas of the Property and to disclose the results of that inspection. However, as some Property defects or conditions may not be discoverable from a visual inspection, it is possible Brokers are not aware of them. If you have entered into a written agreement with a Broker, the specific terms of that agreement will determine the nature and extent of that Broker's duty to you. **YOU ARE STRONGLY ADVISED TO INVESTIGATE THE CONDITION AND SUITABILITY OF ALL ASPECTS OF THE PROPERTY. IF YOU DO NOT DO SO, YOU ARE ACTING AGAINST THE ADVICE OF BROKERS.**

E. YOU ARE ADVISED TO CONDUCT INVESTIGATIONS OF THE ENTIRE PROPERTY, INCLUDING, BUT NOT LIMITED TO THE FOLLOWING:

1. **GENERAL CONDITION OF THE PROPERTY, ITS SYSTEMS AND COMPONENTS:** Foundation, roof, plumbing, heating, air conditioning, electrical, mechanical, security, pool/spa, other structural and non-structural systems and components, fixtures, built-in appliances, any personal property included in the sale, and energy efficiency of the Property. (Structural engineers are best suited to determine possible design or construction defects, and whether improvements are structurally sound.)

2. **SQUARE FOOTAGE, AGE, BOUNDARIES:** Square footage, room dimensions, lot size, age of improvements and boundaries. Any numerical statements regarding these items are APPROXIMATIONS ONLY and have not been verified by Seller and cannot be verified by Brokers. Fences, hedges, walls, retaining walls and other natural or constructed barriers or markers do not necessarily identify true Property boundaries. (Professionals such as appraisers, architects, surveyors and civil engineers are best suited to determine square footage, dimensions and boundaries of the Property.)

3. **WOOD DESTROYING PESTS:** Presence of, or conditions likely to lead to the presence of wood destroying pests and organisms and other infestation or infection. Inspection reports covering these items can be separated into two sections: Section 1 identifies areas where infestation or infection is evident. Section 2 identifies areas where there are conditions likely to lead to infestation or infection. A registered structural pest control company is best suited to perform these inspections.

BIA REVISED 10/02 (PAGE 1 OF 2) Print Date

Buyer's Initials (_____)(_____)
Broker's Initials (_____)(_____)

Reviewed by _____ Date _____

EQUAL HOUSING OPPORTUNITY

410

Property Address: _____ Date: _____

4. **SOIL STABILITY:** Existence of fill or compacted soil, expansive or contracting soil, susceptibility to slippage, settling or movement, and the adequacy of drainage. (Geotechnical engineers are best suited to determine such conditions, causes and remedies.)

5. **ROOF:** Present condition, age, leaks, and remaining useful life. (Roofing contractors are best suited to determine these conditions.)

6. **POOL/SPA:** Cracks, leaks or operational problems. (Pool contractors are best suited to determine these conditions.)

7. **WASTE DISPOSAL:** Type, size, adequacy, capacity and condition of sewer and septic systems and components, connection to sewer, and applicable fees.

8. **WATER AND UTILITIES; WELL SYSTEMS AND COMPONENTS:** Water and utility availability, use restrictions and costs. Water quality, adequacy, condition, and performance of well systems and components.

9. **ENVIRONMENTAL HAZARDS:** Potential environmental hazards, including, but not limited to, asbestos, lead-based paint and other lead contamination, radon, methane, other gases, fuel oil or chemical storage tanks, contaminated soil or water, hazardous waste, waste disposal sites, electromagnetic fields, nuclear sources, and other substances, materials, products, or conditions (including mold (airborne, toxic or otherwise), fungus or similar contaminants). (For more in formation on these items, you may consult an appropriate professional or read the booklets "Environmental Hazards: A Guide for Homeowners ,Buyers, Landlords and Tenants," "Protect Your Family From Lead in Your Home" or both.)

10. **EARTHQUAKES AND FLOODING:** Susceptibility of the Property to earthquake/seismic hazards and propensity of the Property to flood. (A Geologist or Geotechnical Engineer is best suited to provide information on these conditions.)

11. **FIRE, HAZARD AND OTHER INSURANCE:** The availability and cost of necessary or desired insurance may vary. The location of the Property in a seismic, flood or fire hazard zone, and other conditions, such as the age of the Property and the claims history of the Property and Buyer, may affect the availability and need for certain types of insurance. Buyer should explore insurance options early as this information may affect other decisions, including the removal of loan and inspection contingencies. (An insurance agent is best suited to provide information on these conditions.)

12. **BUILDING PERMITS, ZONING AND GOVERNMENTAL REQUIREMENTS:** Permits, inspections, certificates, zoning, other governmental limitations, restrictions, and requirements affecting the current or future use of the Property, its development or size. (Such information is available from appropriate governmental agencies and private information providers. Brokers are not qualified to review or interpret any such information.)

13. **RENTAL PROPERTY RESTRICTIONS:** Some cities and counties impose restrictions that limit the amount of rent that can be charged, the maximum number of occupants; and the right of a landlord to terminate a tenancy. Deadbolt or other locks and security systems for doors and windows, including window bars, should be examined to determine whether they satisfy legal requirements. (Government agencies can provide information about these restrictions and other requirements.)

14. **SECURITY AND SAFETY:** State and local Law may require the installation of barriers, access alarms, self-latching mechanisms and/or other measures to decrease the risk to children and other persons of existing swimming pools and hot tubs, as well as various fire safety and other measures concerning other features of the Property. Compliance requirements differ from city to city and county to county. Unless specifically agreed, the Property may not be in compliance with these requirements. (Local government agencies can provide information about these restrictions and other requirements.)

15. **NEIGHBORHOOD, AREA, SUBDIVISION CONDITIONS; PERSONAL FACTORS:** Neighborhood or area conditions, including schools, proximity and adequacy of law enforcement, crime statistics, the proximity of registered felons or offenders, fire protection, other government services, availability, adequacy and cost of any speed-wired, wireless internet connections or other telecommunications or other technology services and installations, proximity to commercial, industrial or agricultural activities, existing and proposed transportation, construction and development that may affect noise, view, or traffic, airport noise, noise or odor from any source, wild and domestic animals, other nuisances, hazards, or circumstances, protected species, wetland properties, botanical diseases, historic or other governmentally protected sites or improvements, cemeteries, facilities and condition of common areas of common interest subdivisions, and possible lack of compliance with any governing documents or Homeowners' Association requirements, conditions and influences of significance to certain cultures and/or religions, and personal needs, requirements and preferences of Buyer.

Buyer and Seller acknowledge and agree that Broker: **(i)** Does not decide what price Buyer should pay or Seller should accept; **(ii)** Does not guarantee the condition of the Property; **(iii)** Does not guarantee the performance, adequacy or completeness of inspections, services, products or repairs provided or made by Seller or others; **(iv)** Shall not be responsible for identifying defects that are not known to Broker and **(a)** are not visually observable in reasonably accessible areas of the Property; **(b)** are in common areas; or **(c)** are off the site of the Property; **(v)** Shall not be responsible for inspecting public records or permits concerning the title or use of Property; **(vi)** Shall not be responsible for identifying the location of boundary lines or other items affecting title; **(vii)** Shall not be responsible for verifying square footage, representations of others or information contained in Investigation reports, Multiple Listing Service, advertisements, flyers or other promotional material; **(viii)** Shall not be responsible for providing legal or tax advice regarding any aspect of a transaction entered into by Buyer or Seller; and **(ix)** Shall not be responsible for providing other advice or information that exceeds the knowledge, education and experience required to perform real estate licensed activity. Buyer and Seller agree to seek legal, tax, insurance, title and other desired assistance from appropriate professionals.

By signing below, Buyer and Broker each acknowledge that they have read, understand, accept and have received a Copy of this Advisory. Buyer is encouraged to read it carefully.

Buyer Signature	Date	Buyer Signature	Date

Broker Signature	Date	Broker Signature	Date

SURE TRAC
The System for Success™

Published by the
California Association of REALTORS®

BIA REVISED 10/02 (PAGE 2 OF 2)

Reviewed by _____ Date _____

EQUAL HOUSING OPPORTUNITY

BUYER'S INSPECTION ADVISORY (BIA PAGE 2 OF 2)

CALIFORNIA ASSOCIATION OF REALTORS®

EXCLUSIVE AUTHORIZATION TO ACQUIRE PROPERTY
BUYER BROKER COMPENSATION CONTRACT
(C.A.R. Form AAP, Revised 4/02)

1. **EXCLUSIVE RIGHT TO REPRESENT:** _____ ("Buyer")
grants _____ ("Broker")
beginning on (date) _____ and ending at **(i)** 11:59 p.m. on (date) _____ or **(ii)** completion of a resulting transaction, whichever occurs first ("Representation Period"), the exclusive and irrevocable right, on the terms specified in this Agreement, to represent Buyer in acquiring real property or a manufactured home. Broker agrees to exercise due diligence and reasonable efforts to fulfill the following authorizations and obligations. Broker will perform its obligations under this Agreement through the individual signing for Broker below, who is either Broker individually or an associate-licensee (an individual licensed as a real estate salesperson or broker who works under Broker's real estate license). Buyer agrees that Broker's duties are limited by the terms of this Agreement, including those limitations set forth in paragraphs 5 and 6.

2. **AGENCY RELATIONSHIPS:**
   A. **DISCLOSURE:** If the property described in paragraph 4 includes residential property with one-to-four dwelling units, Buyer acknowledges receipt of the "Disclosure Regarding Real Estate Agency Relationships" form prior to entering into this Agreement.
   B. **BUYER REPRESENTATION:** Broker will represent, as described in this Agreement, Buyer in any resulting transaction.
   C. **(1) POSSIBLE DUAL AGENCY WITH SELLER:** (C(1) APPLIES UNLESS C(2)(i) or (ii) is checked below.)
   Depending on the circumstances, it may be necessary or appropriate for Broker to act as an agent for both Buyer and a seller, exchange party, or one or more additional parties ("Seller"). Broker shall, as soon as practicable, disclose to Buyer any election to act as a dual agent representing both Buyer and Seller. If Buyer is shown property listed with Broker, Buyer consents to Broker becoming a dual agent representing both Buyer and Seller with respect to those properties. In event of dual agency, Buyer agrees that: **(a)** Broker, without the prior written consent of Buyer, will not disclose to Seller that the Buyer is willing to pay a price greater than the price offered; **(b)** Broker, without the prior written consent of Seller, will not disclose to Buyer that Seller is willing to sell property at a price less than the listing price; and **(c)** other than as set forth in (a) and (b) above, a dual agent is obligated to disclose known facts materially affecting the value or desirability of the Property to both parties.
   OR (2) SINGLE AGENCY ONLY: (APPLIES ONLY IF (i) or (ii) is checked below.)
   ☐ **(i) Broker's firm lists properties for sale:** Buyer understands that this election will prevent Broker from showing Buyer those properties that are listed with Broker's firm or from representing Buyer in connection with those properties. Buyer's acquisition of a property listed with Broker's firm shall not affect Broker's right to be compensated under paragraph 3. In any resulting transaction in which Seller's property is not listed with Broker's firm, Broker will be the exclusive agent of Buyer and not a dual agent also representing Seller.
   OR ☐ **(ii) Broker's firm DOES NOT list property:** Entire brokerage firm only represents buyers and does not list property. In any resulting transaction, Broker will be the exclusive agent of Buyer and not a dual agent also representing Seller.
   D. **OTHER POTENTIAL BUYERS:** Buyer understands that other potential buyers may, through Broker, consider, make offers on or acquire the same or similar properties as those Buyer is seeking to acquire. Buyer consents to Broker's representation of such other potential buyers before, during and after the Representation Period, or any extension thereof.
   E. **CONFIRMATION:** If the Property includes residential property with one-to-four dwelling units, Broker shall confirm the agency relationship described above, or as modified, in writing, prior to or coincident with Buyer's execution of a Property Contract.

3. **COMPENSATION TO BROKER:**
   NOTICE: The amount or rate of real estate commissions is not fixed by law. They are set by each Broker individually and may be negotiable between Buyer and Broker (real estate commissions include all compensation and fees to Broker).
   Buyer agrees to pay to Broker, irrespective of agency relationship(s), as follows:
   A. **AMOUNT OF COMPENSATION: (Check (1), (2) or (3). Check only one.)**
   ☐ **(1)** _____ percent of the acquisition price AND (if checked ☐) $ _____.
   OR ☐ **(2)** $ _____.
   OR ☐ **(3)** Pursuant to the compensation schedule attached as an addendum _____.
   B. **BROKER RIGHT TO COMPENSATION:** Broker shall be entitled to the compensation provided for in paragraph 3A:
   (1) If Buyer enters into an agreement to acquire property described in paragraph 4, on those terms or any other terms acceptable to Buyer during the Representation Period, or any extension thereof.
   (2) If, within ____ **calendar days** after expiration of the Representation Period or any extension thereof, Buyer enters into an agreement to acquire property described in paragraph 4, which property Broker introduced to Buyer, or for which Broker acted on Buyer's behalf. The obligation to pay compensation pursuant to this paragraph shall arise only if, prior to or within 3 (or ☐ ____) **calendar days** after expiration of this Agreement or any extension thereof, Broker gives Buyer a written notice of those properties which Broker introduced to Buyer, or for which Broker acted on Buyer's behalf.

AAP-11 REVISED 4/02 (PAGE 1 OF 4) Print Date

Buyer and Broker acknowledge receipt of a copy of this page.
Buyer's Initials (_____)(_____)
Broker's Initials (_____)(_____)

EQUAL HOUSING OPPORTUNITY

| Reviewed by |
| Broker or Designee _____ Date _____ |

412

EXCLUSIVE AUTHORIZATION TO ACQUIRE PROPERTY (AAP-11 PAGE 1 OF 4)

Buyer: _____   Date: _____

C. PAYMENT OF COMPENSATION: Compensation is payable:

    (1) Upon completion of any resulting transaction, and if an escrow is used, through escrow.

    (2) If acquisition is prevented by default of Buyer, upon Buyer's default.

    (3) If acquisition is prevented by a party to the transaction other than Buyer, when Buyer collects damages by suit, settlement or otherwise. Compensation shall equal one-half of the damages recovered, not to exceed the compensation provided for in paragraph 3A, after first deducting the unreimbursed expenses of collection, if any.

D. BUYER OBLIGATION TO PAY COMPENSATION: Buyer is responsible for payment of compensation provided for in this Agreement. **However, if anyone other than Buyer compensates Broker for services covered by this Agreement, that amount shall be credited toward Buyer's obligation to pay compensation.** If the amount of compensation Broker receives from anyone other than Buyer exceeds Buyer's obligation, the excess amount shall be disclosed to Buyer and if allowed by law paid to Broker, or (if checked) ☐ credited to Buyer or ☐ other _____.

E. Buyer hereby irrevocably assigns to Broker the compensation provided for in paragraph 3A from Buyer's funds and proceeds in escrow. Buyer agrees to submit to escrow any funds needed to compensate Broker under this Agreement. Broker may submit this Agreement, as instructions to compensate Broker, to any escrow regarding Property involving Buyer and a seller or other transferor.

F. "BUYER" includes any person or entity, other than Broker, related to Buyer or who in any manner acts on Buyer's behalf to acquire property described in paragraph 4.

G. (1) Buyer has not previously entered into a representation agreement with another brokerage firm regarding property described in paragraph 4, unless specified as follows (name other brokerage firm here): _____
_____.

    (2) Buyer warrants that Buyer has no obligation to pay compensation to any other brokerage firm regarding property described in paragraph 4, unless Buyer acquires the following property(ies):_____

    (3) If Buyer acquires a property specified in G(2) above during the time Buyer is obligated to compensate another broker, Broker is neither **(i)** entitled to compensation under this Agreement nor **(ii)** obligated to represent Buyer in such transaction.

4. PROPERTY TO BE ACQUIRED:

Any purchase, lease or other acquisition of any real property or manufactured home described as follows:
_____
_____
_____

Price range: $_____ to $_____

5. BROKER AUTHORIZATIONS AND OBLIGATIONS:

A. Buyer authorizes Broker to: **(i)** locate and present selected properties to Buyer, present offers authorized by Buyer, and assist Buyer in negotiating for acceptance of such offers; **(ii)** assist Buyer with the financing process, including obtaining loan pre-qualification; **(iii)** upon request, provide Buyer with a list of professionals or vendors who perform the services described in the attached Buyer's Inspection Advisory; **(iv)** order reports, and schedule and attend meetings and appointments with professionals chosen by Buyer; **(v)** provide guidance to help Buyer with the acquisition of property; and **(vi)** obtain a credit report on Buyer.

B. For property transactions of which Broker is aware and not precluded from participating in by Buyer, Broker shall provide and review forms to create a property contract ("Property Contract") for the acquisition of a specific property ("Property"). With respect to such Property, Broker shall: **(i)** if the Property contains residential property with one-to-four dwelling units, conduct a reasonably competent and diligent on-site visual inspection of the accessible areas of the Property (excluding any common areas), and disclose to Buyer all facts materially affecting the value or desirability of such Property that are revealed by this inspection; **(ii)** deliver or communicate to Buyer any disclosures, materials or information received by, in the personal possession of or personally known to the individual signing for Broker below during the Representation Period; and **(iii)** facilitate the escrow process, including assisting Buyer in negotiating with Seller. Unless otherwise specified in writing, any information provided through Broker in the course of representing Buyer has not been and will not be verified by Broker. Broker's services are performed in compliance with federal, state and local anti-discrimination laws.

6. SCOPE OF BROKER DUTY:

A. While Broker will perform the duties described in paragraph 5B, Broker recommends that Buyer select other professionals, as described in the attached Buyer's Inspection Advisory, to investigate the Property through inspections, investigations, tests, surveys, reports, studies and other available information ("Inspections") during the transaction. Buyer agrees that these Inspections, to the extent they exceed the obligations described in paragraph 5B, are not within the scope of Broker's agency duties. Broker informs Buyer that it is in Buyer's best interest to obtain such Inspections.

B. Buyer acknowledges and agrees that Broker: **(i)** does not decide what price Buyer should pay or Seller should accept; **(ii)** does not guarantee the condition of the Property; **(iii)** does not guarantee the performance, adequacy or completeness of Inspections, services, products or repairs provided or made by Seller or others to Buyer or Seller; **(iv)** shall not be responsible for identifying defects that are not known to Broker and either **(a)** are not visually observable in reasonably accessible areas of the Property or **(b)** are in common areas; **(v)** shall not be responsible for identifying the location of boundary lines or other items affecting title; **(vi)** shall not be responsible for verifying square footage, representations of others or information contained in Inspection reports; **(vii)** shall not be responsible for providing legal or tax advice regarding any aspect of a transaction entered into by Buyer in the course of this representation; and **(viii)** shall not be responsible for providing other advice or information that exceeds the knowledge, education and experience required to perform real estate licensed activities. Buyer agrees to seek legal, tax, insurance, title and other desired assistance from appropriate professionals.

Buyer and Broker acknowledge receipt of a copy of this page.

Buyer's Initials (_____)(_____)
Broker's Initials (_____)(_____)

Reviewed by _____
Broker or Designee _____ Date _____

EQUAL HOUSING OPPORTUNITY

EXCLUSIVE AUTHORIZATION TO ACQUIRE PROPERTY (AAP-11 PAGE 2 OF 4)

Buyer: _____ Date: _____

C. Broker owes no duty to inspect for common environmental hazards, earthquake weaknesses, or geologic and seismic hazards. If Buyer receives the booklets titled "Environmental Hazards: A Guide for Homeowners, Buyers, Landlords and Tenants," "The Homeowner's Guide to Earthquake Safety," or "The Commercial Property Owner's Guide to Earthquake Safety," the booklets are deemed adequate to inform buyer regarding the information contained in the booklets and, other than as specified in 5B above, Broker is not required to provide Buyer with additional information about the matters described in the booklets.

7. BUYER OBLIGATIONS:

A. Buyer agrees to timely view and consider properties selected by Broker and to negotiate in good faith to acquire a property. Buyer further agrees to act in good faith toward the completion of any Property Contract entered into in furtherance of this Agreement. Within **5 (or ☐ _____) calendar days** from the execution of this Agreement, Buyer shall provide relevant personal and financial information to Broker to assure Buyer's ability to acquire property described in paragraph 4. If Buyer fails to provide such information, or if Buyer does not qualify financially to acquire property described in paragraph 4, then Broker may cancel this Agreement in writing. Buyer has an affirmative duty to take steps to protect him/herself, including discovery of the legal, practical and technical implications of discovered or disclosed facts, and investigation of information and facts which are known to Buyer or are within the diligent attention and observation of Buyer. Buyer is obligated to and agrees to read all documents provided to Buyer. Buyer agrees to seek desired assistance from appropriate professionals, selected by Buyer, such as those referenced in the attached Buyer's Inspection Advisory.

B. Buyer shall notify Broker in writing of any material issue to Buyer, such as, but not limited to, Buyer requests for information on, or concerns regarding, any particular area of interest or importance to Buyer ("Material Consideration").

C. Buyer agrees to (i) indemnify, defend and hold Broker harmless from all claims, disputes, litigation, judgments, costs and attorney fees arising from any incorrect information supplied by Buyer, or from any Material Consideration that Buyer fails to disclose in writing to Broker, and (ii) pay for reports, Inspections and meetings arranged by Broker on Buyer's behalf.

D. Buyer is advised to read the attached Buyer's Inspection Advisory for a list of items and other concerns that typically warrant Inspections or investigation by Buyer or other professionals.

8. DISPUTE RESOLUTION:

A. MEDIATION: Buyer and Broker agree to mediate any dispute or claim arising between them out of this Agreement, or any resulting transaction, before resorting to arbitration or court action, subject to paragraph 8B(2) below. Paragraph 8B(2) below applies whether or not the arbitration provision is initialed. Mediation fees, if any, shall be divided equally among the parties involved. If, for any dispute or claim to which this paragraph applies, any party commences an action without first attempting to resolve the matter through mediation, or refuses to mediate after a request has been made, then that party shall not be entitled to recover attorney fees even if they would otherwise be available to that party in any such action. THIS MEDIATION PROVISION APPLIES WHETHER OR NOT THE ARBITRATION PROVISION IS INITIALED.

B. ARBITRATION OF DISPUTES: (1) Buyer and Broker agree that any dispute or claim in law or equity arising between them regarding the obligation to pay compensation under this Agreement, which is not settled through mediation, shall be decided by neutral, binding arbitration, including and subject to paragraph 8B(2) below. The arbitrator shall be a retired judge or justice, or an attorney with at least five years of residential real estate law experience, unless the parties mutually agree to a different arbitrator, who shall render an award in accordance with substantive California law. In all other respects, the arbitration shall be conducted in accordance with Part III, Title 9 of the California Code of Civil Procedure. Judgment upon the award of the arbitrator(s) may be entered in any court having jurisdiction. The parties shall have the right to discovery in accordance with Code of Civil Procedure §1283.05.

(2) EXCLUSIONS FROM MEDIATION AND ARBITRATION: The following matters are excluded from mediation and arbitration hereunder: **(i)** a judicial or non-judicial foreclosure or other action or proceeding to enforce a deed of trust, mortgage, or installment land sale contract as defined in Civil Code §2985; **(ii)** an unlawful detainer action; **(iii)** the filing or enforcement of a mechanic's lien; **(iv)** any matter that is within the jurisdiction of a probate, small claims, or bankruptcy court; and **(v)** an action for bodily injury or wrongful death, or for any right of action to which Code of Civil Procedure §337.1 or §337.15 applies. The filing of a court action to enable the recording of a notice of pending action, for order of attachment, receivership, injunction, or other provisional remedies, shall not constitute a waiver of the mediation and arbitration provisions.

"NOTICE: BY INITIALING IN THE SPACE BELOW YOU ARE AGREEING TO HAVE ANY DISPUTE ARISING OUT OF THE MATTERS INCLUDED IN THE 'ARBITRATION OF DISPUTES' PROVISION DECIDED BY NEUTRAL ARBITRATION AS PROVIDED BY CALIFORNIA LAW AND YOU ARE GIVING UP ANY RIGHTS YOU MIGHT POSSESS TO HAVE THE DISPUTE LITIGATED IN A COURT OR JURY TRIAL. BY INITIALING IN THE SPACE BELOW YOU ARE GIVING UP YOUR JUDICIAL RIGHTS TO DISCOVERY AND APPEAL, UNLESS THOSE RIGHTS ARE SPECIFICALLY INCLUDED IN THE 'ARBITRATION OF DISPUTES' PROVISION. IF YOU REFUSE TO SUBMIT TO ARBITRATION AFTER AGREEING TO THIS PROVISION, YOU MAY BE COMPELLED TO ARBITRATE UNDER THE AUTHORITY OF THE CALIFORNIA CODE OF CIVIL PROCEDURE. YOUR AGREEMENT TO THIS ARBITRATION PROVISION IS VOLUNTARY."

"WE HAVE READ AND UNDERSTAND THE FOREGOING AND AGREE TO SUBMIT DISPUTES ARISING OUT OF THE MATTERS INCLUDED IN THE 'ARBITRATION OF DISPUTES' PROVISION TO NEUTRAL ARBITRATION."

Buyer's Initials _____/_____	Broker's Initials _____/_____

AAP-11 REVISED 4/02 (PAGE 3 OF 4) Print Date

Buyer and Broker acknowledge receipt of a copy of this page.

Buyer's Initials (_____)(_____)
Broker's Initials (_____)(_____)

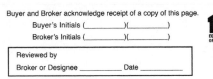

Reviewed by _____
Broker or Designee _____ Date _____

EXCLUSIVE AUTHORIZATION TO ACQUIRE PROPERTY (AAP-11 PAGE 3 OF 4)

Buyer: _____   Date: _____

9. TIME TO BRING LEGAL ACTION: Legal action for breach of this Agreement, or any obligation arising therefrom, shall be brought no more than two years from the expiration of the Representation Period or from the date such cause of action may arise, whichever occurs first.

10. OTHER TERMS AND CONDITIONS, including ATTACHED SUPPLEMENTS: ☑ Buyer's Inspection Advisory (C.A.R. Form BIA-11)

_____
_____
_____
_____
_____

11. ATTORNEY FEES: In any action, proceeding or arbitration between Buyer and Broker regarding the obligation to pay compensation under this Agreement, the prevailing Buyer or Broker shall be entitled to reasonable attorney fees and costs, except as provided in paragraph 8A.

12. ENTIRE CONTRACT: All understandings between the parties are incorporated in this Agreement. Its terms are intended by the parties as a final, complete and exclusive expression of their agreement with respect to its subject matter, and may not be contradicted by evidence of any prior agreement or contemporaneous oral agreement. This Agreement may not be extended, amended, modified, altered or changed, except in writing signed by Buyer and Broker. In the event that any provision of this Agreement is held to be ineffective or invalid, the remaining provisions will nevertheless be given full force and effect. This Agreement and any supplement, addendum or modification, including any copy, whether by copier, facsimile, NCR or electronic, may be signed in two or more counterparts, all of which shall constitute one and the same writing.

Buyer acknowledges that Buyer has read, understands, accepts and has received a copy of this Agreement.

Buyer _____ Date _____
Address _____ City _____ State _____ Zip _____
Telephone _____ Fax _____ E-mail _____

Buyer _____ Date _____
Address _____ City _____ State _____ Zip _____
Telephone _____ Fax _____ E-mail _____

Real Estate Broker (Firm) _____
By (Agent) _____ Date _____
Address _____ City _____ State _____ Zip _____
Telephone _____ Fax _____ E-mail _____

Reviewed by
Broker or Designee _____ Date _____

AAP-11 REVISED 4/02 (PAGE 4 OF 4) Print Date

CALIFORNIA ASSOCIATION OF REALTORS®

SELLER FINANCING ADDENDUM AND DISCLOSURE
(California Civil Code §§2956-2967)

(C.A.R. Form SFA, Revised 10/02)

This is an addendum to the ☐ Residential Purchase Agreement, ☐ Counter Offer, or ☐ Other _____
_____, ("Agreement"), dated _____,
On property known as _____ ("Property"),
between _____ ("Buyer"),
and _____ ("Seller").
Seller agrees to extend credit to Buyer as follows:

1. **PRINCIPAL; INTEREST; PAYMENT; MATURITY TERMS:** ☐ Principal amount $ _____, interest at _____%
   per annum, payable at approximately $ _____ per ☐ month, ☐ year, or ☐ other _____,
   remaining principal balance due in _____ years.
2. **LOAN APPLICATION; CREDIT REPORT:** Within **5 (or ☐ _____) Days** After Acceptance: **(a)** Buyer shall provide Seller a completed
   loan application on a form acceptable to Seller (such as a FNMA/FHLMC Uniform Residential Loan Application for residential one to four
   unit properties); and **(b)** Buyer authorizes Seller and/or Agent to obtain, at Buyer's expense, a copy of Buyer's credit report. Buyer shall
   provide any supporting documentation reasonably requested by Seller. Seller may cancel this Agreement in writing if Buyer fails to
   provide such documents within that time, or if Seller disapproves any above item within **5 (or ☐ _____) Days** After receipt of each item.
3. **CREDIT DOCUMENTS:** This extension of credit by Seller will be evidenced by: ☐ Note and deed of trust; ☐ All-inclusive
   note and deed of trust; ☐ Installment land sale contract; ☐ Lease/option (when parties intend transfer of equitable title);
   OR ☐ Other (specify) _____
   **THE FOLLOWING TERMS APPLY ONLY IF CHECKED. SELLER IS ADVISED TO READ ALL TERMS, EVEN THOSE NOT
   CHECKED, TO UNDERSTAND WHAT IS OR IS NOT INCLUDED, AND, IF NOT INCLUDED, THE CONSEQUENCES THEREOF.**
4. ☐ **LATE CHARGE:** If any payment is not made within _____ **Days** After it is due, a late charge of either $ _____,
   or _____% of the installment due, may be charged to Buyer. **NOTE:** On single family residences that Buyer intends to occupy,
   California Civil Code §2954.4(a) limits the late charge to no more than 6% of the total monthly payment due and requires a grace
   period of no less than 10 days.
5. ☐ **BALLOON PAYMENT:** The extension of credit will provide for a balloon payment, in the amount of $ _____
   plus any accrued interest, which is due on _____ (date).
6. ☐ **PREPAYMENT:** If all or part of this extension of credit is paid early, Seller may charge a prepayment penalty as follows (if
   applicable): _____. Caution: California Civil Code
   §2954.9 contains limitations on prepayment penalties for residential one-to-four unit properties.
7. ☐ **DUE ON SALE:** If any interest in the Property is sold or otherwise transferred, Seller has the option to require immediate
   payment of the entire unpaid principal balance, plus any accrued interest.
8.* ☐ **REQUEST FOR COPY OF NOTICE OF DEFAULT:** A request for a copy of Notice of Default as defined in California Civil
   Code §2924b will be recorded. **If Not,** Seller is advised to consider recording a Request for Notice of Default.
9.* ☐ **REQUEST FOR NOTICE OF DELINQUENCY:** A request for Notice of Delinquency, as defined in California Civil Code §2924e,
   to be signed and paid for by Buyer, will be made to senior lienholders. **If not,** Seller is advised to consider making a Request for
   Notice of Delinquency. Seller is advised to check with senior lienholders to verify whether they will honor this request.
10.* ☐ **TAX SERVICE:**
   A. If property taxes on the Property become delinquent, tax service will be arranged to report to Seller. **If not,** Seller is
   advised to consider retaining a tax service, or to otherwise determine that property taxes are paid.
   B. ☐ Buyer, ☐ Seller, shall be responsible for the initial and continued retention of, and payment for, such tax service.
11. ☐ **TITLE INSURANCE:** Title insurance coverage will be provided to **both** Seller and Buyer, insuring their respective interests
   in the Property. **If not,** Buyer and Seller are advised to consider securing such title insurance coverage.
12. ☐ **HAZARD INSURANCE:**
   A. The parties' escrow holder or insurance carrier will be directed to include a loss payee endorsement, adding Seller to
   the Property insurance policy. **If not,** Seller is advised to secure such an endorsement, or acquire a separate
   insurance policy.
   B. Property insurance **does not** include earthquake or flood insurance coverage, unless checked:
   ☐ Earthquake insurance will be obtained; ☐ Flood insurance will be obtained.
13. ☐ **PROCEEDS TO BUYER:** Buyer will receive cash proceeds at the close of the sale transaction. The amount received will be
   approximately $ _____, from _____ (indicate source of
   proceeds). Buyer represents that the purpose of such disbursement is as follows: _____
14. ☐ **NEGATIVE AMORTIZATION; DEFERRED INTEREST:** Negative amortization results when Buyer's periodic payments are
   less than the amount of interest earned on the obligation. Deferred interest also results when the obligation does not
   require periodic payments for a period of time. In either case, interest is not payable as it accrues. This accrued interest
   will have to be paid by Buyer at a later time, and may result in Buyer owing more on the obligation than at its origination.
   The credit being extended to Buyer by Seller will provide for negative amortization or deferred interest as indicated below.
   (Check A, B, or C. CHECK ONE ONLY.)
   ☐ **A.** All negative amortization or deferred interest shall be added to the principal _____
   (e.g., annually, monthly, etc.), and thereafter shall bear interest at the rate specified in the credit documents (compound interest);
   OR ☐ **B.** All deferred interest shall be due and payable, along with principal, at maturity;
   OR ☐ **C.** Other _____.

*(For Paragraphs 8-10) In order to receive timely and continued notification, Seller is advised to record appropriate notices and/or to
notify appropriate parties of any change in Seller's address.

SFA REVISED 10/02 (PAGE 1 OF 3) Print Date

Buyer's Initials (_____)(_____)
Seller's Initials (_____)(_____)

Reviewed by _____ Date _____

**EQUAL HOUSING
OPPORTUNITY**

SELLER FINANCING ADDENDUM AND DISCLOSURE (SFA PAGE 1 OF 3)

15. ☐ **ALL-INCLUSIVE DEED OF TRUST; INSTALLMENT LAND SALE CONTRACT:** This transaction involves the use of an all-inclusive (or wraparound) deed of trust or an installment land sale contract. That deed of trust or contract shall provide as follows:

    A. In the event of an acceleration of any senior encumbrance, the responsibility for payment, or for legal defense is: _____

    _____ ; OR ☐ **Is not** specified in the credit or security documents.

    B. In the event of the prepayment of a senior encumbrance, the responsibilities and rights of Buyer and Seller regarding refinancing, prepayment penalties, and any prepayment discounts are: _____ ;

    OR ☐ **Are not** specified in the documents evidencing credit.

    C. Buyer will make periodic payments to _____ (Seller, collection agent, or any neutral third party), who will be responsible for disbursing payments to the payee(s) on the senior encumbrance(s) and to Seller. **NOTE:** The Parties are advised to designate a neutral third party for these purposes.

16. ☐ **TAX IDENTIFICATION NUMBERS:** Buyer and Seller shall each provide to each other their Social Security Numbers or Taxpayer Identification Numbers.

17. ☐ **OTHER CREDIT TERMS** _____

18. ☐ **RECORDING:** The documents evidencing credit (paragraph 3) will be recorded with the county recorder where the Property is located. **If not,** Buyer and Seller are advised that their respective interests in the Property may be jeopardized by intervening liens, judgments, encumbrances, or subsequent transfers.

19. ☐ **JUNIOR FINANCING:** There will be additional financing, secured by the Property, junior to this Seller financing. Explain: _____

20. **SENIOR LOANS AND ENCUMBRANCES:** The following information is provided on loans and/or encumbrances that will be **senior** to Seller financing. **NOTE:** The following are estimates, unless otherwise marked with an asterisk (*). If checked: ☐ A separate sheet with information on additional senior loans/encumbrances is attached

	1st	2nd
A. Original Balance	$ _____	$ _____
B. Current Balance	$ _____	$ _____
C. Periodic Payment (e.g. $100/month):	$ _____	$ _____/_____
Including Impounds of:	$ _____	$ _____/_____
D. Interest Rate (per annum)	_____%	_____%
E. Fixed or Variable Rate:	_____	_____
If Variable Rate: Lifetime Cap (Ceiling)	_____	_____
Indicator (Underlying Index)	_____	_____
Margins	_____	_____
F. Maturity Date	_____	_____
G. Amount of Balloon Payment	$ _____	$ _____
H. Date Balloon Payment Due	_____	_____
I. Potential for Negative Amortization? (Yes, No, or Unknown)	_____	_____
J. Due on Sale? (Yes, No, or Unknown)	_____	_____
K. Pre-payment penalty? (Yes, No, or Unknown)	_____	_____
L. Are payments current? (Yes, No, or Unknown)	_____	_____

21. **BUYER'S CREDITWORTHINESS:** (CHECK EITHER A OR B. Do not check both.) In addition to the loan application, credit report and other information requested under paragraph 2:

    A. ☐ No other disclosure concerning Buyer's creditworthiness has been made to Seller;

OR B. ☐ The following representations concerning Buyer's creditworthiness are made by Buyer(s) to Seller:

Borrower _____	Co-Borrower _____
1. Occupation _____	1. Occupation _____
2. Employer _____	2. Employer _____
3. Length of Employment _____	3. Length of Employment _____
4. Monthly Gross Income _____	4. Monthly Gross Income _____
5. Other _____	5. Other _____

22. ADDED, DELETED OR SUBSTITUTED BUYERS: The addition, deletion or substitution of any person or entity under this Agreement or to title prior to close of escrow shall require Seller's written consent. Seller may grant or withhold consent in Seller's sole discretion. Any additional or substituted person or entity shall, if requested by Seller, submit to Seller the same documentation as required for the original named Buyer. Seller and/or Brokers may obtain a credit report, at Buyer's expense, on any such person or entity.

Buyer's Initials (_____)(_____)
Seller's Initials (_____)(_____)

Reviewed by _____ Date _____

SFA REVISED 10/02 (PAGE 2 OF 3)

EQUAL HOUSING OPPORTUNITY

SELLER FINANCING ADDENDUM AND DISCLOSURE (SFA PAGE 2 OF 3)

Property Address: _____ Date: _____

23. CAUTION:

    A. If the Seller financing requires a balloon payment, Seller shall give Buyer written notice, according to the terms of Civil Code §2966, at least 90 and not more than 150 days before the balloon payment is due if the transaction is for the purchase of a dwelling for not more than four families.

    B. If **any** obligation secured by the Property calls for a balloon payment, Seller and Buyer are aware that refinancing of the balloon payment at maturity may be difficult or impossible, depending on conditions in the conventional mortgage marketplace at that time. There are no assurances that new financing or a loan extension will be available when the balloon prepayment, or any prepayment, is due.

    C. If **any** of the existing or proposed loans or extensions of credit would require refinancing as a result of a lack of full amortization, such refinancing might be difficult or impossible in the conventional mortgage marketplace.

    D. In the event of default by Buyer: (1) Seller may have to reinstate and/or make monthly payments on any and all senior encumbrances (including real property taxes) in order to protect Seller's secured interest; (2) Seller's rights are generally limited to foreclosure on the Property, pursuant to California Code of Civil Procedure §580b; and (3) the Property may lack sufficient equity to protect Seller's interests if the Property decreases in value.

If this three-page Addendum and Disclosure is used in a transaction for the purchase of a dwelling for not more than four families, it shall be prepared by an Arranger of Credit as defined in California Civil Code §2957(a). (The Arranger of Credit is usually the agent who obtained the offer.)

Arranger of Credit - (Print Firm Name) _____ By _____ Date _____

Address _____ City _____ State _____ Zip _____

Phone _____ Fax _____

> **BUYER AND SELLER ACKNOWLEDGE AND AGREE THAT BROKERS: (A) WILL NOT PROVIDE LEGAL OR TAX ADVICE; (B) WILL NOT PROVIDE OTHER ADVICE OR INFORMATION THAT EXCEEDS THE KNOWLEDGE, EDUCATION AND EXPERIENCE REQUIRED TO OBTAIN A REAL ESTATE LICENSE; OR (C) HAVE NOT AND WILL NOT VERIFY ANY INFORMATION PROVIDED BY EITHER BUYER OR SELLER. BUYER AND SELLER AGREE THAT THEY WILL SEEK LEGAL, TAX AND OTHER DESIRED ASSISTANCE FROM APPROPRIATE PROFESSIONALS. BUYER AND SELLER ACKNOWLEDGE THAT THE INFORMATION EACH HAS PROVIDED TO THE ARRANGER OF CREDIT FOR INCLUSION IN THIS DISCLOSURE FORM IS ACCURATE. BUYER AND SELLER FURTHER ACKNOWLEDGE THAT EACH HAS RECEIVED A COMPLETED COPY OF THIS DISCLOSURE FORM.**

Buyer _____ Date _____
          (signature)

Address _____ City _____ State _____ Zip _____

Phone _____ Fax _____ E-mail _____

Buyer _____ Date _____
          (signature)

Address _____ City _____ State _____ Zip _____

Phone _____ Fax _____ E-mail _____

Seller _____ Date _____
          (signature)

Address _____ City _____ State _____ Zip _____

Phone _____ Fax _____ E-mail _____

Seller _____ Date _____
          (signature)

Address _____ City _____ State _____ Zip _____

Phone _____ Fax _____ E-mail _____

THIS FORM HAS BEEN APPROVED BY THE CALIFORNIA ASSOCIATION OF REALTORS® (C.A.R.). NO REPRESENTATION IS MADE AS TO THE LEGAL VALIDITY OR ADEQUACY OF ANY PROVISION IN ANY SPECIFIC TRANSACTION. A REAL ESTATE BROKER IS THE PERSON QUALIFIED TO ADVISE ON REAL ESTATE TRANSACTIONS. IF YOU DESIRE LEGAL OR TAX ADVICE, CONSULT AN APPROPRIATE PROFESSIONAL.

This form is available for use by the entire real estate industry. It is not intended to identify the user as a REALTOR®. REALTOR® is a registered collective membership mark which may be used only by members of the NATIONAL ASSOCIATION OF REALTORS® who subscribe to its Code of Ethics.

SURE TRAC
The System for Success™

Published by the
California Association of REALTORS®

Reviewed by _____ Date _____

EQUAL HOUSING OPPORTUNITY

SFA REVISED 10/02 (PAGE 3 OF 3)

418

SELLER FINANCING ADDENDUM AND DISCLOSURE (SFA PAGE 3 OF 3)

CALIFORNIA
ASSOCIATION
OF REALTORS®

CALIFORNIA
RESIDENTIAL PURCHASE AGREEMENT
AND JOINT ESCROW INSTRUCTIONS
For Use With Single Family Residential Property — Attached or Detached
(C.A.R. Form RPA-CA, Revised 10/02)

Date _____, at _____, California.
1. **OFFER:**
  A. **THIS IS AN OFFER FROM** _____ ("Buyer").
  B. **THE REAL PROPERTY TO BE ACQUIRED** is described as _____
      _____, Assessor's Parcel No. _____, situated in
      _____, County of _____, California, ("Property").
  C. **THE PURCHASE PRICE** offered is _____
      _____ Dollars $ _____.
  D. **CLOSE OF ESCROW** shall occur on _____ (date)(or ☐ _____ **Days** After Acceptance).
2. **FINANCE TERMS:** Obtaining the loans below **is a contingency** of this Agreement unless: **(i)** either 2K or 2L is checked below; or **(ii)** otherwise agreed in writing. Buyer shall act diligently and in good faith to obtain the designated loans. Obtaining deposit, down payment and closing costs **is not a contingency.** Buyer represents that funds will be good when deposited with Escrow Holder.
  A. **INITIAL DEPOSIT:** Buyer has given a deposit in the amount of . . . .$ _____
      to the agent submitting the offer (or to ☐ _____), by personal check
      (or ☐ _____), made payable to _____
      which shall be held uncashed until Acceptance and then deposited within **3** business days after
      Acceptance (or ☐ _____), with
      Escrow Holder, (or ☐ into Broker's trust account).
  B. **INCREASED DEPOSIT:** Buyer shall deposit with Escrow Holder an increased deposit in the amount of . .$ _____
      within _____ **Days** After Acceptance, or ☐ _____.
  C. **FIRST LOAN IN THE AMOUNT OF** . . . .$ _____
      (1) NEW First Deed of Trust in favor of lender, encumbering the Property, securing a note payable at
      maximum interest of _____% fixed rate, or _____% initial adjustable rate with a maximum
      interest rate of _____%, balance due in _____ years, amortized over _____ years. Buyer
      shall pay loan fees/points not to exceed _____ (These terms apply whether the designated loan
      is conventional, FHA or VA.)
      (2) ☐ FHA ☐ VA: (The following terms only apply to the FHA or VA loan that is checked.)
      Seller shall pay _____% discount points. Seller shall pay other fees not allowed to be paid by
      Buyer, ☐ not to exceed $_____. Seller shall pay the cost of lender required Repairs
      (including those for wood destroying pest) not otherwise provided for in this Agreement, ☐ not to
      exceed $ _____. (Actual loan amount may increase if mortgage insurance premiums,
      funding fees or closing costs are financed.)
  D. **ADDITIONAL FINANCING TERMS:** ☐ Seller financing, (C.A.R. Form SFA); ☐ secondary financing, . . .$ _____
      (C.A.R. Form PAA, paragraph 4A); ☐ assumed financing (C.A.R. Form PAA, paragraph 4B)
      _____
      _____
  E. **BALANCE OF PURCHASE PRICE** (not including costs of obtaining loans and other closing costs) in the amount of . .$ _____
      to be deposited with Escrow Holder within sufficient time to close escrow.
  F. **PURCHASE PRICE (TOTAL):** . . . .$ _____
  G. **LOAN APPLICATIONS:** Within **7 (or** ☐ _____**) Days** After Acceptance, Buyer shall provide Seller a letter from lender or mortgage loan broker stating that, based on a review of Buyer's written application and credit report, Buyer is prequalified or preapproved for the NEW loan specified in 2C above.
  H. **VERIFICATION OF DOWN PAYMENT AND CLOSING COSTS:** Buyer (or Buyer's lender or loan broker pursuant to 2G) shall, within **7 (or** ☐ _____**) Days** After Acceptance, provide Seller written verification of Buyer's down payment and closing costs.
  I. **LOAN CONTINGENCY REMOVAL: (i)** Within **17 (or** ☐ _____**) Days** After Acceptance, Buyer shall, as specified in paragraph 14, remove the loan contingency or cancel this Agreement; **OR (ii)** (if checked) ☐ the loan contingency shall remain in effect until the designated loans are funded.
  J. **APPRAISAL CONTINGENCY AND REMOVAL:** This Agreement is (**OR,** if checked, ☐ is NOT) contingent upon the Property appraising at no less than the specified purchase price. If there is a loan contingency, at the time the loan contingency is removed (or, if checked, ☐ within **17 (or** ____**) Days** After Acceptance), Buyer shall, as specified in paragraph 14B(3), remove the appraisal contingency or cancel this Agreement. If there is no loan contingency, Buyer shall, as specified in paragraph 14B(3), remove the appraisal contingency within **17 (or** ____**) Days** After Acceptance.
  K. ☐ **NO LOAN CONTINGENCY** (If checked): Obtaining any loan in paragraphs 2C, 2D or elsewhere in this Agreement is NOT a contingency of this Agreement. If Buyer does not obtain the loan and as a result Buyer does not purchase the Property, Seller may be entitled to Buyer's deposit or other legal remedies.
  L. ☐ **ALL CASH OFFER** (If checked): No loan is needed to purchase the Property. Buyer shall, within **7 (or** ☐ _____**) Days** After Acceptance, provide Seller written verification of sufficient funds to close this transaction.
3. **CLOSING AND OCCUPANCY:**
  A. Buyer intends (or ☐ does not intend) to occupy the Property as Buyer's primary residence.
  B. **Seller-occupied or vacant property:** Occupancy shall be delivered to Buyer at _____ AM/PM, ☐ on the date of Close Of Escrow; ☐ on _____; or ☐ no later than _____ **Days** After Close Of Escrow. (C.A.R. Form PAA, paragraph 2.) If transfer of title and occupancy do not occur at the same time, Buyer and Seller are advised to: **(i)** enter into a written occupancy agreement; and **(ii)** consult with their insurance and legal advisors.

RPA-CA REVISED 10/02 (PAGE 1 OF 8) Print Date

Buyer's Initials (_____)(_____)
Seller's Initials (_____)(_____)

Reviewed by _____ Date _____

EQUAL HOUSING
OPPORTUNITY

CALIFORNIA RESIDENTIAL PURCHASE AGREEMENT (RPA-CA PAGE 1 OF 8)

Property Address: _____ Date: _____

C. **Tenant-occupied property: (i) Property shall be vacant** at least **5 (or** ☐ _____) **Days** Prior to Close Of Escrow, unless otherwise agreed in writing. **Note to Seller: If you are unable to deliver Property vacant in accordance with rent control and other applicable Law, you may be in breach of this Agreement.**

OR **(ii)** (if checked) ☐ **Tenant to remain in possession.** The attached addendum is incorporated into this Agreement (C.A.R. Form PAA, paragraph 3.);

OR **(iii)** (if checked) ☐ **This Agreement is contingent** upon Buyer and Seller entering into a written agreement regarding occupancy of the Property within the time specified in paragraph 14B(1). If no written agreement is reached within this time, either Buyer or Seller may cancel this Agreement in writing.

D. At Close Of Escrow, Seller assigns to Buyer any assignable warranty rights for items included in the sale and shall provide any available Copies of such warranties. Brokers cannot and will not determine the assignability of any warranties.

E. At Close Of Escrow, unless otherwise agreed in writing, Seller shall provide keys and/or means to operate all locks, mailboxes, security systems, alarms and garage door openers. If Property is a condominium or located in a common interest subdivision, Buyer may be required to pay a deposit to the Homeowners' Association ("HOA") to obtain keys to accessible HOA facilities.

4. **ALLOCATION OF COSTS** (If checked): Unless otherwise specified here, this paragraph only determines who is to pay for the report, inspection, test or service mentioned. If not specified here or elsewhere in this Agreement, the determination of who is to pay for any work recommended or identified by any such report, inspection, test or service shall be by the method specified in paragraph 14B(2).

A. **WOOD DESTROYING PEST INSPECTION:**

(1) ☐ Buyer ☐ Seller shall pay for an inspection and report for wood destroying pests and organisms ("Report") which shall be prepared by _____, a registered structural pest control company. The Report shall cover the accessible areas of the main building and attached structures and, if checked: ☐ detached garages and carports, ☐ detached decks, ☐ the following other structures or areas _____. The Report shall not include roof coverings. If Property is a condominium or located in a common interest subdivision, the Report shall include only the separate interest and any exclusive-use areas being transferred and shall not include common areas, unless otherwise agreed. Water tests of shower pans on upper level units may not be performed without consent of the owners of property below the shower.

OR (2) ☐ **(If checked)** The attached addendum (C.A.R. Form WPA) regarding wood destroying pest inspection and allocation of cost is incorporated into this Agreement.

B. **OTHER INSPECTIONS AND REPORTS:**

(1) ☐ Buyer ☐ Seller shall pay to have septic or private sewage disposal systems inspected _____.

(2) ☐ Buyer ☐ Seller shall pay to have domestic wells tested for water potability and productivity _____.

(3) ☐ Buyer ☐ Seller shall pay for a natural hazard zone disclosure report prepared by _____.

(4) ☐ Buyer ☐ Seller shall pay for the following inspection or report _____.

(5) ☐ Buyer ☐ Seller shall pay for the following inspection or report _____.

C. **GOVERNMENT REQUIREMENTS AND RETROFIT:**

(1) ☐ Buyer ☐ Seller shall pay for smoke detector installation and/or water heater bracing, if required by Law. Prior to Close Of Escrow, Seller shall provide Buyer a written statement of compliance in accordance with state and local Law, unless exempt.

(2) ☐ Buyer ☐ Seller shall pay the cost of compliance with any other minimum mandatory government retrofit standards, inspections and reports if required as a condition of closing escrow under any Law. _____.

D. **ESCROW AND TITLE:**

(1) ☐ Buyer ☐ Seller shall pay escrow fee _____.

Escrow Holder shall be _____.

(2) ☐ Buyer ☐ Seller shall pay for **owner's** title insurance policy specified in paragraph 12E _____.

Owner's title policy to be issued by _____.

(Buyer shall pay for any title insurance policy insuring Buyer's **lender**, unless otherwise agreed in writing.)

E. **OTHER COSTS:**

(1) ☐ Buyer ☐ Seller shall pay County transfer tax or transfer fee _____.

(2) ☐ Buyer ☐ Seller shall pay City transfer tax or transfer fee _____.

(3) ☐ Buyer ☐ Seller shall pay HOA transfer fee _____.

(4) ☐ Buyer ☐ Seller shall pay HOA document preparation fees _____.

(5) ☐ Buyer ☐ Seller shall pay the cost, not to exceed $ _____, of a one-year home warranty plan, issued by _____

with the following optional coverage: _____.

(6) ☐ Buyer ☐ Seller shall pay for _____.

(7) ☐ Buyer ☐ Seller shall pay for _____.

5. **STATUTORY DISCLOSURES (INCLUDING LEAD-BASED PAINT HAZARD DISCLOSURES) AND CANCELLATION RIGHTS:**

A. **(1)** Seller shall, within the time specified in paragraph 14A, deliver to Buyer, if required by Law: **(i)** Federal Lead-Based Paint Disclosures and pamphlet ("Lead Disclosures"); and **(ii)** disclosures or notices required by sections 1102 et. seq. and 1103 et. seq. of the California Civil Code ("Statutory Disclosures"). Statutory Disclosures include, but are not limited to, a Real Estate Transfer Disclosure Statement ("TDS"), Natural Hazard Disclosure Statement ("NHD"), notice or actual knowledge of release of illegal controlled substance, notice of special tax and/or assessments (or, if allowed, substantially equivalent notice regarding the Mello-Roos Community Facilities Act and Improvement Bond Act of 1915) and, if Seller has actual knowledge, an industrial use and military ordnance location disclosure (C.A.R. Form SSD).

(2) Buyer shall, within the time specified in paragraph 14B(1), return Signed Copies of the Statutory and Lead Disclosures to Seller.

(3) In the event Seller, prior to Close Of Escrow, becomes aware of adverse conditions materially affecting the Property, or any material inaccuracy in disclosures, information or representations previously provided to Buyer of which Buyer is otherwise unaware, Seller shall promptly provide a subsequent or amended disclosure or notice, in writing, covering those items. **However, a subsequent or amended disclosure shall not be required for conditions and material inaccuracies disclosed in reports ordered and paid for by Buyer.**

Buyer's Initials (_____)(_____)
Seller's Initials (_____)(_____)

Reviewed by _____ Date _____

RPA-CA REVISED 10/02 (PAGE 2 OF 8)

420

CALIFORNIA RESIDENTIAL PURCHASE AGREEMENT (RPA-CA PAGE 2 OF 8)

EQUAL HOUSING OPPORTUNITY

Property Address: _____ Date: _____

(4) If any disclosure or notice specified in 5A(1), or subsequent or amended disclosure or notice is delivered to Buyer after the offer is Signed, Buyer shall have the right to cancel this Agreement within **3 Days** After delivery in person, or **5 Days** After delivery by deposit in the mail, by giving written notice of cancellation to Seller or Seller's agent. (Lead Disclosures sent by mail must be sent certified mail or better.)
(5) **Note to Buyer and Seller: Waiver of Statutory and Lead Disclosures is prohibited by Law.**

  B. **NATURAL AND ENVIRONMENTAL HAZARDS:** Within the time specified in paragraph 14A, Seller shall, if required by Law: **(i)** deliver to Buyer earthquake guides (and questionnaire) and environmental hazards booklet; **(ii)** even if exempt from the obligation to provide a NHD, disclose if the Property is located in a Special Flood Hazard Area; Potential Flooding (Inundation) Area; Very High Fire Hazard Zone; State Fire Responsibility Area; Earthquake Fault Zone; Seismic Hazard Zone; and **(iii)** disclose any other zone as required by Law and provide any other information required for those zones.

  C. **DATA BASE DISCLOSURE:** NOTICE: The California Department of Justice, sheriff's departments, police departments serving jurisdictions of 200,000 or more and many other local law enforcement authorities maintain for public access a data base of the locations of persons required to register pursuant to paragraph (1) of subdivision (a) of Section 290.4 of the Penal Code. The data base is updated on a quarterly basis and a source of information about the presence of these individuals in any neighborhood. The Department of Justice also maintains a Sex Offender Identification Line through which inquiries about individuals may be made. This is a "900" telephone service. Callers must have specific information about individuals they are checking. Information regarding neighborhoods is not available through the "900" telephone service.

6. **CONDOMINIUM/PLANNED UNIT DEVELOPMENT DISCLOSURES:**
  A. **SELLER HAS: 7 (or ☐ _____) Days** After Acceptance to disclose to Buyer whether the Property is a condominium, or is located in a planned unit development or other common interest subdivision (C.A.R. Form SSD).
  B. If the Property is a condominium or is located in a planned unit development or other common interest subdivision, Seller has **3 (or ☐ _____) Days** After Acceptance to request from the HOA (C.A.R. Form HOA): **(i)** Copies of any documents required by Law; **(ii)** disclosure of any pending or anticipated claim or litigation by or against the HOA; **(iii)** a statement containing the location and number of designated parking and storage spaces; **(iv)** Copies of the most recent 12 months of HOA minutes for regular and special meetings; and **(v)** the names and contact information of all HOAs governing the Property (collectively, "CI Disclosures"). Seller shall itemize and deliver to Buyer all CI Disclosures received from the HOA and any CI Disclosures in Seller's possession. Buyer's approval of CI Disclosures is a contingency of this Agreement as specified in paragraph 14B(3).

7. **CONDITIONS AFFECTING PROPERTY:**
  A. Unless otherwise agreed: **(i) the Property is sold (a) in its PRESENT physical condition as of the date of Acceptance and (b) subject to Buyer's Investigation rights; (ii)** the Property, including pool, spa, landscaping and grounds, is to be maintained in substantially the same condition as on the date of Acceptance; and **(iii)** all debris and personal property not included in the sale shall be removed by Close Of Escrow.
  B. **SELLER SHALL, within the time specified in paragraph 14A, DISCLOSE KNOWN MATERIAL FACTS AND DEFECTS affecting the Property, including known insurance claims within the past five years, AND MAKE OTHER DISCLOSURES REQUIRED BY LAW (C.A.R. Form SSD).**
  C. **NOTE TO BUYER: You are strongly advised to conduct investigations of the entire Property in order to determine its present condition since Seller may not be aware of all defects affecting the Property or other factors that you consider important. Property improvements may not be built according to code, in compliance with current Law, or have had permits issued.**
  D. **NOTE TO SELLER: Buyer has the right to inspect the Property and, as specified in paragraph 14B, based upon information discovered in those inspections: (i) cancel this Agreement; or (ii) request that you make Repairs or take other action.**

8. **ITEMS INCLUDED AND EXCLUDED:**
  A. **NOTE TO BUYER AND SELLER:** Items listed as included or excluded in the MLS, flyers or marketing materials are **not** included in the purchase price or excluded from the sale unless specified in 8B or C.
  B. **ITEMS INCLUDED IN SALE:**
    (1) All EXISTING fixtures and fittings that are attached to the Property;
    (2) Existing electrical, mechanical, lighting, plumbing and heating fixtures, ceiling fans, fireplace inserts, gas logs and grates, solar systems, built-in appliances, window and door screens, awnings, shutters, window coverings, attached floor coverings, television antennas, satellite dishes, private integrated telephone systems, air coolers/conditioners, pool/spa equipment, garage door openers/remote controls, mailbox, in-ground landscaping, trees/shrubs, water softeners, water purifiers, security systems/alarms; and
    (3) The following items: _____
    _____
    (4) Seller represents that all items included in the purchase price, unless otherwise specified, are owned by Seller.
    (5) All items included shall be transferred free of liens and without Seller warranty.
  C. **ITEMS EXCLUDED FROM SALE:** _____
    _____

9. **BUYER'S INVESTIGATION OF PROPERTY AND MATTERS AFFECTING PROPERTY:**
  A. Buyer's acceptance of the condition of, and any other matter affecting the Property, is a contingency of this Agreement as specified in this paragraph and paragraph 14B. Within the time specified in paragraph 14B(1), Buyer shall have the right, at Buyer's expense unless otherwise agreed, to conduct inspections, investigations, tests, surveys and other studies ("Buyer Investigations"), including, but not limited to, the right to: **(i)** inspect for lead-based paint and other lead-based paint hazards; **(ii)** inspect for wood destroying pests and organisms; **(iii)** review the registered sex offender database; **(iv)** confirm the insurability of Buyer and the Property; and **(v)** satisfy Buyer as to any matter specified in the attached Buyer's Inspection Advisory (C.A.R. Form BIA). Without Seller's prior written consent, Buyer shall neither make nor cause to be made: **(i)** invasive or destructive Buyer Investigations; or **(ii)** inspections by any governmental building or zoning inspector or government employee, unless required by Law.
  B. Buyer shall complete Buyer Investigations and, as specified in paragraph 14B, remove the contingency or cancel this Agreement. Buyer shall give Seller, at no cost, complete Copies of all Buyer Investigation reports obtained by Buyer. Seller shall make the Property available for all Buyer Investigations. Seller shall have water, gas, electricity and all operable pilot lights on for Buyer's Investigations and through the date possession is made available to Buyer.

Buyer's Initials (_____)(_____)
Seller's Initials (_____)(_____)

Copyright © 1991-2003, CALIFORNIA ASSOCIATION OF REALTORS®, INC.
RPA-CA REVISED 10/02 (PAGE 3 OF 8)

Reviewed by _____ Date _____

CALIFORNIA RESIDENTIAL PURCHASE AGREEMENT (RPA-CA PAGE 3 OF 8)

421

Property Address: _____ Date: _____

10. **REPAIRS:** Repairs shall be completed prior to final verification of condition unless otherwise agreed in writing. Repairs to be performed at Seller's expense may be performed by Seller or through others, provided that the work complies with applicable Law, including governmental permit, inspection and approval requirements. Repairs shall be performed in a good, skillful manner with materials of quality and appearance comparable to existing materials. It is understood that exact restoration of appearance or cosmetic items following all Repairs may not be possible. Seller shall: **(i)** obtain receipts for Repairs performed by others; **(ii)** prepare a written statement indicating the Repairs performed by Seller and the date of such Repairs; and **(iii)** provide Copies of receipts and statements to Buyer prior to final verification of condition.

11. **BUYER INDEMNITY AND SELLER PROTECTION FOR ENTRY UPON PROPERTY:** Buyer shall: **(i)** keep the Property free and clear of liens; **(ii)** Repair all damage arising from Buyer Investigations; and **(iii)** indemnify and hold Seller harmless from all resulting liability, claims, demands, damages and costs. Buyer shall carry, or Buyer shall require anyone acting on Buyer's behalf to carry, policies of liability, workers' compensation and other applicable insurance, defending and protecting Seller from liability for any injuries to persons or property occurring during any Buyer Investigations or work done on the Property at Buyer's direction prior to Close Of Escrow. Seller is advised that certain protections may be afforded Seller by recording a "Notice of Non-responsibility" (C.A.R. Form NNR) for Buyer Investigations and work done on the Property at Buyer's direction. Buyer's obligations under this paragraph shall survive the termination of this Agreement.

12. **TITLE AND VESTING:**
   A. Within the time specified in paragraph 14, Buyer shall be provided a current preliminary (title) report, which is only an offer by the title insurer to issue a policy of title insurance and may not contain every item affecting title. Buyer's review of the preliminary report and any other matters which may affect title are a contingency of this Agreement as specified in paragraph 14B.
   B. Title is taken in its present condition subject to all encumbrances, easements, covenants, conditions, restrictions, rights and other matters, whether of record or not, as of the date of Acceptance except: **(i)** monetary liens of record unless Buyer is assuming those obligations or taking the Property subject to those obligations; and **(ii)** those matters which Seller has agreed to remove in writing.
   C. Within the time specified in paragraph 14A, Seller has a duty to disclose to Buyer all matters known to Seller affecting title, whether of record or not.
   D. At Close Of Escrow, Buyer shall receive a grant deed conveying title (or, for stock cooperative or long-term lease, an assignment of stock certificate or of Seller's leasehold interest), including oil, mineral and water rights if currently owned by Seller. Title shall vest as designated in Buyer's supplemental escrow instructions. THE MANNER OF TAKING TITLE MAY HAVE SIGNIFICANT LEGAL AND TAX CONSEQUENCES. CONSULT AN APPROPRIATE PROFESSIONAL.
   E. Buyer shall receive a CLTA/ALTA Homeowner's Policy of Title Insurance. A title company, at Buyer's request, can provide information about the availability, desirability, coverage, and cost of various title insurance coverages and endorsements. If Buyer desires title coverage other than that required by this paragraph, Buyer shall instruct Escrow Holder in writing and pay any increase in cost.

13. **SALE OF BUYER'S PROPERTY:**
   A. This Agreement is NOT contingent upon the sale of any property owned by Buyer.
OR B. ☐ (If checked): The attached addendum (C.A.R. Form COP) regarding the contingency for the sale of property owned by Buyer is incorporated into this Agreement.

14. **TIME PERIODS; REMOVAL OF CONTINGENCIES; CANCELLATION RIGHTS: The following time periods may only be extended, altered, modified or changed by mutual written agreement. Any removal of contingencies or cancellation under this paragraph must be in writing (C.A.R. Form CR).**
   A. **SELLER HAS: 7 (or** ☐ **_____) Days** After Acceptance to deliver to Buyer all reports, disclosures and information for which Seller is responsible under paragraphs 4, 5A and B, 6A, 7B and 12.
   B. **(1) BUYER HAS: 17 (or** ☐ **_____) Days** After Acceptance, unless otherwise agreed in writing, to:
      (i) complete all Buyer Investigations; approve all disclosures, reports and other applicable information, which Buyer receives from Seller; and approve all matters affecting the Property (including lead-based paint and lead-based paint hazards as well as other information specified in paragraph 5 and insurability of Buyer and the Property); and
      (ii) return to Seller Signed Copies of Statutory and Lead Disclosures delivered by Seller in accordance with paragraph 5A.
      (2) Within the time specified in 14B(1), Buyer may request that Seller make repairs or take any other action regarding the Property (C.A.R. Form RR). Seller has no obligation to agree to or respond to Buyer's requests.
      (3) By the end of the time specified in 14B(1) (or 2I for loan contingency or 2J for appraisal contingency), Buyer shall, in writing, remove the applicable contingency (C.A.R. Form CR) or cancel this Agreement. However, if the following inspections, reports or disclosures are not made within the time specified in 14A, then Buyer has **5 (or** ☐ **_____) Days** after receipt of any such items, or the time specified in 14B(1), whichever is later, to remove the applicable contingency or cancel this Agreement in writing: **(i)** government-mandated inspections or reports required as a condition of closing; or **(ii)** Common Interest Disclosures pursuant to paragraph 6B.
   C. **CONTINUATION OF CONTINGENCY OR CONTRACTUAL OBLIGATION; SELLER RIGHT TO CANCEL:**
      (1) Seller right to Cancel; Buyer Contingencies: Seller, after first giving Buyer a Notice to Buyer to Perform (as specified below), may cancel this Agreement in writing and authorize return of Buyer's deposit if, by the time specified in this Agreement, Buyer does not remove in writing the applicable contingency or cancel this Agreement. Once all contingencies have been removed, failure of either Buyer or Seller to close escrow on time may be a breach of this Agreement.
      (2) Continuation of Contingency: Even after the expiration of the time specified in 14B(1), Buyer retains the right to make requests to Seller, remove in writing the applicable contingency or cancel this Agreement until Seller cancels pursuant to 14C(1). Once Seller receives Buyer's written removal of all contingencies, Seller may not cancel this Agreement pursuant to 14C(1).
      (3) Seller right to Cancel; Buyer Contract Obligations: Seller, after first giving Buyer a Notice to Buyer to Perform (as specified below), may cancel this Agreement in writing and authorize return of Buyer's deposit for any of the following reasons: **(i)** if Buyer fails to deposit funds as required by 2A or 2B; **(ii)** if the funds deposited pursuant to 2A or 2B are not good when deposited; **(iii)** if Buyer fails to provide a letter as required by 2G; **(iv)** if Buyer fails to provide verification as required by 2H or 2L; **(v)** if Seller reasonably disapproves of the verification provided by 2H or 2L; **(vi)** if Buyer fails to return Statutory and Lead Disclosures as required by paragraph 5A(2); or **(vii)** if Buyer fails to sign or initial a separate liquidated damage form for an increased deposit as required by paragraph 16. **Seller is not required to give Buyer a Notice to Perform regarding Close of Escrow.**
      (4) Notice To Buyer To Perform: The Notice to Buyer to Perform (C.A.R. Form NBP) shall: **(i)** be in writing; **(ii)** be signed by Seller; and **(iii)** give Buyer at least **24 (or** ☐ **_____) hours** (or until the time specified in the applicable paragraph, whichever occurs last) to take the applicable action. A Notice to Buyer to Perform may not be given any earlier than **2 Days** Prior to the expiration of the applicable time for Buyer to remove a contingency or cancel this Agreement or meet a 14C(3) obligation.

Buyer's Initials (_____)(_____)
Seller's Initials (_____)(_____)

RPA-CA REVISED 10/02 (PAGE 4 OF 8)

| Reviewed by _____ Date _____ |

CALIFORNIA RESIDENTIAL PURCHASE AGREEMENT (RPA-CA PAGE 4 OF 8)

Property Address: _____   Date: _____

   D. EFFECT OF BUYER'S REMOVAL OF CONTINGENCIES : If Buyer removes, in writing, any contingency or cancellation rights, unless otherwise specified in a separate written agreement between Buyer and Seller, Buyer shall conclusively be deemed to have: **(i)** completed all Buyer Investigations, and review of reports and other applicable information and disclosures pertaining to that contingency or cancellation right; **(ii)** elected to proceed with the transaction; and **(iii)** assumed all liability, responsibility and expense for Repairs or corrections pertaining to that contingency or cancellation right, or for inability to obtain financing.

   E. EFFECT OF CANCELLATION ON DEPOSITS: If Buyer or Seller gives written notice of cancellation pursuant to rights duly exercised under the terms of this Agreement, Buyer and Seller agree to Sign mutual instructions to cancel the sale and escrow and release deposits, less fees and costs, to the party entitled to the funds. Fees and costs may be payable to service providers and vendors for services and products provided during escrow. **Release of funds will require mutual Signed release instructions from Buyer and Seller, judicial decision or arbitration award. A party may be subject to a civil penalty of up to $1,000 for refusal to sign such instructions if no good faith dispute exists as to who is entitled to the deposited funds (Civil Code §1057.3).**

15. FINAL VERIFICATION OF CONDITION: Buyer shall have the right to make a final inspection of the Property within **5 (or _____) Days** Prior to Close Of Escrow, NOT AS A CONTINGENCY OF THE SALE, but solely to confirm: **(i)** the Property is maintained pursuant to paragraph 7A; **(ii)** Repairs have been completed as agreed; and **(iii)** Seller has complied with Seller's other obligations under this Agreement.

16. LIQUIDATED DAMAGES: If Buyer fails to complete this purchase because of Buyer's default, Seller shall retain, as liquidated damages, the deposit actually paid. If the Property is a dwelling with no more than four units, one of which Buyer intends to occupy, then the amount retained shall be no more than 3% of the purchase price. Any excess shall be returned to Buyer. Release of funds will require mutual, Signed release instructions from both Buyer and Seller, judicial decision or arbitration award.
BUYER AND SELLER SHALL SIGN A SEPARATE LIQUIDATED DAMAGES PROVISION FOR ANY INCREASED DEPOSIT. (C.A.R. FORM RID)

Buyer's Initials _____ / _____	Seller's Initials _____ / _____

17. DISPUTE RESOLUTION:

   A. MEDIATION: Buyer and Seller agree to mediate any dispute or claim arising between them out of this Agreement, or any resulting transaction, before resorting to arbitration or court action. Paragraphs 17B(2) and (3) below apply whether or not the Arbitration provision is initialed. Mediation fees, if any, shall be divided equally among the parties involved. If, for any dispute or claim to which this paragraph applies, any party commences an action without first attempting to resolve the matter through mediation, or refuses to mediate after a request has been made, then that party shall not be entitled to recover attorney fees, even if they would otherwise be available to that party in any such action. THIS MEDIATION PROVISION APPLIES WHETHER OR NOT THE ARBITRATION PROVISION IS INITIALED.

   B. ARBITRATION OF DISPUTES: (1) Buyer and Seller agree that any dispute or claim in Law or equity arising between them out of this Agreement or any resulting transaction, which is not settled through mediation, shall be decided by neutral, binding arbitration, including and subject to paragraphs 17B(2) and (3) below. The arbitrator shall be a retired judge or justice, or an attorney with at least 5 years of residential real estate Law experience, unless the parties mutually agree to a different arbitrator, who shall render an award in accordance with substantive California Law. The parties shall have the right to discovery in accordance with California Code of Civil Procedure §1283.05. In all other respects, the arbitration shall be conducted in accordance with Title 9 of Part III of the California Code of Civil Procedure. Judgment upon the award of the arbitrator(s) may be entered into any court having jurisdiction. Interpretation of this agreement to arbitrate shall be governed by the Federal Arbitration Act.
(2) EXCLUSIONS FROM MEDIATION AND ARBITRATION: The following matters are excluded from mediation and arbitration: (i) a judicial or non-judicial foreclosure or other action or proceeding to enforce a deed of trust, mortgage or installment land sale contract as defined in California Civil Code §2985; (ii) an unlawful detainer action; (iii) the filing or enforcement of a mechanic's lien; and (iv) any matter that is within the jurisdiction of a probate, small claims or bankruptcy court. The filing of a court action to enable the recording of a notice of pending action, for order of attachment, receivership, injunction, or other provisional remedies, shall not constitute a waiver of the mediation and arbitration provisions.
(3) BROKERS: Buyer and Seller agree to mediate and arbitrate disputes or claims involving either or both Brokers, consistent with 17A and B, provided either or both Brokers shall have agreed to such mediation or arbitration prior to, or within a reasonable time after, the dispute or claim is presented to Brokers. Any election by either or both Brokers to participate in mediation or arbitration shall not result in Brokers being deemed parties to the Agreement.
     "NOTICE: BY INITIALING IN THE SPACE BELOW YOU ARE AGREEING TO HAVE ANY DISPUTE ARISING OUT OF THE MATTERS INCLUDED IN THE 'ARBITRATION OF DISPUTES' PROVISION DECIDED BY NEUTRAL ARBITRATION AS PROVIDED BY CALIFORNIA LAW AND YOU ARE GIVING UP ANY RIGHTS YOU MIGHT POSSESS TO HAVE THE DISPUTE LITIGATED IN A COURT OR JURY TRIAL. BY INITIALING IN THE SPACE BELOW YOU ARE GIVING UP YOUR JUDICIAL RIGHTS TO DISCOVERY AND APPEAL, UNLESS THOSE RIGHTS ARE SPECIFICALLY INCLUDED IN THE 'ARBITRATION OF DISPUTES' PROVISION. IF YOU REFUSE TO SUBMIT TO ARBITRATION AFTER AGREEING TO THIS PROVISION, YOU MAY BE COMPELLED TO ARBITRATE UNDER THE AUTHORITY OF THE CALIFORNIA CODE OF CIVIL PROCEDURE. YOUR AGREEMENT TO THIS ARBITRATION PROVISION IS VOLUNTARY."
     "WE HAVE READ AND UNDERSTAND THE FOREGOING AND AGREE TO SUBMIT DISPUTES ARISING OUT OF THE MATTERS INCLUDED IN THE 'ARBITRATION OF DISPUTES' PROVISION TO NEUTRAL ARBITRATION."

Buyer's Initials _____ / _____	Seller's Initials _____ / _____

Buyer's Initials (_____)(_____)
Seller's Initials (_____)(_____)

Reviewed by _____ Date _____

EQUAL HOUSING OPPORTUNITY

CALIFORNIA RESIDENTIAL PURCHASE AGREEMENT (RPA-CA PAGE 5 OF 8)

Property Address: _____ Date: _____

18. **PRORATIONS OF PROPERTY TAXES AND OTHER ITEMS:** Unless otherwise agreed in writing, the following items shall be PAID CURRENT and prorated between Buyer and Seller as of Close Of Escrow: real property taxes and assessments, interest, rents, HOA regular, special, and emergency dues and assessments imposed prior to Close Of Escrow, premiums on insurance assumed by Buyer, payments on bonds and assessments assumed by Buyer, and payments on Mello-Roos and other Special Assessment District bonds and assessments that are now a lien. The following items shall be assumed by Buyer WITHOUT CREDIT toward the purchase price: prorated payments on Mello-Roos and other Special Assessment District bonds and assessments and HOA special assessments that are now a lien but not yet due. Property will be reassessed upon change of ownership. Any supplemental tax bills shall be paid as follows: **(i)** for periods after Close Of Escrow, by Buyer; and **(ii)** for periods prior to Close Of Escrow, by Seller. TAX BILLS ISSUED AFTER CLOSE OF ESCROW SHALL BE HANDLED DIRECTLY BETWEEN BUYER AND SELLER. Prorations shall be made based on a 30-day month.

19. **WITHHOLDING TAXES:** Seller and Buyer agree to execute any instrument, affidavit, statement or instruction reasonably necessary to comply with federal (FIRPTA) and California withholding Law, if required (C.A.R. Forms AS and AB).

20. **MULTIPLE LISTING SERVICE ("MLS"):** Brokers are authorized to report to the MLS a pending sale and, upon Close Of Escrow, the terms of this transaction to be published and disseminated to persons and entities authorized to use the information on terms approved by the MLS.

21. **EQUAL HOUSING OPPORTUNITY:** The Property is sold in compliance with federal, state and local anti-discrimination Laws.

22. **ATTORNEY FEES:** In any action, proceeding, or arbitration between Buyer and Seller arising out of this Agreement, the prevailing Buyer or Seller shall be entitled to reasonable attorney fees and costs from the non-prevailing Buyer or Seller, except as provided in paragraph 17A.

23. **SELECTION OF SERVICE PROVIDERS:** If Brokers refer Buyer or Seller to persons, vendors, or service or product providers ("Providers"), Brokers do not guarantee the performance of any Providers. Buyer and Seller may select ANY Providers of their own choosing.

24. **TIME OF ESSENCE; ENTIRE CONTRACT; CHANGES:** Time is of the essence. All understandings between the parties are incorporated in this Agreement. Its terms are intended by the parties as a final, complete and exclusive expression of their Agreement with respect to its subject matter, and may not be contradicted by evidence of any prior agreement or contemporaneous oral agreement. If any provision of this Agreement is held to be ineffective or invalid, the remaining provisions will nevertheless be given full force and effect. **Neither this Agreement nor any provision in it may be extended, amended, altered or changed, except in writing Signed by Buyer and Seller.**

25. **OTHER TERMS AND CONDITIONS,** including attached supplements:
    A. ☑ Buyer's Inspection Advisory (C.A.R. Form BIA) _____
    B. ☐ Purchase Agreement Addendum (C.A.R. Form PAA paragraph numbers: _____)
    C. _____
    _____
    _____

26. **DEFINITIONS:** As used in this Agreement:
    A. **"Acceptance"** means the time the offer or final counter offer is accepted in writing by a party and is delivered to and personally received by the other party or that party's authorized agent in accordance with the terms of this offer or a final counter offer.
    B. **"Agreement"** means the terms and conditions of this accepted California Residential Purchase Agreement and any accepted counter offers and addenda.
    C. **"C.A.R. Form"** means the specific form referenced or another comparable form agreed to by the parties.
    D. **"Close Of Escrow"** means the date the grant deed, or other evidence of transfer of title, is recorded. If the scheduled close of escrow falls on a Saturday, Sunday or legal holiday, then close of escrow shall be the next business day after the scheduled close of escrow date.
    E. **"Copy"** means copy by any means including photocopy, NCR, facsimile and electronic.
    F. **"Days"** means calendar days, unless otherwise required by Law.
    G. **"Days After"** means the specified number of calendar days after the occurrence of the event specified, not counting the calendar date on which the specified event occurs, and ending at 11:59PM on the final day.
    H. **"Days Prior"** means the specified number of calendar days before the occurrence of the event specified, not counting the calendar date on which the specified event is scheduled to occur.
    I. **"Electronic Copy" or "Electronic Signature"** means, as applicable, an electronic copy or signature complying with California Law. Buyer and Seller agree that electronic means will not be used by either party to modify or alter the content or integrity of this Agreement without the knowledge and consent of the other.
    J. **"Law"** means any law, code, statute, ordinance, regulation, rule or order, which is adopted by a controlling city, county, state or federal legislative, judicial or executive body or agency.
    K. **"Notice to Buyer to Perform"** means a document (C.A.R. Form NBP), which shall be in writing and Signed by Seller and shall give Buyer at least 24 hours **(or as otherwise specified in paragraph 14C(4))** to remove a contingency or perform as applicable.
    L. **"Repairs"** means any repairs (including pest control), alterations, replacements, modifications or retrofitting of the Property provided for under this Agreement.
    M. **"Signed"** means either a handwritten or electronic signature on an original document, Copy or any counterpart.
    N. **Singular and Plural** terms each include the other, when appropriate.

Buyer's Initials (_____)(_____)
Seller's Initials (_____)(_____)

RPA-CA REVISED 10/02 (PAGE 6 OF 8)

Reviewed by _____ Date _____

EQUAL HOUSING OPPORTUNITY

424

CALIFORNIA RESIDENTIAL PURCHASE AGREEMENT (RPA-CA PAGE 6 OF 8)

Property Address: _____ Date: _____

27. AGENCY:
   A. DISCLOSURE: Buyer and Seller each acknowledge prior receipt of C.A.R. Form AD "Disclosure Regarding Real Estate Agency Relationships."
   B. POTENTIALLY COMPETING BUYERS AND SELLERS: Buyer and Seller each acknowledge receipt of a disclosure of the possibility of multiple representation by the Broker representing that principal. This disclosure may be part of a listing agreement, buyer-broker agreement or separate document (C.A.R. Form DA). Buyer understands that Broker representing Buyer may also represent other potential buyers, who may consider, make offers on or ultimately acquire the Property. Seller understands that Broker representing Seller may also represent other sellers with competing properties of interest to this Buyer.
   C. CONFIRMATION: The following agency relationships are hereby confirmed for this transaction:
   Listing Agent _____ (Print Firm Name) is the agent of (check one): ☐ the Seller exclusively; or ☐ both the Buyer and Seller.
   Selling Agent _____ (Print Firm Name) (if not same as Listing Agent) is the agent of (check one): ☐ the Buyer exclusively; or ☐ the Seller exclusively; or ☐ both the Buyer and Seller. Real Estate Brokers are not parties to the Agreement between Buyer and Seller.

28. JOINT ESCROW INSTRUCTIONS TO ESCROW HOLDER:
   A. The following paragraphs, or applicable portions thereof, of this Agreement constitute the joint escrow instructions of Buyer and Seller to Escrow Holder, which Escrow Holder is to use along with any related counter offers and addenda, and any additional mutual instructions to close the escrow: 1, 2, 4, 12, 13B, 14E, 18, 19, 24, 25B and C, 26, 28, 29, 32A, 33 and paragraph D of the section titled Real Estate Brokers on page 8. If a Copy of the separate compensation agreement(s) provided for in paragraph 29 or 32A, or paragraph D of the section titled Real Estate Brokers on page 8 is deposited with Escrow Holder by Broker, Escrow Holder shall accept such agreement(s) and pay out from Buyer's or Seller's funds, or both, as applicable, the Broker's compensation provided for in such agreement(s). The terms and conditions of this Agreement not set forth in the specified paragraphs are additional matters for the information of Escrow Holder, but about which Escrow Holder need not be concerned. Buyer and Seller will receive Escrow Holder's general provisions directly from Escrow Holder and will execute such provisions upon Escrow Holder's request. To the extent the general provisions are inconsistent or conflict with this Agreement, the general provisions will control as to the duties and obligations of Escrow Holder only. Buyer and Seller will execute additional instructions, documents and forms provided by Escrow Holder that are reasonably necessary to close the escrow.
   B. A Copy of this Agreement shall be delivered to Escrow Holder within **3** business days after Acceptance (or ☐ _____). Buyer and Seller authorize Escrow Holder to accept and rely on Copies and Signatures as defined in this Agreement as originals, to open escrow and for other purposes of escrow. The validity of this Agreement as between Buyer and Seller is not affected by whether or when Escrow Holder Signs this Agreement.
   C. Brokers are a party to the escrow for the sole purpose of compensation pursuant to paragraphs 29, 32A and paragraph D of the section titled Real Estate Brokers on page 8. Buyer and Seller irrevocably assign to Brokers compensation specified in paragraphs 29 and 32A, respectively, and irrevocably instruct Escrow Holder to disburse those funds to Brokers at Close Of Escrow or pursuant to any other mutually executed cancellation agreement. Compensation instructions can be amended or revoked only with the written consent of Brokers. Escrow Holder shall immediately notify Brokers: **(i)** if Buyer's initial or any additional deposit is not made pursuant to this Agreement, or is not good at time of deposit with Escrow Holder; or **(ii)** if Buyer and Seller instruct Escrow Holder to cancel escrow.
   D. A Copy of any amendment that affects any paragraph of this Agreement for which Escrow Holder is responsible shall be delivered to Escrow Holder within **2** business days after mutual execution of the amendment.

29. BROKER COMPENSATION FROM BUYER: If applicable, upon Close Of Escrow, **Buyer** agrees to pay compensation to Broker as specified in a separate written agreement between Buyer and Broker.

30. TERMS AND CONDITIONS OF OFFER:
   This is an offer to purchase the Property on the above terms and conditions. All paragraphs with spaces for initials by Buyer and Seller are incorporated in this Agreement only if initialed by all parties. If at least one but not all parties initial, a counter offer is required until agreement is reached. Seller has the right to continue to offer the Property for sale and to accept any other offer at any time prior to notification of Acceptance. Buyer has read and acknowledges receipt of a Copy of the offer and agrees to the above confirmation of agency relationships. If this offer is accepted and Buyer subsequently defaults, Buyer may be responsible for payment of Brokers' compensation. This Agreement and any supplement, addendum or modification, including any Copy, may be Signed in two or more counterparts, all of which shall constitute one and the same writing.

Buyer's Initials (_____)(_____)
Seller's Initials (_____)(_____)

RPA-CA REVISED 10/02 (PAGE 7 OF 8)

Reviewed by _____ Date _____

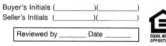

Property Address: _____ Date: _____

31. EXPIRATION OF OFFER: This offer shall be deemed revoked and the deposit shall be returned unless the offer is Signed by Seller and a Copy of the Signed offer is personally received by Buyer, or by _____, who is authorized to receive it by 5:00 PM on the third calendar day after this offer is signed by Buyer (or, if checked, ☐ by _____ (date), at _____ AM/PM).

Date _____ Date _____

BUYER _____ BUYER _____

(Print name) _____ (Print name) _____

(Address) _____

32. BROKER COMPENSATION FROM SELLER:
    A. Upon Close Of Escrow, **Seller** agrees to pay compensation to Broker as specified in a separate written agreement between Seller and Broker.
    B. If escrow does not close, compensation is payable as specified in that separate written agreement.
33. ACCEPTANCE OF OFFER: Seller warrants that Seller is the owner of the Property, or has the authority to execute this Agreement. Seller accepts the above offer, agrees to sell the Property on the above terms and conditions, and agrees to the above confirmation of agency relationships. Seller has read and acknowledges receipt of a Copy of this Agreement, and authorizes Broker to deliver a Signed Copy to Buyer.
    ☐ (If checked) **SUBJECT TO ATTACHED COUNTER OFFER, DATED** _____.

Date _____ Date _____

SELLER _____ SELLER _____

(Print name) _____ (Print name) _____

(Address) _____

(___/___) **CONFIRMATION OF ACCEPTANCE:** A Copy of Signed Acceptance was personally received by Buyer or Buyer's authorized
(Initials) agent on (date) _____ at _____ AM/PM. **A binding Agreement is created when a Copy of Signed Acceptance is personally received by Buyer or Buyer's authorized agent whether or not confirmed in this document. Completion of this confirmation is not legally required in order to create a binding Agreement; it is solely intended to evidence the date that Confirmation of Acceptance has occurred.**

REAL ESTATE BROKERS:
A. **Real Estate Brokers are not parties to the Agreement between Buyer and Seller.**
B. **Agency relationships are confirmed as stated in paragraph 27.**
C. If specified in paragraph 2A, Agent who submitted the offer for Buyer acknowledges receipt of deposit.
D. **COOPERATING BROKER COMPENSATION:** Listing Broker agrees to pay Cooperating Broker **(Selling Firm)** and Cooperating Broker agrees to accept, out of Listing Broker's proceeds in escrow: **(i)** the amount specified in the MLS, provided Cooperating Broker is a Participant of the MLS in which the Property is offered for sale or a reciprocal MLS; or **(ii)** ☐ (if checked) the amount specified in a separate written agreement (C.A.R. Form CBC) between Listing Broker and Cooperating Broker.

Real Estate Broker (Selling Firm) _____
By _____ Date _____
Address _____ City _____ State _____ Zip _____
Telephone _____ Fax _____ E-mail _____

Real Estate Broker (Listing Firm) _____
By _____ Date _____
Address _____ City _____ State _____ Zip _____
Telephone _____ Fax _____ E-mail _____

ESCROW HOLDER ACKNOWLEDGMENT:
Escrow Holder acknowledges receipt of a Copy of this Agreement, (if checked, ☐ a deposit in the amount of $ _____),
counter offer numbers _____ and _____, and agrees to act as Escrow Holder subject to paragraph 28 of this Agreement, any supplemental escrow instructions and the terms of Escrow Holder's general provisions.

Escrow Holder is advised that the date of Confirmation of Acceptance of the Agreement as between Buyer and Seller is _____

Escrow Holder _____ Escrow # _____
By _____ Date _____
Address _____
Phone/Fax/E-mail_____
Escrow Holder is licensed by the California Department of ☐ Corporations, ☐ Insurance, ☐ Real Estate. License # _____

(___/___)   **REJECTION OF OFFER:** No counter offer is being made. This offer was reviewed and rejected by Seller on
(Seller's Initials) _____ (Date)

Published by the
California Association of REALTORS®

RPA-CA REVISED 10/02 (PAGE 8 OF 8)

Reviewed by _____ Date _____

426

CALIFORNIA RESIDENTIAL PURCHASE AGREEMENT (RPA-CA PAGE 8 OF 8)

CALIFORNIA
ASSOCIATION
OF REALTORS®

DISCLOSURE REGARDING
REAL ESTATE AGENCY RELATIONSHIPS
(As required by the Civil Code)
(C.A.R. Form AD, Revised 10/01)

When you enter into a discussion with a real estate agent regarding a real estate transaction, you should from the outset understand what type of agency relationship or representation you wish to have with the agent in the transaction.

SELLER'S AGENT

A Seller's agent under a listing agreement with the Seller acts as the agent for the Seller only. A Seller's agent or a subagent of that agent has the following affirmative obligations:
To the Seller:
  A Fiduciary duty of utmost care, integrity, honesty, and loyalty in dealings with the Seller.
To the Buyer and the Seller:
  (a) Diligent exercise of reasonable skill and care in performance of the agent's duties.
  (b) A duty of honest and fair dealing and good faith.
  (c) A duty to disclose all facts known to the agent materially affecting the value or desirability of the property that are not known to, or within the diligent attention and observation of, the parties.

An agent is not obligated to reveal to either party any confidential information obtained from the other party that does not involve the affirmative duties set forth above.

BUYER'S AGENT

A selling agent can, with a Buyer's consent, agree to act as agent for the Buyer only. In these situations, the agent is not the Seller's agent, even if by agreement the agent may receive compensation for services rendered, either in full or in part from the Seller. An agent acting only for a Buyer has the following affirmative obligations:
To the Buyer:
  A fiduciary duty of utmost care, integrity, honesty, and loyalty in dealings with the Buyer.
To the Buyer and the Seller:
  (a) Diligent exercise of reasonable skill and care in performance of the agent's duties.
  (b) A duty of honest and fair dealing and good faith.
  (c) A duty to disclose all facts known to the agent materially affecting the value or desirability of the property that are not known to, or within the diligent attention and observation of, the parties.

An agent is not obligated to reveal to either party any confidential information obtained from the other party that does not involve the affirmative duties set forth above.

AGENT REPRESENTING BOTH SELLER AND BUYER

A real estate agent, either acting directly or through one or more associate licensees, can legally be the agent of both the Seller and the Buyer in a transaction, but only with the knowledge and consent of both the Seller and the Buyer.

In a dual agency situation, the agent has the following affirmative obligations to both the Seller and the Buyer:
  (a) A fiduciary duty of utmost care, integrity, honesty and loyalty in the dealings with either the Seller or the Buyer.
  (b) Other duties to the Seller and the Buyer as stated above in their respective sections.

In representing both Seller and Buyer, the agent may not, without the express permission of the respective party, disclose to the other party that the Seller will accept a price less than the listing price or that the Buyer will pay a price greater than the price offered.

The above duties of the agent in a real estate transaction do not relieve a Seller or Buyer from the responsibility to protect his or her own interests. You should carefully read all agreements to assure that they adequately express your understanding of the transaction. A real estate agent is a person qualified to advise about real estate. If legal or tax advice is desired, consult a competent professional.

Throughout your real property transaction you may receive more than one disclosure form, depending upon the number of agents assisting in the transaction. The law requires each agent with whom you have more than a casual relationship to present you with this disclosure form. You should read its contents each time it is presented to you, considering the relationship between you and the real estate agent in your specific transaction.

This disclosure form includes the provisions of Sections 2079.13 to 2079.24, inclusive, of the Civil Code set forth on the reverse hereof. Read it carefully.

I/WE ACKNOWLEDGE RECEIPT OF A COPY OF THIS DISCLOSURE AND CHAPTER 2 OF TITLE 9 OF PART 4 OF DIVISION 3 OF THE CIVIL CODE.

BUYER/SELLER _____ Date _____ Time _____ AM/PM

BUYER/SELLER _____ Date _____ Time _____ AM/PM

AGENT _____ By _____ Date _____
        (Please Print)   (Associate-Licensee or Broker Signature)

THIS FORM SHALL BE PROVIDED AND ACKNOWLEDGED AS FOLLOWS (Civil Code § 2079.14):
•When the listing brokerage company also represents the Buyer, the Listing Agent shall give one AD form to the Seller and one to the Buyer.
•When Buyer and Seller are represented by different brokerage companies, then the Listing Agent shall give one AD form to the Seller and the Buyer's Agent shall give one AD form to the Buyer and one AD form to the Seller.

SEE REVERSE SIDE FOR FURTHER INFORMATION

The System for Success™

Published by the
California Association of REALTORS®

EQUAL HOUSING
OPPORTUNITY

AD REVISED 10/01 (PAGE 1 OF 1)   PRINT DATE

Reviewed by _____ Date _____

DISCLOSURE REGARDING REAL ESTATE AGENCY RELATIONSHIPS (AD PAGE 1 OF 1)

CHAPTER 2 OF TITLE 9 OF PART 4 OF DIVISION 3 OF THE CIVIL CODE

2079.13 As used in Sections 2079.14 to 2079.24, inclusive, the following terms have the following meanings:
(a) "Agent" means a person acting under provisions of title 9 (commencing with Section 2295) in a real property transaction, and includes a person who is licensed as a real estate broker under Chapter 3 (commencing with Section 10130) of Part 1 of Division 4 of the Business and Professions Code, and under whose license a listing is executed or an offer to purchase is obtained. **(b)** "Associate licensee" means a person who is licensed as a real broker or salesperson under Chapter 3 (commencing with Section 10130) of Part 1 of Division 4 of the Business and Professions Code and who is either licensed under a broker or has entered into a written contract with a broker to act as the broker's agent in connection with acts requiring a real estate license and to function under the broker's supervision in the capacity of an associate licensee. The agent in the real property transaction bears responsibility for his or her associate licensees who perform as agents of the agent. When an associate licensee owes a duty to any principal, or to any buyer or seller who is not a principal, in a real property transaction, that duty is equivalent to the duty owed to that party by the broker for whom the associate licensee functions. **(c)** "Buyer" means a transferee in a real property transaction, and includes a person who executes an offer to purchase real property from a seller through an agent, or who seeks the services of an agent in more than a casual, transitory, or preliminary manner, with the object of entering into a real property transaction. "Buyer" includes vendee or lessee. **(d)** "Dual agent" means an agent acting, either directly or through an associate licensee, as agent for both the seller and the buyer in a real property transaction. **(e)** "Listing agreement" means a contract between an owner of real property and an agent, by which the agent has been authorized to sell the real property or to find or obtain a buyer. **(f)** "Listing agent" means a person who has obtained a listing of real property to act as an agent for compensation. **(g)** "Listing price" is the amount expressed in dollars specified in the listing for which the seller is willing to sell the real property through the listing agent. **(h)** "Offering price" is the amount expressed in dollars specified in an offer to purchase for which the buyer is willing to buy the real property. **(i)** "Offer to purchase" means a written contract executed by a buyer acting through a selling agent which becomes the contract for the sale of the real property upon acceptance by the seller. **(j)** "Real property" means any estate specified by subdivision (1) or (2) of Section 761 in property which constitutes or is improved with one to four dwelling units, any leasehold in this type of property exceeding one year's duration, and mobilehomes, when offered for sale or sold through an agent pursuant to the authority contained in Section 10131.6 of the Business and Professions Code. **(k)** "Real property transaction" means a transaction for the sale of real property in which an agent is employed by one or more of the principals to act in that transaction, and includes a listing or an offer to purchase. **(l)** "Sell," "sale," or "sold" refers to a transaction for the transfer of real property from the seller to the buyer, and includes exchanges of real property between the seller and buyer, transactions for the creation of a real property sales contract within the meaning of Section 2985, and transactions for the creation of a leasehold exceeding one year's duration. **(m)** "Seller" means the transferor in a real property transaction, and includes an owner who lists real property with an agent, whether or not a transfer results, or who receives an offer to purchase real property of which he or she is the owner from an agent on behalf of another. "Seller" includes both a vendor and a lessor. **(n)** "Selling agent" means a listing agent who acts alone, or an agent who acts in cooperation with a listing agent, and who sells or finds and obtains a buyer for the real property, or an agent who locates property for a buyer or who finds a buyer for a property for which no listing exists and presents an offer to purchase to the seller. **(o)** "Subagent" means a person to whom an agent delegates agency powers as provided in Article 5 (commencing with Section 2349) of Chapter 1 of Title 9. However, "subagent" does not include an associate licensee who is acting under the supervision of an agent in a real property transaction.

2079.14 Listing agents and selling agents shall provide the seller and buyer in a real property transaction with a copy of the disclosure form specified in Section 2079.16, and, except as provided in subdivision (c), shall obtain a signed acknowledgement of receipt from that seller or buyer, except as provided in this section or Section 2079.15, as follows: **(a)** The listing agent, if any, shall provide the disclosure form to the seller prior to entering into the listing agreement. **(b)** The selling agent shall provide the disclosure form to the seller as soon as practicable prior to presenting the seller with an offer to purchase, unless the selling agent previously provided the seller with a copy of the disclosure form pursuant to subdivision (a). **(c)** Where the selling agent does not deal on a face-to-face basis with the seller, the disclosure form prepared by the selling agent may be furnished to the seller (and acknowledgement of receipt obtained for the selling agent from the seller) by the listing agent, or the selling agent may deliver the disclosure form by certified mail addressed to the seller at his or her last known address, in which case no signed acknowledgement of receipt is required. **(d)** The selling agent shall provide the disclosure form to the buyer as soon as practicable prior to execution of the buyer's offer to purchase, except that if the offer to purchase is not prepared by the selling agent, the selling agent shall present the disclosure form to the buyer not later than the next business day after the selling agent receives the offer to purchase from the buyer.

2079.15 In any circumstance in which the seller or buyer refuses to sign an acknowledgement of receipt pursuant to Section 2079.14, the agent, or an associate licensee acting for an agent, shall set forth, sign, and date a written declaration of the facts of the refusal.

2079.17 (a) As soon as practicable, the selling agent shall disclose to the buyer and seller whether the selling agent is acting in the real property transaction exclusively as the buyer's agent, exclusively as the seller's agent, or as a dual agent representing both the buyer and the seller. This relationship shall be confirmed in the contract to purchase and sell real property or in a separate writing executed or acknowledged by the seller, the buyer, and the selling agent prior to or coincident with execution of that contract by the buyer and the seller, respectively. **(b)** As soon as practicable, the listing agent shall disclose to the seller whether the listing agent is acting in the real property transaction exclusively as the seller's agent, or as a dual agent representing both the buyer and seller. This relationship shall be confirmed in the contract to purchase and sell real property or in a separate writing executed or acknowledged by the seller and the listing agent prior to or coincident with the execution of that contract by the seller.
(c) The confirmation required by subdivisions (a) and (b) shall be in the following form.

_____ is the agent of (check one): ☐ the seller exclusively; or ☐ both the buyer and seller.
(Name of Listing Agent)

_____ is the agent of (check one): ☐ the buyer exclusively; or ☐ the seller exclusively; or
(Name of Selling Agent if not the same as the Listing Agent)   ☐ both the buyer and seller.

(d) The disclosures and confirmation required by this section shall be in addition to the disclosure required by Section 2079. 14.

2079.18 No selling agent in a real property transaction may act as an agent for the buyer only, when the selling agent is also acting as the listing agent in the transaction.

2079.19 The payment of compensation or the obligation to pay compensation to an agent by the seller or buyer is not necessarily determinative of a particular agency relationship between an agent and the seller or buyer. A listing agent and a selling agent may agree to share any compensation or commission paid, or any right to compensation or commission for which an obligation arises as the result of a real estate transaction, and the terms of any such agreement shall not necessarily be determinative of a particular relationship.

2079.20 Nothing in this article prevents an agent from selecting, as a condition of the agent's employment, a specific form of agency relationship not specifically prohibited by this article if the requirements of Section 2079.14 and Section 2079.17 are complied with.

2079.21 A dual agent shall not disclose to the buyer that the seller is willing to sell the property at a price less than the listing price, without the express written consent of the seller. A dual agent shall not disclose to the seller that the buyer is willing to pay a price greater than the offering price, without the express written consent of the buyer. This section does not alter in any way the duty or responsibility of a dual agent to any principal with respect to confidential information other than price.

2079.22 Nothing in this article precludes a listing agent from also being a selling agent, and the combination of these functions in one agent does not, of itself, make that agent a dual agent.

2079.23 A contract between the principal and agent may be modified or altered to change the agency relationship at any time before the performance of the act which is the object of the agency with the written consent of the parties to the agency relationship.

2079.24 Nothing in this article shall be construed to either diminish the duty of disclosure owed buyers and sellers by agents and their associate licensees, subagents, and employees or to relieve agents and their associate licensees, subagents, and employees from liability for their conduct in connection with acts governed by this article or for any breach of a fiduciary duty or a duty of disclosure.

(AD BACKER)

REAL ESTATE TRANSFER DISCLOSURE STATEMENT

THIS DISCLOSURE STATEMENT CONCERNS THE REAL PROPERTY SITUATED IN THE CITY OF _____, COUNTY OF _____, STATE OF CALIFORNIA, DESCRIBED AS _____. THIS STATEMENT IS A DISCLOSURE OF THE CONDITION OF THE ABOVE DESCRIBED PROPERTY IN COMPLIANCE WITH SECTION 1102 OF THE CIVIL CODE AS OF _____, 19___. IT IS NOT A WARRANTY OF ANY KIND BY THE SELLER(S) OR ANY AGENT(S) REPRESENTING ANY PRINCIPAL(S) IN THIS TRANSACTION, AND IS NOT A SUBSTITUTE FOR ANY INSPECTIONS OR WARRANTIES THE PRINCIPAL(S) MAY WISH TO OBTAIN.

I

COORDINATION WITH OTHER DISCLOSURE FORMS

This Real Estate Transfer Disclosure Statement is made pursuant to Section 1102 of the Civil Code. Other statutes require disclosures, depending upon the details of the particular real estate transaction (for example: special study zone and purchase-money liens on residential property).

Substituted Disclosures: The following disclosures have or will be made in connection with this real estate transfer, and are intended to satisfy the disclosure obligations on this form, where the subject matter is the same:

__ Inspection reports completed pursuant to the contract of sale or receipt for deposit.

__ Additional inspection reports or disclosures:

_____

_____

II

SELLER'S INFORMATION

The Seller discloses the following information with the knowledge that even though this is not a warranty, prospective Buyers may rely on this information in deciding whether and on what terms to purchase the subject property. Seller hereby authorizes any agent(s) representing any principal(s) in this transaction to provide a copy of this statement to any person or entity in connection with any actual or anticipated sale of the property.

THE FOLLOWING ARE REPRESENTATIONS MADE BY THE SELLER(S) AND ARE NOT THE REPRESENTATIONS OF THE AGENT(S), IF ANY. THIS INFORMATION IS A DISCLOSURE AND IS NOT INTENDED TO BE PART OF ANY CONTRACT BETWEEN THE BUYER AND SELLER.

Seller ___ is ___ is not occupying the property.

A. The subject property has the items checked below (read across):

__Range	__Oven	__Microwave
__Dishwasher	__Trash Compactor	__Garbage Disposal
__Washer/Dryer Hookups		__Rain Gutters
__Burglar Alarms	__Smoke Detector(s)	__Fire Alarm
__TV Antenna	__Satellite Dish	__Intercom
__Central Heating	__Central Air Cndtng.	__Evaporative Cooler(s)
__Wall/Window AirCndtng.	__Sprinklers	__Public Sewer System
__Septic Tank	__Sump Pump	__Water Softener

429

__Patio/Decking   __Built-in Barbecue   __Gazebo

__Sauna

__Hot Tub-Locking Safety   __Pool-Child Resistant   __Spa-Locking Safety

Cover*   Barrier*   Cover*

__Security Gate(s)   __Automatic Garage Door Opener(s)*   __Number Remote Controls

Garage: __Attached   __Not Attached   __Carport

Pool/Spa Heater: __Gas   __Solar   __Electric

Water Heater: __Gas   __Water Heater Anchored,   __Private Utility or

Braced, or Strapped*   Other _____

Water Supply: __City   __Well

Gas Supply: __Utility   __Bottled

__Window Screens   __Window Security Bars

__Quick Release Mechanism on Bedroom Windows*

Exhaust Fan(s) in _____ 220 Volt Wiring in _____ Fireplace(s) in _____

Gas Starter _____ Roof(s): Type: _____ Age: _____ (approx.)

Other: _____

Are there, to the best of your (Seller's) knowledge, any of the above that are not in operating condition? ___Y ___No. If yes, then describe.

(Attach additional sheets if necessary): _____

_____

_____

_____

B. Are you (Seller) aware of any significant defects/malfunctions in any of the following? __ Yes __ No. If yes, check appropriate space(s) below.

___Interior Walls ___Ceilings ___Floors ___Exterior Walls ___Insulation __Roof(s) ___Windows ___Doors ___Foundation ___Slab(s) ___Driveways ___Sidewalks

___Walls/Fences ___Electrical Systems ___Plumbing/Sewers/Septics ___Other

Structural Components (Describe: _____

_____)

If any of the above is checked, explain. (Attach additional sheets if necessary): ____

_____

_____

_____

*This garage door opener or child resistant pool barrier may not be in compliance with the safety standards relating to automatic reversing devices as set forth in Chapter 12.5 (commencing with Section 19890) of Part 3 of Division 13 of, or with the pool safety standards of Article 2.5 (commencing with Section 115920) of Chapter 5 of Part 10 of Division 104 of, the Health and Safety Code. The water heater may not be anchored, braced, or strapped in accordance with Section 19211 of the Health and Safety Code. Window security bars may not have quick-release mechanisms in compliance with the 1995 Edition of the California Building Standards Code.

C. Are you (Seller) aware of any of the following:

1. Substances, materials or products which may be an environmental hazard such as, but not limited to, asbestos, formaldehyde, radon gas, lead-based paint, fuel or chemical storage tanks, and contaminated soil or water on the subject property........   __Yes   __No

2. Features of the property shared in common with adjoining landowners, such as walls, fences, and driveways, whose use or responsibility for maintenance may have an effect on the subject property ....   __Yes   __No

3. Any encroachments, easements or similar matters that may affect your interest in the subject property ....   __Yes   __No

4. Room additions, structural modifications, or other alterations or repairs made without necessary permits ....   __Yes   __No

5. Room additions, structural modifications, or other alterations or repairs not in compliance with building codes ....   __Yes   __No

6. Fill (compacted or otherwise) on the property or any portion thereof ....   __Yes   __No

7. Any settling from any cause, or slippage, sliding, or other soil problems ....   __Yes   __No

8. Flooding, drainage or grading problems ....   __Yes   __No

9. Major damage to the property or any of the structures from fire, earthquake, floods, or landslides ....   __Yes   __No

10. Any zoning violations, nonconforming uses, violations of "setback" requirements ....   __Yes   __No

11. Neighborhood noise problems or other nuisances ....   __Yes   __No

12. CC&R's or other deed restrictions or obligations ....   __Yes   __No

13. Homeowners' Association which has any authority over the subject property ....   __Yes   __No

14. Any "common area" (facilities such as pools, tennis courts, walkways, or other areas coowned in undivided interest with others)   __Yes   __No

15. Any notices of abatement or citations against the property ......   __Yes   __No

16. Any lawsuits by or against the seller threatening to or affecting this real property, including any lawsuits alleging a defect or deficiency in this real property or "common areas" (facilities such as pools, tennis courts, walkways, or other areas coowned in undivided interest with others) ....   __Yes   __No

431

If the answer to any of these is yes, explain. (Attach additional sheets if necessary.)
_____
_____

Seller certifies that the information herein is true and correct to the best of the Seller's knowledge as of the date signed by the Seller.

Seller _____ Date _____

Seller _____ Date _____

III

AGENT'S INSPECTION DISCLOSURE

(To be completed only if the Seller is represented by an agent in this transaction.)

THE UNDERSIGNED, BASED ON THE ABOVE INQUIRY OF THE SELLER(S) AS TO THE CONDITION OF THE PROPERTY AND BASED ON A REASONABLY COMPETENT AND DILIGENT VISUAL INSPECTION OF THE ACCESSIBLE AREAS OF THE PROPERTY IN CONJUNCTION WITH THAT INQUIRY, STATES THE FOLLOWING:

__ Agent notes no items for disclosure.

__ Agent notes the following items:

_____
_____

_____

_____

Agent (Broker

Representing Seller) _____ By _____ Date_____

(Please Print) (Associate Licensee

or Broker-Signature)

IV

AGENT'S INSPECTION DISCLOSURE

(To be completed only if the agent who has obtained the offer is other than the agent above.)

THE UNDERSIGNED, BASED ON A REASONABLY COMPETENT AND DILIGENT VISUAL INSPECTION OF THE ACCESSIBLE AREAS OF THE PROPERTY, STATES THE FOLLOWING:

__ Agent notes no items for disclosure.

__ Agent notes the following items:

_____

_____

_____

_____

Agent (Broker

obtaining the Offer) _____ By _____ Date _____

(Please Print) (Associate Licensee

or Broker-Signature)

V

BUYER(S) AND SELLER(S) MAY WISH TO OBTAIN PROFESSIONAL ADVICE AND/OR INSPECTIONS OF THE PROPERTY AND TO PROVIDE FOR APPROPRIATE PROVISIONS IN A CONTRACT BETWEEN BUYER AND SELLER(S) WITH RESPECT TO ANY ADVICE/INSPECTIONS/DEFECTS

I/WE ACKNOWLEDGE RECEIPT OF A COPY OF THIS STATEMENT

Seller_____Date_____Buyer_____Date_____

Seller_____Date_____Buyer_____Date_____

Agent (Broker

Representing Seller) _____ By _____ Date_____

(Associate Licensee

or Broker-Signature)

Agent (Broker

obtaining the Offer) _____ By _____ Date_____

(Associate Licensee

or Broker-Signature)

SECTION 1102.3 OF THE CIVIL CODE PROVIDES A BUYER WITH THE RIGHT TO RESCIND A PURCHASE CONTRACT FOR AT LEAST THREE DAYS AFTER THE DELIVERY OF THIS DISCLOSURE IF DELIVERY OCCURS AFTER THE SIGNING OF AN OFFER TO PURCHASE. IF YOU WISH TO RESCIND THE CONTRACT, YOU MUST ACT WITHIN THE PRESCRIBED PERIOD.

A REAL ESTATE BROKER IS QUALIFIED TO ADVISE ON REAL ESTATE. IF YOU DESIRE LEGAL ADVICE, CONSULT YOUR ATTORNEY.

(Civil Code Section 1102 et seq.)

APPENDIX V

General Resources

If you need additional help and information, these resources may provide some assistance. For updates and additional links, visit my website, thinkglink.com.

AMERICAN ASSOCIATION OF RETIRED PERSONS (AARP)

601 E. Street NW
Washington, DC
20049
(888) OUR-AARP (888-687-2277)
aarp.org

The AARP offers information, publications, and an excellent website on a variety of topics, targeting Americans age 50 and older.

BANK RATE MONITOR

bankrate.com

Bank Rate Monitor provides excellent information about interest rates for a wide variety of items, including mortgages, credit cards, and automobile financing. Their best information, free to the public, is on the Web, which offers generally excellent articles about improving personal finances.

CONSUMER CREDIT COUNSELING SERVICE (CCCS)

(800) 388-2227

moneymanagement.org/

This organization has offices around the country, and it provides many services to first-time home buyers, including credit and comprehensive housing counseling. These services are confidential and free of charge. More than 1,100 CCCS offices nationwide can prequalify buyers and talk about various mortgage types, and they may be able to connect you with affordable housing programs.

CONSUMER FEDERATION OF AMERICA (CFA)

Headquarters:
1424 16th Street, NW, Suite 604
Washington, DC 20036
(202) 387-6121
consumerfed.org

This nonprofit educational and research organization represents homeowners, prospective homeowners, and home investors.

CONSUMER PRODUCT SAFETY COMMISSION

Washington, DC 20207-0001
(800) 638-2772
Fax: (301) 504-0124
cpsc.gov

Call the toll-free 800 number to lodge

435

a complaint about the safety of houses and buildings or about issues involving smoke alarms, electrical systems, indoor air quality, and home insulation. You can also get recall information and safety tips. If you negotiate the options successfully, an operator will eventually come on the line to take your complaint.

CONSUMER PUBLICATIONS

Pueblo, Colorado 81009
pueblo.gsa.gov

A list of consumer publications is available that may be useful to you as a first-time (or repeat) home buyer.

COUNCIL OF BETTER BUSINESS BUREAUS

Headquarters:
4200 Wilson Boulevard, Suite 800
Arlington, VA 22203-1838
(703) 276-0100
BBBonline.org

This organization is dedicated to consumers and attempts to be an effective national self-regulation force for business. The headquarters personnel can help you find the bureau nearest you.

DEPARTMENT OF HOUSING AND URBAN DEVELOPMENT (HUD)

451 7th Street, SW
Washington, DC 20410
hud.gov
huduser.org

To locate the HUD office nearest to you:
(202) 708-1112
HUD User, a clearinghouse of information:
(800) 245-2691

This agency provides programs for low-income housing, including public housing and privately owned rental housing. It supports housing-related site development and housing rehabilitation through Community Development Block Grants to state and local governments. It also provides support for the residential mortgage market through the Federal Housing Administration (FHA).

There is a local HUD office in nearly every urban area. If you are located outside an urban area, call the HUD office in your state capital or in Washington (DC) to find the office located closest to you.

DEPARTMENT OF VETERANS AFFAIRS (VA)

Loan Guarantee Service
810 Vermont Avenue, NW
Washington, DC 20420
(800) 827-1000
va.gov
E-mail linked through website

This federal agency guarantees a portion of home loans to veterans and regulates the loans' distribution. The VA publishes a free pamphlet about guaranteed home loans for veterans. Call the general number for information on how to contact your local VA office.

The Department of Veterans Affairs also runs a Vendee Financing program, which provides inexpensive financing (with little or no down payment required, and a discount for a cash purchase) of VA-acquired homes. You need not be a veteran to qualify. Check with the Loan Guarantee Service for more information and current qualifications.

FANNIE MAE (FORMERLY FEDERAL NATIONAL MORTGAGE ASSOCIATION)

Headquarters:
3900 Wisconsin Avenue, NW
Washington, DC 20016-2892
(800) 7-Fannie
fanniemae.com
homepath.com

Fannie Mae, the nation's largest source of home mortgage funds, is a congressionally chartered, shareholder-owned company. The company provides lenders with a constant supply of affordable mortgage funds to make available to home buyers. Its special programs increase the availability and affordability of housing for low-, moderate-, and middle-income Americans. If you call the toll-free number, you can order information packets on Community Homebuyers programs, as well as other first-time buyer information.

FREDDIE MAC

Headquarters:
8200 Jones Branch Drive
McLean, VA 22102-3110
(703) 903-2000
freddiemac.com

Freddie Mac is a stockholder-owned corporation that purchases mortgages from lenders and issues mortgage-backed securities. Chartered by Congress in 1970, it helps finance one in six homes. It is considered the "little brother" to Fannie Mae.

HOME INFORMATION CENTER, A UNIT OF THE OFFICE OF AFFORDABLE HOUSING

P.O. Box 7189
Gaithersburg, MD 20898-7189
(800) 998-9999
Fax: (301) 519-5027
comcon.org

Two programs are operative through this organization: The Home Program and Hope 3. The Home Program gives grant money to nonprofit associations. Hope 3 is a single-family-home buyer program using government help properties. For more information on Hope 3, call the 800 number.

INSURANCE INFORMATION INSTITUTE

110 William Street
New York, NY 10038
(212) 346-5500
iii.org

The Insurance Information Institute is a nonprofit communications, educational, and fact-finding organization dedicated to improving the public's understanding of the property/casualty insurance business.

NATIONAL CENTER FOR HOME EQUITY CONVERSION (NCHEC)

National Center for Home Equity Conversion
360 N. Robert, #403
Saint Paul, MN 55101
(651) 222-6775
Fax: (651) 222-6797
Reverse.org

If you're looking for information about reverse mortgages, this is the place to go. NCHEC's executive director, Ken Scholen, has written two excellent books about how reverse mortgages work and how to find a good deal.

NATIONAL COUNCIL FOR STATE HOUSING AGENCIES (NCSHA)

444 North Capitol Street, NW, Suite 438
Washington, DC 20001
(202) 624-7710
Fax: (202) 624-5899
ncsha.org

NCSHA is an advocacy group for low-income housing. It represents state housing finance agencies in all 50 states, plus Puerto Rico and the Virgin Islands. If you are unable to find your state housing finance agency, write to this organization. Hundreds of public agencies have provided financial assistance to first-time home buyers. Generally, there are home-price and family-income limitations. Your state housing agency or real estate agent should be able to point you in the right direction.

NEIGHBORHOOD REINVESTMENT CORPORATION

1325 G St., NW, Suite 800
Washington, DC 20005
(202) 220-2300

437

Fax: (202) 376-2600
nw.org

This organization acts as a national network for affordable housing providers. The headquarters personnel can help you locate the neighborhood housing services nearest you.

RAM RESEARCH

Headquarters:
Rockefeller Center
1230 Avenue of the Americas, 7th Floor
New York, New York 10020
(212) 745-1362
Fax: (917) 639-4005
ramresearch.com

Another good place to go for information on credit cards and interest rates.

STATE PUBLIC INTEREST RESEARCH GROUP

pirg.org and truthaboutcredit.org

Each state has this organization, which represents the public in a variety of matters.

APPENDIX VI

State-by-State Resource Guide

ALABAMA

Websites: Banking—bank.state.al.us
  Real Estate—arec.state.al.us

Complaints about mortgage lenders:
Banking Department
401 Adams Avenue, Suite 680
Montgomery, AL 36130
Telephone: (334) 242-3452

Complaints about real estate brokers:
Alabama Real Estate Commission
1201 Charmichael Way
Montgomery, AL 36106
Telephone: (334) 242-5544

ALASKA

Website: state.ak.us

Complaints about mortgage lenders:
Division of Banking, Securities, and
  Corporations
150 Third Street, Suite 217
Juneau, AK 99801
Website: dced.state.ak.us/bsc/home.htm

Mailing Address:
P.O. Box 110807
Juneau, AK 99811-0807
Telephone: (907) 465-2521
Fax: (907) 465-2549

Complaints about real estate brokers:
Division of Occupational Licensing

Anchorage Investigative Staff
Robert B. Atwood Building
550 W. 7th Avenue, Suite 1500
Anchorage, AK 99501-3567
Telephone: (907) 269-8160
Fax: (907) 269-8156
Website: dced.state.ak.us/occ/home.htm

ARIZONA

Complaints about mortgage lenders:
Arizona State Banking Department
2910 N. 44th Street, Suite 310
Phoenix, AZ 85018
Telephone: (602) 255-4421
Website: azbanking.com

Complaints about real estate brokers:
Arizona Organization Department of Real
  Estate
2910 N. 44th Street
Phoenix, AZ 85018
Telephone: (602) 468-1414
Fax: (602) 468-0562
Website: re.state.az.us
E-mail: Investigations@re.state.az.us

ARKANSAS

Complaints about mortgage lenders:
Arkansas State Banking Department
400 Hardin Road, Suite 100
Little Rock, AR 72211

439

Telephone: (501) 324-9019
Fax: (501) 324-9028
Websites: state.ar.us/bank or state.ar.us/bank/
    complaints.html
E-mail: asbd@banking.state.ar.us

Complaints about real estate brokers:
Arkansas Organization Arkansas
Real Estate Commission
612 South Summit Street
Little Rock, AR 72201-4740
Telephone: (501) 683-8010
Website: state.ar.us/arec/arecweb.html

CALIFORNIA

Websites: dfi.ca.gov or corp.ca.gov/index.htm

Complaints about mortgage lenders:
California Department of Corporations
320 West 4th Street, Suite 750
Los Angeles, CA 90013-2344
Telephone: (800) 622-0620, (213) 576-7500,
(866) 275-2677 (866-ASK-CORP)

71 Stevenson Street, Suite 2100
San Francisco, CA 94105-2980
Telephone: (415) 972-8559, (866) 275-2677
(866-ASK-CORP)

1515 K Street, Suite 200
Sacramento, CA 95814-4052
Telephone: (916) 445-7205, (866) 275-2677
(866-ASK-CORP)

1350 Front Street, Room 2034
San Diego, CA 92101-3697
Telephone: (619) 525-4233, (866) 275-2677
(866-ASK-CORP)

Complaints about real estate brokers:
Website: dre.cahwnet.gov
California Department of Real Estate
Telephone: (916) 227-0864

2201 Broadway
Sacramento, CA 95818
Telephone: (916) 227-0931

1350 Front Street, Suite 3064
San Diego, CA 92101-3687
Telephone: (619) 525-4192

1515 Clay Street, Suite 702
Oakland, CA 94612-1462
Telephone: (510) 622-2552

320 W. 4th Street, Suite 350
Los Angeles, CA 90013-1105
Telephone: (213) 620-2072

2550 Mariposa Mall
Room 3070
Fresno, CA 93721-2273
Telephone: (559) 445-5009

COLORADO

Complaints about mortgage lenders:
Division of Banking
1560 Broadway, Suite 1175
Denver, CO 80202
Telephone: (303) 894-7575
Website: dora.state.co.us/banking/

Complaints about real estate brokers:
Colorado Division of Real Estate
1900 Grant Street, Suite 600
Denver, CO 80203
Telephone: (303) 894-2166
Fax: (303) 894-2683
Website: dora.state.co.us/Real-Estate
E-mail: real-estate@dora.state.co.us

CONNECTICUT

Website: www.state.ct.us/dob/

Complaints about mortgage lenders:
Consumer Credit Division
Connecticut Department of Banking
260 Constitution Plaza
Hartford, CT 06103-1800
Telephone: (860) 240-8170 or (800) 831-7225
Fax: (860) 240-8178
E-mail: banking.complaints@po.state.ct.us

Complaints about real estate brokers:
Department of Consumer Protection
Real Estate and Professional Trades Division
165 Capital Avenue, Room 110
Hartford, CT 06106
Telephone: (860) 713-6135

DELAWARE

Complaints about mortgage lenders:
Office of the Bank Commissioner
    Compliance Staff
555 E. Loockerman Street, Suite 210
Dover, DE 19901
Telephone: (302) 739-4235
Website: state.de.us/bank
E-mail: Dawn.Coffman@state.de.us

Complaints about real estate brokers:
Department of Administrative Services
Division of Professional Regulation
    Real Estate Commission
861 Silver Lake Boulevard
Cannon Building, Suite 203
Dover, DE 19904-2467
Telephone: (302) 744-4500
Fax: (302) 739-2711
Website: professionallicensing.state.de.us/
    index.shtml

FLORIDA

Complaints about mortgage lenders:
Department of Financial Services
200 E. Gaines Street
Tallahassee, FL 32399-0300
Telephone: (850) 413-3100, (800) 342-2762
Website: fldfs.com, dbf.state.fl.us

Complaints about real estate brokers:
Department of Real Estate
400 Robinson Street
P.O. Box 1900
Orlando, FL 32801
Telephone: (407) 245-0800
Fax: (407) 317-7245

GEORGIA

Complaints about mortgage lenders:
Department of Banking and Finance
2990 Brandywine Road, Suite 200
Atlanta, GA 30341-5565
Telephone: (770) 986-1633 or (888) 986-1633
Fax: (770) 986-1654
Website: state.ga.us/dbf

Complaints about real estate brokers:
Georgia Real Estate Commission
International Tower, Suite 1000
229 Peachtree Street, NE
Atlanta, GA 30303-1605
Telephone: (404) 656-3916
Fax: (404) 656-6650
Website: grec.state.ga.us
E-mail: grecmail@grec.state.ga.us

HAWAII

Complaints about mortgage lenders:
Department of Commerce and Consumer
    Affairs
Financial Institutions Division
335 Merchant Street
Honolulu, HI 96813
Telephone: (808) 586-2820

Mailing Address:
    P.O. Box 2054
    Honolulu, HI 96805
Website: www.hawaii.gov or
hawaii.gov/dcca/dfi/

Complaints about real estate brokers:
Hawaii Real Estate Commission
335 Merchant Street, Room 333
Honolulu, HI 96813

Mailing Address:
    P.O. Box 3469
    Honolulu, HI 96801
Telephone: (808) 586-2643
Website: hawaii.gov/hirec
E-mail: hirec@dcca.hawaii.gov

IDAHO

Complaints about mortgage lenders and banks:
Department of Finance
700 W. State Street, 2nd Floor
Boise, ID 83702-0031

Mailing Address:
    P.O. Box 83720
    Boise, ID 83720-0031
Telephone: (208) 332-8000, (208) 332-8005
Toll-Free (within Idaho Only): (888) 346-3378

Fax: (208) 332-8097
Websites: state.id.us/finance/dof.htm or
    finance.state.id.us/industry/industry_home.asp
E-mail: finance@fin.state.id.us

Complaints about real estate brokers:
Idaho Real Estate Commission
633 N. 4th Street
P.O. Box 83720
Boise, ID 83720-0077
Telephone: (208) 334-3285; toll-free:
    (866) 447-5411
Fax: (208) 334-2050
Website: idahorealestatecommission.com/

ILLINOIS

*Complaints about mortgage lenders and real estate
brokers:*
Office of Banks and Real Estate
310 S. Michigan Avenue
Chicago, IL 60604
Telephone: (312) 793-3000

500 E. Monroe Street, Suite 200
Springfield, IL 62701
Telephone-Real Estate: (217) 785-9300
Telephone-Mortgage Lender: (217) 782-3000,
(217) 782-3414
Websites: state.il.us/obr or www.obre.state.il.us

Complaints about credit unions:
Department of Financial Institutions
Credit Union Division
100 W. Randolph Street, Suite 15-700
Chicago, IL 60601
Telephone: (312) 814-2010
or
Credit Union Division
500 Iles Park Place, Suite 510
Springfield, IL 62703
Telephone: (217) 782-2834
Website: state.il.us/dfi/

INDIANA

Complaints about mortgage lenders:
Indiana Department of Financial Institutions
30 S. Meridian Street, Suite 300
Indianapolis, IN 46204

Telephone: (317) 232-3955, (317) 232-6684
Toll-Free in Indiana, (800) 382-4880
Websites: www.dfi.state.in.us/ or in.gov/dfi/

Complaints about credit unions:
Division of Credit Unions
30 S. Meridian Street, Suite 300
Indianapolis, IN 46204
Telephone: (317) 232-5851

Complaints about real estate brokers:
Indiana Professional Licensing Agency
Attn: Indiana Real Estate Commission
302 W. Washington Street, Room E012
Indianapolis, IN 46204
Telephone: (317) 234-3009
Website: in.gov/pla/bandc/estate/
E-mail: pla9@pla.state.in.us

IOWA

Complaints about mortgage lenders:
Iowa Department of Commerce
Division of Banking
200 E. Grand Avenue, Suite 300
Des Moines, IA 50309-1827
Telephone: (515) 281-4014
Websites: state.ia.us/government/com/
    or idob.state.ia.us/

Complaints about credit unions:
Division of Credit Unions
200 E. Grand Avenue, Suite 370
Des Moines, IA 50309-1827
Telephone: (515) 281-6514

Complaints about real estate brokers:
Professional Licensing & Regulation Division
Iowa Real Estate Commission
1920 SE Hulsizer
Ankeny, IA 50021-3941
Telephone: (515) 281-7393 or (515) 281-5910
Fax: (515) 281-7411
Websites: state.ia.us/government/com/prof/
    pro_licens/complaint.html or state.ia.us/
    government/com/prof/home.html

KANSAS

Complaints about mortgage lenders:
Office of the State Bank Commissioner
700 SW Jackson Street, Suite 300
Topeka, KS 66603
Telephone: (785) 296-2266
Website: osbckansas.org/ConsumerAssistance/
    complaints.html

Complaints about real estate brokers:
Kansas Real Estate Commission
3 Townside Plaza, Suite 200
120 SE 6th Avenue
Topeka, KS 66603
Telephone: (785) 296-3411, (785) 296-4996
Website: www.accesskansas.org/krc

KENTUCKY

Complaints about mortgage lenders:
Department of Financial Institutions
1025 Capital Center Drive, Suite 200
Frankfort, KY 40601
Contact: Andie Cubert
Telephone: (800) 223-2579
Fax: (502) 573-8787
Website: dfi.ky.gov/
E-mail: Mary.Cubert@mail.state.ky.us

Complaints about real estate brokers:
Kentucky Real Estate Commission
10200 Lynn Station Road, Suite 201
Louisville, KY 40223
Telephone: (502) 425-4273, (888) 373-3300
Fax: (502) 426-2717
Website: krec.ky.gov/

LOUISIANA

Complaints about mortgage lenders and credit unions:
Office of Financial Institutions
8660 United Plaza Boulevard, 2nd Floor
Baton Rouge, LA 70809

Mailing Address:
    P.O. Box 94095
    Baton Rouge, LA 70804-9095
Telephone: (225) 925-4660
Website: ofi.state.la.us

Complaints about real estate brokers:
Louisiana Real Estate Commission
5222 Summa Court
Baton Rouge, LA 70809

Mailing Address:
    P.O. Box 14785
    Baton Rouge, LA 70898-4785
Telephone: (225) 765-0191
Fax: 2257650637
Website: lrec.state.la.us

MAINE

Complaints about mortgage lenders:
Department of Professional and
    Financial Regulation
Maine Bureau of Banking
124 Northern Avenue
Gardiner, ME 04345

Mailing Address:
    Department of Professional and
        Financial Regulation
    Maine Bureau of Banking
    36 State House Station
    Augusta, ME 04333-0036
Telephone: (207) 624-8527
Fax: (207) 582-7699
Websites: state.me.us/ or
    state.me.us/pfr/pfrhome.htm

Complaints about real estate brokers:
Maine Real Estate Commission
Complaints and Investigations Division
35 State House Station
Augusta ME, 04333-0035
Telephone: (207) 624-8660
Fax: (207) 624-8563
Website:
maine.gov/pfr/olr/categories/cat38.htm

MARYLAND

Complaints about mortgage lenders:
Consumer Credit and Banking Unit
Division of Financial Regulation
500 North Calvert Street, Room 402
Baltimore, MD 21202
Telephone: (410) 230-6097

Complaints about banks:
Banking Unit
Division of Financial Regulation
500 N. Calvert Street, Room 402
Baltimore, MD 21202
Telephone: (410) 230-6102

Complaints about real estate brokers:
Department of Licensing & Regulation
Maryland Real Estate Commission
500 N. Calvert Street, 3rd Floor
Baltimore, MD 21202
Telephone: (410) 230-6230
Website: dllr.state.md.us

MASSACHUSETTS

Complaints about mortgage lenders:
Consumer Assistance Office
Massachusetts Division of Banks
1 South Station, 3rd Floor
Boston, MA 02110
Telephone: (617) 956-1500 ext. 501, (800) 495-
    2265
    ext. 501 (within Massachusetts only)
Fax: (617) 956-1599
Website: state.ma.us/dob/pub_offr.htm
E-mail: susan.sclafani@state.ma.us

Complaints about real estate brokers:
Board of Registration of Real Estate Brokers &
    Salespersons
Massachusetts Real Estate Board
239 Causeway Street, Suite 500
Boston, MA 02114
Telephone: (617) 727-2373
Website: state.ma.us/reg/boards/re

MICHIGAN

Complaints about mortgage lenders or credit unions:
Michigan Financial Institutions Bureau
611 W. Ottowa Street, 3rd Floor
Lansing, MI 48933
Telephone: (517) 373-3470
Toll-Free: (877) 999-6442
Website: Michigan.gov/ofis

Complaints about real estate brokers:
Consumer & Industry Services
Real Estate Commission

P.O. Box 30018
Lansing, MI 48909
Telephone: (517) 241-9202
Website: Michigan.gov/dleg
E-mail: ann.millben@michigan.gov

MINNESOTA

Complaints about mortgage lenders:
Division of Financial Examinations
85 7th Place East, Suite 500
St. Paul, MN 55101
Telephone: (651) 296-2135
E-mail: enforcement.commerce@state.mn.us

Complaints about real estate brokers:
Minnesota Commerce Department
Enforcement Department
85 7th Place East, Suite 500
St. Paul, MN 55101
Telephone: (651) 296-2488
Website: www.state.mn.us

MISSISSIPPI

Complaints about mortgage lenders:
Department of Banking and Consumer Finance
Banking Division
901 Woolfolk Building
501 North West Street, Suite A
Jackson, MS 39201

Mailing Address:
    Banking Division
    P.O. Drawer 23729
    Jackson, MS 39225-3729
Telephone: (601) 359-1031
Website: www.dbcf.state.ms.us/

Complaints about real estate brokers:
Mississippi Real Estate Commission
2506 Lakeland Drive, Suite 300
Flowood, MS 39232

Mailing Address:
    P.O. Box 12685
    Jackson, MS 39236
Telephone: (601) 932-9191
Website: www.mrec.state.ms.us
E-mail: mrec@mrec.state.ms.us

MISSOURI

Complaints about mortgage lenders:
Division of Finance
Harry S. Truman Building, Room 630
P.O. Box 716
Jefferson City, Missouri 65102
Telephone: (573) 751-3242
Fax: (573) 751-9192
E-mail: finance@ded.mo.gov
Website: ded.mo.gov/regulatorylicensing/
    divisionoffinance

Complaints about credit unions:
Division of Credit Unions
Harry S. Truman Building
301 West High Street, Room 720
Jefferson City, MO 65101

Mailing Address:
    P.O. Box 1607
    Jefferson City, MO 65102
Telephone: (573) 751-3419
Website: www.ded.mo.gov/regulatorylicensing/
    creditunion
E-mail: cu@ded.mo.gov

Complaints about real estate brokers:
Missouri Real Estate Commission
3605 Missouri Boulevard
P.O. Box 1335
Jefferson City, MO 65102-1335
Telephone: (573) 751-0038
E-mail: reacom@mail.state.mo.us
Website: pr.mo.gov/appraisers.asp

MONTANA

Complaints about mortgage lenders:
Department of Commerce
Banking and Financial Institutions Division
301 South Park
Helena, MT 59601

Mailing Address:
    P.O. Box 200546
    Helena, MT 59620
Telephone: (406) 841-2920
Fax: (406) 841-2930
Website: discoveringmontana.com/doa/banking

Complaints about real estate brokers:
Montana Board of Realty Regulation
P.O. Box 200513
Helena, MT 59620
Telephone: (406) 444-2961
Website: discoveringmontana.com/dli/bsd

NEBRASKA

Complaints about mortgage lenders:
Financial Institutions Division
Department of Banking and Finance
1200 N. Street, Suite 311
Lincoln, NE 68508

Mailing Address:
    P.O. Box 95006
    Lincoln, NE 68509-5006
Telephone: (402) 471-2171
Website: www.ndbf.org

Complaints about real estate brokers:
Nebraska Real Estate Commission
1200 N. Street, Suite 402
Lincoln, NE 68509
Telephone: (402) 471-2004
Website: www.nrec.state.ne.us

NEVADA

Complaints about mortgage lenders:
Nevada Department of Business and Industry
Financial Institutions Division
Website: fid.state.nv.us/
Carson City:
    406 East 2nd Street, Suite 3
    Carson City, NV 89710-4758
    Telephone: (775) 684-1830
Las Vegas:
    2501 East Sahara Avenue, Suite 300
Las Vegas, NV 89104
Telephone: (702) 486-4120

Complaints about real estate brokers:
Nevada Department of Business and Industry
Nevada Real Estate Division
Carson City:
    Compliance Division
    788 Fairview Drive, Suite 200
    Carson City, NV 89701-5453
    Telephone: (775) 687-4868

Las Vegas:
  2501 E. Sahara Avenue
  Las Vegas, NV 89104-4137
  Telephone: (702) 486-4033
Website: red.state.nv.us/
E-mail: realest@red.state.nv.us

NEW HAMPSHIRE

Complaints about mortgage lenders:
Office of the Banking Commissioner
Banking Department
64B Old Suncook Road
Concord, NH 03301-5127
Telephone: (603) 271-1090
Website: state.nh.us/banking

Complaints about real estate brokers:
New Hampshire Real Estate Commission
25 Capitol Street
State House Annex, Room 434, 4th Floor
Concord, NH 03301
Telephone: (603) 271-2701
Website: nh.gov/nhrec/

NEW JERSEY

Complaints about mortgage lenders:
Department of Banking and Insurance
Consumer Service Unit
P.O. Box 40
Trenton, NJ 08625-0040
Telephone: (609) 984-2777
Website: www.state.nj.us/dobi

Complaints about real estate brokers:
New Jersey Real Estate Commission
P.O. Box 328
Trenton, NJ 08625-0328
Telephone: (609) 292-8280
Website: state.nj.us/dobi/remnu.shtml
E-mail: realestate@dobi.state.nj.us

NEW MEXICO

Complaints about mortgage lenders:
Regulation and Licensing Department
Financial Institutions Division
2550 Cerrillos Road, 3rd Floor
Santa Fe, NM 87505

Telephone: (505) 476-4885
Fax: (505) 476-4670
Website: rld.state.nm.us/fid
E-mail: RLDFID@state.nm.us

Complaints about real estate brokers:
New Mexico Real Estate Commission
First State Bank Building
111 Lomas Boulevard, NW, Suite 410
Albuquerque, NM 87102
Telephone: (505) 841-9120
Fax: (505) 246-0725
Website: state.nm.us/nmrec/

NEW YORK

Complaints about mortgage lenders:
Mortgage Banking Division
New York State Banking Department
One State Street
New York, NY 10004-1417
Telephone: 1-877-BANK-NYS
Website: www.banking.state.ny.us/
E-mail: mortgage@banking.state.ny.us

Manhattan:
  2 Rector Street
  New York, NY 10006-1894
  Telephone: (212) 618-6951
Albany:
  5 Empire State Plaza, Suite 2310
  Albany, NY 12223
  Telephone: (518) 474-2364 or (518) 473-6160
Syracuse:
  333 E. Washington Street
  Syracuse, NY 13202
  Telephone: (315) 428-4049

Complaints about real estate brokers:
Department of State
Division of Licensing Services
84 Holland Avenue
Albany, NY 12208
Telephone: (518) 473-2728
Website: dos.state.ny.us

NORTH CAROLINA

Complaints about mortgage lenders:

Office of the Commissioner of Banks
702 Oberlin Road, Suite 400
Raleigh, NC 27605-0709

Mailing Address:
    P.O. Box 10709
    Raleigh, NC 27605-0709
Telephone: (919) 733-3016
Website: www.banking.state.nc.us/

Complaints about real estate brokers:
North Carolina Real Estate Commission
P.O. Box 17100
Raleigh, NC 27619
Telephone: (919) 875-3700
Website: ncrec.state.nc.us

NORTH DAKOTA

Complaints about mortgage lenders:
Department of Banking and Financial
    Institutions
2000 Schafer Street, Suite G
Bismarck, ND 58501-1204
Telephone: (701) 328-9933
Fax: (701) 328-9955
Website: discoverND.com/dfi
E-mail: dfi@state.nd.us

Complaints about real estate brokers:
North Dakota Real Estate Commission
314 E Thayer Avenue
Bismarck, ND 58501

Mailing Address:
    P.O. Box 727
    Bismarck, ND 58502
Telephone: (701) 328-9749 or (701) 328-9737

OHIO

Complaints about mortgage lenders:
The Ohio Department of Commerce
Division of Financial Institutions
77 South High Street, 21st Floor
Columbus, OH 43215-6120
Telephone: (614) 728-8400
Website: com.state.oh.us/dfi/bnkmain.htm
E-mail: webdfi@dfi.com.state.oh.us
First-Time-Home-Buyer Program
Website: homebuyerohio.com

Complaints about real estate brokers:
Division of Real Estate & Professional
    Licensing
77 S. High Street, 20th Floor
Columbus, OH 43215-6133
Telephone: (614) 466-4100
E-mail: REPLD@com.state.oh.us

OKLAHOMA

Complaints about mortgage lenders:
Oklahoma State Banking Department
4545 N. Lincoln Boulevard, Suite 164
Oklahoma City, OK 73105-3427
Telephone: (405) 521-2782
Website: osbd.state.ok.us

Complaints about real estate brokers:
Oklahoma Real Estate Commission
2401 NW 23rd, Suite 18
Oklahoma City, OK 73107
Telephone: (405) 521-3387
Website: orec.state.ok.us/
E-mail: orec.help@orec.state.ok.us

OREGON

Complaints about mortgage lenders:
Oregon Department of Consumer
    and Business Services
Division of Finance and Corporate Securities
350 Winter Street, NE, Room 410
Salem, OR 97301-3881

Mailing Address:
    Division of Finance and Corporate
        Securities
    P.O. Box 14480
    Salem, OR 97309-0405
Telephone: (503) 378-4140 or (866) 814-9710
Website: cbs.state.or.us/external/dfcs/
E-mail: dcbs.dfcsmail@state.or.us

Complaints about real estate brokers:
Oregon Real Estate Agency
1177 Center Street, NE
Salem, OR 97301-2505
Telephone: (503) 378-4170
Fax: (503) 378-2491
Website: rea.state.or.us
E-mail: orea.info@state.or.us

447

PENNSYLVANIA

Website: www.state.pa.us

Complaints about mortgage lenders:
Department of Banking
333 Market Street, 16th Floor
Harrisburg, PA 17101-2290
Telephone: (717) 787-2665

Complaints about real estate brokers:
Pennsylvania Real Estate Commission
2601 N. Third Street
Harrisburg, PA 17110

Mailing Address:
P.O. Box 2649
Harrisburg, PA 17105-2649
Telephone: (717) 783-3658
E-mail: ST-REALESTATE@state.pa.us

RHODE ISLAND

Complaints about mortgage lenders:
Department of Business Regulation
Banking Division
233 Richmond Street, Suite 231
Providence, RI 02903
Telephone: (401) 222-2405
Website: www.state.ri.us
E-mail: BankInquiry@dbr.state.ri.us

Complaints about real estate brokers:
Department of Business Regulation
Division of Commercial Licensing and
   Regulation
233 Richmond Street, Suite 230
Providence, RI 02903-4230
Telephone: (401) 222-2255
Fax: (401) 222-6654

SOUTH CAROLINA

Myscgov.com

Complaints about mortgage lenders:
Consumer Affairs Department
3600 Forest Drive
Columbia, SC 29250

Mailing Address:
P.O. Box 5757
Columbia, SC 29250-5757

Telephone: (803) 734-4200

Complaints about banks:
SC Board of Financial Institutions
Calhoun Building, 3rd Floor, Room 309
1015 Sumter Street
Columbia, SC 29201

Mailing Address:
P.O. Box 12549
Columbia, SC 29211
Telephone: (803) 734-2001

Complaints about real estate brokers:
Department of Labor Licensing & Regulation
South Carolina Real Estate Commission
110 Centerview Drive
Kingstree Building, Suite 201
Columbia, SC 29210

Mailing Address:
P.O. Box 11847
Columbia, SC 29211-1847
Telephone: (803) 896-4400
Website: llr.state.sc.us

SOUTH DAKOTA

Complaints about mortgage lenders:
Division of Banking
Department of Commerce and Regulation
$217^{1}/_{2}$ West Missouri
Pierre, SD 57501-4590
Telephone: (605) 773-3421
Website: state.sd.us
BANK-HOM.htm
E-mail: bankinfo@state.sd.us

Complaints about real estate brokers:
South Dakota Real Estate Commission
425 E. Capital Street
Pierre, SD 57501
Telephone: (605) 773-3600
Website: state.sd.us/sdrec

TENNESSEE

Complaints about mortgage lenders:
Division of Consumer Affairs
500 James Robertson Parkway
Nashville, TN 37243-0600
Telephone: (615) 741-4737

448

Fax: (615) 532-4994
Website: state.tn.us/consumer/

Complaints about real estate brokers:
Tennessee Real Estate Commission
Davy Crockett Tower
500 James Robertson Parkway
Nashville, TN 37243-1151
Telephone: (800) 342-4031 or (615) 741-2273
Fax: (615) 741-0313
Website: state.tn.us/commerce/boards/trec/
    index.html

TEXAS

Complaints about mortgage lenders:
State Finance Commission
2601 North Lamar Building
Austin, TX 78705-4294
Telephone: (512) 475-1300
Fax: (512) 474-1313
Website: fc.state.tx.us/

Complaints about real estate brokers:
Texas Real Estate Commission
1101 Camino La Costa
Austin, TX 78752

Mailing Address:
    P.O. Box 12188
    Austin, TX 78711-2188
Telephone: (512) 459-6544
or (800) 250-8732
Website: trec.state.tx.us
E-mail: enforce@trec.state.tx.us

UTAH

Complaints about mortgage lenders:
Department of Financial Institutions
324 S. State Street, Suite 201
Salt Lake City, UT 84111

Mailing Address:
    Financial Institutions
    P.O. Box 146800
    Salt Lake City, UT 84114-6800
Telephone: (801) 538-8830
Fax: (801) 538-8894
Website: dfi.utah.gov/

Complaints about real estate brokers:
Department of Commerce
Utah Division of Real Estate
Heber M. Wells Building
160 E. 300 South, 2nd Floor
Salt Lake City, UT 84111

Mailing Address:
    P.O. Box 146711
    Salt Lake City, UT 84114-6711
Telephone: (801) 530-6747
Website: www.commerce.state.ut.us

VERMONT

Complaints about mortgage lenders:
Department of Banking, Insurance, Securities
    & Health Care Administration
89 Main Street
Drawer 20
Montpelier, VT 05620-3101
Telephone: (802) 828-3301
Website: Bishca.state.vt.us

Complaints about real estate brokers:
Office of Professional Regulation
Vermont Real Estate Commission
Heritage Building
81 River Street
Drawer 9
Montpelier, VT 05609
Telephone: (802) 828-3256
Website: vtprofessionals.org

VIRGINIA

Complaints about mortgage lenders:
Department of Banking
Tyler Building
13006 Main Street
Richmond, VA 23219

Mailing Address:
    Bureau of Financial Institutions
    P.O. Box 640
    Richmond, VA 23218
Telephone: (804) 371-9657
Website: www.state.va.us/scc/division/banking

Department of Professional and
Occupational Regulation
3600 W. Broad Street

Richmond, VA 23230-4917
Telephone: (804) 367-8500
Website: www.state.va.us/dpor

WASHINGTON

Complaints about mortgage lenders:
Washington Department of Financial
    Institutions
150 Israel Road, SW
Tumwater, WA 98501

Mailing Address:
    P.O. Box 41200
    Olympia, WA 98504-1200
Telephone: (360) 902-8700 or (800) 372-8303
    (in Washington)
Website: www.wa.gov/dfi/

Complaints about real estate brokers:
Department of Licensing
Business and Professions Division
Real Estate Program
2000 4th Avenue, W, 2nd Floor
Olympia, WA 98502

Mailing Address:
    P.O. Box 9015
    Olympia, WA 98507-9015
Telephone: (360) 586-4602
Website: dol.wa.gov
E-mail: RealEstate@dol.wa.gov

WEST VIRGINIA

Complaints about mortgage lenders:
West Virginia Division of Banking
1900 Kanawha Boulevard, E

Building 3, Room 311
Charleston, WV 25305-0240
Telephone: (304) 558-2294
Website: www.state.wv.us/banking

Complaints about real estate brokers:
1033 Quarrier Street, Suite 400
Charleston, WV 25301-2315
Telephone: (304) 558-3555

WISCONSIN

*Complaints about mortgage lenders and
    real estate brokers:*
Department of Regulation and Licensing
P.O. Box 8935
Madison, WI 53708-8935
Telephone: (608) 266-2112
Website: drl.wi.gov/

WYOMING

Complaints about mortgage lenders:
Division of Banking
Herschler Building 3E
122 W. 25th
Cheyenne, WY 82002
Telephone: (307) 777-7797
Website: audit.state.wy.us/banking/default.htm

Complaints about real estate brokers:
Wyoming Real Estate Commission
2020 Carey Avenue, Suite 100
Cheyenne, Wyoming 82002-0180
Telephone: (307) 777-7141
Website: realestate.state.wy.us/

GLOSSARY OF REAL ESTATE TERMS EVERY HOME BUYER SHOULD KNOW

A

Abstract (of Title)   A summary of the public records affecting the title to a particular piece of land. An attorney or title insurance company officer creates the abstract of title by examining all recorded instruments (documents) relating to a specific piece of property, such as easements, liens, mortgages, etc.

Acceleration Clause   A provision in a loan agreement that allows the lender to require the balance of the loan to become due immediately if mortgage payments are not made or there is a breach in your obligation under your mortgage or note.

Addendum   Any addition to, or modification of, a contract. Also called an amendment or rider.

Adjustable-Rate Mortgage (ARM)   A type of loan whose prevailing interest rate is tied to an economic index (like one-year Treasury bills), which fluctuates with the market. There are three types of ARMs, including one-year ARMs, which adjust every year; three-year ARMs, which adjust every three years; and five-year ARMs, which adjust every five years. When the loan adjusts, the lender tacks a margin onto the economic index rate to come up with your loan's new rate.

ARMs are considered far riskier than fixed-rate mortgages, but their starting interest rates are extremely low, and in the past 5 to 10 years, people have done very well with them.

Agency   A term used to describe the relationship between a seller and a broker, or a buyer and a broker.

Agency Closing   The lender's use of a title company or other party to act on the lender's behalf to close on the purchase of a home or to refinance a loan.

Agent   An individual who represents a buyer or a seller in the purchase or sale of a home. Licensed by the state, an agent must work for a broker or a brokerage firm.

Agreement of Sale   This document is also known as the contract of purchase, purchase agreement, or sales agreement. It is the agreement by which the seller agrees to sell you his or her property if you pay a certain price. It contains all the provisions and conditions for the purchase, must be written, and is signed by both parties.

Amortization   A payment plan that enables the borrower to reduce debt gradually through monthly payments of principal and interest. Amortization tables allow you to see exactly how much you would pay each month in interest and how much you repay in principal, depending on the amount of money borrowed at a specific interest rate.

Annual Percentage Rate (APR)   The total cost of your loan, expressed as a percentage rate of interest, which includes not only the loan's interest rate, but factors in all the costs associated with making that loan, including closing costs and fees. The costs are then amortized over the life of the loan. Banks are required by the federal Truth-in-Lending statutes to disclose the APR of a loan, which allows borrowers a common ground for comparing various loans from different lenders.

Application   A series of documents you must fill out when you apply for a loan.

Application Fee   A onetime fee charged by the mortgage company for processing your application for a loan. Sometimes the application fee is applied toward certain costs, including the appraisal and credit report.

Appraisal   The opinion of an appraiser, who estimates the value of a home at a specific point in time.

Articles-of-Agreement for Deed   A type of seller financing that allows the buyer to purchase the home in installments over a specified period of time. The seller keeps legal title to the home until the loan is paid off. The buyer receives an interest in the property—called equitable title—but does not own it. However, because the buyer is paying the real estate taxes and paying interest to the seller, it is the buyer who receives the tax benefits of homeownership.

Assumption of Mortgage   If you assume a mortgage when you purchase a home, you undertake to fulfill the obligations of the existing loan agreement the seller made with the lender. The obligations are similar to those that you would incur if you took out a new mortgage. When assuming a mortgage, you become personally liable for the payment of principal and interest. The seller, or original mortgagor, is released from the liability, and should get that release in writing. Otherwise, he or she could be liable if you don't make the monthly payments.

B

Balloon Mortgage   A type of mortgage that is generally short in length but is amortized over 25 or 30 years so that the borrower pays a combination of interest and principal each month. At the end of the loan term, the entire balance of the loan must be repaid at once.

Broker   An individual who acts as the agent of the seller or buyer. A real estate broker must be licensed by the state.

Building Line or Setback   The distance from the front, back, or side of a lot beyond which construction or improvements may not extend without permission by the proper governmental authority. The building line may be established by a filed plat of subdivision, by restrictive covenants in deeds, by building codes, or by zoning ordinances.

Buydown   An incentive offered by a developer or seller that allows the buyer to lower his or her initial interest rate by putting up a certain amount of money. A buydown also refers to the process of paying extra points up front at the closing of your loan in order to have a lower interest rate over the life of the loan.

Buyer Broker   A buyer broker is a real estate broker who specializes in representing buyers. Unlike a seller broker or conventional broker, the buyer broker has a fiduciary duty to the buyer, because the buyer accepts the legal obligation of paying the broker. The buyer broker is obligated to find the best property for a client and then negotiate the best possible purchase price and terms. Buyer brokerage has gained a significant amount of respect in recent years, since the National Association of Realtors has changed its code of ethics to accept this designation.

Buyer's Market Market conditions that favor the buyer. A buyer's market is usually expressed when there are too many homes for sale, and a home can be bought for less money.

C

Certificate of Title A document or instrument issued by a local government agency to a homeowner, naming the homeowner as the owner of a specific piece of property. At the sale of the property, the certificate of title is transferred to the buyer. The agency then issues a new certificate of title to the buyer.

Chain of Title The lineage of ownership of a particular property.

Closing The day when buyers and sellers sign the papers and actually swap money for title to the new home. The closing finalizes the agreements reached in the sales agreement.

Closing Costs This phrase can refer to a lender's costs for closing on a loan, or it can mean all the costs associated with closing on a piece of property. Considering all closing costs, it's easy to see that closing can be expensive for both buyers and sellers. A home buyer's closing costs might include: lender's points, loan origination or loan service fees; loan application fee; lender's credit report; lender's processing fee; lender's document preparation fee; lender's appraisal fee; prepaid interest on the loan; lender's insurance escrow; lender's real estate tax escrow; lender's tax escrow service fee; cost for the lender's title policy; special endorsements to the lender's title policy; house inspection fees; title company closing fee; deed or mortgage recording fees; local municipal, county, and state taxes; and the attorney's fee. A seller's closing costs might include: survey (which in some parts of the country is paid for by the buyer); title insurance; recorded release of mortgage; broker's commission; state, county, and local municipality transfer taxes; credit to the buyer for unpaid real estate taxes and other bills; attorney's fees; FHA fees and costs.

Cloud (on Title) An outstanding claim or encumbrance that adversely affects the marketability of a property.

Commission   The amount of money paid to the broker by the seller (or, in some cases, the buyer), as compensation for selling the home. Usually, the commission is a percentage of the sales price of the home, and generally hovers in the 5 to 7 percent range. There is no "set" commission rate. It is always and entirely negotiable.

Condemnation   The government holds the right to "condemn" land for public use, even against the will of the owner. The government, however, must pay fair market price for the land. Condemnation may also mean that the government has decided a particular piece of land, or a dwelling, is unsafe for human habitation.

Condominium   A dwelling of two or more units in which you individually own the interior space of your unit and jointly own common areas such as the lobby, roof, parking, plumbing, and recreational areas.

Contingency   A provision in a contract that sets forth one or more conditions that must be met prior to the closing. If the contingency is not met, usually the party who is benefiting from the contingency can terminate the contract. Some common contingencies include financing, inspection, attorney approval, and toxic substances.

Contractor   In the building industry, the contractor is the individual who contracts to build the property. He or she erects the structure and manages the subcontracting (to the electrician, plumber, etc.) until the project is finished.

Contract to Purchase   Another name for Agreement of Sale.

Conventional Mortgage   A conventional mortgage means that the loan is underwritten by banks, savings and loans, or other types of mortgage companies. There are also certain limitations imposed on conventional mortgages that allow them to be sold to private institutional investors (like pension funds) on the secondary market. For example, as of 2004, the loan must be less than $359,650, otherwise it is considered a "jumbo" loan. Also, if you are buying a condominium, conventional financing decrees that the condo building be more than 70 percent owner-occupied.

Co-op   Cooperative housing refers to a building, or a group of buildings, that is owned by a corporation. The shareholders of the corporation are the people who live in the building. They own shares—which gives them the right to lease a specific unit within the building—in the corporation that owns their building and pay "rent" or monthly maintenance assessments for the expenses associated with living in the building. Co-ops are relatively unknown outside of New York, Chicago, and a few other cities. Since the 1970s condominiums have become much more popular.

Counteroffer   When the seller or buyer responds to a bid. If you decide to offer $100,000 for a home listed at $150,000, the seller might counter your offer and propose that you purchase the home for $140,000. That new proposal, and any subsequent offer, is called a counteroffer.

Covenant   Assurances or promises set out in the deed or a legally binding contract, or implied in the law. For example, when you obtain title to a property by warranty, there is the Covenant of Quiet Enjoyment, which gives you the right to enjoy your property without disturbances.

Credit Report   A lender will decide whether to give you a loan based on your credit history. A credit report lists all of your credit accounts (such as charge cards), and any debts or late payments that have been reported to the credit company.

Cul-de-Sac   A street that ends in a U shape, leading the driver or pedestrian back to the beginning. The cul-de-sac has become exceptionally popular with modern subdivision developers, who use the design technique to create quiet streets and give the development a nonlinear feel.

Custom Builder   A home builder who builds houses for individual owners to the owners' specifications. The home builder may either own a piece of property or build a home on someone else's land.

D

Debt Service   The total amount of debt (credit cards, mortgage, car loan) that an individual is carrying at any one time.

Declaration of Restrictions   Developers of condominiums (or any other type of housing unit that functions as a condo) are required to file a condominium declaration, which sets out the rules and restrictions for the property, the division of ownership, and the rights and privileges of the owners. The "condo dec" or "homeowner's dec," as it is commonly called, reflects the developer's original intent and may only be changed by unit-owner vote. Other types of declarations include the homeowners' association dec and town house association dec. Co-op dwellers are governed by a similar type of document.

Deed   The document used to transfer ownership in a property from seller to buyer.

Deed of Trust   A deed of trust or trust deed is an instrument similar to a mortgage that gives the lender the right to foreclose on the property if there is a default under the trust deed or note by the borrower.

Deposit   Money given by the buyer to the seller with a signed contract to purchase or offer to purchase, as a show of good faith. Also called the earnest money.

Down Payment   The cash put into a purchase by the borrower. Lenders like to see the borrower put at least 20 percent down in cash, because lenders generally believe that if you have a higher cash down payment, it is less likely the home will go into foreclosure. In recent years, however, lenders have become more flexible about cash down payments; recently, lenders have begun accepting cash down payments of as little as 2 percent.

Dual Agency   When a real estate broker represents both the buyer and the seller in a single transaction, it creates a situation known as dual agency. In most states, brokers must disclose to the buyer and to the seller whom they are representing. Even with disclosure, dual agency presents a conflict of interest for the broker in the transaction. If the broker is acting as the seller broker and the subagent for the seller (by bringing the buyer), then anything the buyer tells the broker must by law be brought to the seller's attention. If the broker represents the seller as a seller broker and the buyer as a buyer broker in the same transaction, the broker will receive money from both the buyer and the seller, an obvious conflict of interest.

Due on Sale Clause   Nearly every mortgage has this clause, which states that the mortgage must be paid off in full upon the sale of the home.

E

Earnest Money   The money the buyer gives the seller up front as a show of good faith. It can be as much as 10 percent of the purchase price. Earnest money is sometimes called a deposit.

Easement   A right given by a landowner to a third party to make use of the land in a specific way. There may be several easements on your

457

property, including for passage of utility lines or poles, sewer or water mains, and even a driveway. Once the right is given, it continues indefinitely, or until released by the party who received it.

Eminent Domain   The right of the government to condemn private land for public use. The government must, however, pay full market value for the property.

Encroachment   When your neighbor builds a garage or a fence, and it occupies your land, it is said to "encroach on" your property.

Encumbrance   A claim or lien or interest in a property by another party. An encumbrance hinders the seller's ability to pass good, marketable, and unencumbered title to you.

Escrow Closing   A third party, usually a title company, acts as the neutral party for the receipt of documents for the exchange of the deed by the sellers for the buyer's money. The final exchange is completed when the third party determines that certain preset requirements have been satisfied.

Escrow (for Earnest Money)   The document that creates the arrangement whereby a third party or broker holds the earnest money for the benefit of the buyer and seller.

Escrow (for Real Estate Taxes and Insurance)   An account in which monthly installments for real estate taxes and property insurance are held—usually in the name of the home buyer's lender.

F

Fee Simple   The most basic type of ownership, under which the owner has the right to use and dispose of the property at will.

Fiduciary Duty   A relationship of trust between a broker and a seller or a buyer broker and a buyer, or an attorney and a client.

First Mortgage   A mortgage that takes priority over all other voluntary liens.

Fixture   Personal property, such as a built-in bookcase, furnace, hot water heater, and recessed lights, that becomes "affixed" because it has been permanently attached to the home.

Foreclosure   The legal action taken to extinguish a homeowner's right and interest in a property, so that the property can be sold in a foreclosure sale to satisfy a debt.

G

Gift Letter A letter to the lender indicating that a gift of cash has been made to the buyer and that it is not expected to be repaid. The letter must detail the amount of the gift and the name of the giver.

Good Faith Estimate (GFE) Under RESPA, lenders are required to give potential borrowers a written good faith estimate of closing costs within three days of an application submission.

Grace Period The period of time after a loan payment due date in which a mortgage payment may be made and not be considered delinquent.

Graduated-Payment Mortgage A mortgage in which the payments increase over the life of the mortgage, allowing the borrower to make very low payments at the beginning of the loan.

H

Hazard Insurance Insurance that covers the property from damages that might materially affect its value. Also known as homeowner's insurance.

Holdback An amount of money held back at closing by the lender or the escrow agent until a particular condition has been met. If the problem is a repair, the money is kept until the repair is made. If the repair is not made, the lender or escrow agent uses the money to make the repair. Buyers and sellers may also have holdbacks between them, to ensure that specific conditions of the sale are met.

Homeowners' Association A group of homeowners in a particular subdivision or area who band together to take care of common property and common interests.

Homeowner's Insurance Coverage that includes hazard insurance, as well as personal liability and theft.

Home Warranty A service contract that covers appliances (with exclusions) in working condition in the home for a certain period of time, usually one year. Homeowners are responsible for a per-call service fee. There is a homeowner's warranty for new construction. Some developers will purchase a warranty from a company specializing in new construction for the homes they sell. A homeowner's warranty will warrant the good working order of the appliances and workmanship of a new home for between 1 and 10 years; for example, appliances might be covered for one year while the roof may be covered for several years.

Housing and Urban Development, Department of Also known as HUD, this is the federal department responsible for the nation's housing programs. It also regulates RESPA, the Real Estate Settlement Procedures Act, which governs how lenders must deal with their customers.

I

Inspection The service an inspector performs when he or she is hired to scrutinize the home for any possible structural defects. Inspections may also be done to check for the presence of toxic substances, such as leaded paint or water, asbestos, radon, or pests, including termites.

Installment Contract The purchase of property in installments. Title to the property is given to the purchaser when all installments are made.

Institutional Investors or Lenders Private or public companies, corporations, or funds (such as pension funds) that purchase loans on the secondary market from commercial lenders such as banks and savings and loans. Or they are sources of funds for mortgages through mortgage brokers.

Interest Money charged for the use of borrowed funds. Usually expressed as an interest rate, it is the percentage of the total loan charged annually for the use of the funds.

Interest-Only Mortgage A loan in which only the interest is paid on a regular basis (usually monthly), and the principal is owed in full at the end of the loan term.

Interest Rate Cap The total number of percentage points that an adjustable-rate mortgage (ARM) might rise over the life of the loan.

J

Joint Tenancy An equal, undivided ownership in a property taken by two or more owners. Under joint tenancy there are rights of survivorship, which means that if one of the owners dies, the surviving owner rather than the heirs of the estate inherits the other's total interest in the property.

L

Landscape   The trees, flowers, planting, lawn, and shrubbery that surround the exterior of a dwelling.

Late Charge   A penalty applied to a mortgage payment that arrives after the grace period (usually the 10th or 15th of a month).

Lease with an Option to Buy   When the renter or lessee of a piece of property has the right to purchase the property for a specific period of time at a specific price. Usually, a lease with an option to buy allows a first-time buyer to accumulate a down payment by applying a portion of the monthly rent toward the down payment.

Lender   A person, company, corporation, or entity that lends money for the purchase of real estate.

Lessee   You, or the person leasing the property.

Lessor   The owner of the property who is leasing it to you.

Letter of Intent   A formal statement, usually in letter form, from the buyer to the seller stating that the buyer intends to purchase a specific piece of property for a specific price on a specific date.

Leverage   Using a small amount of cash—say, a 10 or 20 percent down payment—to purchase a piece of property.

Lien   An encumbrance against the property, which may be voluntary or involuntary. There are many different kinds of liens, including a tax lien (for unpaid federal, state, or real estate taxes), a judgment lien (for monetary judgments by a court of law), a mortgage lien (when you take out a mortgage), and a mechanic's lien (for work done by a contractor on the property that has not been paid for). For a lien to be attached to the property's title, it must be filed or recorded with local county government.

Listing   A property that a broker agrees to list for sale in return for a commission.

Loan   An amount of money that is lent to a borrower, who agrees to repay it plus interest.

Loan Commitment   A written document that states that a mortgage company has agreed to lend a buyer a certain amount of money at a certain rate of interest for a specific period of time, which may contain sets of conditions and a date by which the loan must close.

461

Loan Origination Fee   A onetime fee charged by the mortgage company to arrange the financing for the loan.

Loan-to-Value Ratio   The ratio of the amount of money you wish to borrow compared with the value of the property you wish to purchase. Institutional investors (who buy loans on the secondary market from your mortgage company) set up certain ratios that guide lending practices. For example, the mortgage company might only lend you 80 percent of a property's value.

Location   Where property is geographically situated. "Location, location, location" is a broker's maxim that states that where the property is located is its most important feature, because you can change everything about a house except its location.

Lock-In   The mechanism by which a borrower locks in the interest rate that will be charged on a particular loan. Usually, the lock lasts for a certain time period, such as 30, 45, or 60 days. On new construction, the lock may be much longer.

M

Maintenance Fee   The monthly or annual fee charged to condo, co-op, or town house owners, and paid to the homeowners' association, for the maintenance of common property. Also called an assessment.

Mortgage   A document granting a lien on a home in exchange for financing granted by a lender. The mortgage is the means by which the lender secures the loan and has the ability to foreclose on the home.

Mortgage Banker   A company or a corporation, like a bank, that lends its own funds to borrowers in addition to bringing together lenders and borrowers. A mortgage banker may also service the loan (i.e., collect the monthly payments).

Mortgage Broker   A company or individual that brings together lenders and borrowers and processes mortgage applications.

Mortgagee   A legal term for the lender.

Mortgagor   A legal term for the borrower.

Multiple Listing Service (MLS)   A computerized listing of all properties offered for sale by member brokers. Buyers may only gain access to the MLS by working with a member broker.

N

Negative Amortization A condition created when the monthly mortgage payment is less than the amount necessary to pay off the loan over the period of time set forth in the note. Because you're paying less than the amount necessary, the actual loan amount increases over time. That's how you end up with negative equity. To pay off the loan, a lump-sum payment must be made.

O

Option When a buyer pays for the right or option to purchase property for a given length of time, without having the obligation to actually purchase the property.

Origination Fee A fee charged by the lender for allowing you to borrow money to purchase property. The fee—which is also referred to as points—is usually expressed as a percentage of the total loan amount.

Ownership The absolute right to use, enjoy, and dispose of property. You own it!

P

Package Mortgage A mortgage that uses both real and personal property to secure a loan.

Paper Slang usage that refers to the mortgage, trust deed, installment, and land contract.

Personal Property Movable property, such as appliances, furniture, clothing, and artwork.

PITI An acronym for Principal-Interest-Taxes-and-Insurance. These are usually the four parts of your monthly mortgage payment.

Pledged Account Borrowers who do not want to have a real estate tax or insurance escrow administered by the mortgage servicer can, in some circumstances, pledge a savings account into which enough money to cover real estate taxes and the insurance premium must be deposited. You must then make the payments for your real estate taxes and insurance premiums from a separate account. If you fail to pay your taxes or premiums, the lender is allowed to use the funds in the pledged account to make those payments.

Point   A point is 1 percent of the loan amount.

Possession   Being in control of a piece of property, and having the right to use it to the exclusion of all others.

Power of Attorney   The legal authorization given to an individual to act on behalf of another individual.

Prepaid Interest   Interest paid at closing for the number of days left in the month after closing. For example, if you close on the 15th, you would prepay the interest for the 16th through the end of the month.

Prepayment Penalty   A fine imposed when a loan is paid off before it comes due. Many states now have laws against prepayment penalties, although banks with federal charters are exempt from state laws. If possible, do not use a mortgage that has a prepayment penalty, or you will be charged a fine if you sell your property before your mortgage has been paid off.

Prequalifying for a Loan   When a mortgage company tells a buyer in advance of the formal application approximately how much money the buyer can afford to borrow.

Principal   The amount of money you borrow.

Private Mortgage Insurance (PMI)   Special insurance that specifically protects the top 20 percent of a loan, allowing the lender to lend more than 80 percent of the value of the property. PMI is paid in monthly installments by the borrower.

Property Tax   A tax levied by a county or local authority on the value of real estate.

Proration   The proportional division of certain costs of homeownership. Usually used at closing to figure out how much the buyer and seller each owe for certain expenditures, including real estate taxes, assessments, and water bills.

Purchase Agreement   An agreement between the buyer and seller for the purchase of property.

Purchase Money Mortgage   An instrument used in seller financing, a purchase money mortgage is signed by a buyer and given to the seller in exchange for a portion of the purchase price.

Q

Quit-Claim Deed   A deed that operates to release any interest in a property that a person may have, *without a representation that he or she actually has a right in that property.* For example, Sally may use a quit-claim deed to grant Bill her interest in the White House, in Washington, DC, although she may not actually own, or have any rights to, that particular house.

R

Real Estate   Land and anything permanently attached to it, such as buildings and improvements.

Real Estate Agent   A state-licensed individual who acts on behalf of the seller or buyer. For his or her services, the agent receives a commission, which is usually expressed as a percentage of the sales price of a home and is split with his or her real estate firm. A real estate agent must either be a real estate broker or work for one.

Real Estate Attorney   An attorney who specializes in the purchase and sale of real estate.

Real Estate Broker   An individual who is licensed by the state to act as an agent on behalf of the seller or buyer. For his or her services, the broker receives a commission, which is usually expressed as a percentage of the sales price of a home.

Real Estate Settlement Procedures Act (RESPA)   This federal statute was originally passed in 1974 and contains provisions that govern the way companies involved with a real estate closing must treat each other and the consumer. For example, one section of RESPA requires lenders to give consumers a written good faith estimate within three days of making an application for a loan. Another section of RESPA prohibits title companies from giving referral fees to brokers for steering business to them.

Realtist   A designation given to an agent or broker who is a member of the National Association of Real Estate Brokers.

Realtor   A designation given to a real estate agent or broker who is a member of the National Association of Realtors.

Recording   The process of filing documents at a specific government office. Upon such recording, the document becomes part of the public record.

Redlining The slang term used to describe an illegal practice of discrimination against a particular racial group by real estate lenders. Redlining occurs when lenders decide certain areas of a community are too high risk and refuse to lend to buyers who want to purchase property in those areas, regardless of their qualifications or creditworthiness.

Regulation Z Also known as the Truth in Lending Act. Congress determined that lenders must provide a written good faith estimate of closing costs to all borrowers and provide them with other written information about the loan.

Reserve The amount of money set aside by a condo, co-op, or homeowners' association for future capital improvements.

S

Sale-Leaseback A transaction in which the seller sells property to a buyer, who then leases the property back to the seller. This is accomplished within the same transaction.

Sales Contract The document by which a buyer contracts to purchase property. Also known as the purchase contract or a contract to purchase.

Second Mortgage A mortgage that is obtained after the primary mortgage, and whose rights for repayment are secondary to the first mortgage.

Seller Broker A broker who has a fiduciary responsibility to the seller. Most brokers are seller brokers, although an increasing number are buyer brokers, who have a fiduciary responsibility to the buyer.

Settlement Statement A statement that details the monies paid out and received by the buyer and seller at closing, also known as the HUD-1.

Shared Appreciation Mortgage A relatively new mortgage used to help first-time buyers who might not qualify for conventional financing. In a shared appreciation mortgage, the lender offers a below-market interest rate in return for a portion of the profits made by the homeowner when the property is sold. Before entering into a shared appreciation mortgage, be sure to have your real estate attorney review the documentation.

Special Assessment An additional charge levied by a condo or co-op board in order to pay for capital improvements, or other unforeseen expenses.

Subagent A broker who brings the buyer to the property. Although subagents would appear to be working for the buyer (a subagent usually ferries around the buyer, showing him or her properties), they are paid by the seller and have a fiduciary responsibility to the seller. Subagency is often confusing to first-time buyers, who think that because the subagent shows them property, the subagent is "their" agent, rather than the seller's.

Subdivision The division of a large piece of property into several smaller pieces. Usually a developer or a group of developers will build single-family or duplex homes of a similar design and cost within one subdivision.

T

Tax Lien A lien that is attached to property if the owner does not pay his or her real estate taxes or federal income taxes. If overdue property taxes are not paid, the owner's property might be sold at auction for the amount owed in back taxes.

Tenancy by the Entirety A type of ownership whereby both the husband and wife each own the complete property. Each spouse has an ownership interest in the property as his or her marital residence and, as a result, creditors cannot force the sale of the home to pay back the debts of one spouse without the other spouse's consent. There are rights of survivorship whereby upon the death of one spouse, the other spouse would immediately inherit the entire property.

Tenants in Common A type of ownership in which two or more parties have an undivided interest in the property. The owners may or may not have equal shares of ownership, and there are no rights of survivorship. However, each owner retains the right to sell his or her share in the property as he or she sees fit.

Term The length of a mortgage. A typical mortgage term will be 15 or 30 years.

Title Refers to the ownership of a particular piece of property.

Title Company The corporation or company that insures the status of title (title insurance) through the closing and may handle other aspects of the closing.

Title Insurance   Insurance that protects the lender and the property owner against losses arising from defects or problems with the title to the property.

Trust Account   An account used by brokers and escrow agents, in which funds for another individual are held separately and not commingled with other funds.

U

Underwriter   One who underwrites a loan for another. Your lender will have an investor underwrite your loan.

V

Variable Interest Rate   An interest rate that rises and falls according to a particular economic indicator, such as Treasury bills.

Void   A contract or document that is not enforceable.

Voluntary Lien   A lien, such as a mortgage, that a homeowner elects to grant to a lender.

W

Waiver   The surrender or relinquishment of a particular right, claim, or privilege.

Warranty   A legally binding promise given to the buyer at closing by the seller, generally regarding the condition of the home, property, or other matter.

Z

Zoning   The right of the local municipal government to decide how different areas of the municipality will be used. Zoning ordinances are the laws that govern the use of the land.

Alphabetical Listing
of Websites

Alabama
    (arec.state.al.us)
    (bank.state.al.us)
    (state.al.us)
Alaska
    (dced.state.ak.us/bsc/home.htm)
    (dced.state.ak.us/occ/home.htm)
    (state.ak.us)
American Association of Retired Persons (AARP)
    (aarp.org)
American Society of Home Inspectors
    (ashi.com)
Arizona Organization Department of Real Estate
    (re.state.az.us)
Arizona State Banking Department
    (azbanking.com)
Arkansas
    (state.ar.us/bank)
    (state.ar.us/bank/complaints.html)
Arkansas Organization Arkansas Real Estate Commission
    (state.ar.us/arec/arecweb.html)
Arkansas State Banking Department
    state.ar.us/bank/banking1.html

Bank of America
    bankofamerica.com
Bank Rate Monitor
    (bankrate.com)

California
    (corp.ca.gov/index.htm)
    (dfi.ca.gov)
    (dre.cahwnet.gov)

California Department of Real Estate
  (dre.ca.gov)
Century 21
  (century21.com)
  (keyword Century21 if you're on America Online)
Coldwell Banker
  (coldwellbanker.com)
Colorado Division of Banking
  (dora.state.co.us/banking/)
Colorado Division of Real Estate
  (dora.state.co.us/Real-Estate)
Connecticut
  (state.ct.us/dob/)
Consumer Credit Counseling Service (CCCS)
  (moneymanagement.org/)
Consumer Federation of America (CFA)
  (consumerfed.org)
Consumer Product Safety Commission
  (cpsc.gov)
Consumer Publications
  (pueblo.gsa.gov)
Council of Better Business Bureaus
  (BBBonline.org)
Countrywide Home Loans
  (countrywide.com)

Delaware Department of Administrative Services
  (professionallicensing.state.de.us/index.shtml)
Delaware Office of the Bank Commissioner
  (state.de.us/bank)
Department of Housing and Urban Development (HUD)
  (hud.gov)
  (huduser.org)
Department of Veterans Affairs (VA)
  (va.gov)

Ebay
  (ebay.com)
E-Loan
  (eloan.com)
EPA toxin link
  (epa.gov/opptintr/)

Fannie Mae (formerly Federal National Mortgage Association)
  (fanniemae.com)
  (fanniemae.com/homebuyers/homepath)
  (homepath.com)
Federal Emergency Management Agency (FEMA)
  (fema.gov)

Florida Department of Financial Services
   (fldfs.com)
Florida Department of Banking and Finance
   (dbf.state.fl.us)
Freddie Mac
   (freddiemac.com)
Free Credit Report
   (annualcreditreport.com)

Georgia Real Estate Commission
   (grec.state.ga.us)
Georgia Department of Banking and Finance
   (state.ga.us/dbf)
Georgia Real Estate Commission
   (greab.state.ga.us/)

Hawaii
   (hawaii.gov)
Hawaii Department of Commerce and Consumer Affairs
   hawaii.gov/dcca/dfi/
Hawaii Real Estate Commission
   (hawaii.gov/hirec)
HomeAdvisor
   (homeadvisor.com)
Home Information Center (a unit of the Office of Affordable Housing)
   (comcon.org)

Idaho Department of Finance
   (state.id.us/finance/dof.htm) or
   (finance.state.id.us/industry/industry_home.asp)
Idaho Real Estate Commission
   (idahorealestatecommission.com/)
Illinois Department of Financial Institutions
   (state.il.us/dfi/)
Illinois Office of Banks and Real Estate
   (state.il.us/obr) or (obre.state.il.us)
Ilyce Glink
   (thinkglink.com)
Indiana Department of Financial Institutions
   (dfi.state.in.us/) or (in.gov/dfi/)
Indiana Real Estate Commission
   (in.gov/pla/bandc/estate
Insurance Information Institute
   (iii.org)
International Real Estate Digest
   (ired.com)
Iowa
   (state.ia.us/)

471

Iowa Department of Commerce
(idob.state.ia.us/)
(state.ia.us/government/com/)
Iowa Real Estate Commission
state.ia.us/government/com/prof/home.html
(state.ia.us/government/com/prof/pro_licens/complaint.html)

Kansas Office of the State Bank Commissioner
(osbckansas.org/ConsumerAssistance/complaints.html)
Kansas Real Estate Commission
(accesskansas.org/krec/)
Kentucky Department of Financial Institutions
(dfi.ky.gov/)
Kentucky Real Estate Commission
(krec.ky.gov)

Louisiana Office of Financial Institutions
(ofi.state.la.us)
Louisiana Real Estate Commission
(lrec.state.la.us)

Maine
(state.me.us/)
Maine Department of Professional and Financial Regulation
(state.me.us/pfr/pfrhome.htm)
Maine Real Estate Commission
(maine.gov/pfr/olr/categories/cat38.htm)
Mapping sites
(geocities.com)
Maryland Department of Licensing and Regulation
(dllr.state.md.us)
Massachusetts
(state.ma.us/dob/pub_offr.htm)
Massachusetts Real Estate Board
(state.ma.us/reg/boards/re)
Michigan Financial Institutions Bureau
(Michigan.gov/ofis)
Michigan Consumer & Industry Services
(Michigan.gov/dleg)
Microsoft's House and Home
(houseandhome.msn.com)
Minnesota
(state.mn.us)
(www.commerce.state.mn.us)
Mississippi Department of Banking and Consumer Finance
(dbcf.state.ms.us/)

Mississippi Real Estate Commission
 (www.mrec.state.ms.us)
Missouri Division of Credit Unions
 (ded.mo.gov/regulatorylicensing/creditunion)
Missouri Division of Finance
 (ded.mo.gov/regulatorylicensing/divisionoffinance)
Missouri Real Estate Commission
 (pr.mo.gov/appraisers.asp)
Montana Board of Realty Regulation
 (discoveringmontana.com/dli/bsd)
Montana Division of Banking and Financial Institutions
 (discoveringmontana.com/doa/banking)
MyFICO (credit history and score)
 (myfico.com)

National Association of Exclusive Buyer's Agents
 (naeba.com)
National Association of Realtors
 (realtor.com)
National Center for the Home Equity Conversion (NCHEC)
 (reverse.org)
National Council for State Housing Agencies (NCSHA)
 (ncsha.org)
Nebraska Financial Institutions Division
 (ndbf.org)
Nebraska Real Estate Commission
 (nrec.state.ne.us)
Neighborhood Reinvestment Corporation
 (nw.org)
Nevada Department of Business and Industry
 (fid.state.nv.us/)
Nevada Real Estate Division
 (red.state.nv.us/)
New Hampshire Office of the Banking Commissioner
 (state.nh.us/banking)
New Hampshire Real Estate Commission
 (nh.gov/nhrec/)
New Jersey Department of Banking and Insurance
 (state.nj.us/dobi)
New Jersey Real Estate Commission
 (state.nj.us/dobi/remnu.shtml)
New Mexico Real Estate Commission
 (state.nm.us/nmrec/)
New Mexico Regulation and Licensing Department
 (rld.state.nm.us/fid)
New York
 (dos.state.ny.us)

New York State Banking Department
(banking.state.ny.us)
North Carolina Office of the Commissioner of Banks
(banking.state.nc.us)
North Carolina Real Estate Commission
(ncrec.state.nc.us)
North Dakota Department of Banking and Financial Institutions
(discovernd.com/dfi)

Ohio
(com.state.oh.us/dfi/bnkmain.htm)
(homebuyerohio.com)
Oklahoma Real Estate Commission
(orec.state.ok.us/)
Oklahoma State Banking Department
(osbd.state.ok.us)
Oregon
(cbs.state.or.us/external/dfcs/)
Oregon Real Estate Agency
(rea.state.or.us)

Pennsylvania
(state.pa.us)

Quicken.com
(quicken.com)
Quicken Loans
(quickenloans.com)

Ram Research
(ramresearch.com)
RE/MAX
(remax.com)
Real Estate Café
(realestatecafe.com)
RealEstate.com
(realestate.com)
Realtor.com
(realtor.com)
Rhode Island
(state.ri.us/)

School Districts
(schoolmatch.com)
South Carolina
(Myscgov.com)

South Carolina Department of Labor, Licensing and Regulation
(llr.state.sc.us)
South Dakota
(state.sd.us)
South Dakota Real Estate Commission
(state.sd.us/sdrec)
State Public Interest Research Group
(pirg.org and truthaboutcredit.org)

Tennessee
(state.tn.us)
Tennessee Division of Consumer Affairs
(state.tn.us/consumer/)
Tennessee Real Estate Commission
(state.tn.us/commerce/boards/trec/index.html)
Texas Real Estate Commission
(trec.state.tx.us)
Texas State Finance Commission
(fc.state.tx.us/)

Urban Development
(hud.gov)
Utah Department of Financial Institutions
(dfi.utah.gov/)
Utah Division of Real Estate
(commerce.state.ut.us)

Vermont Department of Banking, Insurance, Securities & Health Care
Administration
(bishca.state.vt.us)
Vermont Real Estate Commission
(vtprofessionals.org)
Virginia Department of Banking
(state.va.us/scc/division/banking)
Virginia Department of Professional and Occupational Regulation
(state.va.us/dpor)

Washington Department of Financial Institutions
(wa.gov/dfi/)
Washington Department of Licensing
(dol.wa.gov/)
West Virginia Division of Banking
(state.wv.us/banking)
Wisconsin
(wisconsin.gov)
Wisconsin Department of Regulation and Licensing
(drl.wi.gov/)

Wyoming Division of Banking
(audit.state.wy.us/banking/default.htm)
Wyoming Real Estate Commission
(realestate.state.wy.us/)

Yahoo!
(yahoo.com)

Acknowledgments

When I look back over the past dozen years or so since I started thinking about the first edition of this book, I am amazed by how far the real estate world has come.

So much today is taken for granted: using the Web safely to search for information, apply online for a mortgage, and peruse homes (photos and videos!) for sale anywhere in the United States and many places around the world; women (and their salaries) being treated, by and large, the same as men; single women and men and young home buyers (25 years or younger) being treated with respect by real estate agents and mortgage lenders; home values rising at several times the rate of inflation; and creative financing that permits home buyers to design the loan that works best for their own personal finances—much the way you'd decide whether you want granite, slate, or marble as a kitchen countertop.

Keeping up to date on the ins and outs of the residential real estate world takes plenty of help. Over the years, I've interviewed countless agents, brokers, lenders, attorneys, economists, developers, and builders, not to mention the myriad of spokespeople from national trade organizations, lobbying firms, and governmental and quasi-governmental housing agencies. They have been kind, considerate, and helpful over the years, and I am grateful for their assistance.

I am also thankful to the thousands of home buyers, sellers, and homeowners who have sent e-mail and letters and have agreed to be interviewed over the course of my career as a real estate and personal finance journalist. Whether you were on the record, or off, your stories helped shape this book, as they shape my columns, television news segments, and radio programs each week.

Helping to make it all happen—and making sure I don't get lost in the details—are some very talented individuals. A big round of applause goes to my fabulous assistants: Rebeca Beeman, Jaime Alpert, and Elizabeth Horevitz, who keep me on deadline and as focused as possible.

I am also grateful for the friendship, counsel, and support of: Ralph Martire, Ellen Fiedelholtz, Thea Flaum, Ellyn Rosen, Leo Shaw and Gene Galperin, Beth and Mark Kurensky, Sarah and Michael Alter, Emanuele and Gerhard Plaschka, Lance Gams, Joni and Hal Alpert, Condace Pressley, Todd Mark, Pete Spriggs, and Greg Moceri. The Random House team is, as always, top-notch: My editors, Annik La Farge and Mario Rojas, contributed immeasurably to this third edition, and I couldn't ask for a better publicist than Brian Belfiglio, who makes magical things happen every day.

My family continues to put up with the best and worst of this eclectic life I've chosen, offering their love and support. I especially wish to thank my sisters, Shona Glink Kitei and Phyllis Glink, who are kind, thoughtful, and encouraging; and my mother, Susanne Kraus Glink, who, with more than 20 years of experience, remains one of the best (and top-selling!) real estate agents in Chicago. She introduced me to this crazy business, opened my eyes to some of its deepest, darkest secrets; told me some hilarious (but true!) stories; and repeatedly suggested that I write a book.

Finally, I would never have finished without the unstinting help of my husband and best friend, Samuel J. Tamkin, the world's best real estate attorney, and one hell of an editor—who now cowrites our weekly, nationally syndicated "Ask the Lawyer" column—who continues to believe all my wildest dreams will come true.

Index

489

Also by Ilyce R. Glink

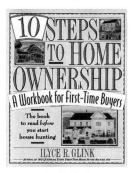

10 Steps to Home Ownership
0-8129-2531-9. $15.00 paperback

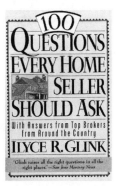

100 Questions Every Home Seller Should Ask
0-8129-2406-1. $15.00 paperback

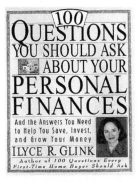

**100 Questions You Should Ask
About Your Personal Finances**
0-8129-2741-9. $19.00 paperback

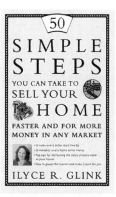

**50 Simple Steps You Can Take to Sell Your Home
Faster and for More Money in Any Market**
0-609-80933-4. $14.00 paperback

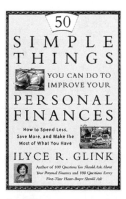

**50 Simple Things You Can Do to Improve
Your Personal Finances**
0-8129-2742-7. $14.00 paperback

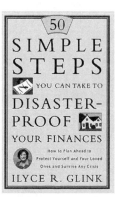

**50 Simple Steps You Can Take to
Disaster-Proof Your Finances**
0-609-80995-4. $14.00 paperback

Wherever books are sold

THREE RIVERS PRESS
NEW YORK

CrownPublishing.com

tend to be larger than homes built 20 years ago. Typically you'll have two and a half baths in a four-bedroom home. Twenty years ago, it was more common to have four bedrooms and two baths. Fifty years ago, you might have had three bedrooms and only one and a half baths. Today's newly built homes typically contain central air, loads of appliances, fireplaces, and lofted spaces. You may have a two- or three-car garage, upgraded wiring, double-paned windows, granite or marble countertops, and a basement with a high ceiling. One of the reasons your new house is so expensive is that you're typically paying a portion of the *impact fees*, charged to developers by the community to cover the costs of development (including sewer lines, more roads, and more students in the local schools). If money is an issue, you'll probably want to find an existing house that you can later fix up with all the amenities of a newly built house.

2. The neighborhood may not be established. New construction typically takes place in cornfields. That's because it's difficult to find a vacant, large *infill* plot of land in a city, and it isn't as profitable for large, production developers to build homes piecemeal. So developers looking to put up 100 to 500 homes at a time typically purchase acreage farther and farther out from the city center. Whole new communities spring up, but the retail and service development for these new communities usually lags behind. When you first move into a new community, you might have to drive five miles for a gallon of milk. (And if you have young kids at home, all those milk runs can really add up the mileage on your car.) Also, developers sometimes pick less favorable school districts or communities in order to find affordable land. So your brand-new home may not be in the best school district, or even in your suburb of choice. Does that mean you shouldn't buy a home in a new development? No. It simply means you need to think about where you're going to go shopping, work out, drop off the cleaning, fill up the car, and school your children before you sign the purchase offer.

3. Make sure your developer is well funded. One of the dangers in buying new construction early on in the life of the project is that the developer may run out of cash before the project is done. (Back in 2003 and 2004, that happened to several high-profile brand-new condo buildings in Chicago. The developer went broke, and the finance company had to take over the buildings.) If that's the case, your home could plummet in value, as the investors look to recapture their investment by selling the homes below the price you paid. Few developers are going to give you their financial statements to look at, so be sure to thoroughly check out the background of the developer by searching the Internet for news about the developer, checking with the Better Business Bureau, and even contacting your state to check out any possible complaints filed against the company. You shouldn't have trouble with a large, well-known company that has completed various successful projects over many years, but do your homework. Visit residents who live at other developments the builder has completed, and see how well the homes have held up. Also ask if the owners have any complaints about the developer or the development. A series of disgruntled homeowners should be a red flag.

4. Quality new construction may appreciate at the same speed or even more rapidly than an existing home. If you purchase a home from a reputable, quality developer, and the development itself is a quality project, your home should not only retain its value but also appreciate in value, even though other, newer projects have opened up. But beware: In a low-quality development, homes can come apart faster than they were originally put together. Although your home may still go up in value, you may spend more than the appreciation you gain in repairing big problems.

5. Do you want to live in a new home? Or do you want to fix up a home? New construction means everything is about as perfect as it's going to get. These days, no matter what the price range, you should be able to customize your home to some degree, take advantage of options and upgrades, and choose your own colors and carpet. You also get a home specifically designed to your needs. If you require a home office, for example, most new-construction house plans feature a first-floor space that could function as a separate home office. Your newly constructed home should require almost no maintenance. (Why? Everything is new.) So if you're looking for a house that's about as maintenance-free as can be (without going into a maintenance-free community we talked about earlier), new construction might be perfect for you. When you buy new construction, however, your home will appreciate only as fast as the general area. If you are looking to build in value, you'll probably want to choose a fixer-upper home. (See Question 7 for more information on looking at and purchasing fixer-upper homes.)

> ### *Matt and Annie's Story*
>
> As the saying goes, it's location, location, location. Matt and Annie bought a new house for $400,000. They spent another $70,000 to build out the attic, add some beautiful landscaping, and spruce up the family room.
>
> Five years later, they sold their house for $800,000! Why did they do so well? They were among the first to buy in what ended up becoming a very hot, trendy, expensive development. Their lot, although not directly on the water, had a nice view from the second floor. And it was easily accessible to the nearby downtown metro area. Matt and Annie pocketed a lot of cash, but what they did next was an even smarter move. They bought another house for $500,000, in cash, in the same general area but a less expensive neighborhood. As a result, instead of making monthly mortgage payments, they are using the cash they would have spent on a mortgage to build up their children's college funds, create a solid emergency fund, and take a vacation.

This old adage is really true: If it seems too good to be true, it probably is. And that goes for everything, from new construction to stock tips. If the developer is promising you the moon, and you can't get any independent confirmation that this person is an honest, reputable businessperson, watch out. Also, if you can't overcome some misgivings about the value you're getting for an investment in a property, don't sign the papers. At a minimum, finish reading this book before you make a final decision on purchasing a new or existing home.

WHAT ARE THE ADVANTAGES AND DISADVANTAGES OF BUYING A HOME THAT NEEDS RENOVATION? WHAT DO BROKERS MEAN BY "OVERIMPROVED"?

QUESTION 7

Brokers like to say that three kinds of formerly owned homes are available to buy:

1. Move-in condition. This is a house that's about as close to perfection as possible. There's no decorating or renovation required. All you have to do is move in your furniture (or purchase the sellers' furniture, if that's an option) and start living.

2. Good condition. When you hear brokers refer to a home like this, it generally means the home's "bones," or structure, are in fine shape, and the amenities and appliances are in good working order. On the other hand, you might not like the decor. Gold velvet flocked wallpaper and olive green shag carpeting might be your taste, or it might not. In this type of house, which accounts for most of the homes on the market, you might need to repaint the walls, strip the floors, or replace the carpeting.

3. Handyman's special or the fixer-upper. With a handyman's special (no offense intended to all of the handy women out there), you can expect to see anything from a home needing minor repairs to a home that requires a gut job to be livable.

When it comes to the question of the advantages and disadvantages of buying a home that needs renovation, the answer depends on how much money you have to spend. Most first-time buyers have limited cash reserves. Usually the down payment is a stretch, let alone finding money to decorate or renovate a home. Also, fewer people today have the time, know-how, or interest to actually do much of the renovation themselves, and hiring renovators or decorators can be expensive. If the option of buying a new home is available to you, purchasing new construction can be cheaper and easier in the long run.

If, however, you have the time and cash to put into renovating a home, there are significant advantages to be gained. You might be able to purchase a bigger home in a better neighborhood. You may be able to purchase a two-flat or two-family home and fix it up, then rent out one unit and live at a far reduced cost. And, of course, one of the best reasons to buy a fixer-upper is to maximize the investment you make in your home.

Angela and Tom's Story

When Angela and Tom went looking for houses, they realized they couldn't afford to buy anything worthwhile in their top choices for location. So instead of looking at single-family homes, they looked for a two-family house.

They found one that needed a substantial bit of repair. But they also could see that the house would make a terrific single-family home once they could afford to do the renovation and live without the additional rental income.

After six years, and several substantial increases in their annual income due to job changes, Angela and Tom finally had the cash to do the renovation and live without the renter's monthly contribution to the mortgage. Best of all, the neighborhood had appreciated tremendously in value. By renovating their home to just above the neighborhood standard, they were able to significantly increase its value. Today the house is a showpiece, and Angela and Tom are busy squirreling money away for their young daughter's college education.

But It Doesn't Always Work Out This Well

There are also disadvantages to fixing up a home. Renovation and decorating create mess and chaos; understand ahead of time that during the period of the renovation (and for some time thereafter), your house will never be clean. Construction and renovation almost *always* take more time than you plan for. And more than one relationship has been known to end over the turmoil and tumult of construction.

When you look at a home that needs renovation or a gut job (taking a house down to its structural bones or guts), you need to understand exactly how much work would be required and acquire a realistic ballpark estimate of how much that work will cost.

Unless your broker is also a contractor, his or her estimate of how much renovation work costs will likely be dead wrong. Do not rely on his or her estimate. Instead, hire a contractor or architect to tour the home with you before you make an offer. A contractor's or architect's ballpark estimate of renovation and construction costs will be close enough for you to decide how much you want to pay for the home. Just remember, when renovating, expect the unexpected—and add 10 to 15 percent to your expert's ballpark estimate. Renovation almost always costs more, and takes more time, than you think it will. One contractor's best guess: Double the time and add 25 percent to the final bill, and you won't be sorry.

For example, if you're in a neighborhood of renovated homes that sell for $275,000, and you see a house that requires a new kitchen, new electrical wiring, repainting, refinishing of floors, and three new windows to make it livable, you must take into consideration the cost of construction and subtract that (or most of that) from the list price. If the house is listed for $275,000 and you figure the renovation will cost $60,000, then the effective list price of that house for you should be around $215,000. And, depending on whether the market is fast or slow (i.e., it's a buyer's or seller's market), you might offer something around the $210,000 range. If, however, every house in the neighborhood needs similar renovations, then $275,000 might be an appropriate price for the property. In that case, you also need to think what the house will be worth once the renovations are complete. If you pay $275,000, and then put in $60,000, will the property be worth at least $335,000 when you're done?

Another problem with renovation is that buyers sometimes think they can buy a cheap house and create the house of their dreams. Sometimes that strategy works, but when it doesn't, watch out. When the time comes to sell the house (in five to seven years), you may find you have a white elephant: a house whose value far outstrips the other homes in the neighborhood.

This is called *overimproving* your home. You can overimprove your home to the point where you'll never be able to get your money out of it. Try to avoid the situation of selling a $400,000 house in a $100,000 neighborhood.

Daniel's Story

About 10 years ago, Daniel bought a house that needed a new kitchen. He loves to cook, so he put an $18,000 kitchen into a $160,000 house, and he planned to do other repair and renovation work. One day, his broker stopped by to say hello and look at his construction work. After admiring his beautiful new kitchen, the broker cautioned Daniel not to spend so much money that he would want to ask more than $250,000 for the house.

"The neighborhood won't support a house that's worth more than that. I'll have trouble selling it," the broker told Daniel. At that point, he hadn't overimproved the house, but he had to be careful about where he spent his renovation dollars.

A few years later, Daniel sold his house for $230,000 and made about $30,000 in profit, after expenses. It was nice to pocket some profit, but his timing was a little off. His neighborhood was about to pop. Recently, I heard that the house he used to own sold for more than $500,000. If Daniel had stayed in his house a few extra years, until the neighborhood values caught up with his improvements, he would have pocketed more than $300,000 in profits.

Not all neighborhoods explode in value the way Daniel's did, but many homes do have the potential to increase in value—if you make the right home improvement choices.

Sally and Andy's Story

Sally and Andy make a great living. Together, they earn nearly $550,000 per year. When they decided to buy a home (it wasn't their first, but a third home), it was a 4,000-square-foot condominium in a nice building. They paid $600,000 for the condo and spent another $700,000 completely gutting the place. They created a fancy one-bedroom apartment, with a den that also functioned as a guest bedroom, and a gourmet cook's kitchen.

And then one day, at age 48, Sally got pregnant. Realizing their home wouldn't work for a baby and a nanny, they decided to sell. They put the condo on the market for nearly $1 million, even though nothing in the building had ever sold for nearly that much. Had they sold for that price, they would have lost about $300,000 in renovation costs, not to mention another $60,000 in broker's commission.

But the condo didn't sell. Then they lowered the price another $100,000. The house took another year to sell. By that time, the couple had bought a house elsewhere and had been carrying two loans for nearly nine months. They lost a substantial amount of cash on the transaction.

If you're thinking about buying a home that needs renovation, be careful to consider what other renovated homes in your neighborhood are selling for in the marketplace.

SHOULD MY FIRST HOME BE AN INVESTMENT?

Young and single individuals age 21 to 25 are the fastest-growing portion of first-time buyers. Although some of these home buyers are purchasing homes that they will live in, others are purchasing these homes as investments. Why? It's clear that the stock market, though a solid long-term investment, isn't the only way to make money. When the stock market goes through a down period, as it did from 2000 to 2004, and real estate values shoot up, as they have for the last decade or more, intelligent people are going to wonder if there maybe isn't a different investment to be made.

Real estate has long stood the test of time as an investment. It generally appreciates slowly, at just above the rate of inflation. Portfolio managers have long used real estate to hedge their other investments, since it typically moves out of synch with stocks and bonds. For most of us, our biggest investment in real estate will be our own homes. But what if you're not quite ready to live in a big house? That's where buying a first home as an investment property can make a lot of sense. In some ways, real estate is a rather flexible investment: You can buy a single-family house, a town house, or a multifamily building that may have as few as two units in it or as many as six or eight units. Multifamily units are nice investments over the long run because you can live in one of the units and rent out the others. As rents rise, you can, and should, have the long-term goal of raising rents enough to cover the amount you pay to live—and more.

Michael's story is typical of the letters I often receive from readers and visitors to my website.

Michael's Story

Michael had been renting a one-bedroom condo in a building on Chicago's lakefront. He had been thinking about buying a place, so when the owner of another unit in the building decided to sell, Michael bought it, thinking he'd move into it.

But the owner of the condo Michael was renting offered him a fabulous deal to stay. He looked at the numbers and decided he could make at least 10 percent on his money by simply renting out the other unit, which was more than he could make by keeping the money in the bank or investing it in the stock market. So he continued to rent the one-bedroom in which he had been living and rented out the other unit.

Yet another condo in the building came on the market, and Michael bought that one as well and rented it out for a substantial profit. Finally a third unit came on the market and Michael bought it and moved into his own home. All three condos have doubled in value since Michael bought them. He is now collecting enough income from the other two condos to not only pay the bills but also all of the expenses of his own condo—so he lives for free.

There are thousands of stories like Michael's. When I was in Atlanta a few years ago speaking at a personal finance conference for Newstalk 750 WSB (the radio station I work for), I met a woman who started out like Michael and ended up owning 40 properties.

"You should tell people that it really works," she said. When I asked her why she was attending the conference (instead of giving one of her own), she replied, "Because I always learn something from someone here. And if I don't learn anything, at least I feel like I already know more than most people here."

I thought that was an amazing lesson: A heaping dose of self-confidence is key to making a successful investment, whether in real estate or the stock market. Do your homework, make sure the numbers add up, and then step forward.

These are important lessons for any first-time home buyer.

Should you buy a first home as an investment rather than as a primary residence? The younger you are when you buy your first home, the wealthier you'll be later in life. If you're not ready to buy a home to live in, the smartest move you could make might be to buy something and rent out.

Lisa and Jaime's Story

Neither Lisa nor her twin sister, Jaime, are ready to buy a primary residence. In their senior year of college, these 21-year-olds aren't ready for a big house of their own. But what about buying one and renting out rooms to their friends?

Lisa is planning on going to medical school, which means she'll need a place to live on campus for at least another four years. Jaime wants to get into the real estate world. So they've come up with the idea of buying a house near where Lisa will attend medical school. They'll fix it up, rent out bedrooms to Lisa's classmates, and with any luck, the house will pay for itself.

This plan has a lot of "what-ifs." For example, what if Lisa can't rent out the bedrooms? What if the house has problems that have to be fixed? What if someone forgets to pay the mortgage?

On the other hand, real estate around college campuses continues to rise at about the same speed as college tuition. Pick a good school, and provide a decent place to live for students, and you should have a good investment. Plus, if Lisa is living in the house at the same time, she'll have some control over how trashed the house gets—which should be less with medical students than your typical college student (get those thoughts of *Animal House* out of your head).

Whether this particular plan Jaime and Lisa have works remains to be seen. But buying a home as an investment before you buy a home to live in can be an excellent idea no matter how old you are.

I have heard from hundreds of friends, readers, viewers, and thinkglink.com visitors throughout the past few years who want my advice about buying a first home as an investment. Many of these individuals went ahead and bought their first home as investments. Although some of these real estate investments have made more money than others, many have turned out well. Better yet, many of these first-time buyers are hungry to make another real estate investment. Remember: The younger you are when you buy your first home, the wealthier you'll be later in life.

Jerry's Story

Jerry put 10 percent down on a building that was being converted from industrial space to condominiums. He intended to move into the property, but when the building finally opened (several years after he had put down his cash), he realized the unit had appreciated so much that he could reap a huge profit by selling. Then he realized he could more than cover his expenses by renting it out at the current market rate. So he kept the rental unit and ended up buying a second property (a single-family house) not too far from where he worked.

Keep in mind that while many real estate investment stories have happy endings, the road also can be a bit bumpy along the way.

Ed's Story

Ed put down cash on a building that was being converted from rental units to condominiums. Like Jerry, he originally thought he would move into the unit. When the time came, he realized the market rents would more than cover his investment, so he rented out the condominium.

And that's where the trouble started. After two months of rental payments, Ed's renter skipped out, causing some minor damage to the unit and leaving Ed with a mortgage payment, real estate taxes, and a homeowner's insurance bill but without any investment income. To cover all that plus his own rent, Ed ran up a few thousand dollars on his credit card.

Ed decided to sell. Another problem emerged: He couldn't sell the unit. It took nearly eight months to sell. Lesson learned: Real estate is a far less liquid (meaning, easily salable) investment than a share of stock.

The good news is that overall, Ed wound up making about 30 percent on the cash he originally invested in his property. The property had
appreciated significantly, and when all was said and done, he pocketed
more than $35,000 for his efforts.

Investment Property Gotchas

Before you buy a home as an investment, here are a few things to keep
in mind.

1. It's still all about location. Whether you're buying your first
home to live in or rent out, location counts. Read Question 3 to understand why agents say it doesn't just matter what suburb or neighborhood you choose but where your property is placed on a block. If
you're buying a condo or town house, location refers to where your
unit is placed inside the building as well. (One of Ed's problems was
that his rental condo was on the first level, rather than higher up in the
building.)

**2. Make sure the numbers work before you sign the contract
to purchase.** Whether you live in your new home or rent it out,
real estate costs money to buy and maintain. Make sure you feel
comfortable with carrying the costs of the rental unit (assuming you
can't get it rented) over a period of months. Talk to local rental
agents about how much rent they think the unit could fetch. If there
are monthly condo or homeowners' association fees, make sure you
add those in, too.

3. Give yourself a financial cushion. You want to have some
extra cash on hand, just in case something breaks or you're without a
renter for an extended period of time. One of my own rental properties was vacant for nine months after the terrorist attacks on September 11, 2001.

4. Create an exit strategy for yourself and the property. You
probably won't keep this rental property for the rest of your life. At
some point, you'll want to sell. Figure out what has to happen to trig-
ger the sale. You might want to use the cash for a different property.
Or you might move to another state. If you can't rent it for several
months or a year, then perhaps you'll list the property.

49

5. Think about how difficult it will be to sell this investment before you buy it. If you buy a home that's been on the market for a while, there's probably a reason it hasn't sold. Figure out the reason and see if it can be corrected—before you make an offer to purchase. If you can't fix "the problem" with the property but know it will make a great investment, then you should buy it. But remember that if you purchase a property priced well below similar homes in the area, and whatever problem or drawback the property has can't be fixed, you may find that it appreciates much more slowly than neighboring properties and could take a lot longer to sell.

2

How Do I Look for a Home?

HOW DO I START MY SEARCH FOR THE HOME OF MY DREAMS? SHOULD I LOOK ON THE INTERNET?

There are two ways to find the right home: You can work with a real estate broker, or you can do it yourself. Most of this book is slanted toward buyers who work with real estate agents or brokers, but let's spend a few minutes examining how you can find a home on your own—and why you might choose to do it that way.

QUESTION 9

FSBOs

If a seller chooses to sell his or her home without the assistance of a real estate agent or broker, it's called "for sale by owner." You might also see the acronym *FSBO*, which is pronounced "fizz-bo." Homeowners choose to sell their homes themselves for two reasons: (1) they think they can handle all the details, and (2) they won't have to pay a commission to the real estate agents who help get the home sold.

How many homes are sold as FSBOs? No one really knows. The best studies seem to suggest that anywhere from 15 to 35 percent of homeowners choose to sell without a broker. The National Association of Realtors (NAR) will tell you the number is closer to the 15 percent range. Other industry observers suggest the true number of FSBOs ranges quite a bit higher than that. Some experts suggest that as the Internet matures, the number of FSBOs will naturally increase, but so far the only thing I see increasing are the number of websites where sellers can list their homes for sale by owner.

You'll find FSBOs listed in your local newspaper's real estate classi-fied advertisements under "Houses for Sale." You might also find them listed in alternative newspapers, weekly or monthly neighbor-hood newspapers, and local magazines. Since 1996 the Internet has ex-ploded with literally thousands of real-estate-related websites. One bunch, dedicated solely to FSBOs, includes sites like ForSaleBy-Owner.com, which as we went to press for this edition was widely rec-ognized as the leading FSBO site. There are also thousands of local FSBO sites.

With the Internet, however, things change frequently. When I wrote the second edition of this book, a website called Owners.com was the leading FSBO site. It basically invented the genre. Several years ago, it went out of business and the man who started it sold the website name and went to work for someone else. Although this incar-nation of ForSaleByOwner.com may be the leading FSBO website now, that could change in the future. If you decide to sell by owner or look for a home that is for sale by owner in your neighborhood, the best idea is to go to Google or Yahoo and type "FSBO" into the search browser. Start your search with those results.

Of course, one of the best ways to find a FSBO property to pur-chase is to walk around the neighborhoods you've targeted as being acceptable. FSBO homes usually have a sign posted outside letting prospective buyers know they are for sale.

If you decide you want to tour the inside of a FSBO, simply call the telephone number in the advertisement or on the sign and make an appointment. The homeowner will then give you a tour of his or her home. This can be awkward, as you should be looking for every fault and every reason *not* to buy the home. And yet, you don't want to in-sult the homeowner, just in case you *do* want to buy the home. Internet listings are helpful here, too, because many websites allow you to see photos of the home's exterior and interior. As the Internet becomes more developed, and technology becomes cheaper, you'll soon be able to download video and audio "tours" of a prospective home. (Some metro areas have audio tours that are available when you drive by a home. Simply call the number listed on the sign and you can listen to the agent's description of the home.)

Going It Alone

One new, and rather disturbing, trend is for first-time buyers to look for property without the benefit of an agent representing them. Why does this happen? When first-time buyers go to a new construction development, they often go by themselves. The moment you sign in without an agent, you are considered "unrepresented," and it may be difficult to later introduce an agent into the process. From that point on, you are dealing with the developer on your own, usually through a salesperson who represents the developer exclusively. Other times, home buyers simply (and mistakenly) believe they'll get a better deal if they approach a seller about his or her home (whether it is listed or not). They figure the seller will only have to pay a half commission, and that leaves 2.5 to 3 percent of the purchase price negotiable.

Here's the real truth: Whether you come with an agent or not, the seller has already signed a commission agreement with his or her agent promising to pay the total commission regardless of whether the buyer comes with an agent or not. If the buyer has an agent, then the seller's agent agrees to split the commission paid with the buyer's agent. Otherwise, the seller's agent gets it all.

When it comes to FSBOs, buyers again believe they'll be better off without an agent. And, in some cases, they will be. But more often, first-time buyers don't understand how a local marketplace works, and they don't have a clear idea of what a property is worth. An agent can help here. Otherwise, you could easily wind up overpaying for your home.

Now that you know that, why would you want to look for a home without an agent? Frankly, I don't think you should. As a home buyer, you're in the enviable position of having *buyer brokerage* (where the agent owes his or her fiduciary duty to you, not the seller—see Question 13 for more details) available to you, without having to pay for it out of pocket (the seller still pays the commission). Why wouldn't you want to have a smart person, who supposedly knows the area and housing stock, take you around and share a career's worth of knowledge?

The advantages of having a broker seem obvious, and yet I hear more and more stories every day about buyers going it alone. All sellers, but particularly FSBOs, tend to be greedy. They're hoping to save the 6 or 7 percent, not share it with you, the home buyer. So when you start the negotiations, they may come down 6 or 7 percent, but because they've started out with such a high price, you're still paying more than you should and not reaping the benefit of the commission savings.

Many home buyers like FSBOs because it makes them feel as if they are seeing everything that's out there on the market. Of course, they aren't, because the majority of homes for sale are listed with brokers in a computerized system called a *multiple listing service* (MLS). Access to the MLS used to be restricted to member brokers and their clients. In the days before the Internet, access to the MLS data was so tightly guarded that brokers weren't even allowed to give listing books (telephone-book-size listing books printed every other week with the new listings) to their clients to peruse. Today, you can find almost all listing information online at any number of websites, including Realtor.com (the website of the NAR), HouseandHome.msn.com, Yahoo.com, and on broker's individual sites, which may be listed at the International Real Estate Digest website (ired.com). For more websites, check the listings in the Alphabetical Listing of Websites. Also, check back at thinkglink.com, as I'll continue to update the listings in this book online.

first time buyer tip

If you're going to purchase a home that's a FSBO, be sure you get a good real estate attorney to help you draw up the contract. You'll need an attorney even if you live in a state like California, where attorneys typically aren't used. That's because you'll want someone to enforce the disclosures the seller is required to make to you, the buyer—disclosures he or she may not realize must be delivered at certain times before the home closes. Also, you'll want to make sure to hire a professional home inspector to thoroughly scrutinize the home before you close.

New Construction

Let's explore what happens when you shop for a newly built home. Developers, who have already set aside the amount of money to pay a commission to a broker who brings a buyer to the development, love it when consumers come without representation. That's because they save the 3 percent they would have paid to the buyer broker. The developer's salespeople love it when you come without representation, because they typically get a higher commission or a bonus.

As a buyer, however, you'll find it easier and less time-consuming if you go with a buyer broker or agent to see several new construction developments. Developers will tell you that you don't need a broker—but they'll pay the commission should you choose to use one. I'm going to reiterate an important point: *If you don't bring a broker with you to the model, and if you don't protect your broker by signing in under his or her name, you may not be allowed to bring in that broker later. Effectively, you will have no representation in your deal.*

Once in a while, the developer will lower the cost of the new construction by the amount that he or she would have paid in brokerage commission fees. Mostly, though, the developer won't. More likely, developers will give you extra upgrades for free or at a reduced cost. The truth is, a good broker may be able to extract the same concessions or even more—that's what negotiation is all about.

Again, be sure you have a good real estate attorney who can eyeball your new construction contract (the standard forms typically favor the builder and give the buyer few, if any, rights or recourse).

new construction tip

Although it isn't common to hire an inspector for new construction, it's an excellent idea to have someone look in during the four crucial stages of building: (1) after the foundation is poured; (2) after the framing is up; (3) after the house is wired and plumbed; and (4) just before the walls are closed in. By having your professional home inspector stay on top of the builder during the construction, you'll have someone who can point out mistakes or shoddy workmanship while these errors can be remedied less expensively—and on the builder's dime, not yours. You'll also want to do a final walkthrough before closing, and make sure you have your *punch list* (your list of items that still need to be finished before the house is completed).

Using a Broker

If you decide you don't want to look for a place to buy by yourself, your other option is to use a broker. Brokers come in all different shapes, sizes, and personalities. The benefits of using a real estate agent or broker can be significant:

1. Eyes and Ears. A good broker is supposed to be your eyes and ears, prescreening homes on the market, finding out why the home is for sale, and selecting the ones he or she thinks might be right for you.

2. Less Legwork. Your broker is supposed to do at least some of your legwork by walking through these homes to further eliminate those that won't meet your needs and wants.

3. Guide You. A good broker will make your appointments for you, chauffeur you around from showing to showing, help you understand the good and bad about a house, provide you with enough information to create an offer, and then present that offer to the seller and seller broker.

4. Educate You. A good broker will educate you about the home-buying process and the local real estate market. He or she should be able to point out the good and the bad, so you can make an informed decision.

By tapping into the local MLS, brokers can pull up all kinds of information, including:

- A list of all homes available in your price range or in your desired location
- The homes' amenities, square footage, most recent tax bill, number and size of bedrooms and bathrooms
- How long a particular home has been listed for sale
- The original price plus any price reduction
- The home's address and the listing broker's telephone number
- A photo of the exterior of the home, and possibly the interior, and perhaps even a video tour
- A list of similar homes that have sold recently and the relevant data
- Other pertinent and interesting facts and figures, such as the lot size, the way the house faces, and the listing broker's description

first time buyer tip

Remember, brokers are only as good as you let them be. If you choose to use a broker or agent, you'll have to learn the difference between conventional, buyer, and discount brokers. You'll also have to learn how much to tell your broker, and when complete honesty may not be entirely appropriate.

first time
buyer tip

Everyone comes with baggage; that is, their own personal collection of aches, pains, and problems. And the older we are, the more baggage we seem to tote around. It works the same way with a home. The older the home is, the more likely it is going to have problems, quirks, oddities, and other items that seem to make it less than perfect. I'll talk about this more as we move through the home-buying process, but remember this: Buying a home is the American dream, but the reality of the house is what you have to live with.

Using the Internet to Find Your New Home

Just before the first edition of this book went to press at the end of 1993, I decided to get an e-mail address. Although the Web was in its infancy (America Online perhaps had 2 or 3 million members—if only I'd bought the stock at that time!), it seemed to me that e-mail would make communications a lot faster than the post office, which perennially seems to have problems just getting the mail delivered on time. And if it was easier and faster to send an e-mail, perhaps more readers would feel comfortable writing and asking their own questions.

So a few days before the first edition's final press date, I hooked up to AOL and put my e-mail address in the preface. I was fortunate in that my e-mail address of choice—my name—was available. (Then again, how many Ilyce Glinks do you know?) In the first year, I received far more letters to my post office box than to my e-mail address. But starting in 1995, the amount of e-mail dwarfed the so-called snail mail by about 10 to 1. Today, I receive hundreds of e-mails a week from readers, viewers, and thinkglink.com visitors. I receive perhaps two to three snail-mail letters in my post office box.

The use of the Internet as a tool for personal communications, however, has been surpassed by the incredible speed with which the business community has taken to the World Wide Web, and that includes the world of real estate. And as in other industries, the Internet is forcing profound changes to the core of the industry. These changes are important because they directly affect how you will buy and finance your home.

Up until, say, 1996, the way people bought homes had been fairly static for centuries. All of the key information—which homes were listed for sale and how much they cost—resided with a few licensed real estate agents and brokers, who zealously (some might say jealously) guarded it. Access to the information was severely limited. How limited? As late as the late 1980s, books of house listings were printed every other week. Agents who were members of the local MLS (there were typically a dozen or more in a major metropolitan area) would have a copy and you could make an appointment with the agent to see the current listing book. If the agent really liked you, you might be given an old copy of a listing book under cover.

You wanted to buy a house? You either worked with a licensed agent, or you trolled the newspaper listings over the weekend looking for FSBOs.

But in the mid-1990s, computers and the Internet began to open up new opportunities to companies wanting to move in and disseminate real estate information on a larger scale. Multiple-listing services (MLS) began to merge into one or two metropolitan MLSs, which cooperated fully with each other and gave all licensed agents who were members (no matter where they were located) access to the data.

Internet companies put everything up on the Web, free to anyone who had a computer and modem. After a few expensive false starts, the data about which homes were for sale started getting posted on the Internet for anyone to see. Suddenly, by going to Yahoo! or Realtor.com, you could tap into as many as 2 million listings and find out the listing price, the number of bedrooms and bathrooms, how much the seller paid in taxes, and all sorts of previously private information.

Both the industry consolidation and the Internet advances were met with a great deal of skepticism and cynicism by both agents and brokers, as well as the real estate reporters who covered the industry.

first time
buyer tip

The dissemination of listing data is fine, except it sets up one of the biggest problems for consumers shopping for a home on the Internet: *If you contact the listing broker for more information about a particular listing and you are either not represented or you do not inform the listing broker at the time of contact that you are represented, there is a very real chance that you will end up in a dual agency situation, with the listing broker owing her loyalty to neither you nor the seller. That would mean you'd be spending the largest amount you've ever spent on anything without anyone guiding you along the way.*

The key to making real estate brokers happy about the dissemination of the listing data was to put in their e-mail address as the contact name for more information about the property. (And not putting FSBO properties on the same sites that carry Realtor listings.)

Today, literally hundreds of thousands of real-estate-related sites exist on the Internet.

The Best and the Worst of the Internet

As with any information system, there are some good things and bad things about using the Internet as a way to shop for a home or a mortgage loan.

The Good News
The Internet is a good place to:

1. Identify potential cities or neighborhoods. Mapping sites like Mapquest.com allow you to look at the geographical shape of an area and make selections based on distance to work, school, or your house of worship. Other sites will place addresses on the map for you, along with various points of interest. Future versions of mapping sites will allow you to name the stores, restaurants, or addresses of interest and have the site plot them out for you.

2. Learn more about that city or neighborhood. Many cities have their own sites, which discuss everything from sports and recreational opportunities, to cultural offerings, shopping and restaurants. Other companies, such as a local real estate company, may also put neighborhood information up on the Web.

3. Choose a school district. Various sites offer links to school ratings programs, including SchoolMatch.com, which ranks schools based on an independent evaluation. They also can assist you in finding the right program to meet your children's needs. It's easy to log on to a state's department of education to find school scoring statistics as well. Also, many school districts host their own websites, which include dates, contact information, teacher résumés, calendars, photos of students, and other information that can help you evaluate a school.

4. Get a taste of what's on the market. You'll be able to see some, even many, of the homes that are for sale in a given marketplace. Many of the sites offer color photos, 360-degree photos, and even videos of the interior and exterior of the homes.

5. Check out the demographics and statistics that define a neighborhood. Many sites, including HouseandHome.msn.com, offer information on who is living in a particular neighborhood and what kind of crime you might encounter while living there. Also, if you log onto a search engine like Google or Yahoo! and enter "crime statistics" and your neighborhood or city, you'll quickly track down the information you're looking for.

6. Shop around for a home loan. You can easily apply online for a mortgage with all types of lenders, including a portal mortgage lender that aggregates many lenders into one site, an individual mortgage broker, a national lender, or an Internet company that offers a slew of the top lenders from which to choose. In the past few years, legislation was signed that will permit you to sign loan documents with an electronic signature. This means that someday you'll be able to close on your home electronically, without paying a visit to a local title or escrow company.

The Bad News
Unfortunately, the Internet:

1. Doesn't offer information on every home that's for sale in every neighborhood. If you rely solely on the Internet to shop for a home, you're probably missing some, if not a lot of, homes. Also, even the most inclusive of websites, like Realtor.com, may not include every listing that is available for sale locally. That's because some companies have withdrawn their data from the national sites (to reserve it for their own websites and keep sales in-house), and other companies do not belong to the local MLSs that feed into the national sites.

2. Might be out of date. Although some sites claim to update their information daily, if not several times during the day, the truth is, they can't update anything unless the information has been sent to them from the individual brokerage firms. In some cases, that happens frequently (daily), but in other cases, it might happen weekly or even monthly. In a hot sellers' market, like the one we experienced during the latter half of the 1990s and into the early 2000s, when homes sold in a matter of days (or minutes), keeping listings up to date is tough, if not impossible.

3. You'll get steered toward the seller broker for more information. Although the seller broker knows what's going on, you don't want to end up in a dual agency situation—which is what might happen if you e-mail a seller broker for more information about a particular listing and you don't mention that you're already represented by a buyer's agent. Or you could wind up with no representation at all, if the seller's agent continues working only for the seller.

4. Isn't like walking around a neighborhood. Getting to know a city or neighborhood through an Internet site is a good idea, but it isn't even close to going there in person and experiencing the area as a would-be resident. You may like a *house* on the Internet but be horrified by the actual *neighborhood* once you get there. Until you visit and see for yourself, you'll never really know.

5. Can't provide you with an electronic closing. Although electronic signatures have been legislated, meaning they're legal, the technology and rules for implementation weren't quite there by the time we went to press. So you can shop for a home and loan online, but you'll eventually have to sign real papers, and go through a real closing. With any luck, you've actually gone to see the home at least once or twice, and you've followed a home inspector through a general house inspection. As for a true electronic closing, we might get there one day, or we might not.

6. Can overwhelm you with information. What the Internet does best is to provide you with information so you can make an informed decision on your own. And you can have access to that information at any time of the day or night. Want to apply for a loan at 3 A.M.? No problem. On the other hand, with hundreds of thousands of real-estate-related websites to peruse, you can get easily overwhelmed if you don't know where to go and what to look for.

The truth is, many real estate websites are a waste of time. Either the information is duplicated on larger websites, or you're getting information that is supposedly objective but is provided by someone who wants your business.

Nevertheless, according to the latest figures, more than 70 percent of Americans start their search for a home on the Internet. Another new trend is that home buyers are purchasing homes—sight unseen—through the Internet. In my mind, these buyers are taking a huge risk (what if the home isn't what it seems to be in the photos and video seen on the Internet?), but sometimes it works out.

> ### *Fred's Story*
>
> Fred lived in the San Francisco area and was told at work he was being transferred to Boston in the next two weeks. The problem was that Fred was going to be traveling nonstop (for his job) and didn't have time to fly out to look for a place to live.
>
> Late one night, he went to his home office, fired up his computer, and started searching Boston real estate in his price range. He looked up neighborhoods, the different types of homes that were available, and found a few things he liked. Next, he went to a couple of mortgage sites and ended up applying for a loan online.
>
> By the next night, he was approved for his mortgage and had called several agents to talk to them about various properties they represented. By the third day, when he left for a two-week business trip to Asia, he had made a successful offer on a property without ever seeing it. At the end of his trip he came back to San Francisco, packed up, put his stuff in storage, and flew to Boston. He closed on the property a few weeks later and had his things moved into his new place.
>
> Fred likes the home he bought and because of a hot seller's market in the Boston neighborhood he chose, he felt he had to move quickly. Time constraints and travel prevented him from visiting Boston ahead of time, but fortunately, it worked out okay.

If you're going to buy a home sight unseen, keep these issues in mind:

1. Protect yourself as best you can. Put in the usual inspection and financing contingencies as well as an attorney approval rider (see Questions 36, 37, and 38 for details). If, for some reason, the seller won't accept a mortgage contingency, try to include a contingency that allows you to withdraw from the sale if the house doesn't appraise out in value. (That is, if the bank's appraiser comes back and says the house isn't worth what you're paying for it.)

2. Find out as much as possible about the neighborhood and block. Look up crime statistics, try to find photos online, look for a neighborhood or block association that can provide more information, and try to talk to someone who lives nearby. Talk to the local village hall or building department to make sure no new highways, train depots, commercial developments, or dumps will be located nearby. Study local maps to figure out whether your property will be surrounded by other similar properties or something entirely different.

3. Ask the agent to send you a complete set of digital photos of the interior and exterior of the property. It's probably less important if you're buying a condominium or a unit in a maintenance-free town house development. It's more important to see what the exterior of the property looks like if you're buying a single-family house.

Getting Started and Helping Out

By the time you've decided to buy a house, you'll be ready to go full speed ahead. Even the fastest agent won't be quick enough once you've made the mental commitment to becoming a home buyer. You'll probably want to dive in and help find the perfect home. If you sit back and wait, you'll likely end up frustrated. Take the lead and assist your broker, but be ready to sit back and listen when he or she has information to share.

When starting your home search, your first stop should be the World Wide Web. Start by searching through the major online listing services (see the Alphabetical Listing of Websites for a list of good sites, like Realtor.com, or visit thinkglink.com for a complete updated list). If you don't have access to a computer at home or at work, check out your local library. Most libraries now offer free access to the Internet, and the librarians are trained to help you with your search. You can also access the Internet through online cafés, where, for a small hourly fee, you can use their equipment to tap into the Web. In Cambridge, Massachusetts, in the shadow of Harvard University, housing activist Bill Wendel runs the Real Estate Café, where you can tap into not only the Internet but also Bill's expertise.

Each of the national chains, including Century 21 (century21.com or keyword Century21 if you're on America Online), Coldwell Banker (coldwellbanker.com), RE/MAX. (remax.com), and ERA (era.com), offer loads of different information, not only about their own national base of listings but also about the various cities and towns in which they're located. Individual offices sometimes have their own sites that contain local listings. You can get the website address either by looking at newspaper advertisements in your local weekend real estate section or by calling the office directly. You can also go online to the International Real Estate Digest (ired.com) website. This site lists many different real-estate-related websites and will often review them.

As we mentioned before, listings on the Web are only as good as the people who input the information and then upload it to the database.

Often, the listings are old or sold. By the time you log on, they're gone. Also, and I'll talk about this more in the next couple of questions, if you contact a listing by e-mail for more information on a particular house, you may end up in a *dual agency* situation, where the listing broker also becomes your buyer broker. The bottom line is, unfortunately, you'll have no independent representation. (See Question 14 for more details on dual agency.)

The Internet has loads of mortgage information as well. See Question 60 for more information on how to shop and apply for a loan online.

No matter how much you think you love a house you found online, don't make an offer until you've actually stepped through its portals in person. If you must make an offer sight unseen, be sure you include the regular home inspection, financing, and attorney approval (if applicable in your state) contingencies in order to protect yourself.

WHAT IS THE DIFFERENCE BETWEEN A REAL ESTATE AGENT AND A REAL ESTATE BROKER? WHAT IS A REALTOR?

Real estate professionals go by a few different names, although the distinction shouldn't matter much to you, the first-time buyer. The only caveat here is to make certain the broker or agent you choose to work with is a licensed real estate professional. All real estate brokers and sales agents are licensed and regulated by each state. Most states have laws that require brokers and agents to post their licenses in a visible place. If you're not certain your agent is licensed, simply ask to see the license. Or you can call the state agency that regulates real estate agents and brokers in your state and verify the license. (See Appendix VI on page 439 for a list of regulating agencies in each state.)

What's the difference between a real estate agent and a real estate broker? To the average home buyer or seller, there isn't much difference. Either an agent or a broker can help you successfully complete your home purchase. To become a real estate agent, an individual must complete the required number of hours of classes and pass the agent's exam. To become a broker, the agent must then take additional classes, have a specified amount of experience in the field (usually a year), and pass another exam. Both agents and brokers are typically required to take a certain number of hours of continuing education courses, and they may also take additional courses to garner a few extra letters after their name.

Having a real estate broker's license confers certain privileges, including the right to open, run, and own a real estate office, and to work independently without an office. A real estate agent must work for a broker, who is responsible for that agent's actions.

Is it better to work with a broker than a sales agent? Not necessarily. Although it would seem that a broker may have more experience or be more knowledgeable than an agent, that isn't always the case. Plenty of excellent sales agents have chosen not to become brokers because they have no intention of ever running their own office. (For example, my mother, Susanne, a top-selling agent in Chicago for more than 20 years, has never taken the broker classes or exam.) The experience and knowledge of an agent who has been working in an area for 15 years will far surpass that of a brand-new broker. You should find the most experienced professional to work with you, regardless of whether he or she is an agent or broker.

Realtors vs. Non-Realtors

What is the difference between a broker who is a Realtor and a broker who is not? A Realtor is a broker or agent who belongs to the National Association of Realtors (NAR) and subscribes to that organization's code of ethics and conduct. There are around 2 million real estate agents and brokers in the United States, of which about half belong to the NAR.

Is it better to work with a Realtor than a broker who is not a Realtor? Not necessarily. As we'll talk about in the next few questions, you want to find the best, most knowledgeable, and most reliable broker or agent. Don't worry about titles, designations, and how many letters follow his or her name.

Agents and brokers can assist you equally well in the purchase of property. In fact, an agent with 15 years of experience might be able to better help you than a brand-new broker, who has a total of 1½ years of experience.

HOW DO I CHOOSE THE RIGHT AGENT OR BROKER?

Finding a broker or agent who meets your needs and personality can be tougher than it sounds. Buyers who have the worst experiences are often those who just walk into or call their neighborhood shop and ask for anyone at random. That is *not* how you find a good agent or broker. It might, however, give you a huge headache.

Connie is director of career development and advertising for a real estate firm located in Overland Park, Kansas. She has her broker's license and had sold real estate for more than 14 years. Connie believes every buyer, but especially a first-timer, should carefully interview several agents and brokers. Here are some of her recommendations: "Have them describe to you how they go about assisting a buyer. Try to get a feel for the agents' philosophy on working with buyers. Try to get a feel for their background and experience level. And be sure to ask them for a résumé. If you're thinking about letting someone represent you in the transaction, I think it's reasonable to expect to see a copy of their résumé."

Connie says she'd be leery of any agent who lets you walk into his or her office and then immediately bundles you into his or her car and shows you homes. The agents need to interview you, she says. "And first-time buyers generally need an education on the purchase process and an understanding of what their options are in the transaction."

Although Connie recommends working with a heavily experienced agent ("Why should you be the guinea pig?" she asks), she says sometimes brand-new agents offer excellent service. "That depends on their training and support. It can be a good situation. But more often than not, the more experienced the agent, the more transactions he or she handles in a year, the more situations they're confronted with, the more insight into the closing process they will have."

Making a Good Match

In addition to looking for an experienced agent, try to find one who suits your personality. If you're an early bird, don't choose someone habitually late. If you're allergic to smoking, don't choose a smoker. If you're extremely organized, don't choose a broker who is constantly losing his or her keys. Over time, or on long days of multiple showings, these little personality quirks will make you crazy.

It's also important to find someone who won't push you into making a decision before you're ready. You want a broker who will tell you the facts and will help you compare the differences between properties, but you don't want someone who will scare you or pressure you into purchasing a home. Unfortunately, some brokers and agents do pressure buyers to buy. If that happens, you must be tough enough to back away from that pressure and find yourself a new agent. You can also talk with the agent's managing broker about the situation. One of the managing broker's jobs is to smooth out the bumps between agents and brokers.

> Working with a real estate agent is a little like short-term marriage. Even in the best of circumstances, the pressure will mount and you may not always like what's happening, or how a situation is being handled. But since you'll be in such close proximity for an undetermined amount of time—at least three to six months from start to closing—it's a good idea to find someone with whom you're compatible.

How do you find a good broker or agent? As in choosing a doctor or an attorney, most people are referred to a broker by their friends or a family member who has recently bought or sold a home and had a good experience. If you're moving across state lines and don't know anyone in your hometown-to-be, you may want to contact a relocation company, who can assist you with the sale of your existing home (if you already own a home) and the purchase of your new home. There are also plenty of referral sites on the Internet, like HomeGain.com, which can refer you to several qualified agents, allowing you to take the interview process from there. If your company is moving you, the company may have an ongoing relationship with a broker or brokerage firm in your new location. Although it's certainly wise to interview a broker who is referred by someone you know, also interview several other agents who frequently work in your area. Aunt Jeanne's suburban agent may not be the most effective agent to help you find a downtown loft.

> Don't let your mother, father, or sibling foist someone on you or try to guilt you into using a family member or friend. If one of your relatives is a real estate agent, by all means sit down and interview that individual. But make sure that's only one of a small handful of agents whom you interview before you hire someone. I typically recommend talking to three agents to start, and adding a fourth or fifth if you still don't feel as though you've found the right person.

Here are a few other suggestions:

1. Open your local newspaper to the real estate section and see who runs the biggest ads, week in and week out.

2. If you ask friends, neighbors, or relatives for referrals, make sure they had a great experience with the agent they used. You don't want to use someone who doesn't provide a good real estate experience.

3. Visit open houses and spend some time talking to the real estate agents about homes in the neighborhoods. Ask these listing brokers to define what makes a great buyer's agent. Ask them who, in addition to themselves, they'd want their own children to use.

4. Call your local board of Realtors and ask for the names of agents who sold the most property last year.

Things You Can Do

Despite any horror stories you may have heard, the vast majority of first-time buyers have good, if not great, experiences with their agents. But to ensure you're working with the right person, take on the responsibility of interviewing several agents before you make your final selection. If you simply take a friend or relative's suggestion, you may find yourself working with the wrong broker and looking in the wrong neighborhoods at homes that are too expensive.

Sixteen Questions You Should Ask Real Estate Agents Before You Hire One

Here are some questions you should ask each time you interview a real estate agent:

1. How many years have you been in the real estate business?

2. How many years have you been with this company?

3. How many real estate transactions did you complete in each of the last two years?

4. What was the dollar volume of your transactions in each of the last two years?

5. What percentage of your business is with home buyers? What percentage of your home-buyer business is with first-time buyers?

6. How old are your clients, on average? Do they have children?

7. What was the price range (lowest to highest) of the homes you helped your clients buy and sell last year?

8. What would you say is the average price of the homes you helped your clients buy and sell?

9. Are you an exclusive buyer broker? Do you ask home buyers to sign an exclusivity contract? Do you charge an up-front fee that is later applied to the commission?

10. What are the primary neighborhoods or communities in which you work?

11. How familiar are you with the schools, crime statistics, and demographics of the various neighborhoods? (Hint: Brokers are forbidden from "steering" you to one neighborhood or another for any reason. For the same reason, they may choose to tell you where to go to get information on crime or schools but opt not to tell you themselves.)

12. What style of home do you most frequently work with? (If you're looking for a four-family apartment building and they're more familiar with single-family houses, it might not be a good fit.)

13. Are you a smoker or a nonsmoker? (If this is important to you.)

14. How many home buyers or sellers do you work with at a given time? (You're trying to find out how much time you'll get from the agent.)

15. How frequently will I hear from you? How do I reach you? Can I e-mail you? Or phone you at home? Are you planning any extended vacations in the next six months?

16. Do you work with an assistant? Will I be working with the assistant or with you?

You can find out a lot about an agent just by the way he or she answers these questions. If the person bristles and seems reluctant to share information with you, that may be a sign of things to come. If the agent is open and friendly, and you develop a connection on the phone, you may have found someone with whom you'll enjoy working.

first time
buyer tip

Going It Alone

As I've said before, I don't see any benefit to purchasing a home without a buyer broker's help. Although more and more buyers tell me they are *shopping* on their own, if they purchase something that's listed on the local MLS, they are not necessarily *buying* on their own. They are buying with the assistance of a dual agent, also known as a *transactional agent*, a *facilitator*, or *nonagent*, depending on which state you live in.

That means you're essentially making the largest single purchase of your life without any representation at all. (For more information on dual agents, transactional agents, facilitators, and nonagents, see Question 14.)

WHAT IS A SELLER (OR CONVENTIONAL) BROKER? WHAT ARE THE SELLER BROKER'S RESPONSIBILITIES TO ME?

First things first: There is a wide gulf between a seller broker, also known as a conventional broker, and a buyer broker. Buyer brokers (and exclusive buyer brokers) represent the interests of the buyer (see Question 13). Seller brokers represent the interests of the seller.

It seems obvious, but there's a lot of crossover that makes it confusing.

In theory, the broker works for the person who pays his or her commission. A seller broker means the seller pays the commission. A buyer broker means the buyer is responsible for paying the commission.

But wait! Didn't I just say that even if you use a buyer's agent, the seller will pay the commission? Yep. And, in practice, that's generally how it works. In many states, any broker who works with a buyer, who is not a dual agent, automatically becomes a buyer broker—even if the seller pays the commission. But if, for some reason, the seller doesn't pay the commission, the buyer would then be responsible for paying it.

Since I first wrote this book buyer brokerage has gone mainstream. In the early 1990s, there were more conventional brokers than buyer brokers. Today, buyer brokerage has been accepted by the NAR and written into almost all state statutes. We'll talk more about this in Question 13.

When a seller or conventional broker brings the buyer to the deal, he or she is also called the *subagent*. Even though a subagent will take you, the buyer, around to see various houses and appears to work in your best interests, your broker is still a seller broker. He or she has a fiduciary responsibility to the seller, rather than to you, the buyer. The seller broker is required by law to represent the seller's best interest, not yours. These distinctions have caused a tremendous amount of confusion for buyers, who quite naturally assume that the person taking them around, showing them houses, telling them the inside scoop, and buying them coffee and dinner works for them.

Let's be clear on one point: If you haven't hired a buyer broker and signed an exclusivity contract with him or her, and if you're not living in a state that mandates buyer brokerage, you're most likely working with a seller or conventional broker.

In many states, subagency has been eliminated. In these states, if an agent is working for a buyer, he or she is a buyer's agent. If the agent is working for the seller, he or she is a seller's agent. That clears up some of the confusion. If the subagent (bringing the buyer to the table) or buyer broker is also the listing broker, he or she is known as a dual agent.

Agency Disclosure

It's all so confusing—far more than it needs to be. To counteract some of the confusion, many states have adopted "agency disclosure" laws that require brokers to disclose to the buyer whom they actually represent in a given deal. In some states, brokers and agents must make that disclosure in writing. If you live in a state that requires a written disclosure form, you might get something that looks like the following. (See Appendix IV for a complete form.)

When you sign the form, you're saying that you understand who is working for you, and whether the agent is working for you or for the seller. *If you don't understand what the form says or what it means, don't sign it.*

Things a Seller's Agent Cannot Do for You

If you're a buyer working with a subagent, there are certain things seller brokers may not do according to the law, which varies slightly from state to state. In general, he or she:

1. Cannot tell you what to offer for the property. Because they work for the seller, subagents are supposed to help the seller get his or her list price. If you're in an extremely hot market, like during the latter half of the 1990s, you may pay list price or even above list price. In a soft market, one that favors the buyer, you'll probably pay less than list price, perhaps a lot less. Either way, how much you pay will put you in conflict with the obligation the seller broker has to the seller.

2. Cannot tell you which home to buy if you are deciding between two. A seller broker works for each seller and may work for multiple sellers. If a seller broker, for example, shows you five houses in a given day, he or she has technically worked for five sellers. That's confusing, but it boils down to this: If you like two homes, the seller broker actually works for two sellers simultaneously, and so should not help you choose one home over the other. (Can you see now why buyer brokerage is so much more appealing?)

3. Cannot point out the defects of a home, unless they are material, hidden defects. The seller broker cannot say anything or do anything that will influence you not to buy a property. Material hidden defects must be disclosed, however, because they are not visible to the naked eye. For more information on seller disclosure, see Question 47. You'll find a copy of one state's seller disclosure form in Appendix IV.

4. May only provide you with comparable data upon request. Seller brokers must provide you with all the information you need to come up with a reasonable offer. Ask your broker (buyer or seller) to provide you with a list of "comps" detailing how much other homes in the neighborhood, similar in size and amenities to the one you like, sold for in the past six months. Also ask the broker to provide you with a list of current similar listings and their list prices. It's important to know the difference between the asking and sales price of homes in the area. Finally, ask for the average number of list days. This will help you figure out whether you're in a fast market (seller's market) or slow market (buyer's market).

Of course, some seller brokers will give you all these things without you asking for them. It's understandable why they do it: Brokers rely on referrals for their business to grow. If everyone refers two buyers or sellers, the agent's or broker's client list pyramids. After a few years, he or she could have a client list numbering in the hundreds. Whether you work with a seller's agent or a buyer's agent, an agent:

- *Wants* you to have a good experience when you buy a home.
- *Wants* it to be easy.
- *Wants* you to like them.
- *Wants* you to refer your friends to them.

Before you start believing that conventional brokers won't be able to help you buy a home as effectively as a buyer broker, let me reassure you: That is not always the case. For dozens of years, conventional brokers were the only game in town. They've helped millions of buyers successfully purchase homes. If you have a choice, however, go with a buyer's agent.

20/20 hindsight

Many seller brokers pride themselves on being full-service firms, and because they have every incentive to close the deal—after all, they get paid only at the closing—the broker should be delighted to provide you with the names of various mortgage brokers, inspectors, and attorneys. Ask for several recommendations for each service. That way you can properly interview the prospective attorney or inspector and choose the best person for the job. In addition, many real estate companies now own mortgage firms. Undoubtedly, they'll give you the name of their in-house or affiliated lender, who may or may not give you a great deal. But you won't know that until you shop around and compare prices.

The various changes in state laws governing brokers who are sub-agents of the seller require that you be more aware of the shifting nature of the relationship. However, a good broker (whether buyer or seller) will be responsive to your needs. That puts the onus on you to be well informed about what you want and how you intend to get it.

Remember, you want to work with the very best broker you can. A great seller broker may be a better choice for you than a lousy buyer broker who doesn't really know the particular neighborhood of interest to you. But typically, any broker who works with a buyer is now considered a buyer agent, barring any dual agency.

first time buyer tip

WHAT IS A BUYER BROKER? WHAT IS AN EXCLUSIVE BUYER'S AGENT? SHOULD I USE ONE?

We've established that the broker works for the person who pays the commission. Traditionally, that's the seller. For an increasing number of buyers, however, the conventional broker's role poses a conflict of interest. These buyers ask: How can a broker have my best interest at heart when he or she is being paid by the seller? How can a broker help me find the best property at the best price when he or she is bound legally and financially to serve the seller's best interest?

If you find yourself having these qualms about traditional broker-age, you may want to consider buyer brokerage. Although buyer bro-kerage has been around for nearly 20 years, it only became popular during the 1990s. In the latter half of the 1990s, many states around the country changed their laws to designate buyer agency. Today, if you're a buyer and are working with a broker, that broker automati-cally becomes a buyer's agent. If you're a seller, the broker functions as a seller broker.

But we're getting a little bit ahead of ourselves. A buyer's agent is one who is ethically and legally bound to put the buyer's interests ahead of all else in a real estate transaction. The buyer's agent owes the buyer, not the seller, his or her fiduciary duty—*even if the seller will ul-timately pay the agent or broker's commission.*

The buyer's agent's duties are not at all dissimilar to the way a nice seller broker might have treated you. The buyer broker will hunt for homes that are appropriate for your needs and budget. He or she will help you negotiate every facet of the contract, striving to get you the best price and terms. Some buyer brokers will even help you find the best mortgage and homeowner's insurance with the most favorable terms. Then the broker will help you with any of the other niggling closing details and show up at the closing to collect his or her check.

A buyer broker may want you to sign an *exclusivity agreement.* This agreement states that you will not work with any other buyer's agents within a defined period of time. As with all real estate contracts, it is ne-gotiable. The agent may want you to put down a fee of some sort (re-fundable at closing). Whether or not you pay it is up to you; however, I don't think it's necessary to pay a buyer's agent to prove that you're committed to working with him or her. Likewise, I would make sure that the exclusivity agreement includes a definite time limit and allows you to cancel the agreement if you decide not to purchase a home or simply because you've found someone else you'd rather work with.

There Are Buyer's Agents and
There Are *Exclusive* Buyer's Agents

The most common form of buyer's agency is *designated agency*, which means the agent is a buyer's agent when working with a home buyer and a seller's agent when working with a seller.

That means your buyer's agent might also be a listing agent and may in fact have several homes currently listed for sale that may be right for you. The possible conflict of interest is, of course, that you'll be shown one of these listings and find yourself in a dual agency situation—where the same agent is representing both sides in the same transaction. Although you can ask your buyer's agent to give you to another agent in his or her office to go through the offer-counteroffer process, you may feel bad because you've developed a strong attachment to your buyer's agent. More important, you've probably told him or her some personal information about how much you can really spend on a house. If your buyer's agent becomes a dual agent, can you trust him or her not to reveal your financial secrets to the seller? That kind of disclosure could really destroy your negotiating power.

first time
buyer tip

We all talk too much about ourselves to our buyer's agents. It just happens because you spend so much time together. Don't lose any sleep if you've let slip some vital piece of financial information. But try not to talk, at any time, about exact numbers, just in case the quoted amount comes back to haunt you.

Another way around the potential dual agency conflict of interest is to hire an *exclusive buyer's agent*. Exclusive buyer's agents never take listings. They represent only buyers. In the mid-1990s, exclusive buyer's agents were viewed with skepticism and scorn by the regular brokerage community. In Massachusetts, for example, there were even stories (which I was unable to verify directly) that exclusive buyer brokers were discriminated against when it came to setting up showings. One exclusive buyer's agent claimed he had been physically assaulted by another real estate agent who was unhappy with his client's bid for a property!

Fortunately, those stories are few and far between, and in the years since I published the second edition of this book, they have pretty much faded away completely. Exclusive buyer's agency clearly has become much more accepted over the years, although it remains far more popular on the east and west coasts than in the center or southern sections of the country. The fear that these agents are "extremists" looking to kill all the deals has dissipated. Best of all, where before you might have found only one or two exclusive buyer's agents in an entire metropolitan area, more have joined the ranks so that home buyers have a larger choice of people with whom they can work.

web

resources

If you're looking for an exclusive buyer's agent (EBA), you might want to check out the National Association of Exclusive Buyer Agents (www.naeba.com), a nonprofit organization dedicated to improving the image and numbers of EBAs around the country. They can recommend you to their members who must abide by their tough code of ethics. Most EBAs will also be members of the National Association of Realtors (NAR), which didn't even recognize buyer's agency as a legitimate form of real estate agency until the early 1990s.

A Difference in Perception

If you're wondering how a buyer broker might treat you differently from a seller broker, you're not alone. If the seller broker breaks the law by providing you with insights and information about various sellers and their homes and advises you on which house to bid and on how much to offer, then there may not be a great difference in service. (Then again, the seller could be liable to the seller for breaching his or her fiduciary duty to the seller. But that's not your concern.)

On the other hand, a buyer broker is completely on your side, bound by contract and the law to provide you with all of the information you need to buy your dream house at the lowest price possible and on the most favorable terms.

Sharon, a sales agent in west suburban Chicago, says: "When I'm working for the seller, my job is to bring in the best offer. When I'm working as a buyer broker, I feel free to give that kind of advice as well as to suggest different pricing (strategies) my clients may offer."

Experts say buyers generally have trouble with two facets of buyer brokerage: the exclusivity agreement and the payment for services rendered. When a buyer opts for buyer brokerage, he or she is often asked to sign an exclusivity agreement. According to most of these contracts, the buyer agrees to work only with the buyer broker for a certain length of time. If the buyer purchases a home within the exclusivity period, he or she will owe the broker a fee.

Sounds simple enough, but buyers, who are used to changing agents at will, sometimes find the idea of exclusivity disquieting. If you feel that a 90-day exclusivity period is too long, offer a 30-day term that is renewable. A good buyer broker will understand your nervousness (you're not the first to feel this way) and should be happy to make you feel comfortable. Thirty days will be enough time for you to decide if you like the buyer broker's service.

Payment of the buyer brokerage fee is another issue buyers struggle with—particularly first-time buyers who are often short on cash. You should know that it is the fee that guarantees the buyer broker's loyalty. Buyer brokerage fees can be paid either as a flat payment, hourly, or as a percentage of the purchase price of the home.

The Real World

In the real world, however, the buyer broker's compensation often ends up being paid by the seller. What happens is the seller's agent agrees to split the commission with the buyer broker, just as the seller's agent would agree to split the commission with a conventional broker. Where the fee issue might come into play is if you end up buying a FSBO with the help of your buyer's agent. But there, too, it usually gets worked out. Either the seller pays a half commission (2½ or 3 percent) to the buyer's agent, or the purchase price of the home is raised to cover the commission.

Other Issues and Concerns

Do buyer brokers ever pressure their clients to buy something if their exclusivity contract is about to expire? Most brokers say no, but first-time buyers Dawn and Bill don't agree. They said they've had a nasty experience with a buyer broker who applied enormous pressure and even took the couple to court. (The judge threw the broker's case out of court and forced him to pay both sides' legal fees.) Some real estate attorneys confide that they've seen some agents present their clients with a choice of four houses and pressure them to purchase one, and quickly. Again, I think that reputable agents do not act in this way. Your job is to find a reputable agent.

There are many reasons for choosing to work with a buyer broker, but the most obvious one is hardly ever mentioned. Because the buyer pays the buyer broker, he or she is free to bring the buyer to any property that is available, including FSBOs.

Mark's Story

Mark is an architect who purchases homes and small apartment buildings for rehabilitation and resale. He is always on the lookout for a deal and has hired a couple of agents to look for these types of properties in different parts of town.

Although Mark has had some luck calling sellers directly, he has directed the agents he works with to pursue FSBO properties. He guarantees them their share of the commission when the deal goes through.

Frequently he purchases FSBO properties with a buyer broker, and he recently closed on such a house. "The property wasn't listed in the multiple listing service. A conventional broker wouldn't have even found it," he said.

Is buyer brokerage the right choice for you? That depends on how comfortable you are with the concepts of exclusivity and being responsible for the broker's commission. When Mark buys a FSBO property, he makes sure the seller will pay the half commission his broker is entitled to. If the seller won't, Mark adjusts his offer and pays the commission out of his own pocket.

More buyers, especially first-timers, are choosing buyer brokers because they like having someone represent them. Some companies who transfer employees from one location to another, and pay their moving costs, ask the relocation company to give their employees a buyer broker option. Even some websites, which originally listed only the listing broker as a contact, now suggest you might want to contact your own buyer broker first.

As when making any selection, interview a buyer broker and (if it's an option, because it isn't in many states) a conventional broker and decide who will be able to help you the most.

QUESTION 14

WHAT IS A DUAL AGENT? WHAT IS A TRANSACTIONAL BROKER? WHAT IS A NONAGENT?

Dual agency occurs when the same real estate broker or agent represents both sides in the same transaction. A dual agent represents both the buyer and seller in the purchase and sale of a single property.

The problem with dual agency is the inherent conflict of interest in having the same person represent two sides of a single deal. How can the buyer broker have a fiduciary relationship with the buyer, and do everything in his or her power to help the buyer purchase the home for the best possible price and on the best possible terms, if he or she is also acting as a seller broker, trying to get the seller the most money possible? It's impossible for a single broker or agent to represent the best interests of opposing sides in a single transaction—no matter what anyone tries to tell you!

Another form of dual agency occurs when the selling broker and buyer's agent work for the same firm. Although not all states recognize this as dual agency, some do because it's possible that the listing agent and buyer's agent will share confidential information in some informal exchange that could be harmful to their client. The firewall separating buyer's agents and seller's agents can seem dangerously thin (or nonexistent) in some offices.

Because of the inherent conflicts of interest, the NAR, the nonprofit trade association with nearly 1 million agents and brokers as members, has tried over the years to give new names to dual agency that appear to lessen this inherent conflict of interest.

Two new terms of choice include *transactional brokerage* or *nonagency.* If your buyer broker happens to bring you to one of his or her listings and you fall in love with it and want to make an offer, the buyer broker may cease to become your broker and may assume the role of a *transactional broker.* This means that the broker will help the transaction through to the close, without having a fiduciary duty to either the buyer or seller.

The problem with transactional brokerage is that the buyers and sellers lose and the broker wins. Neither the buyer nor the seller have a broker in their pocket to guide and advise them, but the seller pays the full commission, as if he and the buyer were receiving everything they bargained for from their full-service brokers.

Nonagency is another name for transactional brokerage, except it's more honest. Again, the agent does not work for either the buyer or seller, but shuffles papers back and forth and helps the deal go through.

Is dual agency a bad thing? Sometimes, because the broker knows both sides really well, he or she can help smooth over a difficult situation and find the common ground that permits the deal to happen. In that case, dual agency is a good thing. But when the buyer and seller have developed a trusting, personal relationship with their agent and then suddenly find themselves nonrepresented by their agent who is stuck in the middle, the lack of representation can cause real problems.

What should you do if you're presented with a dual agency situation? If you're the buyer, you can always request that your agent choose whether he or she wants to represent either the seller or you. If the agent chooses the seller, ask the agent or the managing broker of the firm to assign another agent to you. That way, you'll have full representation in the construction and negotiation of your contract.

Whether you're working with a buyer's agent or a conventional agent, you may run into an uncomfortable situation, either because there is dual agency or because the agent isn't giving you the kind of service you're expecting. If you've tried to speak to the agent about the situation and aren't getting any satisfaction, you may want to talk to the managing broker of the firm. It's the managing broker's responsibility to make sure that all of the home buyers and sellers are happy with the service they're receiving. The managing broker can sit down with you and your agent to help resolve any problems.

WHAT IS THE TYPICAL REAL ESTATE COMMISSION? HOW IS IT SPLIT?

Although this is more a question for sellers, it's important for buyers to be aware of how much commission is actually being paid. By law, there is no standard real estate commission. It's entirely negotiable, and real estate agents must tell you that. They might, however, give you a general range of commissions, say, 5 to 7 percent. More often than not, sellers will offer to pay 5 to 5.5 percent of the selling price of the property to their broker, who then splits the commission in half with the subagent who brought the buyer to the table. (These days the seller's agent will often split the commission unequally, keeping the bigger portion for him- or herself.)

(Today, most MLSs around the country recognize buyer brokerage and automatically pay the buyer's agent his or her share of the commission.)

Even though it is the seller who typically pays the commission, buyers should be aware of the commission rates and whether it is a buyer's or seller's market in their area. If it's a seller's market—where there are more qualified buyers than homes for sale—the commission might be somewhat below the rate typically acceptable for that area. If the commission is normally 6 percent, it might be 5.5 percent or less, because the demand is high for the seller's property and the seller broker doesn't have to work too hard to make the sale.

You might also see far more FSBOs in a seller's market. If there is a huge demand for property, sellers may put up a website featuring information about their home, as well as advertise in the local newspaper and put up a large "For Sale" sign on their front lawn. Savvy sellers will hope that they can get away with paying only a half commission to the buyer's agent and pocket the other half of the commission they'd normally pay to the listing agent.

If it's a buyer's market—where there are more sellers than qualified buyers—you might find the seller offering more than the typical commission to entice brokers to bring prospective buyers to tour the house. If the typical commission is 6 percent, the seller might offer 7 percent, with 4 percent going to the agent who brought the buyer to the table. Although most agents won't try to sell you a piece of property just because it has an extra-high commission (or other bonuses) attached, they might bring you to see it.

A disturbing new trend is the unequal distribution of the commission between the seller and buyer brokers. Typically the commission is split 50/50, but sometimes the seller agent will take a larger portion of the commission. I've seen deals where the seller agent gets a 3 percent commission and the buyer agent gets just 2 or 2½ percent. Although this new trend wouldn't seem to affect a home buyer, it might. I'm not suggesting your agent would ever pressure you to buy a home strictly because of the commission split (although this, in fact, does happen once in a while), but you will likely be shown homes where the commission split is equal or favors the buyer broker before you are shown homes where the reverse is true. Sellers who permit this kind of unequal commission split to go on are doing themselves no favors. Buyers should insist on seeing everything that's available in their price range, regardless of the commission split.

QUESTION 16

WHAT IS A DISCOUNT BROKER? WHEN SHOULD I USE ONE?

The idea that you can buy something for less is extremely appealing in America. We have discount clothing stores, food stores, drugstores, and whole towns built up around outlet malls. Is it surprising that the demand for discount real estate brokerage has continued to grow?

Here's the basic concept. The discount real estate broker gives you the names and addresses of properties for sale from the local multiple-listing service (MLS), but you do all the legwork, look at every home that might possibly be right for you, work out your own mortgage, present your own contract, submit your own counteroffer, arrange for your own inspectors, and do your own walk-through. For your "sweat equity," the discount broker will give you a portion of the commission he or she receives.

Why should the discount broker receive anything if you're doing all the work? Good question. To begin with, the discount broker has access to the MLS, which lists all the properties for sale in the area. That's where you find out all the information about homes for sale, such as their size, price, and number of bedrooms and bathrooms. It's a very useful list to have, and access to all these details is strictly limited to member agents and brokers and their clients. By sharing the commission with the discount broker, you're essentially buying access to the local MLS.

"But wait!" you say. "What about the Internet? Can't I get all the listings from a website?"

Possibly. But the amount of information you'll receive generally isn't enough to take any action other than calling your own broker or the listing broker. You typically won't get an address (though, in a few years, competition may dictate that the address of the property be posted, and in some cases it is already available), specific information about the size of the lot and house, or the amount of last year's tax bill. As listing information available on the Internet improves, it's possible that this information will become available. But right now, it's generally not widely available.

The Dollars and Cents of Discount Brokerage

Here's a look at how the dollars and cents of discount brokerage works.

Discount brokerage firms give back up to 50 percent of their share of the commission at closing. On a $300,000 property, your share might be as much as $4,500. That $4,500 might well pay the points for your mortgage or cover the cost of repainting the interior of the house after you move in. And although $4,500 may not seem like it's worth the effort, discount brokers say that some home buyers, particularly first-time buyers, need every nickel to buy a home and are willing to put in the time and effort it takes.

As we discussed earlier, real estate companies that work with the buyer typically receive about half the commission the seller pays to his or her listing agent's company. If the commission is 6 percent of the sales price, each side gets 3 percent. In conventional brokerage, the company then splits its 3 percent with the real estate agent, so each side gets 1.5 percent of the price.

(In some real estate companies, the split between the company and the agent is quite uneven. A top-producing agent may receive as much as 90 or even 95 percent of the commission received by her real estate firm.)

A discount broker splits his or her 3 percent commission with you, minus any "extras." And this is where you need to take care. The discount brokerage firm puts a price tag on every service it provides for you, including every telephone call or each showing. A minimum number of showings are usually included in the deal, but if the broker shows you any additional properties, the fees for these pay-as-you-go services are deducted from your portion of the commission.

For example, a discount brokerage firm in Chicago deducts somewhere between one and four percentage points from the commission refund for each service it performs. If a client needs the broker to place a follow-up call to the lender, the company would reduce the refund by 1 percent for each call. If the total possible refund is $4,500, each phone call would cost $45.

Sandra's Story

A first-time buyer, Sandra needed every penny to put into the purchase of her home. She saw an ad for a discount broker, which she thought seemed like a great deal, and called.

Later, she told me she had been thinking that she'd just do some of the work and receive about $2,000 back from the agent.

Things didn't turn out quite as she had planned. First, it was a really tight seller's market. By the time the discount broker got around to setting up showings, the homes had sold. Sandra spent hundreds of hours scouring neighborhoods, real estate classified advertising, the Internet—anywhere she thought there might be an appropriate home for sale.

After a few short weeks, the discount broker informed her that she had used up her allotment of "free time" and would now be charged for everything the broker had to do, from phone calls to setting up appointments. She would even be charged for the ultimate negotiation of the contract.

"I'd given myself a thorough education of the marketplace, and for that I'm grateful," Sandra said later. "But I also realized the value of a full-service agent in a market that's so tight that you need to be in the inner circle of agents to have any chance at all of a successful bid."

Sandra fired the discount broker and hired a full-service broker who worked with the biggest company in town. Within a few weeks, she'd found a house and made a successful offer to purchase.

The general caveat for real estate services holds true here also: Don't necessarily use the first broker you find. Try to locate more than one discount broker in your area and then interview each at length. Ask for a résumé and references. Then call those references and ask how much time they put into their home purchase and how much money they received back from the broker. Discount brokerage is best used by home buyers who have a clear idea of what they want, or who have been through the process before. But first-time buyers who are willing to put in a little "sweat equity" might be able to save a little money.

HOW MUCH SHOULD MY BROKER KNOW ABOUT THE AMOUNT I CAN AFFORD TO SPEND ON A HOME?

As we discussed earlier, all conventional or seller brokers have a fiduciary responsibility to work on the seller's behalf. They must do everything they can (legally, morally, and ethically) to get the seller the highest price from the buyer. Buyer brokers have a written fiduciary responsibility to the buyer. They must do everything in their power to help the buyer purchase the home for the best price possible and on the best possible terms.

84

The reason for this separation of duties is clear. The seller pays the commission of both brokers, the one who lists and shows the property, and the subagent, who brings the ready, willing, and able buyer to the table.

But since most seller agents act as buyer agents when working with buyers, the whole notion of agency representation is a bit sticky. So play it safe. When it comes to your finances, you should play your cards extremely close to the vest. As a general rule, **NEVER disclose to your agent the maximum amount you can afford to pay for a home.**

Why? Although the buyer broker is supposed to hold your intimate thoughts, feelings, and finances in confidence, that buyer broker may show you one of his or her listings and then become a dual agent. Or your buyer broker might decide to represent the seller and another buyer broker will be assigned to handle your negotiation. Either way, your former buyer broker now knows how much you can afford to spend—and you may end up spending that, even if you didn't intend to.

Mark and Amy's Story

Mark and Amy recently discussed their search for the perfect home on Long Island. Like most first-time buyers, they had a general idea of the process, but only a vague concept of the fine lines the real estate world has drawn between broker-seller and broker-buyer relationships.

Mark and Amy found a beautiful house in a tiny, wooded community on Long Island, about an hour and a half from Manhattan. The house was listed at $350,999. They put in a low-ball offer for $260,000 but told "their" agent (who in fact was a seller broker and not a buyer broker) that they would go as high as $300,000.

That turned out to be a strategic mistake. By telling the broker they were willing to spend as much as $300,000 for the property, they were precluded from getting the property for less.

Why? "Their" broker was obligated not only to bring the seller the $260,000 offer but also to inform the seller that the buyers would go as high as $300,000. If the seller had responded favorably to the lower bid, he or she might have been persuaded to sell the property for less than $300,000. But once informed that the buyers would go as high as $300,000, the seller had no incentive to make the deal for less than that amount.

If, as required by law, Mark and Amy's broker actually told the seller that the couple was willing to bid as much as $300,000, then their effective bid would have been $300,000 rather than the $260,000 they actually offered.

As it happens, Mark and Amy didn't buy that particular house. After this episode, they changed to a buyer's agent and simply didn't disclose any information about their finances.

Exclusive Buyer Brokers and Agents

As you can see, there is a danger in disclosing any information about your finances to either a conventional or buyer's agent. But what about an exclusive buyer's agent? An EBA will never represent a seller, so there is no potential conflict of interest, right? That's the general idea.

But it's possible that your EBA will represent other home buyers interested in the same neighborhood, home type, and price point that you are. If you make an offer for a house and your EBA also has another set of clients interested in that property, and you've disclosed how much you can pay for the house, the EBA might (I'm not saying "would," I'm saying "might" because things happen and people talk) let it slip how much you can pay. Then the other couple may have a slight advantage when it comes to putting together an offer.

Protecting Yourself

The best way to protect yourself is the easiest: *Don't disclose your financial situation or intent.* Never tell your broker the top price you'd be willing to pay for a piece of property. Simply reassure the agent that you've been preapproved for a loan and are interested in looking at homes priced from, say, $200,000 to $250,000. Always assume that whatever financial information you convey to the broker might be transmitted (perhaps inadvertently) to the other side. If your agent or broker offers to assist you in getting a mortgage (or asks directly to see your financial statements), politely accept the name of a few lenders he or she does business with regularly, and then decline to go into specifics.

Although I hope nothing bad happens to you in your search for, and purchase of, a home, the best protection is to prepare for the worst.

For more information on how to figure out how much you can spend on a home, see Question 28 on page 118.

86

Brokers will often tell me that they can't represent a home buyer effectively if they don't know how much the buyer(s) can spend on a home. I'm not sure that's true. Some of the best agents I know simply like to be in complete control of the situation, and that includes knowing about their client's finances. But wanting to know and needing to know are separate issues. Just because you're asked how much you can afford to spend doesn't mean you have to give out a top number. Also, just because you've been told you can spend a certain amount doesn't mean you'll want to go that high. As long as you can truly afford to spend whatever range you give your agent (and getting preapproved for a loan is a good way to go), then the agent needn't know anything else.

HOW DO I KNOW IF MY BROKER IS DOING A GOOD JOB?

Whether you use a buyer broker or a conventional agent, the first point of business is to assist you in finding a property that's suitable and affordable.

A broker or agent is doing a good job if he or she listens closely to your wants and needs and asks you thoughtful follow-up questions that prompt further introspection and explanation. Whether or not the agent is doing a good job becomes more apparent once you start seeing some homes. Do the homes you're shown match up with what you've told the broker you want and need? Do they match up with the priorities on your wish list and reality check?

If your broker is totally off the mark, assume she or he hasn't been paying attention. Or perhaps you didn't communicate effectively and honestly. If you aren't honest with yourself about what you want and need, it'll be hard to discuss it openly with someone else, so your broker may end up showing you the wrong kind of property. (See Question 1 for more details about a wish list and reality check.)

Get Clued In

Here are some ways to know whether your broker is doing a good job:

1. Do you feel the broker is paying attention to you? Or does his or her attention wane when you're speaking?

2. Does the agent ask you a lot of questions? Has the agent ever asked you why you're looking for a four-bedroom home or one that has an exercise studio? By asking, the agent may be able to better understand your motivations.

3. If you've worked with the agent several times and all the properties you've been shown were not even close matches to what you'd hoped you would see, you might have a problem.

4. If you're working with a buyer broker and the seller suddenly seems to know your every move during the negotiation, your agent might be spilling the beans (perhaps unwittingly) and violating his or her fiduciary duty to you, the buyer.

5. If your broker never returns your phone calls, or takes several days to do so, that's a clear signal that he or she is not being conscientious.

If It Isn't Going Well, Take Action

If you decide that your agent isn't doing a good job, don't hesitate to speak with the agent's managing broker. Again, one of the most important functions of the managing broker's job is to ensure that the customers of the firm are happy. If you're not satisfied with the response you receive from the managing broker, feel free to file a complaint with the agency that regulates real estate agents in your state. (See Appendix VI on page 439 for a list of all state real estate agencies and commissions.)

Unless you've signed a buyer brokerage exclusivity agreement, you have the option to find another agent or broker at any time. Most agents will allow you to break an exclusivity agreement if you're really unhappy, because they don't want you to cut into their referrals by discussing how unhappy you are. If you can't break your exclusivity agreement, or the agent wants you to pay him or her additional money to break the agreement, simply wait out the expiration date of the contract. No one can make you work with someone you don't like.

HOW CAN I HELP IN THE SEARCH
FOR A HOME IF I USE A BROKER?

QUESTION 19

Brokers across the country say the most important thing you can do is be *honest* about what you really want in a home and what you actually need.

Most buyers think they're being honest, but they may not turn their vision into usable information for the broker. You can say you need a four-bedroom house, but if you don't tell the broker that you need that fourth bedroom for an office, you're not being as helpful as you could. Why? A prospective house may have other spaces for an office—such as a third-floor attic that offers privacy—but they may not meet the official definition of a "bedroom."

After honesty, brokers ask that buyers be flexible with their time and responsive to their calls. If a broker agrees to spend an entire Saturday with you, and sets up a day of showings, it's extremely frustrating if you decide to cancel Friday night or Saturday morning.

Of course, it's perfectly acceptable to cancel if there is a true emergency. If that's the case, communicate that to the broker and reschedule. But remember, weekends are prime time for real estate agents. If they set aside the time for you and you cancel, it's lost time to them. It would be hard for them to reschedule new showings for different buyers on such short notice.

Here's a short course on home buyer etiquette:

1. Honesty is the best policy. Whether you're telling the broker what you really want or need in a home or telling the agent specifically why you did or did not like a particular home, if you're not honest and open, you make the job tougher than it has to be.

2. Be available. If you're going to be out of town on business, or tied up in meetings, let the broker know the times you're not going to be available to look at property or talk about prospective homes. On the other hand, return your agent's calls promptly, and have a backup number in case the agent calls with an urgent message about a property. You might have either received an answer to your offer, or a new, hot property has come on the market in the neighborhood you want.

3. Don't have unrealistic expectations. Your agent may be the best in town, but she's not a miracle worker. If you call her up on Saturday morning and ask her to book in a day of showings, it's probably not going to happen. The weekends are the busiest times for an agent and book up quickly. Also, booking open houses (even if both sides use Internet-based house-showing software) takes time and some back and forth. If you want to spend a Saturday or Sunday looking at open houses, make sure to reserve your agent's time at least a few days, if not a week, in advance.

4. Loyalty. Agents like loyal buyers. Don't work with two full-time agents at the same time. The real estate community is small, and word gets around fast. Also, if you've taken up six months of an agent's time, and things are going well, it's not nice to suddenly switch to your relative or to a discount broker to close the sale. Legally, of course, you may have the right to switch at any time (barring an exclusivity agreement), but that doesn't make it right. If you want to use Aunt Edna because she'll give you a portion of her commission back, use her for the entire process. Don't waste another broker's valuable time.

Helping Out

As we discussed earlier, if you're like every other first-time buyer, the moment you decide to seriously look for a home, you'll be energized—if not consumed—by the process. You'll want to do everything in your power to find the right home fast!

You can help your agent by using the Internet to look for properties that might be for sale, and scouring the real estate "for sale" ads in the local paper. If your broker has a good handle on the local market, he or she has probably seen most of the properties for sale. But if you see something interesting in the paper, ask about it.

first time buyer tip

You'll probably be tempted to visit some open houses as you walk around the neighborhood. That's fine, but be sure to sign in as represented by your agent. That's called "protecting the broker." By signing in as someone's client, you're putting the seller and seller's agent on notice that you are represented. If you don't sign in your broker at an open house, and you later try to go back with your agent and make an offer, the selling broker might put up a fight and say that you were his or her client for that particular house—making the listing broker a dual agent and entitled to the entire commission. Make sure you sign in your broker at each and every open house.

Finally, you can help your agent by trying to learn everything you can about the neighborhoods you've chosen. Walk around and try them on for size. Visit the local grocery store, dry cleaner, schools, and parks. Drive around at various times of the day so you can experience "rush hour" traffic. Get a feel for the people who live and work there. Educate yourself rather than relying on your broker for lessons.

HOW SHOULD I INTERPRET THE HOME DESCRIPTION IN THE LOCAL NEWSPAPER OR IN BROKER LISTING SHEETS?

QUESTION 20

The key to understanding real estate ads is to assume that the broker is putting the best face on a bad situation.

That's not to say that there aren't some fabulous homes out there. There are, and they may be worth every penny of their list price. I'm also not saying that brokers are being dishonest. Most of them aren't.

But if Mr. Smith's apartment has a four-inch-wide view of the ocean sandwiched between two towers, I'll bet you even money that Mr. Smith's broker will put "ocean view" somewhere in the newspaper ad.

Brokers know that most people want to have a good view from their windows—even if they're going to be away at work during the day and will see it only at night. (Actually, I've always been amazed at people who want to have a view of Lake Michigan or any other body of water, because at night it's completely black and you can't see anything anyway.) Usually the most expensive property is congregated around whatever view is the star attraction: In Chicago, it's Lake Michigan; in Boston, it's the Charles River; in San Francisco, it's the bay; in New York . . . well, in New York, everything is expensive. But the Manhattan buildings that overlook Central Park are *really* expensive.

When you read an advertisement, how do you distinguish between an apartment that really has a great view from one that has a four-inch-wide strip of blue? How can you tell a home that's really in move-in condition from one that needs to be completely redecorated?

That's the tough part. But remember: The broker will usually be very specific about a true feature. If the kitchen is new with top-brand appliances, the ad may say, "gourmet kitchen with top appliances." If the view really does include Lake Michigan (or Central Park, or the river, the bay, or whatever), it will say so.

Be Sure to Read Between the Lines

If you don't know a specific building or neighborhood well, you might want to try and read between the lines of an advertisement. Here's a list of key phrases to watch for and what they may mean (in a tough, cynical world):

Phrase	*What It Might Mean*
Fantastic View	Could be the best view of your life; or there might be little, if any, view, and you might have to crane your neck out the window to see it.
Treetop View	The apartment is about four floors up. During the summer your view may be blocked by leaves.
Just Renovated	Probably needs a minimal amount of redecorating—unless the seller's red walls and chintz everywhere don't agree with your ideas about good taste.
Move-In Condition	May be in pristine condition, or you may just need to paint.
Needs Work	Could mean anything from a home that needs new paint and carpet to major structural renovation.
Handyman's Special	Probably a gut job; it's likely the home needs serious renovations and may even be unlivable.
"As Is" Condition	The home may have some serious problems that will emerge with a home inspection report; the house may be filthy, and the seller doesn't want to clean it up; or the seller simply wants to be done with the deal, without having a prospective buyer try to negotiate the price down because of the condition; or a combination of all three.
Bright and Sunny	Maybe the home has a southern exposure, or maybe every room is painted bright yellow, or maybe there is 10,000 watts' worth of lightbulbs, all of which will be turned on during your showing.
Dollhouse	A word brokers often use to describe a home that is too small to accommodate a growing family; it may also be too small to accommodate a regularly sized individual.

Oversized Rooms	Don't expect Queen Elizabeth's great hall; could mean truly large rooms or anything more than nine-by-nine feet.
Street Parking	The broker is telling you the home doesn't come with a parking space, implying that you can park easily on the street. However, if the home is located in a congested metro neighborhood, or an area that doesn't permit street parking from 2 A.M. to 6 A.M., or an area that doesn't allow parking on the street in case of a "snow emergency" (anything over two inches), don't believe it unless you see for yourself. It isn't always easy or desirable to park on the street.
Deeded Parking Space	You get a parking space. It could be indoors, outdoors but covered, or simply outdoors, but it's yours—even if it is too small for your vehicle.
Round-the-Clock-Security	Could mean a 24-hour doorman (though brokers usually say this), a nighttime security person patrolling the premises, a television security system, or a buzzer system.
Newer Mechanicals	Might have been replaced last year or five years ago. You may have to replace expensive mechanical systems within five years.
Newer Roof	You may have to replace the roof within five years, or it may be just fine.
Needs New Roof	Don't be surprised to find signs of water damage from recent roof leaks. Check for brown water marks on the ceiling and buckling hardwood floors during your showing. Next question: Does the roof need a "tear-off," where several layers of old roofing must be pried off and replaced? Or could you, for a lot less money, add another layer of asphalt shingles?
Oversized Lot	In Chicago, which has one of the smallest "regular" lot sizes in the country, an oversized lot could mean something as small as 30 by 125 feet. (A standard lot in Chicago is 25 by 125 feet, so you'd be getting a few extra blades of grass.)

What About Square Feet?

The concept of square footage requires a bit more explanation. As you tour different homes, brokers will give you a listing sheet for the property. On it you'll see that the size of the unit is given in square feet. You'll remember from your high school geometry class that a square foot is a two-dimensional square measuring one foot by one foot. You'll often see it expressed as 1′ × 1′ or 10′ × 10′ (a room measuring 10 feet by 10 feet, or 100 square feet).

Entire homes are measured the same way. But the truth is, the actual square footage of a home as presented on paper can be a bit deceptive. Over the years, I've received dozens of letters from readers who felt that the square footage was misrepresented on the home, and they paid a larger amount because they thought the house was actually bigger than it is. *Pricing a home based on its square footage isn't exactly the best way to go and should be considered only along with other methods of determining value.* Here's why.

If your listing sheet says a particular home has 2,000 square feet, you may assume it's a big house. But when you get there, it may not feel that large. Why? Because a home's square footage is supposed to be calculated by measuring the exterior perimeter of the home. So in addition to losing the interior wall space, you also lose the exterior wall space. Although it doesn't sound like much, it can be. You'll also lose space to closets (people don't really count the square footage of a small closet, but it can add up), mechanicals, and chimney vents.

Brokers want you to think you're getting the most for your money, so they'll put down the largest number for the home's square footage that they can get away with. In my former residence, a vintage co-op built in the 1920s, our unit was listed as having as few as 1,700 square feet to as many as 2,300 square feet. The difference in measurement—600 square feet—is an entire condominium in New York City!

Bobbi's Story

When Bobbi bought her Manhattan condo, the property was listed as having 1,800 square feet, but it felt smaller. Bobbi bought the apartment next door, advertised as having at least 500 square feet, and planned to add it to her unit. Together, Bobbi thought she would have 2,300 square feet.

When the architect she hired did the drawings to combine the units, the new unit turned out to have only 2,000 square feet. Why? The original unit actually had 300 square feet of living space less than was originally advertised. The larger number could be justified if you measured around the exterior of the unit (and perhaps included a share of hallway space and the storage closet in the building basement).

Don't rely on the listing sheet for an accurate assessment of a home's true square footage. If you want to know how many square feet are in the home, either measure the house's exterior, or ask if the sellers have an architectural plan of the unit. After a while, you'll have a sense of how big 2,000 square feet really is and will be able to "guesstimate" how large other homes are based on how big they feel.

Developers have their own set of tricks for increasing a house's square footage on paper. For example, some developers will include an attached garage when calculating square footage. Others will include the attic, a crawl space, or the basement, whether it is or isn't finished. What is the true measure of square footage? Again, you should measure around the perimeter of the house or condo and use that as a base. Also, garages (whether attached or not), basements, unfinished attic spaces, and other spaces that are not legal by local code are typically not included in the square footage assessment. Use the architectural drawings that accompany the information kit the developer has prepared and make your own determination of size.

If you make an offer based on a certain price per square footage and later find out the unit doesn't have quite that much space, don't beat yourself up about it. Remember, if the house was big enough for you when you thought it had 2,000 square feet, it's still probably big enough even if it only has 1,850 square feet.

NOW THAT I CAN SHOP FOR A HOME ON THE INTERNET OR BUY FROM A DEVELOPER, DO I NEED AN AGENT? CAN I GET A BETTER DEAL IF I BUY A HOUSE WITHOUT AN AGENT?

We live in a do-it-yourself world. Stroll up and down the aisles of any home improvement store, and you suddenly feel capable of tackling any home-related project. Regrout the tile in the bathroom? No problem. Install cabinets or a hardwood floor? No problem. Rewire the house? No problem. Stores like Home Depot and Lowe's have plenty of experienced staff on hand to help you plan out your renovation or home improvement project down to the tiniest detail. As you walk through the exit, with hundreds or thousands of dollars in materials and equipment, your confidence level is high. You know you can complete the project and it's going to look great.

As you start carrying in the bags from the car, reality sets in. A little later, when the caulk pops out in a big goop, you know you're in trouble. It isn't quite as easy as it looks. It'll still get done, but it may take you a whole lot longer, cost more, and cause more angst than if you hired someone with experience to help.

Similarly, when it comes to buying a house, many home buyers feel they have the knowledge, tools, and savvy to buy a house on their own. For sure, the Internet provides easy access to a huge amount of information like house listings, interest rates, and credit scores. And knowledge is power.

The only thing the Internet doesn't do is provide years of experience to filter the vast amount of information that's available. That's the biggest benefit you'll receive by hiring a great agent to help with this purchase. Because even though you're reading this book, and I'm walking you through the process of buying a home, I'm not there, in person:

- To point out the stain on the ceiling that could indicate the presence of a leak, or the mold on the basement walls, or the absence of gutters

- To remind you that even though you're "in love" with this house, the other one you saw four days ago better suits your needs and wants

- To be your eyes and ears when new properties come on the market, so you don't waste your time seeing homes that aren't right for you and your family

- To tell you the ugly wallpaper, cat-scratched floor, and diaper stench can be removed and the house buffed and polished back to pristine condition, building in extra value for your hard-earned dollars

- To make sure the seller gives you all of the state-mandated disclosures

- To be the buffer between you and the seller when the negotiations get tough, or the seller pulls a fast one, or the inspection doesn't go well

- To tell you there will always be another house, and even though it seems like this was the "perfect house," the next one that comes along will be even better

It's true that with an agent, you may not be able to move as quickly as you'd like. There is someone else whose schedule must be accommodated, who probably isn't going to be working at 3:00 A.M. when you're up, scrolling through listings online because you're so excited you can't sleep. You may feel dragged down by the weight of having someone else on board.

When you're considering the single biggest, most-expensive purchase of your life, however, there is a benefit to not leaping before you look. An experienced agent will offer you the perspective of someone who has seen the house you think you want to buy go on and off the market a half dozen times over a couple of decades.

Can you buy a house without an agent? Absolutely. No law requires you to use an agent to buy or sell real estate. But for home buyers, particularly first-time buyers, it seems foolhardy. After all, you get the benefit of all this experience for nothing because the seller typically pays the commission.

As for getting a better deal, you won't get one with a property that's listed. As we've discussed earlier, on day one the seller signed a contract agreeing to pay his or her agent a set commission (typically a percentage of the sales price) when the home is sold. It doesn't matter whether you're represented by an agent or you come solo. It's unlikely that you'll get a better deal out of a seller when you are negotiating on your own behalf.

What about a FSBO? There's a good chance you'll overpay for the property, simply because you haven't seen all the properties on the market. Even if you live in the neighborhood, you might not know the true value of a home that is for sale.

> ### *Jacki's Story*
>
> Jacki owns a house on a double lot. She also owns a building with three apartment units. One day, she called my husband, Sam, who is a real estate attorney, to ask how complicated it would be to swap her three-unit building for the property next door to the house she owns. "It would be an even trade," she said.
>
> Sam asked her about the property next door. It turned out to be a little run-down. On the other hand, her three-unit property is in pristine condition, the apartments are bigger, and it's fully rented. Sam said it seemed to him that her rental property might be worth more than her neighbor's property. He advised her to have a real estate agent come out and take a look, especially because the neighbor's property was already listed with a real estate agent.
>
> Even though she had lived in the neighborhood for 30 years, next door to this property, Jacki wasn't sure how much everything was worth. If she traded her property evenly, she might have lost a quarter of a million dollars of value.

Almost all home buyers, but particularly those buying for the first time or purchasing new construction, will do better by having an experienced agent on their home-buying team.

WHAT DO I NEED TO KNOW ABOUT BUYING A HOUSE THAT'S FOR SALE BY OWNER (FSBO)?

Whether you buy a property that's listed or is a FSBO, most of what you have to do stays the same. The questions in this book should be asked whether you're buying an existing, listed property, a FSBO, or new construction. But a few specific issues should be kept in mind when looking for a FSBO.

1. It's easy to overpay for a FSBO. The biggest mistake home buyers make when buying FSBOs is overpaying for the property. It's not just that you can't compare one house to another in terms of size and amenities. With a FSBO, you need to think about the possible financial impact of issues and neighborhood changes that aren't readily apparent. For example, if the developers of a six-story apartment building have received approval to build on the lot behind the

FSBO property, the seller may not be legally obligated to share that tidbit of information with you—but it could dramatically (and most likely negatively) affect the value of the property. If you don't know what's going on in the immediate vicinity of the property, it could hurt you.

2. The seller won't automatically reduce the sales price. Another mistake home buyers make is thinking the seller will reduce the sales price by the amount of the commission he or she isn't paying. If you believe the home is worth what you're offering, versus what the seller is asking, you may need to back that up with some relevant sales data.

3. Some properties come with problems attached. Homeowners sell without a broker for two reasons, and both have to do with money: (1) the seller doesn't want to pay a commission, and (2) prospective agents have told the seller that the property won't sell for as much money as the seller wants, so the seller decides to sell by owner in order to set a higher price (and hopefully fool a buyer). When the seller and prospective agents differ on the value of a property, it often has to do with the seller not realizing that any problems that may be attached to the property might lower the intrinsic value. In other words, if the property backs up to a cornfield, that fact might have a positive effect on the price. If the cornfield is slated to be turned into a subdivision of town houses, however, it could have a negative effect on the price. Do your investigation ahead of time and then, before you make an offer, think about how hard it might be to resell this property in the future.

4. Don't undernegotiate. Often, first-time buyers don't know whether it's a buyer's market or a seller's market. Not knowing can undercut your negotiation power when it comes to dealing with a FSBO. Make sure you know what you want out of the deal, and how much you're willing to pay, and then hold firm. Don't allow a seller to talk you into paying more than you want (or can).

5. Make sure the seller gives you the required disclosures. State laws require sellers to make various disclosures. If you're buying directly from the seller, without an agent, make sure you get all of the disclosure forms you're entitled to receive. If you work with an attorney (which I think is an excellent idea anyway, but particularly if you're not working with an agent), he or she should help guide you in this area. If not, talk to your escrow or title company about forms and contracts.

6. Don't give the seller your earnest money. When you make an offer to purchase, you'll typically include a good faith deposit check along with the signed contract. If no brokers are involved, determine who will hold the earnest money. Never pay it directly to the seller. Instead, see whether the escrow company, the title company, or other third party will act as an intermediary and keep the funds safe. Another option is to have one of the attorneys (either yours or the seller's) hold it for you.

7. Make sure you buy an owner's title policy in addition to the lender's title. In some states, the buyer pays for the title insurance policy. In other states, it's up to the seller. If the seller traditionally buys the title policy, make sure yours does. If the buyer pays for title in your state, you can work with your escrow agent or title officer to order the title.

8. Get your documents in order. In many parts of the country, real estate agents help buyers and sellers get their documents organized so that the property can close. If you're doing this on your own, you'll want to check with your attorney or escrow agent or title officer to be sure you haven't forgotten anything. You don't want to show up at the closing and find out there is a problem.

9. Be careful which contract forms you use. If you're using an attorney, he or she should be able to provide you with a contract and contingencies that protect your rights. If you aren't using an attorney, ask the escrow agent or title officer to help you gather the contracts and forms you need. Although some, or maybe all (depending on the state), of these contracts and forms are on the Web, be careful about which form you use. Whether you are in an escrow state (where escrow agents or title companies have forms), or in other states (where forms are on the Web), take care in selecting the contract because these are the words, sentences, and paragraphs that are supposed to protect you in this huge purchase.

10. Don't take the seller's word—check it out yourself. A common mistake home buyers make is taking the seller or the seller broker at his or her word. When you're spending a few hundred thousand dollars, it's important to check out everything yourself. Insist on a professional home inspection and a final walk-through. If something doesn't look right or doesn't pass inspection, spend what is necessary to ensure the house is okay. Once you close, it's expensive and heartbreaking to have to sue the seller. The time to check things out is now.

3

How Do I Identify What I Like and Need in a Home?

Knowing which of two or three different properties is right for you is the key to *selectivity*. Over the next few questions we'll talk about ways to hone your natural sense of selectivity and apply it toward your home purchase.

QUESTION 23

HOW DO I BECOME SELECTIVE WHEN CHOOSING A HOME? HOW DO MY WISH LIST AND REALITY CHECK HELP ME?

The issue of selectivity is very tough if you're a first-time buyer. Nearly every home is going to look a lot better than the cramped one-bedroom apartment you've been renting for the past five years (or better than your old room at home in which you've been living rent-free since college).

It's important, however, not to jump at the first house that appears to meet your needs. Why? Because in addition to meeting your basic needs, you might also be able to get a few things you want. And if the house later turns out not to have met as many needs as you first thought, you'll be glad you gave yourself a few days to get over that first rush of house adrenaline.

Joanne's Story

Joanne set up 10 showings for a couple who were first-time buyers. The couple went to the first home and fell in love with it. They wanted to make an offer on the spot. But Joanne, an agent in Pompton Plains, New Jersey, has a policy: Never let a first-time buyer purchase a home at the first showing.

"First showings are all about emotion," she says. "You have to get some distance and some perspective before choosing the right home."

Joanne showed the rest of the homes to the couple. They liked 3 of the 10, including the first. And then they had to choose. They ended up choosing the first, but for reasons that hadn't even occurred to them when they first decided it was "*the* home."

Relatives and friends can lend perspective. Mike, a sales associate in York, Pennsylvania, says family members can help first-time buyers become more selective about a home, especially if they come to the first showings and feel like they're part of the process. "If they come only for the second showing, they feel compelled to find something wrong with the house," Mike explains.

Learning how to be selective doesn't just mean relying on your friends or relatives to tell you which way to turn. Although listening to their advice and opinions (especially if they conflict with yours) will help develop your selectivity (particularly if you become selective about whose advice you're going to take), selectivity is also about defining and refining your own tastes and trusting your own judgment. It's about putting aside emotion in favor of reason and logic.

Starting the Process

You start the process by determining how much you know about the type of home you'd like to buy. Let's say you aren't sure whether to live in a condo, buy a ranch home, or purchase new construction. You shouldn't limit yourself the first time out. Have your real estate agent show you a wide variety of homes, including the ranch, condominiums, a town house, and a subdivision under construction. Compare the styles and feel of each environment. Once you've identified which housing style you like best—maybe it's the subdivision under construction—have your broker set up a showing of a handful of houses that fall into your price range, size, location, and amenity requirements.

Next, compare what you like and dislike about each of the homes you've seen. After each showing, Joanne provides her buyers with a listing sheet that includes a photograph of each home. "When we get back in the car, I immediately ask them to write down what they liked and didn't like about the house. After they've seen five or six homes, I ask them to prioritize the top two or three they're most interested in," Joanne says.

Joanne recommends you look at the properties that come closest to your needs and wants. Then, begin to eliminate those that don't add up. Try to limit the list of homes you love to no more than two or three. If another "fabulous" home comes up, compare it with the others you "love," and try to identify which are the *new* top two.

When you're in a hot seller's market, the process of learning how to be selective might mean that homes in which you're interested wind up selling to other parties. That's because homes move faster than you do. It's painful to lose a house that might be right, but it's more painful to purchase a home quickly, just for the sake of doing it, and then realize that it isn't right.

Selectivity isn't easy. It forces you to make decisions about what you like and don't like. Also, some of the issues aren't clear-cut. Each home will have pluses and minuses. One may be in a good school district; another might have four oversized bedrooms and a nice backyard. Your wish list and reality check can help. If you've been honest about your priorities and understand that reality will temper the amenities you'll get with your first home, the lists should help you step back and take most of the emotion out of the decision. (For more information on how to make a wish list or reality check, see Question 1 on page 14.)

Billy's Story

As a young lawyer fresh out of law school, Billy found himself with a huge salary and no deductions. He'd lived in rental apartments all his life (his parents never bought) and decided to purchase a home before his work assignments got too busy.

Of course, work kicked in immediately at the firm, and Billy ended up taking quick looks (if that) at apartments and making blind offers. He relied on his agent to do the looking and then made an offer based on her assessment of how good or bad the condo was.

Needless to say, it wasn't a great way to go. Billy ended up buying a condo that's just so-so.

If you're thinking about buying new construction, you've got to focus even more on selectivity. You need to be selective about the contractor or builder or developer you choose. In addition, you need to be selective about the location within the development, as well as where the development itself is located in the neighborhood or suburb. You must then be selective about which options you add onto the purchase price—or you'll quickly go broke trying to upgrade everything in the home. New construction involves so many decisions that it's easy to get confused. Again, go back to your wish list and reality check and figure out what selective means to you in the context of a newly built home.

WHEN I GO TO A SHOWING, WHAT SHOULD I LOOK FOR?

QUESTION
24

The most important thing you can do at a showing is to step back and view the home objectively. For your purposes, that house, condo, or town house isn't a home but a physical dwelling: four walls, a floor, and a roof. Brokers say first-time buyers often get caught up in the moment. A rush of attention is thrust upon them, with brokers willing to do almost anything to get buyers to like the properties they are visiting.

Mary, a sales agent in San Antonio, Texas, says she tries to have people look dispassionately at the homes that are for sale. She tells her first-time buyers to inspect everything—every nook and cranny, every corner of the house. Pick up the rugs to inspect the condition of the floor, she recommends. Open every door. Poke through the closets.

"I actually prefer to show a vacant house rather than one with furniture in it because by the time the buyers get halfway through, they're looking at the antique sewing machine, not the bones of the house. Inevitably, conversation turns to the great bedspread or grandfather clock," Mary says.

For some people, seeing through the decoration is the hardest part of buying the right home. If you have an aversion to bright colors, prints, checks, or plaids and you see a house with blue, yellow, and orange walls, you may have trouble focusing on how beautiful the structure of the home is because you're repulsed by the decoration. Your emotional reaction might be to turn and walk right out the door and miss a potentially terrific home simply because someone has different taste.

Sara and Jeff's Story

Sara and Jeff are minimalists. It's an understatement to call their taste "spare," because it almost looks like no one lives in their home. They prefer white walls, hardwood floors or white carpeting, and a few pieces of starkly designed furniture and artwork arranged artfully in a room. Living in their home is quiet and peaceful, Jeff says. It's almost a Zenlike experience.

So imagine their frustration when they went house hunting. Brightly colored rooms, loud-print wallpaper, and more mess and clutter than they'd ever seen. They looked at beautiful homes but were unable to visualize how a can of white paint would have helped a red room become an area they'd enjoy living in.

Eventually, they ended up purchasing a loft in a commercial building that was being renovated and converted into residential units. They found it easier to deal with blueprints than with reality.

On Your First Showing

When you schedule your first showing, you're looking for a home that meets your basic needs:

1. **Is it within the right distance to work, church, family and friends?**
2. **Does it have enough bedrooms and bathrooms?**
3. **Is there enough storage space?**
4. **Is there parking?**
5. **Is it safe?**
6. **Is it in the right school district?**

If the home meets the basic requirements, then start to look for how many wish list items it includes. (*Note:* These are my suggestions and are to be used as an example. Go back to your own wish list and reality check to remind yourself about what's important to you.)

1. **Is there an extra bedroom and/or bathroom?**
2. **Is there a double vanity in the second bathroom?**
3. **Is there a garden or deck?**
4. **Is there a separate laundry room?**

5. **Is there a basement or crawl space? Is it convertible into usable space?**
6. **Is the garage attached?**
7. **Can the kids walk to school and after-school activities?**
8. **Is there a wood-burning fireplace or a gas fireplace?**
9. **What is the condition of the house—its appliances, roof, foundation, walls, mechanicals, wiring, and so on?**

Remember, start with the general items and then get more specific.

If you're having trouble remembering which home had more of the features you want, or are finding it difficult to rank the homes based on their amenities, try this simple rating system. Assign five points to each item in the top five spots on your wish list and reality check. Assign one point to the remaining items on each list. As you go through each house, check off all the features it has on the wish list and reality check. Add up the points and put that number at the top of the listing sheet. This method should help you nonemotionally rank the homes you've seen. If you want to be more specific, make a few copies of your wish list and reality checks and attach the checked-off copies to the individual listing sheets.

HOW CAN I REMEMBER EACH HOME WHEN I'VE SEEN SO MANY?

It's difficult to keep all the homes straight in your head, particularly if you've toured more than 10 houses. Brokers know that after buyers see just 5 or 6 homes, their recall of each one becomes confused, and it's not unusual to visit 10 or more open houses in one Sunday afternoon. My mother, Susanne, a real estate agent in Chicago, recently showed a couple 20 properties over a day and a half. They were visiting from out of town and had requested to see everything that was available on the market in their neighborhood of choice that they could afford. By the end of the second day, my mother said they were completely frazzled—and more than just a bit confused about which property had which amenity.

New subdivision developers know that prospective buyers might visit as many as 5 different subdivisions, each with 5 to 8 model homes in a weekend. That's 25 to 40 model homes to keep straight—a virtually impossible task!

Is your head swimming yet? You need to create a method to the real estate madness. Here are a few suggestions for keeping the houses organized in your mind:

1. Keep a written log. Include the date you saw the house, time of the showing, and who was there (your broker, the seller broker, the owner, your mother, your father-in-law, etc.). I suggest you purchase a spiral-bound notebook and keep a dated log of each house you've seen. You can either attach listing sheets here or in a three-ring binder (see my later suggestion).

2. Photocopy and enlarge a map of the areas in which you're most interested. As you go through an area, use a yellow highlighter to mark the streets you've looked at. Use a different-colored highlighter (red, blue, or green) to mark the various homes you've actually seen in the area. You'll also want to mark the local schools, shopping, transportation routes and houses of worship. When my husband, Sam, and I were looking for the house in which we now live, Sam marked the train lines and train stations in red. Since we only had one car at that time, he knew he'd be walking to the train station, and about a half-mile was the maximum amount of distance he was willing to go.

3. Put the listing sheet given to you to good use. A listing sheet should contain all of the important information about a house, including the list price, size, lot size, number of bedrooms and bathrooms, and any extra amenities. Choose a few specific or spectacular or memorable things (lime-green kitchen, beautiful greenhouse, attached four-car garage, sauna in basement, pine floors, plastic imitation-wood paneling in basement) about the house, and write them down on the back of the listing sheet. Sketch out the floor plan. Either staple these listing sheets into the spiral-bound notebook you bought, or invest in a cheap three-ring binder. Punch holes in your listing sheets and organize them by date. If a house sells, note the selling price on its listing sheet. If you don't receive a listing sheet, create one based on what you saw during the showing.

4. Staple a completed wish list and reality check to the listing sheet. It should help remind you what attracted you to the house in the first place.

5. Create your own photo reference file. Invest in or borrow an instant-print camera and a few packs of film. Better yet, use a digital camera (see below). Take several photos of each property, including one of the front door and the address. At night, you can arrange the photos so each house's photos are together. If you forget which property belongs to which photo, go online to the website of the company listing the property and look it up. The beauty of the Internet today is that listing agents often post at least one photo of the property, and sometimes many photos or even a virtual tour of different rooms. So it's easier than ever, even weeks later, to coordinate the photos you took with those on the website to help you remember which photo belongs to which house. If you're printing up hard copies of the photos, whether on your color printer at home or at your neighborhood pharmacy, be sure to mark each photo with the address of the house. Better yet, staple it to your listing sheet. (Be sure to ask the listing agent for permission to take an interior photo. You do not need anyone's permission to take an exterior photo of the home.)

6. Make videos; they're even better. If you take along your video camera, or if you have a cell phone with video capabilities, you can record your thoughts and feelings about a house as you record the interior and exterior of the home, as well as the neighborhood. Also, you'll get more of a sense of what the house feels like with your video camera. (Again, ask permission. Sometimes sellers are understandably nervous about someone having a video or photograph of the interior contents of their home.)

7. Go digital. With a digital camera (they're getting cheaper and better by the day), you can actually download your photos onto your computer and keep an electronic record of homes you've viewed. You'll always know where the file is (especially if you create a folder for houses you've seen and then name each file with the address of a particular house), and you'll be able to send photos of the homes you've seen to your relatives and friends. You can also pull down photos of the homes that you've seen on the Internet. Sites like Realtor.com (www.realtor.com) and HomeAdvisor (www.homeadvisor.com), among others, often show photos of the homes that are listed for sale.

8. Give future residents a chance to express their feelings. If you're buying the home with another person (spouse, significant other, business partner, child, parent, friend, etc.), be sure the other people involved have a chance to write down what they think about the house. Purchasing a house with other people means buying by committee; you don't get to make a unilateral decision. If you have children over the age of eight (or perhaps younger, if they are precocious), they will have definite likes and dislikes about a house. I'm not telling you to rely solely on their judgments, but they should certainly be included in the process, perhaps at the second or third showing.

Many developers will put together information packets that explain the concept behind the subdivision and will offer floor plans of the various models offered for sale. There may be four to eight different models (or more) for sale, and you may visit that many model homes, so it may be tough to keep everything straight. Model home designers, also known as "merchandisers," strive to create something memorable that will also make you feel at home. An empty-nester couple might see themselves in a house that has the master bedroom on the first floor and guest rooms upstairs. A family with young children might remember a house that has a bedroom with two cribs (for the twins the imaginary mother is expecting). By taking photos of the exterior and interior of model homes, you'll be able to personalize each information package. This should help you keep the subdivisions—and their developers—apart.

HOW DO I KNOW WHEN IT'S TIME FOR A SECOND SHOWING?

Whether you go for a second showing depends on your reaction to a home. If the house appears to meet your needs and wants, and you like the home, your agent may set up a second showing.

Brokers say you'll know when you're ready for a second showing. It usually happens after you've seen four to five houses. You may have followed all the suggestions for remembering which house is which, but you can't seem to place that one house you remember really liking. Or you still like a particular house better than all the others you've seen and want to go back for an extended look.

Brokers may schedule first showings 20 minutes apart so that you can see five to six homes in a morning or afternoon, including travel time. Fifteen minutes should be enough time for you to decide whether the home is a possibility. You'll say either "Maybe" or "Forget it." (As you get further along the path, you may be able to make up your mind in five minutes or less, but that's a lot of pressure to put on a first showing, when you're new to the game.)

Second showings are longer; they start at about a half-hour in length. During a second showing you'll want to reconfirm that the things you liked about the house the first time are still appealing. Or you may decide that the house really isn't right and cross it off your list. If you do like the house, the second showing is where you should begin to examine the home's structure and mechanicals. Although you'll hire a home inspector to do a professional home inspection on the house, each inspection will set you back between $300 and $600 (or more), depending on the size of the property. If you know what to look for, you can spot problems early on in the game and save yourself some money.

Here are some physical things to check out during a second showing:

1. Overall impression of the exterior. Does the house seem in good shape? Is it sound? Step back: Are the lines of the house straight? Does the roof sag? If the house is brick, is the mortar between the bricks cracked or chinked? Is the paint peeling? Is the aluminum siding dented, dirty, or in really good shape? Is the sidewalk cracked around the house? Does it appear to pitch in toward the house (which might cause leaking into the basement) or slope away from the house?

2. Roof. Are the shingles curling or lifting? Ask the agent (or owners, if they're there) how old the roof is and whether there have been any problems. A new roof, if properly installed, should last between 15 and 25 years. If the house has a tile or slate roof, it could last for 50 to 100 years or more, but it might be expensive to fix or replace.

3. Windows and door frames. Are they in good shape? Are there storm windows? Has the caulk dried out and pulled away? Are they cracked? Can you feel air blowing in? Are the frames square? Are there cracks in the plaster above the door frames?

4. Overall impression of the interior. Does the home appear to be sound? Do the wood floors creak when you walk on them? Are they pitched in any one direction? Are the stairs shaky? Is the kitchen or bath linoleum tile peeling or bubbled? Are there discolored patches on the walls or ceiling? Are there other signs of leaks? Is the plaster cracked? Is the paint or wallpaper peeling? Are the walls and ceiling straight? Do doors, cupboards, and drawers open easily? Is the house clean?

5. Attic or crawl space. Is there insulation? Has it been laid out properly? Is there a fan? Are there air leaks? Is there poor ventilation?

6. Plumbing and electricity. Turn on all the faucets in the sinks, showers, and bathtubs. Is everything working? Do they drain well? How's the water pressure? Does the water have a funny smell? Does the home use city water or have its own well? Do the lights seem to work? Check the fuse box or circuit breaker. Are there enough electrical outlets? Or is everything connected with extension cords? Are there enough telephone jacks?

7. Basement. Are there cracks in the walls or foundation? Does it smell musty, stale, or damp? Does the basement leak? Is the house in a floodplain? (The listing agent may or may not know the answer to this question. You may have to find out independently by visiting the local village or city hall.)

8. Mechanicals. How old are the hot water heater and furnace systems? Is there an air-conditioning system or are there window units? How old are the window units and do they come with the house? Does the listing agent have any information on the heating, electricity, or water bills?

9. Pests. Is there evidence of termites? Cockroaches? Mice? Check any wooden beams for tiny holes or piles of sawdust.

Seat Yourself

Second showings take the selectivity issue we've been talking about a step further. In a second showing, you should sit down on the furniture and try to imagine living in the home. You should look around and think about where you would put *your* furniture. Ask yourself these questions:

- How would you feel about coming home to this house after a hard day's work?
- Where would you relax?
- Can you see yourself cooking in the kitchen?

- Will your armoire fit into the living room?

- Is the bedroom quiet enough for sleeping?

- Go outside to the garden and sit for a while. Will you feel comfortable grilling in the backyard? Do you like the garden as is or will you want to redo the landscaping?

- Open up the windows and listen to the sounds of the neighborhood. Are there noisy wind chimes? Children? Dogs? Dump trucks? Airplanes? Is the house on a flight path? Are you listening to a nearby or distant highway? Local traffic? Frequently used train tracks? Are there other noises?

- Do you feel relaxed in the house?

At this point, you might be able to make up your mind about the house. For some first-time buyers, the second showing clinches their decision and they make an offer. However, other first-time buyers need a third, or even fourth, showing.

Third Showings

After living in our co-op for a few years, Sam and I decided to sell and buy a house. We put the apartment on the market and a couple came and looked at it on five separate occasions.

The rule of thumb is, if you don't have a contract in hand when you come for the *fifth* showing, don't come at all. If you ask for a third showing, the brokers and seller are naturally going to think you're really interested. They're going to expect you to make a serious offer.

If the third showing comes and goes and there's no offer, the seller is going to begin to get impatient. If you then call and ask for a fourth showing, the brokers will have to persuade the seller to go along with it. It's a lot of work preparing a house for a showing. The seller has to clean the house, pack everyone off, and basically clear the decks. It's a major maneuver, because most of our homes don't look like those featured in *Architectural Digest* or *House Beautiful* (and my apologies to those of you who maintain homes to these standards).

By the time you ask for a fifth showing, the seller has given up on you and is more interested in the next buyers who are scheduled to come through the door. If you do put in an offer after a fifth showing, the seller may not treat it very seriously (especially if it's a low-ball offer) because you've wasted his or her (and everyone else's) time.

I can hear you howling, "But I wanted to be sure! It's a big invest-ment—the single biggest investment of my life!" All that's true, but five showings is a great inconvenience to a seller, particularly if there's no offer. I don't want you to rush and make a bad decision. And the seller will deal with whatever happens. But over time, as you become more familiar with the process of buying a home, your ability to make a decision will naturally speed up.

By the way, our fifth-showing buyer never made an offer. We even-tually took the home off the market and lived there for three more years before selling to a doctor who was moving to Chicago from New York.

Making an Offer on the First Showing

Some brokers say first-time buyers don't really need a second, third, or fourth showing. They say if you've been honest with the broker and honest with yourself in filling out your wish list and reality check, the broker will lead you to several homes, each of which could work for you.

Sales agent Mike says he tries to eliminate the need for second showings by picking homes that most closely match the buyer's needs and wants. He does, however, encourage second showings if the buyer initially sees the house at night. "If I've done a good job," he notes, "they'll be ready to make an offer after only two outings. My first-time buyers rarely need to see more than 10 properties [to find the one they love]."

Some immigrant first-time buyers, who speak little or no English and work with agents who speak their own language (one national real estate company once boasted it had agents who, between them, spoke at least 75 different languages), get fewer choices than that. My hus-band, Sam, has worked with many Hispanic buyers who were shown two or three houses and told to choose between them. They were so grateful to be able to buy a house—*any* house—that it didn't even occur to them to ask if there were others on the market that they could look at.

Rarely will two or three homes be enough to see, if you've never bought a home before. Never let anyone show you just two houses and tell you to choose between them. (We'll get to that situation later.) Ten homes might be the right number for some buyers, but 50 or even 110 homes might be the right number for you.

When Sam and I were looking to buy the house we now own, we looked at perhaps 125 or even 150 houses over a four-year period. Many were open houses on the weekends. Some were showings. None were right, especially as our way of thinking began to evolve. We changed neighborhoods and locations and finally made our way to a suburb of Chicago, some 17 miles north of where we were originally looking to buy. On the other hand, when we were deciding to purchase a loft for Sam's office, in downtown Chicago, his need to be close to the train, in a certain part of town, and for a certain price, eliminated all but one building. And because that building only had one condo for sale that met the price and size criteria, the choice, in retrospect, was easy.

When you're going through the process of buying a home, it's easy to get sucked into the buyer–broker relationship and start letting the broker make your decisions for you. What you really have to do is step back and analyze whether this home is right for you. Try not to think about whether the *broker* thinks it's a good choice.

hindsight

WHEN DO I KNOW I'VE FOUND THE RIGHT HOUSE?

QUESTION 27

What is most important thing you can learn about buying a home? **There is more than one right home for you.**

Reread and remember those two lines. Some buyers get so overcome with emotion that they become fixated on one particular property. They focus all of their energy and attention on one property that (1) they may not get or (2) for which they may pay too much.

There *is* more than one right home for you.

When you go out looking, try to retain a steady perspective. Don't get emotionally involved with the seductive process of buying a home. Don't get intellectually tangled up in the thousands, even hundreds of thousands, of dollars you're going to spend. Don't worry about whether you've secured or damaged your prospects for a golden retirement.

Real estate attorneys routinely advise their clients *not* to fall in love with a piece of property. "It's not wise because if you fall in love with a house and then have the inspection and something's terribly wrong, you're going to want to buy the house anyway, and that may not be in your best interests," says one attorney.

Sometimes real estate agents or brokers will seem to encourage you to fall in love with a house. They'll say things like, "Isn't it beautiful?" or "I could spend my whole life here," or "You'll be so happy here," or "Don't you just love this place?"

Of course they want you to fall in love with this house, because then you'll buy it. They'll receive their commission and go onto the next first-time buyer. You, on the other hand, will end up spending the next five to seven *years* in that home. Despite the admonitions *not* to fall in love with a home, *not* to become fixated on one particular piece of property, people do it all the time. Including me.

I fell in love with our vintage co-op with a wood-burning fireplace. We could have bought a newly built house we saw on a huge lot (for Chicago, it was big—about 30 feet by 165 feet) in a nice neighborhood. In the first five years after purchase, it would have nearly doubled in value. But no, I was completely enamored with this 24-hour doorman, no-parking building. I saw all of the pluses and none of the minuses—an oh-so-typical symptom of "first-timeritis."

Sixteen years, two houses, three investment condos, thousands of newspaper columns and magazine articles, and four books on real estate later, I can tell you that falling in love with a house is exactly the *wrong* thing to do. If you don't keep some objectivity during the buying process, you'll be suckered in before you know it.

About That Objectivity . . .

There is a difference between falling in love with something you've seen and recognizing that you could buy a piece of property and successfully live there for whatever length of time.

Sales agent Joanne says she can tell when her buyers find the right house by the look of joy on their faces. "If they sit down on the couch, it's a good sign. If they're trying to decide where to put their furniture, it's a very good sign. If they've got a special glow on their faces, it's the right house."

You may not be the type to blush easily, but you get the idea. You'll have a chemical reaction to a house that's a good choice. And there may be more than one house to which you respond in this way.

Over time—say, in a few years—the home that's right today may seem small and cramped for your growing family. You'll change, and as your fortunes increase, today's dream home may seem a little like a starter home. You'll reset your sights on that golf course development, or a better neighborhood or school district. Your cozy kitchen will suddenly seem too small for your growing family.

"Where did all that space go?" you'll wonder. And then it will be time to find your next "right" house.

4

How Do I Know What I Can Afford to Spend?

HOW MUCH CAN I AFFORD?

How much *house* can you afford?

The answer most real estate experts give is this: If you can afford to rent and have cash for a down payment, you can probably afford to buy. But the easiest way to find out how much you can afford is to get prequalified or preapproved for your loan.

When you get *prequalified*, you essentially tell the lender (either on the phone, in person, or online) how much you earn and what debts you have. The lender crunches those numbers through a formula and comes up with an actual mortgage amount you can afford to support.

When you get *preapproved*, you may need to provide the lender with documentation like checking or bank account statements, a recent pay stub from work, or perhaps the last two years' of income tax forms. If you go online for your preapproval, many online lenders (e.g., E-Loan) do a "lite" version, requiring only that you answer the questions truthfully. The paperwork is done during the verification stage of the loan.

The biggest difference between getting prequalified and preapproved for a loan is this. When you get preapproved for your loan, the lender is actually *committing in writing to funding your loan*, providing the house appraises out in value (and assuming that your paperwork checks out). With a prequalification, there is no commitment from the lender, but you have an idea of what you can afford.

As technology continues to advance, it will likely be possible for you to get preapproved for your loan within seconds on an Internet mortgage lending site, including receiving a written commitment from a lender via e-mail. Currently, many online lenders are set up to grant loan approvals electronically within minutes. In addition, various websites are in the process of setting up behind-the-scenes databases and software that will allow you to apply by providing just a social security number (or part of your social security number) and filling out a short form that will include a few extra pieces of information, like your name, current address, and where you work. Then a company, with the information you've provided, will be able to reach out to various sources that have electronic information about you (e.g., credit history, credit score, IRS tax return, etc.) and instantly provide you with your loan approval. My guess is that all of this will not only happen, but become routine, before I write the next edition of this book.

Prequalification

The nice thing about prequalification is that you typically do not need to tie yourself in by paying an application fee and actually applying for the mortgage. You can save that until after you've found the home you want to buy, and then you can comparison shop to find the best mortgage deal. Lenders will be delighted to prequalify you in a preliminary way, with no obligation, because it means they get an opportunity to pitch their wares to you.

Prequalifying is a relatively painless process. The lender will ask you a few simple questions about your debts and assets and apply your numbers to the debt-to-income ratios that lenders on the secondary market require. Then, the lender will tell you how much mortgage your income will support.

You may hear about secondary market lenders during the course of your purchase. These are companies like Fannie Mae and Freddie Mac, which purchase loans from mortgage companies that make loans to consumers like you. By guaranteeing retail lenders a steady source of cash, secondary market lenders help keep the mortgage market "liquid," which keeps mortgages affordable for home buyers. Even though you may see an advertisement for Fannie Mae or Freddie Mac, and perhaps will visit their websites to get more information about the home-buying process, you won't do business directly with them. For more information about the secondary market, mortgages, and buying a home, visit these websites at www.homepath.com (which is Fannie Mae's consumer website) and www.freddiemac.com.

Figure It Out Yourself

If you are paying $600 per month in rent, and you assume the home you're buying will require about $100 per month in real estate taxes and insurance, you're left with $500 per month. Based on an annual rent payment of $6,000 ($500 multiplied by 12) you can manage a mortgage of about $60,000, if you assume the interest rate is 10 percent. If you assume an interest rate of 7 percent, your annual rent payment will support a mortgage of $85,714.

Three percentage points in interest (the difference between 10 percent and 7 percent) makes a huge difference in affordability. Sliding interest rates can drastically affect how much house you can afford to buy. At 4 percent interest, which may be the starting point for some adjustable-rate mortgages (ARMs), $500 per month can support a $150,000 mortgage (though at that price, you may have to put away more for real estate taxes and insurance).

In the past decade, homeownership has become more affordable than almost any other time in the last half century. Mortgage interest rates have fallen from a high of 18 percent in 1982 to 10 percent at the end of the 1980s, to the 6.5 to 8 percent range for most of the 1990s, to around 5.3 percent for a 30-year fixed-rate mortgage (a 46-year low) during the early 2000s. In 2004, Federal Reserve Bank chairman Allan Greenspan began raising the short-term federal funds rate for the first time in four years. Rates for the 10-year bond, to which the interest rates for 30-year mortgages are tied, began to rise as well.

If interest rates are 10 percent, you can afford to buy something that costs somewhere between two (if you're conservative) and two and a half times your income. This assumes, however, that you have 20 percent in cash to put down on a house and little, if any, long-standing debt (like your car loan or credit card debt). If interest rates are at 7 percent, you may be able to purchase a home that costs more than three times your gross annual income (again, providing you have down payment money and no debt).

For example, if your combined family income minus debt payments is $50,000 per year, and the interest rates are at 10 percent (which, by the way, is the historical average), conventional wisdom suggests that you can afford to buy a house that costs around $100,000. If interest rates are 8 percent, your $50,000-per-year income might stretch far enough to buy a home that costs between $150,000 to $190,000, depending on how much you can put down in cash.

Debt-to-Income Ratios

How do mortgage lenders specifically determine how much you can afford to pay? Primary lenders (the retail companies that lend to consumers like you) and secondary markets have developed debt-to-income lending ratios through years of trial and error.

All lenders more or less follow the same ratios. They've determined that you can afford to pay between 28 and 36 percent of your gross income in debt service. That means that, altogether, your mortgage principal and interest payments, real estate taxes, insurance, and car loan and credit card payments may not exceed 36 percent of your gross monthly income.

As lenders have become more sophisticated about lending to different types of borrowers, and have developed a myriad of creative loans that can be somewhat personalized for each home buyer, several of the largest secondary market players (which control the way the vast majority of mortgages are made) have somewhat relaxed this debt-to-income ratio. Fannie Mae and Freddie Mac, the nation's two largest investors in home mortgages, are federally charted private corporations mandated to provide financial products and services that increase the availability and affordability of housing for low-, moderate-, and middle-income Americans.

Because these companies are in competition with one another to purchase, repackage, and resell the largest amount of residential mortgages, they are continually developing new loan products to help more consumers achieve their homeownership dreams. At the beginning of the 1990s, for example, Fannie Mae decided it would extend the upper limit of the debt-to-income ratio from 36 to as much as 40 or even 42 percent. Freddie Mac quickly jumped in and created loans that do the same thing. On FHA loans (backed by the Federal Housing Authority), the upper limits on the debt-to-income ratios have been extended to as much as 43 percent. For special homeownership programs backed by Community Development Block Grant (CDBG) funds, the ratios can be even higher, with down payment assistance provided.

Although the extra 3 to 6 percent doesn't sound like much, this is groundbreaking stuff. Suddenly, if your family's gross annual income is

$50,000, and interest rates are 10 percent, you can buy a house worth $125,000 to $140,000, a significant difference in many communities. If interest rates are 7 percent, you may be able to spend up to four times your annual income (depending on how much other debt you're carrying).

Calculating How Much Loan Payment You Can Carry

Let's put aside the issue of the down payment for a moment and talk about how much of a monthly loan payment your income will carry. Some experts suggest you should aim to spend 25 percent of your gross monthly income (GMI) on your housing expenses; others say you can spend up to 33 percent. Compared with the 36 to 41 percent of gross monthly income that your lender will allow you to put toward your total debt payment, 25 and even 33 percent seem sort of conservative. Ultimately, you decide how much of your income you want to spend each month on housing; that is, how aggressive or conservative you can be without incurring more debt because of your other living expenses.

Get out a pencil and fill in your personal finance facts on the Maximum Monthly Payment Worksheet.

Let's say your gross monthly income is $5,000 ($60,000 per year). Multiply by 25 percent ($1,250) or 33 percent ($1,667). Let's say you have a car loan ($150 per month), and you're paying off a credit card balance ($100 per month):

$$\$1,250 - \$250 = \$1,000$$

or

$$\$1,667 - \$250 = \$1,417$$

In this example, you'd be able to spend between $1,000 and $1,417 per month on your principal and interest payments, real estate taxes, and insurance. If real estate taxes are $100 per month ($1,200 per year) and insurance is another $50 per month, that will leave you between $850 and $1,267 to spend on a mortgage.

Here's how to calculate the amount of mortgage you can afford to carry: Multiply the net amount you can spend ($850 to $1,267) by 12 (for an annual mortgage amount), then divide that number by the current prevailing interest rate (say, 8 percent for a 30-year fixed-rate loan).

WORKSHEET

Maximum Monthly Payment

1. Gross monthly income from all sources: _____

2. Multiply by the percentage of GMI you want to spend (Hint: Multiply by .25 for 25 percent of your income, .33 for 33 percent of your income, or .36 for 36 percent of your income):
   × _____

3. Subtract present monthly debt service:

   Credit cards _____

   Car loans _____

   School loans _____

   Charge accounts _____

   Other personal debt _____

   Total debt: _____

4. Subtract your total debt: − _____

5. Your maximum monthly payment is: = _____

25 percent of gross income: $850 × 12 = $10,200 ÷ .08 = $127,500

33 percent of gross income: $1,267 × 12 = $15,204 ÷ .08 = $190,050

So how much house can you afford? Assume you add a 20 percent down payment to each of these mortgage amounts (divide $127,500 or $190,050 by 5 and add that number to the total):

$127,500 + $25,500 = $153,000

$190,050 + $38,010 = $228,060

According to these calculations, on a $60,000-per-year income, assuming you have 20 percent to put down in cash, you'd be able to afford a home that costs between $153,000 and $228,060.

The 8 percent interest rate allows you to purchase a home between two and a half and nearly four times your income! And the lower interest rates go, the further your hard-earned dollars will stretch.

Use the worksheet on page 125 to figure out the approximate price you can afford to spend on a home.

Finding the Comfort Level

Just because you *can* afford to spend up to four times your income doesn't mean you *have* to. It's extremely important to find a level of payment that's comfortable for you and your family based on how you like to spend your money. Although you may be technically able to afford a $150,000 home, making those mortgage payments might mean your family will have to give up other luxuries like summer camp or new clothes for school.

Remember, no one says you have to spend every nickel you have on your home.

Figuring Out Your Budget

Finding your comfort zone is most easily accomplished if you're on top of your expenses. If you know what you spend, you know which expenses can be redirected toward paying the costs associated with home ownership.

WORKSHEET
Estimated Purchase Price

25 Percent Gross Monthly Income   **33 Percent Gross Monthly Income**

GMI* _____   _____

          × .25 _____   × .33 _____

Less: Monthly debt – _____   – _____

          = _____   = _____

× 12 months   = _____   = _____

Current rate of
interest   ÷ _____   ÷ _____

          = _____   = _____

(Amount of mortgage you can afford)

Down payment   + _____   + _____

          = _____   = _____

(Approximate purchase price of house)

*Gross Monthly Income (GMI)

The first thing to do is figure out where the money goes each month. Use the Monthly Expenditures Checklist on pages 128 and 129 to help you determine what you're spending your salary on each month.

Be honest. If you routinely spend $16.99 a week on the newest CD or DVD, put it in. If you rent two videos per week, put it in. If you eat lunch out with your friends four days a week, put it in. Later on, when you're trying to figure out how to save enough money for a down payment, you'll know exactly where to make the cut.

Adding It All Up

Are your monthly expenditures more than your monthly after-tax take-home pay? Are the two numbers closer together than they ought to be? If they are, you're out of balance financially, which could be a problem when you try to get a loan.

An important part of being a homeowner is taking responsibility for your finances. Most first-time buyers (and even those who are repeat buyers) have to make some trade-offs because homeownership is expensive. By cutting back on your budget now, you'll be steps ahead after you move in and want to spend some more money to dress the place up. Look over the list and begin to determine which expenses can be eliminated or cut down. (For more hints on budgets, credit, and finance, check out my book *100 Questions You Should Ask About Your Personal Finances*, or visit my website, thinkglink.com)

One-Stop Shopping

These days, many decent-sized real estate firms also own little side businesses to which they try to steer business. These businesses typically include a mortgage brokerage, title company, home inspectors, alarm companies, housecleaning services, and various other products and services homeowners typically use.

In addition to selling you a house—or selling your house for you—the real estate agent will also suggest (sometimes gently, sometimes strongly) that you use the brokerage firm's side companies for your other real estate needs. Here are the arguments that will be presented to you:

1. The price is competitive with anything else you'll find out there. Is it? Have you shopped around? Often, these real estate company-owned mortgage firms won't give you the best price until you get a great price elsewhere and then go back to negotiate. At that point, unless they're willing to beat the price by, say, 5 or 10 percent, you should think about why you'd want to do business with a company that takes an only-when-caught approach to fees.

2. It's convenient. "I [the broker] will be able to stay on top of them for you." How good was your broker at staying on top of the details of your purchase or sale? That could be a valuable clue to the attention other details involved in the transaction will get.

Let's review again where you can go to get prequalified and preapproved:

- You can go online to BankRate.com to check out current interest rates on various types of mortgage programs.
- You can click through to various lenders through that site or call them to see if the rates offered online are available.
- You can go to national lenders' websites, like Countrywide Home Loans (Countrywide.com) or Bank of America (BankofAmerica.com).
- You can go to a website that aggregates many lenders on one site, like Eloan.com, HouseandHome.com (Microsoft's homeowner's website), or LendingTree.com, and have them bid for your business.
- You can call a lender to be prequalified or even preapproved over the phone.
- You can visit a lender's office in person. Face-to-face stuff is nice, but it may actually take longer than if you go online, where everything is automated.

Some of the best mortgage programs are available exclusively online (see Chapter 8 for more information), but be sure to get everything in writing. Every lender, including online lenders, is required to live up to the rules in RESPA (Real Estate Settlement Procedures Act), which is governed by the Department of Housing and Urban Development. You should get, in writing, a good faith estimate (see Question 69 on page 252) as well as a statement committing to funding your loan (pending the successful appraisal of the property) if you're getting prequalified.

3. "We've used them extensively and they provide good service." Is it mentioned that the firm gets a fee—known in rougher times as a "kickback"—for every home buyer or seller steered toward

MONTHLY EXPENDITURES CHECKLIST

Use this checklist to figure out exactly where your money goes each month. If you have other expenses that aren't listed, add them in at the bottom.

Expenses	Amount Spent Per Month
Rent	_____
Electricity	_____
Gas	_____
Telephone/Online	_____
Auto Loan/Lease Payment	_____
Auto Insurance	_____
Health Insurance	_____
Renter's Insurance	_____
Life Insurance	_____
Other Insurance	_____
Monthly Savings	_____
Retirement Contribution	_____
Children's Education Fund	_____
Credit Card Debt	_____
School Loans	_____
Other Monthly Debt Payments	_____
Grocery/Pharmacy/Sundry Bills	_____
Weekly Transportation	_____
Care for an Aging Parent or Relative	_____
Charity contributions	_____
Medical/Dental Bills	_____

Expenses	Amount Spent Per Month
Restaurants/Ordering In	_____
Entertainment	_____
Health Club/Working Out	_____
Recreation	_____
Child Care/Babysitters	_____
Children's Expenses (lessons/camp/clothing, etc.)	_____
School Tuition	_____
Housecleaning Expenses	_____
Vacations (divide your annual expense by 12 to find out the monthly expenditures	_____
Books/CDs/Tapes/Videos/DVDs	_____
Newspaper/Magazine Subscriptions	_____
Laundry/Dry Cleaning	_____
Yard Work/Landscaping (for rental)	_____
Gifts	_____
Major Purchases (stereo/computer)	_____
Furniture/Decorating	_____
Clothing	_____
Miscellaneous Expenses (morning cup of gourmet coffee, snacks, lottery tickets)	_____
Other _____	_____
_____	_____
_____	_____
_____	_____
_____	_____
_____	_____
Monthly Total	_____

Note: If you're going to enter in a clothing purchase under "clothing" but are carrying it as a debt on your credit card, only enter it once. If you put it in under "clothing," make sure you enter only the amount of interest you pay on your credit card, not the minimum amount due (which includes a tiny bit of principal in addition to all that hefty interest).

that company? In some areas, the agent's bonus is determined by how many clients he or she sends to other companies owned by the firm.

The process of looking for a home and shopping for a mortgage is usually stressful, arduous, and time-consuming. I'm all for one-stop shopping to expedite the process, but I strongly believe you'll get the cheapest and best loan after you've shopped around. If nothing else, you'll have the satisfaction of knowing that the best mortgage lender was right under your nose the entire time. Shopping online is easy and fast, and studies have shown that you can get a good deal with an on-line lender. But start with the Maximum Monthly Payment Worksheet on page 123, and you'll have a pretty good idea of how much you can afford to borrow to purchase your new home.

Real estate companies really, really, *really* want you to use their other services because it's a way for them to build their business and fatten the bottom line without having to pay the costs of bringing in new business. But even if a line on your agency disclosure agreement (or listing agreement, when it comes time to sell your home) says "Check here if you want to use XYZ Title Company," and you check it off, you can always change your mind. Don't ever let anyone try to pressure you into using a product or service that you haven't thoroughly checked out and priced out. Remember, you're the customer.

QUESTION 29

HOW MUCH WILL IT COST TO OWN AND MAINTAIN A HOME?

In the movie *The Money Pit*, Tom Hanks ends up throwing his life savings into renovating his home. Maintaining a home often feels the same way.

Calculating the costs of homeownership appears to be easy: If you can afford your mortgage, insurance, and real estate taxes, you can afford to own a home, right? Unfortunately, that's not always the case. Some costs of homeownership, hidden from renters, can lighten the wallet and break the bank.

Calculating these costs is a lot tougher than predicting your mortgage payments because they're variable by nature and given to change. If the principal, interest, real estate taxes, and insurance (PITI) are the fixed costs involved with owning a home, utility payments are semi-fixed, and everything else is a variable.

Here are the basic expenses you will be responsible for when you actually buy your home:

- Mortgage payments of principal and interest, paid monthly, or bi-monthly, if you have a loan that requires you to make payments every other week.

- Real estate taxes, paid annually or in two installments, or paid monthly with the mortgage, if you escrow your insurance and taxes.

- Homeowner's insurance policy premium, paid monthly with the mortgage, if you escrow your insurance and taxes, but sometimes paid separately annually or semiannually.

- Homeowner's assessments or co-op monthly assessments.

- Utilities, including electricity, gas, cable, cable modem, satellite, online service, and so on.

- Trash and garbage collection, including recycling as required by your local municipality.

- Water and sewage (may be separate or billed together).

- Repairs and maintenance of the interior and exterior of the home (includes everything from washing windows to replacing the roof or painting the interior and exterior).

- Landscaping and grounds maintenance (including driveway resurfacing, as needed, plus all the regular stuff).

- Snow removal (for those living in colder climates).

How much do these items cost? For some, like landscaping, water, and the utilities, the answer depends greatly on season and usage. Your mortgage and insurance payments will likely be fixed and remain the same. Utilities will go up and down with the seasons and will likely drift higher. Repairs and maintenance of the house depend on the condition the home was in when you bought it. If the boiler is on its last legs when you bought the home, you may have to pay for a new one shortly after the closing.

It is less expensive to keep up with the maintenance rather than to defer it. Plan to put at least $3,000 to $5,000 in a home improvement fund so that you have the cash you need to make emergency repairs or regular maintenance. A new roof could cost $3,000 to $20,000, while a new hot water heater might cost $600 to $1,500, plus installation. Consider purchasing a home warranty (for existing homes only, not for new construction). Although it doesn't cover structural problems, it will pay to fix or replace any appliance or electrical or mechanical system that was working on the day of closing through the first year you own your home. Best of all, many sellers will pick up the cost of a home warranty as a marketing tool. See Question 42 for more information.

The whole point of buying new construction is that you won't have to touch the house for the next 10 years, right? That may be true with some things, like the roof, mechanical systems, and appliances (hopefully!), but new construction carries with it a whole other set of problems, including the possibility that the builder didn't install some items properly. Although you'll find most of these soon after you've moved in, make sure that the caulking around the bathtubs, showers, and sinks stays in place, and that you don't let exterior painting go for too long. The last thing you want is a nearly brand-new house looking disheveled and run-down.

Real Estate Taxes

Real estate taxes are another matter. From every corner of the United States, homeowners cry out that their property taxes are too high. Formulas for calculating property taxes differ from state to state, but the general feeling is that you can expect to pay anywhere between 1 and 3 percent of the market value of the home.

For example, if your home has a market value of $100,000, it's likely that you might pay anywhere between $1,000 and $3,000 or more per year in property taxes, depending on where you live. In Chicago, if you own a $250,000 condo in the Gold Coast (the fanciest part of town), you might pay up to 70 percent more in real estate taxes than the person who owns a $250,000 bungalow on the city's southwest side. Is it fair? Not really. Currently in California, homeowners pay 1 percent of the sales price of the home, no matter when they bought it. If you paid $100,000 for a California bungalow 25 years ago, you're still paying around $1,000 in property taxes.

You can't escape property taxes, but you can fight them. See Chapter 12 for useful information on how to lighten your property tax burden.

General Maintenance

What kinds of specific expenses might you encounter in your first few years of homeownership? General maintenance and upkeep of your home can be expensive. Brokers say would-be homeowners often forget to consider the basics for the exterior and interior of the home.

Cold-weather and warm-weather climates exact their own peculiar punishments on a home. Severe winter weather can wreak havoc on driveways, gutters, the roof, and exterior paint, not to mention the time spent shoveling. Depending on the amount of snow, you may want to invest in a snowblower. (Or consider joining your new neighbors to pay for snow removal during the season.) In addition, your driveway may need a coat of sealant from time to time to prevent cracking.

Landscaping and a garden are year-round issues. If you live in the Deep South, your garden will require constant care and attention to avoid becoming a jungle. In the North, you'll have at least three seasons of gardening.

Another maintenance concern is the exterior upkeep of the home. Brick homes may need expensive tuck-pointing to keep the walls from leaking. Clapboard or shingle houses need painting every few years to stay weather-tight and may require new shingles or boards from time to time. Even homes with aluminum or vinyl siding have portions that require some painting or, at the very least, washing. (Aluminum or vinyl siding tends to be the cheapest alternative in the long run. These sidings require little maintenance beyond the occasional cleaning, experts say.)

Repairing or patching the roof can be an ongoing expense. A particularly severe winter or windstorm can rip shingles right off the roof. If you live in the house long enough, you will one day have to replace the roof, though a new roof should last 20 years and usually comes with a warranty.

It's a good idea to use a professional home inspector or structural engineer to give any home the once-over before you buy. If you're purchasing an older home, an inspection is almost a "must," even if you're buying in "as is" condition. A good inspector (and real estate agent) should point out the age of the home and remind you that you might have to replace the roof or other appliances and mechanical systems within the next few years.

Maintaining the interior of a home can also be expensive. Older windows may need recaulking or a new sash. You may want to purchase storm windows to improve energy efficiency. Bathroom tiles may need regrouting. If your wood floors have a polyurethane finish, you'll need to buff them down and reapply that finish every two to three years, or risk damaging the floor. Hardwood floors with a wax finish should be cleaned and buffed every two to three years as well.

Older homes may need rewiring, a new hot water heater, or a new furnace right away. Depending on how long you plan to live in the house, odds are you'll replace most of the major mechanical systems. Even newer mechanicals require yearly upkeep, however; filters need to be changed and systems need to be cleaned. Although basements and attics might seem like ideal storage facilities, they require maintenance as well. Basement walls may require treatment for mold and cracks. Attics may need extra insulation. Other issues may arise as the house—especially a brand-new home—settles.

Being a good neighbor means being there in case of an emergency, and helping out if you can. But it also means keeping your home looking good so that the neighborhood continues to improve and appreciate in value. Maintenance and landscaping are the essence of that unspoken agreement you make when you buy into a neighborhood. If it's part of the bargain you aren't willing to keep, perhaps you should rethink your homeownership plans, or purchase a different type of home that doesn't require as much work.

WHAT ARE ASSESSMENTS? DO ALL TOWN HOUSES, CONDOS, AND CO-OPS HAVE THEM?

Assessments are fees that you, the owner, pay for the upkeep of property held jointly with other owners. You'll have to pay some sort of monthly or annual assessment if you choose to buy a condo, co-op, or town house. If your single-family home is located in a particular type of subdivision that has common property (like a private playground, security gate, clubhouse, etc.), a homeowners' association may assess you for a share of the maintenance of that common property.

Regardless of the type of property, your proportionate share of the upkeep of the property should be assessed based on your percentage of ownership. If you own 1 percent of the property, then you will pay 1 percent of the upkeep.

Many different areas and amenities may be part of the common area, including a parking garage or parking spaces, recreational amenities (clubhouse, health club or workout facilities, tennis courts, private lake or lagoon), land, the roof and exterior walls of condos, town houses, and co-ops, lobby, security, doormen, and so on. Part of the upkeep of these common areas includes liability insurance coverage as well.

Paying Your Assessment

How do you pay an assessment? Assessments are usually billed monthly by the homeowners' association. Some single-family homeowners' associations bill on a yearly basis; some bill twice a year. Whenever it comes, the bill is expected to be paid promptly, and if it is not, the association is entitled to bill you for late fees and even to take you to court to force you to sell your home to pay for late assessments.

If you're thinking about buying a town house, condo, co-op, or single-family house that would require payment of an assessment, be aware that the lender will consider the assessment to be another fixed expense (like paying down a car loan or credit card balance) and will include the assessment in the debt-to-income ratio. That means you will have less money to spend to buy a home.

For example, if you have $1,000 per month to spend on housing expenses and the monthly assessment of the condo you've had your eye on is $200, you really only have $800 to spend on your housing expenses.

Another thing: Assessments usually go up. Every condo, co-op, or town house association has a board of directors that oversees the costs, repairs, and maintenance done to the property. They have the power to impose "special assessments" to pay for large-scale capital improvements, including a new roof, new deck, new elevators, new windows, tuck-pointing, and a hundred other things.

Protect Yourself: Read

How can you protect yourself? Before you close on a condo, co-op, or town house, request copies of the last two to three years of budgets and board minutes to familiarize yourself with ongoing issues of maintenance, problems, and long-range planning. Also request a copy of the current year's budget and next year's project budget (if available). Reading board minutes can bore you to tears, or it can be like a juicy gossip rag. You won't know the people, but if you move in, they'll be your neighbors.

Reading the board minutes will quickly get you up to speed on any major capital improvements the board may be planning. In that case, you may have an advantage when negotiating the price of the home. If you read the minutes and find out that the board is planning to levy a three-year special assessment to cover the cost of windows that were replaced five years earlier, you should try to get your seller to lower his or her price to at least recoup some of that cost. (After all, the seller enjoyed the use of those windows for five years.)

20/20 hindsight

When you ask for a copy of the board minutes, also request a copy of the rules and regulations of the building. Many properties have pet restrictions, which you'll want to know before making your offer.

5

Putting Together the Deal

HOW DO I DECIDE WHAT TO OFFER FOR THE HOME?

QUESTION 31

If you've been prequalified or preapproved by a mortgage lender, or you've figured it out for yourself how much new debt you can manage, you already know your uppermost financial limit. That's the number you can't go beyond, unless interest rates change, or you earn more, win the lottery, or inherit a bundle.

However, what you can afford to spend has nothing to do with how much a seller is asking for his or her house. The seller wants the most money possible. You want to pay the least amount of money. The rest is subject to negotiation.

But we're getting ahead of ourselves. It's important to determine how much a house is worth *before* you make an offer. (This would seem obvious, but plenty of buyers get caught up in the heat of the moment—especially in a hot seller's market—and just offer up a number.)

The answer to the question of worth lies with your broker or agent. He or she has access to the sales data that can tell you what homes in the neighborhood are selling for, and how long they took to sell. Because of the differences in the fiduciary responsibilities between a buyer broker and a seller broker, however, you'll have to proceed on a slightly different course to get this information and put it to use.

If you're using a buyer broker, and I'm assuming he or she is at least competent, if not fabulous, it should be relatively easy to ask the buyer broker for "comps" (comparable properties that have recently sold in your neighborhood). Once you have the comps, you and your buyer

137

broker can begin an ongoing discussion about what the comps mean and how they apply to various homes in which you're interested.

If you're working with a seller broker, he or she is required by law in most states to provide you with everything you need to make an informed decision on how much to offer. However, you may have to specifically request that the seller broker provide you with recent sale comps, as well as the listing prices for similar homes in the neighborhood. You may also request information on the number of days a particular home has been on the market.

What Are Comps?

Comps are homes that have recently been sold and are similar in size, location, and amenities to the home on which you want to bid. Comps give you an idea of what other sellers have been paid for their homes. Finding out the listing prices is also important, because comparing the list prices with the sale prices tells you exactly what percentage of their sales price sellers are getting. (Study after study has found that homes sell, *on average*, for 6 percent below list price. But that assumes the home is not overpriced and that the market is well balanced, with an even number of buyers and sellers. If a home is well priced, it is listed at or just a bit above what comparable homes in the neighborhood have sold for. In the hot seller's market we saw during the latter half of the 1990s, many sellers received list price—or more—for their homes.)

Here's How It Works

Let's say House A was listed at $400,000 and sold for $384,000 (Seller A received 96 percent of the list price); House B was also priced at $400,000 and sold for $380,000 (Seller B received 95 percent of the list price). Home A and Home B are nearly identical homes in more or less the same good physical condition. Seller C, however, put a few extras into House C, such as a wood-burning fireplace and upgraded carpet. The home was priced at $450,000, and the seller received $422,500 (Seller C received 95 percent of the list price).

House D comes on the market priced at $450,000. You pay a visit to House D and discover it is in the same condition as Houses A and B. Based on the sales prices of other homes in the subdivision, how much would you pay for the house? Sellers A, B, and C received around 95 percent of their list prices, but their homes were competitively priced. Seller D's home is not competitively priced.

If you know the most you want to offer Seller D for the house is $380,000 (95 percent of $400,000, which is amount at which the house should be priced), you have to make a decision about the lower amount that you want to offer initially.

Unless you're in a heated situation where several parties are bidding on the same house you want (see Question 41, "What Do I Do in a Multiple-Bid Situation?"), or if you're in a tight seller's market (sellers are getting almost exactly what they want for their properties, in a very short amount of time), *never offer the list price for a home.* Instead, offer between 5 and 10 percent *below* the maximum price you want to pay for the home. If you've decided you're not going to pay any more than $380,000 for Seller D's home, then you may want to consider an initial offer of $375,000. That's the start of negotiation.

Of course, the trick is to know what you want to pay for a property *before* you make your first offer. And instead of emotion, that decision should be based on logic and reasoning. If you can't get a clear idea of how much to offer based on the comps your broker has provided to you, then ask him or her for another set of comps. And if your search goes on for more than three months, you'll need another set, as the market continually changes.

If you're working with a buyer broker, feel free to ask what he or she would pay for the house. Buyer brokers, because they owe their fiduciary loyalty to you, the buyer, should be forthcoming with how much they think a property is worth. If your seller broker is less forthcoming, ask how much he or she would allow his or her children to pay for the home. Remember that the seller broker has a fiduciary responsibility to the seller. According to a strict interpretation of the law, the seller broker can't do anything but suggest you pay the list price.

If you have a dual agent (representing both sides), a nonagent, or a transactional agent working with you, the effect is the same as working with a seller broker. Ask for the information you need and an explanation for any data you don't understand. Finally, if you feel lost and can't get what you need from your transactional agent, dual agent, or nonagent, go to the managing broker of the firm and ask to have a buyer broker assigned to work with you.

Making an Offer for New Construction

Making an offer for a new home that has yet to be built is in some ways more complex than making an offer for an existing house. At least with the existing home, all of the appliances, tile, wall coverings, window treatments, and siding are already there. With new construction, often you'll be buying from blueprints, or perhaps after seeing a model home built and decorated for your viewing pleasure.

Part of the offer and negotiation process includes the myriad of choices—everything from what kind of tiles and carpet you want, to whether you want to upgrade to the full basement with the extra tall ceiling and a concrete floor. Do you want to add on a fourth bedroom upstairs instead of the double-high entryway (I think maximizing your interior space is always a savvy choice)? Do you want the three-car garage with the option in the future of making one of the bays into an office?

As a standard rule, developers rarely negotiate down on price, unless they're stuck with a final unit or two that won't sell for whatever reason. More typically, the lowest prices will be offered when the development first opens for business. As sales activity heats up, the price of homes in subsequent phases (you'll often hear about Phase I, Phase II, and Phase III of a development) will rise.

Developers make a *lot* of money on options and upgrades. It's far too easy to walk into a $300,000, four-bedroom, two-and-a-half-bath house and then spend another $100,000 (yes, you read that right) on options and upgrades the salesperson convinces you are must-haves. New studies show that the average new construction home buyer will spend more than 10 percent of the purchase price on options and upgrades. On a $300,000 house, that's more than $30,000 in upgrades. Although it's generally easier and cheaper to add these things in the beginning, to ensure maximum leverage in your negotiation process, visit a bunch of competing subdivisions and price out the various packages other developers give to home buyers. (If this process sounds a lot like buying a new car, you're getting the hang of it. The big difference is that new cars depreciate in value, and you're hoping that your new home will appreciate.)

Being the first to buy into a new subdivision often means you get the best price and perhaps the best upgrade package on the options that are available. The risk is that the subdivision will fail to sell out, the developer will go belly-up, and the investors will take over and offer the remaining properties at a price far below what you paid. If you're buying the last unit, the developer may offer you a deal on the price or upgrades simply because he wants to sell out the development and move on.

When you make your offer, you can try to negotiate the developer down on price. But you'll probably have better luck asking for more options and upgrades. For example, you might pay full price but receive upgrades on appliances, wiring, carpet, and tile choices. If you're one of the first to buy into a condo development and the parking is being sold separately, you may be able to get the developer to throw in the space for nothing, or to give you two spaces at a discount.

Janet's Story

When Janet was in her early 30s, she became editor of a real estate section of a major metropolitan newspaper. After editing the section's stories for a while, she decided she should stop paying rent and instead purchase a home.

She talked to all of the real estate writers to find out which developer had the best reputation and settled on a converted school that was being turned into condominiums. She was one of the first people to buy into the development, and armed with her information from her writers, she negotiated all kinds of extras and upgrades when she purchased the unit.

Her big coup, however, was getting the developer to throw in her parking space for free. Two weeks later, the developer started charging $15,000 for the spot. Four years later, Janet got married and sold her unit—for a big profit!

HOW DO I MAKE AN OFFER?

An offer includes three basic pieces: (1) the address or description of the property; (2) *consideration*, or the price you are prepared to pay; and (3) the date on which the closing will take place.

A valid offer can be written on anything, including a paper napkin, and can read as follows: "I, Ilyce R. Glink, offer to buy 1 Willow Lane for $125,500, to close on July 13, 2001."

Although property has been bought and sold this way for centuries, making an offer today is usually a bit more complex. In some states, the broker customarily uses a "Contract to Purchase" form when making an offer. In other states, the broker has a preprinted "Offer for Purchase" form. Whichever form is used, you will generally sit with the broker and discuss all sorts of issues such as:

1. Contingencies (see Questions 35 to 38);
2. Earnest money, also known as your *good faith deposit* (Question 34).
3. Any requests you may have for personal property (such as appliances, lamps, attached bookcases, and so on).

After you fill in and sign the form, your broker will then present the offer to the seller and his or her broker. If you are buying a FSBO, you will have to make the presentation yourself. If you don't understand the contract and its implications, *don't sign it.* Consult a real estate attorney first.

first time buyer tip

As the Internet facilitates the sale of homes, more sellers may try to sell without a broker's help and save the 5 to 7 percent commission. If 15 to 20 percent of homes are sold today without a broker's assistance, in 10 years perhaps 20 to 30 percent (or more—although agents don't like to hear you say it) of homes could be sold by owner. The savvy home buyer needs to know how to make a quality offer that any seller, represented or not, will be happy to accept, and how to sound good while presenting an offer. Essentially, in a presentation, you go over the offer for purchase with the seller, point by point, discussing things like price, closing date, date of possession, and any contingencies. As long as you're calm and professional, and consult with a real estate attorney ahead of time, you'll do just fine if you end up presenting without the assistance of a broker.

Typically, buyers represented by brokers do not attend the offer presentation. But sometimes they wait nearby.

Leo and Genna's Story

Leo and Genna looked at 50 homes before they found the one they wanted to buy. It was a nice-looking three-bedroom, two-and-a-half-bath house with a big living room, dining room, and sunroom facing a small porch and backyard.

Because there was so much interest in the property, Leo and Genna decided right on the spot (at the first showing) to make an offer. They sat at the kitchen table with their broker and drew up the offer, then waited while the broker went upstairs to present the offer to the sellers.

Although this was their first purchase, Leo and Genna took the time to thoroughly investigate the neighborhood and market before looking at homes. These savvy first-time buyers knew almost immediately how much they were going to offer for the house. They had seen many similar homes in the neighborhood and knew the range of selling prices over the previous six months. That knowledge enabled them to act fast when the time was right.

The Pressure Cooker

Sometimes, getting what you want hinges on how quickly you're able to act under pressure. Even at its best, making an offer can feel like a pressure cooker. Don't allow yourself to be sucked in to a point where you're no longer able to rationally discuss the offer and its implications. If you're finding yourself dragged along by the current, perhaps against your will, take a time-out. Remember, there is more than one right house for you.

If you're the typical homeowner, you're going to move between five and seven times in your life. There will always be another house. If you fall prey to the notion that this home is the only one for you, you may offer too much for it, thereby making it an imperfect choice.

Making an offer for a newly constructed home often means sitting down with the developer's agent and your agent (if you have one) and working out the price plus the upgrades and options to be included in the price. If the developer is mobbed with offers, you may have to make a reservation or be wait-listed for a home, and you may not find out until later whether you are actually going to be able to purchase it.

new construction tip

WHAT GOES INTO THE ACTUAL OFFER TO PURCHASE OR CONTRACT TO PURCHASE?

QUESTION 33

An *offer to purchase* is usually a much simpler document than a *contract to purchase*. Why? Because the contract to purchase must get much more specific about the property description, fixtures, exclusions, and all the necessary legal language for property transfer, rights to sue for specific performance (if the buyer or seller backs out of the contract on a whim), damages, brokers' fees, and so on.

Every city and state will have its own real estate or Realtor (member of the National Association of Realtors) association that provides standard form contracts for the purchase and sale of real estate. You should also be able to get the contracts you need from your real estate attorney, if you are buying a house without an agent. In a pinch, preprinted forms are available at local stationery stores, although you will need to consult with an attorney to find out if these preprinted forms favor the seller or the buyer in the transaction (rarely are they neutral). *Although the contracts are similar, real estate laws vary from state to state.*

Remember that contracts tend to be written from the seller's perspective. (Originally all brokers were seller brokers and that bias tends to remain.) As a buyer you should look over the forms carefully and probably will want to hire a real estate lawyer to help you sort them out.

If you're purchasing new construction from a developer or builder, you'll probably use the developer's contract, which will likely be written to favor the developer. Some developers will allow attorneys to modify the contract to make it more evenhanded. *Do not attempt to modify the contract yourself. Engage a real estate attorney to assist you, especially if you are not working with an agent.*

Offer to Purchase

Let's look at an offer to purchase real estate contract, which starts out like a letter. It is addressed:

To: _____

    seller(s) _____

There is a place for the date of the offer. Then:

The property herein referred to is identified as follows: _____
(Fill in the address of the property.)

I hereby offer to buy said property, which has been offered to me by _____ (Fill in name of the seller broker), as your broker, under the following terms and conditions:

The contract now allows you to check off whether you will pay for the property by check or cash. Next comes how much you will pay for the property, and in what stages:

$_____ is paid herewith as a deposit to bind this offer.

$_____ is to be paid as an additional deposit upon the execution of the purchase and sale agreement provided for below.

$_____ is to be paid at the time of delivery of the Deed in cash, or by certified, cashier's, treasurer's or bank check.

Next comes a statement that tells the seller that the offer is only good until a certain time on a certain date. The seller has until then to accept the offer or it becomes invalid. If the seller counteroffers, further negotiation would take place.

When an offer is acceptable, the seller is notified that the offer is contingent upon the execution of the standard purchase and sale agreement.

Next comes the closing date:

A good and sufficient Deed, conveying a good and clear record and marketable title shall be delivered at 12:00 Noon on _____, 2005, at the appropriate Registry of Deeds, unless some other time and place are mutually agreed upon in writing.

After another paragraph, in which the buyer promises to forfeit the deposit if he or she does not fulfill his or her obligations, and one that says "time is of the essence," there is a space to write in any additional terms and conditions, or to attach any riders.

Finally, the document is signed by the buyers, and the receipt for the deposit at the bottom of the page is filled out.

The standard purchase and sale agreement form can be two or three times as long. (See Appendix IV for a complete form.)

Real estate attorneys say that most buyers never read the contract. *But you should.* Although each contract will vary by state or even city, most of the main issues and points will be similar.

The following list walks you through the contract, point by point:

1. Parties. Fill in the name of the seller and buyer.

2. Description. Give the address, title reference, and description of the property. For example: "The land with the buildings thereon, numbered 391 Waverley Avenue, Newton, Massachusetts, Middlesex County, being shown as Lot B on a 'Plan of Land in Newton belonging to Katherine F. Cameron,' E. S. Smithe, Surveyor, dated May 1914, recorded with Middlesex South Registry Deeds Book 4741 and more particularly described in deed to Seller dated May 27, 1977, recorded at Middlesex South Registry Deeds in Book 13200, Page 450."

3. Buildings, Structures, Improvements, Fixtures. This is a general list of the buildings, structures, and improvements that are included with the sale. You should delete, exclude, or add anything appropriate. In particular, list items that the sellers could take with them but should be part of the deal: the dishwasher, washer, dryer, and refrigerator. The disposition of some of these items will be decided based on local custom. For example, in downtown Chicago, all appliances stay with the house. In the northern and western suburbs, refrigerators, washers, and dryers generally go with the sellers to their new home. (Your agent can fill you in on the local custom if you're not aware of it.)

4. Title Deed. Specifically note any restrictions, easements (rights other people may have to use your property or otherwise restrict your use of the property), rights, or obligations that you are willing to accept on your title and delete those that you are not. Your attorney will help you with this.

5. Plans. The plans should have already been approved and recorded in advance by the seller, and they should comply with all laws, allowing a clear transfer to the buyer.

6. Registered Title. Some states have a registration system for title.

7. Purchase Price. Fill in the amount and write out the amount to be paid as a deposit, the amount of the escrow (that is, money held in trust by a third party) "upon execution of this agreement," and the remainder at closing.

8. Time for Performance: Delivery of Deed. State the time, date, and place for closing.

9. Possession and Conditions of Premises. A statement that says the buyer is to receive full possession, free of tenants and occupants, at closing; that the property does not violate any building or zoning laws; and that the buyer shall be entitled to inspect the premises before closing.

10. Extension to Perfect Title or Make Premises Conform. A provision that gives the seller 30 days to correct any problems with the property's title.

11. Failure to Perfect Title or Make Premises Conform. A statement that says, should the seller fail to deliver good title, the buyer's money will be refunded.

12. Buyer's Election to Accept Title. If something impairs the property's title, such as a mechanic's or tax lien, the buyer can elect to take the property as is, subject to the lien, and deduct the lien amount from the purchase price. Should a disaster occur, such as a fire, the buyer can elect to take the home as is and be compensated from the insurance proceeds, or take a reduction in the price of the home to cover the damage.

13. Acceptance of Deed. Acceptance of the deed at closing means that the seller has fulfilled all duties and obligations under the contract.

14. Use of Money to Clear Title. The seller may leave behind money at closing to pay off any liens against the property.

15. Insurance. The seller promises to maintain a certain amount of insurance. The amount is usually negotiated but should be sufficient to cover the cost of restoring the property after a fire or other disaster.

16. Adjustments. A prorated list of expenses (like water or assessments) and taxes for the portion of the month or year the seller owned the house until closing. The buyer is credited at closing for these expenses.

17. Adjustment of Unassessed and Abated Taxes. Taxes that have not yet been assessed for the year are usually prorated based on the prior year's taxes according to a local formula.

18. Broker's Fee. Spells out who gets the commission and how much.

19. Broker's Warranty. Names the brokers and verifies that they are licensed.

20. Deposit. The escrow agreement and a statement of who will receive the interest on the account.

21. Buyer's Default and Damages. If the buyer fails to buy the property, the seller may keep the earnest money or sue the buyer for damages.

22. Release by Husband or Wife. The spouse agrees to release any claim. The release is omitted if the seller is divorced or widowed.

23. Broker as Party. A statement that the brokers are a part of the contract.

24. Liability of Trustee, Shareholder, Beneficiary. Included if one of the parties is represented by a trustee; otherwise, omitted.

25. Warranties and Representations. The promises the seller makes to the buyer regarding the conditions of the property.

26. Mortgage Contingency Clause. A standard clause on some contracts; otherwise, added as a rider. (See Question 36.)

27. Construction of Agreement. Legal language that sets up the contract as a contract.

28. Lead Paint Law. Recently enacted federal rules require sellers who live in properties built before 1978 to disclose that a home may have lead. Some states have gone further. In Massachusetts, if a child under the age of six resides in any residential premises where paint, plaster, or other material contains dangerous levels of lead, the owner must remove or cover the paint to make it safe for children.

29. Smoke Detectors and Other Certifications. Where required (e.g., in Massachusetts), the seller agrees to provide a certificate from the local fire department stating the property is equipped with smoke detectors. In Illinois, a seller must provide a certificate saying the water bill has been paid.

30. Additional Provisions. The place for any additional riders.

For complete copies of a contract to purchase, see Appendix IV.

Condominium Contracts

The difference between purchasing a condo and purchasing a single-family home is slight. When you purchase a condo, you are buying real estate plus an interest in the common areas managed by the homeowners' association.

Sometimes real estate sales contracts for condominiums contain special provisions that are not applicable to single-family houses. For example, some condo boards have the right of first refusal when a condo unit is sold. This allows the board to purchase the unit if it decides that the purchase is in the best interest of the condo building. In a sales contract, the seller will agree to procure the release or waiver of any option or right of first refusal.

Co-op Contracts

When you purchase a co-op, you're not really purchasing real estate. You purchase personal property in the form of shares in the corporation that owns the building. You become a tenant and pay "rent" (a monthly maintenance assessment fee) for the right to live there. Co-op contracts are entirely different from condo or single-family contracts.

WHAT IS THE EARNEST MONEY? WHO HOLDS IT? WHEN DO I GET IT BACK?

The *earnest money*, also known in some places as a *good faith deposit*, is an amount of cash that the buyer puts up to show he or she is serious about purchasing the property. The money represents the buyer's commitment to buy and acts as an unofficial option on the property. After receiving an earnest money check, the seller will usually stop showing the property and wait to see if the buyer can get a mortgage.

Earnest money is important to the transaction because it shows the seller that the buyer is operating in good faith (hence the name, "earnest"). The bigger the deposit, the more the seller is reassured that "This buyer is serious." It also ties the buyer to the property and keeps him or her from looking for additional properties.

How Much Good Faith Do I Have to Show?

Usually, home buyers offer 5 to 10 percent of the sales price of the house in cash as the earnest money. The money is typically held by the seller's broker, and is an amount large enough that almost any buyer will think twice about walking away from the house on a whim.

If you don't have 10 percent in cash, then put down 5 percent. Sometimes a buyer will attach a $1,000 check to the offer to purchase to show initial good faith. The rest of the deposit, or earnest money, is due when the contract is signed by both parties, or shortly thereafter.

Who Holds the Earnest Money?

The money typically goes into an escrow account held by the seller broker, but this is largely a matter of local custom or it can be negotiated. The buyer usually is credited for the interest earned on his or her money.

When Do I Get the Earnest Money Back?

If the sale goes through, the earnest money, plus interest, is often used as part of the cash down payment given to the seller. If the sale does not go through because of a reason covered by a contingency in the contract (if, e.g., the buyer could not get a mortgage), the seller should sign a release of escrow and refund the earnest money to the buyer. The earnest money should also be refunded to the buyer if the sale does not go through because of a problem on the seller's side. If, however, the buyer backs out of the deal for no reason at all, or for a reason that is not covered by a contingency, return of the earnest money may be subject to negotiation.

What If the Seller Won't Give Back the Earnest Money?

Before a buyer can get back earnest money, the seller needs to sign a *release of escrow*. If the buyer and seller disagree over who is entitled to the earnest money, and the attorneys can't resolve the issue, the broker has two options: (1) to hold the money until the disagreement is resolved or (2) in some states, to turn over the funds to the state real estate commission or agency for mediation, or to local courts for litigation. Ask your buyer broker to explain your state law and local customs regarding this matter.

In the real world, brokers hate to be put in this position. Even though they legally can't release the funds until the seller and buyer have resolved their differences, they become the focal point for everyone's frustration at the situation. But if they turn over the funds to either party before a resolution is reached, they could lose their license.

If you can't resolve who is entitled to the good faith estimate, or the seller refuses to release the funds, you may have to sue to get your cash back. If this happens to you, consult with a real estate attorney for details on the legal options available to you.

WHEN I MAKE AN OFFER, WHAT CONTINGENCIES SHOULD I INCLUDE?

QUESTION
35

Ilyce and Sam's Story

When the first edition of this book was published in 1994, my publisher sent me on a book tour. Around the same time, we'd grown tired of our 1920s co-op overlooking Lake Michigan in Chicago and were looking to buy a house.

We looked for more than four years, trying to find the right home. And in that time, we saw perhaps 125 houses. (Who knows? It could have been a lot more.)

While I was traveling on my book tour, Sam continued house hunting. And homes were selling quite quickly at that time. During one trip, he found a couple of houses he liked very much. After we talked on the phone, and he described the home in detail, he made an offer.

He included the usual cadre of contingencies, including an attorney approval rider, a financing contingency, and an inspection contingency. He also included an "Ilyce has to love it" contingency.

What this special contingency said was essentially this: When Ilyce comes back into town, she has to come and see the house. If she doesn't like it, we can back out of the deal.

Lucky thing, because as it turned out, I wasn't wild about the house when I saw it. The sellers had accepted the contingency, and we did back out of the deal.

Although the market in the late 1990s and early 2000s was considerably hotter than in the mid-1990s, this kind of contingency is making a resurgence—through the Internet. Home buyers are now making offers for property through the Internet—sight unseen (except for 360-degree photos or a video of the property available online).

So the "We have to love it when we finally see it" contingency is becoming somewhat more popular. (I don't recommend making an offer sight unseen on *any* property, but if you're so inclined, I may have a bridge in Brooklyn you'd be interested in buying.)

Your Everyday, Garden Variety Contingencies

Let's start out with a definition: A *contingency* allows you to back out of a contract for a specific reason. Typically, three contingencies accompany a contract to purchase: (1) financing or mortgage; (2) inspection; and (3) attorney approval. Each of these is explained in Questions 36, 37, and 38.

Many other contingencies might appear in a contract for purchase, including:

- Sale of your prior residence (but not for first-time buyers)
- Admittance to certain clubs (e.g., if you are buying a home near a private golf course, you might make the purchase contingent on your acceptance to the club)
- Approval by the condo or co-op boards
- Pest inspection, asbestos, radon, lead, water (may be separate contingencies or lumped under inspection)
- Compliance with building codes
- Liking it in person, if you are bidding on a home sight unseen (except perhaps through the Internet)

You can attach almost any contingency you like to your offer to purchase, but remember, having odd contingencies, in addition to the mortgage, inspection, and attorney approval, could give the seller grounds for refusing your contract.

WHAT IS A MORTGAGE OR FINANCING CONTINGENCY?

A mortgage or financing contingency gives you a way to back out of the contract to purchase if you cannot get a lender to give you a mortgage commitment.

The contingency will generally require you to be specific about the type of mortgage you are seeking as well as require you to seek mortgage approval within a specified period of time, generally 45 to 60

152

days. You must be reasonable about the mortgage's parameters, and usually you must agree to look for a mortgage at the current prevailing rate of interest.

The contingency is meant to protect you in case you can't find financing. Here is the mortgage contingency from the Greater Boston Real Estate Board. Remember, although this contingency form's wording may not be viable in your state, many stationery stores will carry contingency forms you can purchase.

FINANCING CONTINGENCY FOR MASSACHUSETTS

In order to help finance the acquisition of said premises, the BUYER shall apply for a conventional bank or other institutional mortgage loan of _____, payable in no less than _____ years at an interest rate not to exceed _____. If despite the BUYER's diligent efforts a commitment for such a loan cannot be obtained on or before _____, 20__, the BUYER may terminate this agreement by written notice to the SELLER(S) and/or the Broker(s), as agent for the SELLER, prior to the expiration of such time, whereupon any payments made under this agreement shall be forthwith refunded and all other obligations of the parties hereto shall end. In no event will the BUYER be deemed to have used diligent efforts to obtain such commitment unless the BUYER submits a complete mortgage loan application conforming to the foregoing provisions on or before _____, 20__.

(Provided courtesy of the Greater Boston Real Estate Board.)

The mortgage contingency should be included in the contract. If it is not, be sure to ask your broker or real estate attorney to make an addendum to the contract.

What do you do if you're in a really tight bidding war, with several other parties all looking for a way to differentiate their bids? If you've been preapproved for your loan, you'll get your financing as long as the house appraises out in value. The lender has committed to it in writing. In an extreme situation, you could change your financing contingency to read that purchase of the home is contingent only upon the house appraising out in value by the lender's appraiser. The risk is, of course, that the lender will back out of the deal for some reason. With a written commitment, the lender has to follow through, unless the company goes belly-up. This type of contingency may give you the edge you need to complete a winning bid. Before you do this, however, consult with your real estate attorney.

WHAT IS THE INSPECTION CONTINGENCY?

This contingency gives you the right to have a house inspector come and examine the property before you close on the purchase.

Again, the purpose of the contingency is to protect you from buying a home that may have serious hidden structural problems or material defects. When you add an inspection contingency to the contract, make sure it covers both the home and the property on which it sits. You might also want to have a separate contingency for each of the following:

- Radon
- Asbestos
- Lead
- Toxic substances
- Mold
- Water
- Pests, including termites, mice, rats, roaches, and so on

Although a recently passed federal law requires sellers of homes built before 1978 to disclose if they have lead in their homes, the sellers may not know. If the home is old, and you're planning to do any renovation work, you may uncover decades-old lead-based paint that could then get sanded into the air, creating a potentially danger-ous situation—especially for children. Inexpensive products are available in any hardware store to help test for lead (and mold). One of the easiest looks like a cigarette butt. Basically you swab it over a windowsill, next to a pipe, or anywhere else you suspect lead. If the test swab turns red, lead is present. Like asbestos, lead is only dan-gerous if it is ingested. Babies can and do pick up tiny pieces of paint to stick in their mouths (my first son, Alex, didn't do it, but our sec-ond, Michael, couldn't resist). It's worth a few bucks to make sure you know what's lurking in the house you're about to purchase.

Generally, the inspection contingency will require you to have your inspection within 5 to 10 days after the seller accepts the offer. Other-wise, you may lose the right to withdraw from the contract. Keep this in mind when scheduling your various tests.

Here is a sample inspection contingency addendum. Remember, this contingency wording may not be viable in your state, but any stationery store will carry contingency forms you can purchase.

INSPECTION CONTINGENCY FOR MASSACHUSETTS

The BUYER may, at his own expense and on or before _____, 20__, have the property inspected by a person engaged in the business of conducting home inspections. If it is the opinion of such inspector that the property contains serious structural, mechanical, or other defects, then the BUYER shall have the option of revoking the Offer by written notice to the SELLER and/or the Broker, as your agent, prior to the expiration of such time, which notice shall be accompanied by a copy of the inspector's opinion and any related inspection report, whereupon all deposits made by the BUYER to you shall be forthwith refunded and this Offer shall become null and void and without further recourse to any party.

(Provided courtesy of the Greater Boston Real Estate Board.)

Sometimes buyers hope that the inspection will turn up small, fixable problems with the property so that they can get additional money from the seller at closing. The real purpose of the inspection contingency, however, is to protect you from purchasing property that may have serious, expensive, or unfixable problems. Like the mortgage contingency, the inspection contingency should be either written into the contract or attached to it as a rider or addendum.

When Don't I Need an Inspection?

I'm often asked whether *every* home buyer should have his or her future home inspected. The short answer is yes.

However, if you've been living in your home for the past five years as a renter, and you've been responsible for the entire upkeep of the property, then perhaps you know what problems exist with the plumbing, heating, and electrical systems (e.g., the back right burner on the stove doesn't work and the air-conditioning compressor is on its last legs).

But most home buyers haven't lived in the property they're going to purchase. They don't even know where the water shut-off valves are. If that's the case with you, you should definitely pay for a professional home inspection.

Some brokers say that if you're moving into a condo or co-op apartment building, you have relatively little risk of something big popping up. That's because with a condo you only own what's inside your unit plus a share of the common elements of the property. With a co-op, you don't even own that. You own shares in the corporation that owns your property, and you pay a monthly rental fee (the maintenance or assessment) for the unit that the shares represent.

In a condo or co-op, the only things for which you're responsible are interior electrical work, appliances, and plumbing fixtures (and sometimes not even those). Your financial liability, should something go wrong, is slight.

So why, you're probably thinking, should any condo or co-op buyer pay for a professional inspection? Because a good inspector will tour the common elements of the property—look at the building heating, electrical, and plumbing systems, and check out the roof, the foundation, the parking structure, and the windows.

When we moved into our co-op, the inspector found that some members of the building's board of directors had tapped in, illegally, to the electrical panel, dangerously overloading it. Our inspector was required to report it to the city, which fined the building (and made us less than popular). The building eventually corrected the problem, for which it had to assess the residents.

By having the inspection, you learn not only how your own property works, but also what problems may exist in a condo or co-op—problems you'll have to pay for during the time you live there.

WHAT IS THE ATTORNEY APPROVAL OR ATTORNEY RIDER?

Before you sign any contract or offer, *consult with someone who can advise you about the purchase and its legal consequences.* In some states, that's the real estate attorney's job. In others, the broker will advise you. **Be aware that real estate agents and brokers are not attorneys and are not supposed to give you legal advice.** If they give you legal advice about changing the contract, be aware that the advice may not be correct. If the advice they give you is incorrect, you may not be able to go back and sue them for giving you bad legal advice since they are not attorneys.

The attorney contingency or rider essentially gives your attorney the right to make changes to the contract, or to reject a contract that doesn't protect you.

If you are working with a seller broker and that broker is the person who is supposed to advise you of your legal rights under the contract, there may be a serious conflict of interest. If you have any qualms at all about being counseled by your real estate broker or sales agent, consult an attorney. Spending between $250 and $750 for an attorney is a small price to pay when you're making the biggest investment of your life (if your first home costs in excess of $750,000, the cost for an attorney may rise as well). When all the fees and costs are pinching your wallet, try to imagine how expensive and time-consuming it would be if something *really* went wrong.

Do not assume that, just because you have an attorney rider, your attorney can remove you from the deal if you suddenly discover you have made a mistake in the offer (usually, offering too high a price for the home). Although some attorneys do try to cover for their clients' mistakes by rejecting the contract, this is unprofessional. If you have any questions about the offer or contract, consult an attorney *before* making the offer or signing your name.

For more information about why attorneys are important, and how to hire a good one, see Questions 44 and 45.

In some states, the offer for purchase is worded in such a way that there is no need for an attorney approval rider. It would say, for example: "This offer to purchase is subject to a contract that is agreeable to both parties." If you aren't sure whether or not your offer is worded in that way, attach an attorney rider.

Here is a sample attorney approval contingency that is valid in the State of Illinois. Remember, this language may not be valid in your state, but your broker or a local stationery store should have a rider that will work for you:

ATTORNEY APPROVAL RIDER FOR STATE OF ILLINOIS

It is agreed by and between the parties hereto as follows: That their respective attorneys may approve of, make modifications, other than price and dates, mutually acceptable to the parties. Approval will not be unreasonably withheld, but, if within _____ days after the date of acceptance of the Contract, it becomes evident agreement cannot be reached by the parties hereto, and written notice thereof is given to either party within the time specified, then this Contract shall become null and void, and all monies paid by the Purchaser shall be refunded. In the absence of written notice within the time specified herein, this provision shall be deemed waived by all parties hereto, and this contract shall be in full force and effect.

(Provided courtesy of the Chicago Association of Realtors.)

6

Negotiating the Deal

HOW DOES THE NEGOTIATION PROCESS WORK?

Whether you're negotiating to buy or sell a home, the terms and conditions of a divorce settlement, or what salary, benefits, and bonus you'll accept with your new job, negotiation is about give-and-take.

David Falk, Michael Jordan's agent throughout his basketball career, says negotiations are most successful when everyone walks away happy. The person who holds the stronger hand usually gets to give less and take more, but in a successful negotiation, both sides end up compromising.

That's what you want when it comes to buying your home as well. You don't want the seller to take you for a ride, nor do you want to ride the seller, or he or she will begin to like you a lot less and the move will become a lot more difficult. Emotions run high in something as personal as selling a home. And when negotiations get tough, emotions become embittered arms-at-war.

Happy Homeowners

Unlike a judge's settlement, where both sides may end up profoundly unhappy with the result, a successful house negotiation can leave everyone feeling like winners—and that's the goal. As a buyer, you want the sellers to feel they are getting a fair price for their home. You want them to bask in the glow of having made a good deal so they will

QUESTION
39

159

be nice to you when you tromp through with the inspector, your spouse, your friends, your decorator, and your parents.

You want that niceness to extend through to the closing, so the sellers do not make you crazy with all kinds of nonsense at the end. You want them to like you so they will feel good about selling their home to someone who will love it as much as they have. (As we'll discuss later, the emotional component to homeownership is stronger than for just about any other type of financial investment.)

At the same time, you also want to feel as though you paid a fair price for the home. Nothing is worse than finding out the day after you've signed the contract that you overpaid for the house—except than fighting with the sellers over items you thought were included with the price, but that they intend to take (stealing, you may call it). The nastiness can leave a bad taste in your mouth. And in your attitude about your home.

Negotiating Fairly

How do you negotiate fairly? How do you end up with good feelings on all sides of the table? First, enlist your broker's (or attorney's, if you choose not to work with a broker) help in keeping everyone's emotions at bay. Brokers are good at this. It's probably one of the most important parts of their job. They must present your offer as something worthwhile, not insulting. You must rely on them to make you seem like a serious buyer.

Once you write up the offer with your broker, it's up to the broker to present the offer. This is the first step of the negotiation. The broker will present your offer to the sellers and, usually, the seller broker. This can take place in an office, but usually your broker will go to see the sellers in their home, where they are most comfortable. Then, perhaps over a cup of coffee, your broker will tell the sellers exactly how much you are willing to pay for their home, the conditions under which you'll purchase the home, and when.

Sometimes it doesn't happen like this. Once in a while, especially if the sellers are out of town, or if they work odd hours, an offer will be communicated over the telephone or by fax. But usually it is done in person. After all—as my mother, Susanne, the agent, likes to say—this is a very personal business. When your broker leaves, the sellers and their broker will discuss the offer.

Unless a full-price offer is offered or the sellers are quite desperate, they will almost never take your first offer. Everyone understands that the first offer is a little bit (or quite a lot) below what you expect to pay for the property. The key to a successful negotiation is to remember that it's a psychological game.

In a bidding-war situation, you may get only one opportunity to make an offer. The best-bid offer can be frightening to construct. You want to get the property, but you don't want to overpay for it. In that case, you'll have to rely on your broker to steer you through, based on his or her years of knowledge and experience in home sales in the neighborhood. See Question 41 for more ideas on how to win in a multiple-bid situation.

Offer and Counteroffer

Here's how making an offer works. Let's say the home is priced at $100,000. You think that's close, but still a slightly higher price than you think is fair. You offer $90,000, or 10 percent less than the asking price. The sellers now assume you'll be willing to compromise somewhere in the middle, say, $94,000 to $96,000. The sellers then make a calculated guess: Are you willing to go up to $96,000? Or will you only go up to $95,000? Or will you stop at $94,000? If the sellers want to cut to the chase, they may instruct their broker to present a "split the difference" counteroffer. If accepted, you'd pay $95,000 for the property.

Sometimes negotiations get tough. If the sellers think the $100,000 price is fair and don't want to go much lower, they may come back in much lower increments—say, $1,000. Then you must decide whether to match those increments or make a final offer. Making the last offer is like saying "I call" in a card game. The sellers might come down $2,500 and say that $97,500 is a final offer, take it or leave it. Or you might put in a take-it-or-leave-it offer of $95,000 and put the ball in the sellers' court. If you turn the negotiation into a power struggle, it could quickly turn nasty. Keeping things on a more even pace is a better, if not downright friendly, way to keep the negotiations moving ahead step by step.

That doesn't mean you shouldn't play up your strengths. If you can't afford to pay more than $95,000, have your broker tell the sellers that you are making your very best offer and while you can't be more flexible on the price, you really love the house and would be more flexible on the closing date. You're never going to know what the sellers' hot points are. They may be much more concerned about the closing date than the extra $5,000. They may also be more interested in turning their home over to people who really love it. That's where you can use a seller's emotional attachment to his or her home to your great advantage.

The Low-Ball Bid

If you decide you love a home that's either too expensive or way over your budget, you have a choice: You can walk away and find somewhere else to live, or you can make a low-ball offer.

Although there is no one set definition of a low-ball offer, several things can be said to describe one. First, it is usually more than 10 percent below the asking price of the home; second, sellers usually find them insulting, which means the seller broker must plead with them to reconsider and make a counteroffer; third, it gives a decidedly negative cast to the negotiation process.

Sometimes a low-ball offer works; other times, it doesn't. A lot depends on the broker's presentation and the desperation of the seller. It also depends on whether you're in a buyer's market or seller's market. If you're in a hot seller's market, where there are too many buyers for the homes that are available for sale, expect to pay close to, at, or in excess of the list price for the home. A low-ball bid in an evenly paced market might be considered highly insulting in a hot market. In fact, many sellers wouldn't even respond to such a bid, even though you might be perfectly willing to raise your initial offer.

For example, if you decide to offer $80,000 for a home priced at $100,000 and enclose with your offer comps of other like homes in the neighborhood that recently sold for $75,000, the seller may consider your offer. But if you offer $50,000 for a house that's well priced at $100,000, few sellers would even dignify the offer with a response. As the buyer, you have the right to make whatever offer you want, and your broker must present that offer to the seller. But that doesn't mean you won't tick off the seller.

The Bidding War

A bidding war occurs when more than one buyer is interested in purchasing the same home. In the late 1990s, the market all over the United States was so hot that bidding wars erupted over properties that sellers couldn't sell even a year or two earlier.

Usually the seller broker will ask for bids from the interested parties. The broker will then present the bids to the seller, who will decide which offer to respond to. Often you'll find out there is another interested party and your broker will encourage you to make your very best bid; that is, no negotiation. If you want to offer $95,000, then that's what you put in the bid. If you think the other party is going to offer $95,000, and you really want the house, offer a little more.

The key problem with the negotiation step in the home-buying process is that it's extremely pressured. Your broker will tell you to stay close to the telephone so that you won't miss "The Call." You'll be on pins and needles, wondering if your bid is going to be accepted or rejected. Try not to get so worked up about your bid that you can't concentrate on anything else. Take a walk. See a movie. Get your mind off of it. Putting some space between you and your offer, not to mention the whole negotiation process, will help you gain some much-needed perspective.

Marla and David's Story

Marla and David were certain that they'd never be able to buy a home. They had plenty of cash to make a significant down payment and extra funds for closing costs and fees and the cash reserves lenders require. They had excellent credit and had even been approved for a mortgage.

What was killing them was the heat of the market.

Every time they went to make an offer on a house, it sold before they could even see it. If they were lucky enough to get their bid considered, it was one of several bids in a hotly contested bidding war.

After losing six houses in bidding wars, plus another half dozen homes they couldn't even bid for, Marla and David sat down for a long talk. They discussed their strategy for finding and bidding on houses, as well as their broker's approach.

They decided to become much more aggressive. They told their agent that she had to be much more aggressive in finding properties for them earlier, almost anticipating the market. And they decided to be much more aggressive in the type of offer they presented.

They got the next house they bid on.

Negotiation Survival Strategies

Marla and David used some of the following ideas when putting together their final, winning bid. Although some sellers and their agents may find some of these strategies to be too aggressive—or offensive or even unethical—they may help you capture the home of your dreams. Use them sparingly, and only when you're facing a relentless seller's market.

Aggressive Negotiation Strategies

1. Don't be afraid to initially offer the list—or even above the list—price. Yes, you're telling the sellers you'll pay at least that much for their home. And you may even go up from there. But nothing gets a seller's attention like an offer that contains the number he or she was hoping to see.

2. Remove as many contingencies as you can. The first contingency to go should be your financing contingency—*if* you've been approved (and have received the lender's commitment in writing) and *if* you're sure that the house is going to appraise out and that the lender won't go out of business before you close. In an aggressive situation, some brokers advise their clients that being preapproved is the same as being an all-cash buyer. The next contingency to go should be the inspection contingency. Unless you're worried about a structural element like the foundation or roof, most flaws can be fixed later. Finally, if you have to, you can let go of the attorney approval rider. Although your attorney (if you're in a state that uses attorneys) can still negotiate your contract language for you, he or she can't yank you out of a deal simply because the contract doesn't protect you. A tough situation calls for tough measures.

3. Make an open-ended offer. If the seller agent calls around for a "best bid," make an offer that really counts. Some extra-aggressive folks have won houses in tough bidding wars by offering to pay $1,000, $5,000, or a specific percentage more than the highest bid. For example, instead of listing a price, your offer might read: "The buyer agrees to pay 2 percent more than the highest bid."

4. Offer to let the seller choose the closing time. If you line up your ducks ahead of time, you may be able to close within a week or two, rather than in two to three months. By letting the seller choose the closing time that suits him or her best, you're throwing a big bone to the wolves.

5. Create several offer packages and allow your broker to pick the one that's going to get the job done. In a multiple-bid presentation, the buyer brokers will often present one after another, allowing each broker to hear the others' bids. Although it's not quite on the up and up ethically, some brokers have their buyers create multiple offers, which they keep in separate envelopes in their brief-cases. Then they angle to be the last to make their presentation. After hearing the other bids, they simply pull out of their briefcase the one that'll take the cake.

Real estate markets can change on a dime. A hot buyer's market or hot seller's market rarely will last for years, although as I write this, we're in our ninth year of the hottest seller's market ever (fueled by the lowest interest rates in 46 years), which came on top of about a six-year buyer's market in the west and northeast portions of the country. The bottom line is: Markets do change, and real estate has cyclical highs and lows. If you are overly aggressive, you risk purchasing property at the all-time high price (especially if you're only going to hold it for a short period of time), and then watching your home lose half of its value overnight (as happened in Boston, New York, and Southern California in the late 1980s). Consider stepping aside for a few months and waiting until the heat subsides. If it doesn't, you should at least be able to look at the market unemotionally, and with a more seasoned eye.

20/20 hindsight

When you're immersed in the process of looking for a home to buy, and you've been disappointed time and time again, it's easy to start feeling as though you'll never find the right house—or even if you find it, you'll never be able to buy it. The truth is, plenty of houses come on the market every day. If you don't get a particular house, another will come along that will seem even more wonderful and perfect than the house you lost. *There will always be another house.*

Negotiating into the Future

It's hard to imagine a negotiation for anything—be it an art auction, real estate, or even a lawsuit—that wouldn't take place in person, or at least over the telephone. But that's what appears to be happening.

The success of eBay (www.ebay.com), an Internet-based auction site for just about anything from old stuffed animals and trading cards to furniture, has led to an explosion of online negotiation. Everyone is trying to help everyone buy things electronically. There's even a site that allows two sides in a lawsuit to negotiate toward the middle. Each side sends an offer (what will be paid or accepted) into the site, and the two sides get closer and closer until they're $5,000 or less apart. Then the computer finds the right number in the middle. Both parties pay relatively little and save hundreds, if not thousands (or a percentage of the winnings) in attorneys' fees.

When I first wrote this book, going online and getting an e-mail address from America Online was about the last thing I did (in November 1993) before this book went to press. (Yes, I wish I had thought to buy stock at that time in the company, but alas, I can't lay claim to that one.) At that time, I couldn't have imagined that by the end of the 1990s, millions of people would go online to peruse all homes that are listed for sale with multiple listing services (MLSs) nationwide. I didn't dream people would make offers for homes they'd seen only on the Internet. I could barely imagine buyers and owners getting excellent, complete information about the mortgage process, let alone applying online for a home loan.

As I write this third edition, there are websites that catalog every condo building in Chicago and provide such information as the condo declaration and the floor plans. Other websites allow buyers and sellers and their agents to schedule showings electronically (essentially, you log online to see whether the showing time you want is available), eliminating the need for all of those follow-up phone calls. There are websites that can help you search out the true value of a home and others that will send your contact information to 10 top agents in your area so they can contact you about buying or selling property. And then there is eBay's real estate division, in which buyers bid for homes in an open forum.

The Internet, in the incarnation in which it currently exists, is but 10 years old—basically in its infancy. It's hard to imagine what innovation or revolution the next 10 years will bring to the real estate industry. But you can count on technology continuing to change the way homes are bought and sold.

HOW DO I MAKE A COUNTEROFFER?

A *counteroffer* is what happens after the initial contract is presented. You make the offer. The seller responds by countering your offer with another offer. Any response from you or the seller, after the initial offer presentation, is a counteroffer.

Making a counteroffer is actually simpler than making the first offer because you're in the driver's seat. A counteroffer means that the seller has responded to your offer. Responding to your offer means that the seller believes you are a serious buyer and that your offer is valid.

Before responding to the seller's counteroffer, make sure you understand the psychological implications behind it. In making your counteroffer, you can either match the seller's decrease in price with an equal increase, or jump up more to make the seller feel better about the deal. The choice is yours.

Once you've decided how much to offer in this next round, talk to your broker. It's usually unnecessary to draw up an entirely new contract, although customs vary from state to state and county to county. At this stage, the broker usually modifies the existing offer and calls the seller broker, who relays the new offer to the sellers.

Once you make your offer, you'll be hard-pressed to do anything until you've heard back from the broker regarding your counteroffer. To ensure you hear something quickly, consider limiting the time in which your offer is valid. If you put down specific terms—"This offer expires within 24 hours" or ". . . by the end of the business day on Wednesday"—you will force the seller to respond within your time frame, not his or hers.

QUESTION 41

WHAT DO I DO IN A MULTIPLE-BID SITUATION?

Whenever there aren't enough homes on the market for all the home buyers who wish to purchase them, you have what's known as a seller's market. And when the list price is the starting point for negotiations instead of a home-run finish for the seller, you know you're in a really hot market.

In this kind of home-buying climate, many people often bid on the same home at the same time, resulting in a multiple-bid offer.

When this happens, you have only a few choices:

1. Make an offer at or above the list price. How high you go depends on how badly you want the house.

2. Make your best offer first. Don't wait for a second round of negotiations. If the seller asks for your "best offer," don't assume there will be a counteroffer phase of the negotiations.

3. Offer a "clean" contract. A "clean" offer is usually one with few, if any, contingencies. As mentioned, consider eliminating the home inspection contingency, the financing contingency, and the attorney approval rider.

4. Be as flexible as possible. Offer the seller his or her choice of closing dates. Consider allowing the seller to take some of the fixtures, like a dishwasher or refrigerator, that might have ordinarily stayed with the house.

5. Consider adding an "appraisal" contingency. If you have to remove the financing contingency, consider substituting an appraisal contingency, which will allow you to cancel the deal if the house doesn't appraise out in value—that is, if the bank's appraised value of the home is less than the purchase price.

6. Back off. Often an agent will counsel buyers to back off in a multiple-bid situation, reasoning that the likely outcome will be to pay too much for the property. Sometimes both buyers back off and the seller's agent will go to the various buyers and ask them to come back and bid, diffusing the situation.

7. Don't panic. You may not get the property at first, but sometimes deals have a way of unwinding. The other buyers might drop out of the deal for some reason and the seller will come back to you.

It would be nice if every story had a happy ending. But in a hot market, sometimes things just don't work out.

Mark and Lisa's Story

Mark and Lisa were tired of shopping for their first home. They had spent virtually every moment of free time looking over the past couple of months. In Southern California, where they were looking, homes were selling in minutes or hours, rather than days or weeks, and home prices were zooming up before their very eyes.

"We felt like we were watching our future profits slip away because we could not find a house to buy in our price range," Mark explained.

After losing out on several properties when they didn't offer enough cash, Mark and Lisa made an offer for a town house. The town house had some good points and some not-so-great-but-livable things. Although it was in the neighborhood they wanted, at 1,500 square feet, it was quite a bit smaller than the space they'd hoped to get. It was listed for $300,000, about $30,000 more than they wanted to spend, though certainly affordable by a mortgage lender's standards.

This town house seemed perfect. Their agent, sensing yet another set of buyers about to throw in the towel, suggested they use a tried-and-true method for getting their offer accepted: Make a full price offer without any contingencies, and write a letter telling the sellers how much they wanted to buy the town house, and what good neighbors they would be. The wife, a television writer, wrote a beautiful letter. The agent included the letter with the full-price, no contingency offer and the promise that the seller could choose the closing date. The buyers waited. At the end of the day, the seller countered their offer—$10,000 above the list price.

Lisa thought the seller countered above asking because she and Mark sounded so desperate in their letter, but their broker said two more offers had come in for the property, each of which was above the list price. Lisa and Mark mulled it over and decided to take a pass on the property.

Remember, if you're on the losing end of a multiple-bid situation, there will always be another house.

QUESTION 42

WHAT IS A HOME WARRANTY? WHAT KIND CAN I GET FOR NEW CONSTRUCTION? WHAT ABOUT A PREVIOUSLY OWNED HOME?

The concept of a home warranty sounds pretty good: If something breaks, the foundation cracks, or the roof leaks, all you have to do is call an 800 number and someone will come out and fix it for free (you may have to pay a flat fee for the service call, like an insurance deductible).

Another cliché unfortunately holds true: If it sounds too good to be true, in most cases, it is.

Although existing and new home warranties should work this way in theory, in practice you will often incur extra headaches and extra expenses on the road to fixing the problem.

There are two types of home warranties: a homeowner's warranty for new construction, and a homeowner's warranty for previously owned homes. Let's look at new construction first.

New Home Warranties

New construction basically means you'll be the first person to live in your newly built home. And, today, many developers are building semicustom homes; they allow you to choose your own style of home, decor, cabinetry, floor coverings, appliances, and bathroom fixtures. You may even have a choice of options—a basement, a sunroom, an attic, a two- or three-car garage, an extra bedroom, and upgrades— carpeting, floor coverings, cabinetry, fixtures, and so on.

In the past, developers of new construction provided a new home warranty backed by one of two or three organizations that created a pool of money to cover structural problems with new homes. It worked pretty well until a rash of undercapitalized, sleazy developers built shoddy homes and didn't put in enough money to cover the problems that later developed. That left one of the organizations short of funds and unable to pay the claims.

But real estate attorneys say reputable developers of new construction will often back up their own work, and this should be one of the criteria on which you select a new home. Usually, the developer will provide a door-to-door warranty for one year on nearly everything in the home. The manufacturers of your new appliances and mechanical systems cover part of this warranty. The developer might also extend the warranty to 5 or 10 years for specific major components, such as the roof, hardwood floors, or the fireplace.

I can't stress this enough: It's vital to know exactly what kind of service your developer will provide to you once you've bought his or her home, and what structural items and mechanical systems have what kind of warranty. If the developer refuses to warrant anything, watch out. That refusal might mean that the developer is sleazy, or has built a shoddy project, or has something to hide.

Juanita's Story

Juanita bought a town house in a new development on the west side of Chicago. After she moved in, she started having problems with a few minor leaks, which caused her floorboards to buckle.

The paint in one of her bathrooms started peeling, and the deck didn't look like it was connected correctly. She contacted the architect, who happened to buy a unit in the same development (a good sign, I'd say). Before the architect could respond to her complaints and concerns, Juanita hired a professional home inspector to go through her unit, pointing out all the things that weren't built right.

Juanita sent a three-page letter to the architect, developer, and the developer's attorney. Although the home inspector's final conclusion was that it would cost about $1,000 to fix all of the little problems, his report was so scary to Juanita that nothing the developer could say would make it right.

Although Juanita had lived in the unit for a year, she decided she wanted out. The developer agreed to buy back the unit and pay for some of her closing costs. He intends to fix the relatively minor problems and resell the unit—for an additional $60,000.

What Juanita didn't realize was that the price of her town home had skyrocketed in the year she'd lived there, giving the developer a huge return on his investment.

The time to reaffirm that your new home has a warranty is when you're negotiating for the home. Your attorney can step in and request a new home warranty, then make it a condition of buying the home. At the very least, not having a home warranty for new construction means you have no recourse (other than expensive litigation) should something go wrong. *Make sure you get all warranties in writing. Keep the documents in a safe, easily accessible place.*

20/20 hindsight

In Juanita's case, everyone ends up a winner. Juanita gets her money back. She bought from a quality developer who backed up his product. The developer is happy because he'll resell the town house and make a huge profit. The architect is happy because she no longer has a neighbor in the development who is unhappy with the work. Bottom line: It's incredibly important to buy from a quality developer, one who will back up his or her product a year or more after the sale.

first time buyer tip

When buying new construction, check out other homes built by the developer to see how the homes have stood the test of time. Are the homeowners happy with their residences? If you're buying in an established—or semiestablished—subdivision, knock on doors and ask the owners what they like and dislike about their home. Ask about everything, from how well the mechanical systems work to how quickly the developer fixed items on the punch list (a list of items not finished to your satisfaction by closing). Check out other, older subdivisions the developer has built and see what complaints, if any, turn up. Check for complaints that may have been filed against the developer with your local chamber of commerce, Better Business Bureau, and your local state attorney's office. Remember: "The best defense is a good offense." Find out ahead of time what you're up against.

Existing Home Warranties

The majority of first-time buyers will be buying previously owned homes, those that are up for resale. As we've discussed, these older homes are also referred to as "existing" homes in real estate jargon.

More than 25 years ago, several companies began providing home warranties for preowned homes. Although this type of homeowner warranty was slow to catch on at first, it has grown by leaps and bounds in the last few years, fueled by our increasingly litigious society and some recent court rulings that have placed more responsibility on the seller to disclose problems in the home. More than a million existing home warranties were purchased in 2003, about half of which were for homes in California. Nearly all home buyers in California purchase a home warranty or have one purchased for them by the seller. In other parts of the country, the number of homeowners who purchase warranties ranges from 8 to 20 percent.

Unlike new construction warranties, which cover all types of problems, including expensive structural problems, existing home warranties are actually service contracts. Many people confuse them with insurance; in many states, they are indeed regulated by the state department of insurance.

Like service contracts, existing home warranties cover the costs to repair or replace a broken appliance or plumbing system over and above a deductible, which the home warranty industry refers to as a service fee. But home warranties are limited in scope. A typical policy covers the furnace, air-conditioning, kitchen appliances, water heater, trash compactor, electrical system (fuses and interior wiring), and interior plumbing. But there are serious exclusions. For example, if a pipe bursts because something gets stuck, it's covered. If a pipe bursts because it freezes, however, it's not covered. Commonly, separate warranties must be purchased for refrigerators, washers, and dryers, not to mention swimming pools and spas.

Homeowner warranties do not cover preexisting problems. If an appliance works on the day of closing, it's covered. Otherwise, it's not. And these warranties don't cover everything in your home. Most important, they do not cover structural problems, such as a crack in the foundation walls or basement floor, or a leaky roof. Industry experts say warranties are designed to cover those appliances and plumbing and electrical systems that are in working condition when the home is sold.

Usually the seller purchases a home warranty, which is paid for out of the closing proceeds. The buyer is responsible for the service fees, should there be any need to call the toll-free number. Sometimes, a seller broker will purchase the warranty for the buyer. And, increasingly, buyers who are not given a warranty with the home are purchasing it themselves. The cost runs from less than $350 to more than $600 for a year of coverage.

Neither buyers nor sellers pay much attention to the service fee, but it gets charged every time, and buyers have to foot that bill. On some home warranties, the deductible or service fee can run as much as $150 per call. Most service fees range from $35 to $75 per call.

Are existing home warranties worth it? "If you look at a home in terms of the kinds of things that can go wrong in the first year, it's a pretty good deal [for the buyer]," says a spokesperson for the Home Warranty Association of California. "It's inevitable in a resale house: Some things are going to break down. Water heaters can explode. Furnaces can go out.

Air conditioners can break. Without a home warranty, you'd probably spend $1,000 to repair a furnace or $2,500 to replace it," he adds.

One individual, who was starting up a home warranty company (there are fewer than 10 that provide coverage nationwide, although there are a couple dozen in California), says his research showed that new home-owners living in an existing home called the toll-free number at least once during the year. If that's true, and you can get the seller to pick up the bill, there's no reason *not* to have a home warranty.

In some states, home warranties are completely *unregulated.* In other states, the department of insurance regulates the home warranty. If the home you are considering comes with a home warranty, check out the company for any reports of nonpayment of claims. Also check for complaints that have been filed with the Better Business Bureau, your state attorney's office, and the attorney general's office.

Don't mistake a home warranty for homeowner's insurance coverage. A home warranty typically only lasts for the first year you live in your home. Generally, it cannot be extended. It also doesn't cover the types of damage covered by a homeowner's insurance policy, nor does it have the liability component. The simplest way of putting it is this: Neither new home warranties nor existing home warranties are insurance. They are by-products of the insurance industry. You still need to buy a homeowner's insurance policy.

To find out more about home warranties in general, log onto the Home Warranty Association of California's website (warrantyassn.com).

WHAT DOES THE CONTRACT REALLY SAY AND WHAT ARE MY OBLIGATIONS UNDER IT?

QUESTION 43

The real estate contract, also called a purchase and sale agreement or an offer to purchase, contains certain provisions that deal with the transfer of title to property between two parties. It also has certain provisions that deal with what happens to the property if it's destroyed before the deal is closed.

Price and title (the actual ownership interest in a house) are most important. Why? Because you have to know what you're buying and how much you're paying for it.

- With a single-family house, you're usually buying a house, the land on which it sits, and the things in it.
- With a condo or town house, you are buying the space between the walls, floor, and ceiling of a building and the things in it.
- With a co-op, you're buying shares in a corporation that owns the property. These shares are equal to the unique value of your unit. (You're actually "renting" your unit.)

The sellers are supposed to deliver to you good title to the house, condo, town house, or co-op. If they're including personal property in the sale, like a washing machine or refrigerator, they must also give you good title to these items as well.

How are the sellers going to guarantee and deliver good title?

Before we get into the meat of it, let's first define *good title*. Ownership with good title means the individual who owns the property owns it free of defects, easements, liens, and mortgages (except the owner's current mortgage), and free from any matters that would impair the use of the home as a residential dwelling. There's nothing more complicated about it.

Basic Elements of a Contract to Purchase

The basic elements of a contract include: the assurance of good title, the deed, conveyance (that is, transfer to your ownership) of personal property like bookshelves or light fixtures, the payment method, the sales price, and the closing location. Other elements of the contract are of slightly lesser importance.

Of all the basic issues, title is the most important. This example may illustrate one problem.

Sarah and Bob's Story

The Indiana Dunes, which is on the southern tip of Lake Michigan, is a beautiful stretch of sand and water, punctuated, at times, with a glimpse of the far-off skyline of Chicago. Generations of Chicago and Indiana residents have gone there to rest, play, and enjoy the shore.

Years ago, Sarah and Bob decided to purchase a vacation house at the Indiana Dunes. They agreed to pay $200,000 and signed the contract. In the contract, the seller sold them the house with a Quit Claim Deed, which essentially sold Sarah and Bob every interest he owned in the house.

Everything would have been fine, had Sarah and Bob bothered to do a title search on the property. What they would have found might have made them change their minds. They were so enamored with the idea of spending weekends and summers in their new vacation home, however, that they neglected to learn what was going on in the community. If they had been reading the local papers, they would have known why the seller was willing to sell them the property at what seemed to them to be a great deal.

The seller sold them a house he owned on land he had leased from the federal government, and the government had decided not to renew the land leases for some of the home in the Indiana Dunes. This decision, which reversed generations of policy, was made to protect the shore from becoming too populated too close to the beach. Those homeowners, some of who recently had paid big bucks for vacation homes on the beach, had bought limited occupancy; the government leases had just 10 years left before they ended.

At a price tag of $200,000 and with only 10 years to live there, Sarah and Bob were facing a steep tab of $20,000 per year. They could never resell the property and recoup their investment, so they tried to fight the decision, but to no avail.

A purchase and sale agreement usually provides that the seller must give the purchasers a warranty deed. That deed warrants that the seller has good title to the property and that he or she will defend you against others who may claim to have an ownership interest in the home you are buying. If the seller has only a leasehold interest in the property, then he or she can sell only that leasehold interest, and not title to the property.

first time buyer tip

Checking out the title for problems, liens, and encumbrances is the only way to ensure that you'll never have a long-lost relative or friend of the seller laying claim to your home. And to make sure you don't lose out if someone does "pop out of the woodwork," purchase an owner's title insurance policy to protect you from anything the title company missed in its search.

Under the typical purchase contract, the buyer is obliged to purchase the property, for a certain amount of money, at a certain time, provided the seller guarantees good title.

SHOULD I USE A REAL ESTATE ATTORNEY? SHOULD I SIGN ANYTHING BEFORE MY ATTORNEY REVIEWS IT?

QUESTION

44

No state requires you to hire a real estate attorney. In fact, real estate professionals in some states—California, Arizona, and Indiana, for example—actively discourage the use of an attorney. Instead, buyers and sellers are encouraged to rely on real estate brokers and the local title or escrow company to close the deal.

Whether or not you need a real estate attorney depends on how familiar you are with the workings of the real estate industry. I've talked to attorneys and brokers all over the country, and, except in a few states like California, they overwhelmingly recommend that first-time buyers use attorneys.

There are several good reasons for this. Real estate attorneys:

- Are the only people involved in the transaction who do not have a vested interest in seeing you close on the deal. Real estate brokers and mortgage lenders, for example, don't get paid until the deal closes.
- Act as another layer, removing emotion from the deal.
- Can negotiate the finer points of the deal for you.
- Can protect you from getting a bad deal should problems arise or should the negotiation turn nasty.
- Can work with the real estate brokers to organize and finalize details of the closing.
- Can work with the lender to make sure documentation is prepared correctly and is sent to the closing at the right time.
- Can explain the legal consequences of the deal and any terms you may not understand.
- Are a good buy for the money, as they usually work for a fixed fee.
- May be able to get you a reduced fee from the title company (which works on volume).
- Track all the little details that ensure a smooth closing.
- Provide you with a closing book that neatly organizes all the documents involved with your house closing.

Penny Wise, Pound Foolish

You may think you're making a smart move by not hiring a real estate attorney and saving yourself the fee. But when you consider a $60,000, $100,000, or $200,000 investment (which is the cost of your home), trying to save $400 to $600 isn't so smart. Some people could research all of the minutiae involved in selling or buying a home and save themselves the expense of a real estate attorney. But the vast majority of us don't do this on a daily basis, and we won't be prepared to deal with the consequences if something out of the ordinary happens or we've overlooked a detail.

What would you do, for example, if your seller dies the day before closing? What would you do if you lost your job the week before closing and could no longer qualify for the mortgage? And what if a long-lost relative of the sellers turns up a few days before closing to lay claim to the home? What if the house you're supposed to close on the following week is destroyed by fire, flood, tornado or a hurricane?

In the interests of full disclosure, I want you to know that I'm married to a real estate attorney. For nearly 20 years, I've watched Sam help literally thousands of individuals purchase and sell their homes. Most of the time, the deals go pretty well, but there's always a chance that something will crop up.

For example, in one instance the sellers, who were angry about moving, ripped out all of the alarm wiring in the house just before the closing. In another case, a real estate broker contacted a homeowner about selling to her clients and then persuaded the seller to give a "loan" to the buyer's mother-in-law, who then gifted the funds to the buyers. Not illegal, per se, as long as it was disclosed to the end lender. (The mortgage broker was in on the deal, too.) Sometimes home buyers and sellers don't know what they're doing, or they fall prey to a bad-apple real estate agent or mortgage lender who uses them to further their own agendas. There are bad real estate attorneys, too. But a good real estate attorney can help you successfully negotiate the minefield of homeownership, helping you buy or sell—and to enjoy the experience.

In 2004, Sam and I started writing a syndicated column that answers some of the legal questions home buyers and sellers ask. It's called "Ask the Lawyer." If you'd like to ask Sam a question, e-mail him through my website, thinkglink.com.

The attorney's fee is minuscule even if you're purchasing a $100,000 home. On a bad deal, that fee could save you a tremendous amount of heartache, not to mention money, to fix whatever problems crop up.

No one hires an attorney for the good times. Protect yourself in case your dream of homeownership turns into a nightmare.

Signing on the Dotted Line

You can sign any contract, as long as it contains the absolute right for your attorney to review the document and approve it. If the contract or document does not contain that absolute right, then *do not sign it* unless you're sure you understand all of its provisions.

As I mentioned earlier, most attorney riders give your attorney the limited right to cancel the contract on the basis of his or her review of the contract. If you're going to use a real estate attorney, and you're not sure you understand the terms of the contract you're signing—for example, if you're not sure there is an absolute right for your attorney to review and approve the document—then show it to your attorney *before* you sign it.

HOW DO I FIND A REAL ESTATE ATTORNEY? HOW MUCH SHOULD HE OR SHE CHARGE ME?

Not all real estate attorneys are competent, let alone good. And it's important to find one who will help, rather than hinder, the deal. Finding a good real estate attorney is like finding a good broker. First, ask your broker and friends for recommendations. You want someone experienced, someone who has handled a minimum of 50 closings within each of the past three years. If you're purchasing new construction, or building a new home on land that you already own, hire an attorney who is very familiar with new construction contracts and can protect you in case the developer defaults or builds a shoddy product that doesn't conform to code.

After you get several names, call the attorneys and ask how much they charge and what they will do for that fee. Don't be embarrassed to ask about fees. It's crucial that you know how much you're getting for your money.

How They Charge

Some attorneys (especially those in medium or large law firms) charge by the hour. In the largest firms, you can expect to pay $150 to $400 per hour, depending on who does your closing. (The young associates have the cheap hourly rates, and the senior partners charge the most.) You'll also be charged for photocopies, facsimiles, computer research time, and the time it takes to actually travel to and attend the closing.

Other attorneys, especially solo practitioners, charge a flat fee. The flat fee can range from $350 to more than $1,000, depending on what you're buying. It's not unusual for attorneys to charge more for new construction, especially if the deal won't close for a year or more. A lot of extra work is involved in one of those deals. Also, if you're buying a very large or expensive home, typically you'll be charged a higher flat fee because of the work involved in negotiating the contract. Try to find someone who will charge you a flat fee for his or her time. That way, if there is a problem with the closing, you won't be charged for all those extra hours.

Sam says that if a buyer calls and tells him "My closing is a piece of cake," he can almost always predict that it won't be. Typically, such a home buyer has an unrealistic expectation of what is involved in a home closing and may have unknowingly created more problems that Sam will have to untie. Even the "easy" real estate deals can be technical and complicated to close successfully.

Looking solely at how much attorneys charge for their services is not necessarily the best way to choose your attorney. For this, the biggest investment of your life, ask yourself whether you feel comfortable telling this person all the intimate details of your financial life. It's vital that you feel comfortable with, and perhaps even a bit close to, your attorney.

Think About This

When you're interviewing your attorney, think about the attorney's response to these questions:

1. How busy are you right now? How many house deals are you handling? Some real estate attorneys handle upward of 300 transactions per year. That means they basically don't have time to sneeze—or you're working with an associate, paralegal, or assistant. You want someone who has enough time to handle you not only for the closing but also for the entire transaction. Think about it this way: Do you want to feel like you're relaying messages to the doctor through the nurse or the secretary, or do you want to talk to the doctor directly?

2. How many closings do you do each year? Make sure your attorney completes at least 50 residential real estate closings each year. Then you'll know he or she has the experience necessary in residential transactions. Don't hire your cousin the litigator, or your friend Harold, who negotiates airplane leases for a living. These folks probably didn't even do their own house deals.

3. How much do you charge? If it seems as though the attorney isn't charging enough, he or she may be part of a network of attorneys who do their own title work. In that case, they also get compensated from a title company (or another firm that employs real estate attorneys to do title work), if you choose to work with that title company. Is it a bad thing? Perhaps not. If something goes wrong with the title, the attorney could be liable. Either way, you won't know what the story is until you ask.

4. Are you involved in any deals that would conflict with mine right now? It's happened more than once. A buyer calls up an attorney only to find out the same attorney is already representing the seller. No attorney worth his or her salt will suggest he or she can handle both sides of the same transaction, *even* if you agree to sign a document that says you know it and approve it. If there is a conflict, ask your attorney to recommend you to another real estate attorney.

The old cliché is true: You get what you pay for.

5. Do you have an engagement letter I can sign? Attorneys should present you with an engagement letter that outlines the things the attorney will do to help you negotiate and close on your real estate transaction. The letter should also state the fee. The better attorneys do this; all attorneys should (or at the very least, they should give you this information verbally). Ask the attorney you select to prepare one for you to sign.

181

new construction tip

If you're hiring an attorney to handle your new construction purchase, make sure at least one-third of the attorney's practice is new construction. Not all new construction is the same. For example, a single-family home in a development in the far suburbs is going to be different from a new construction *infill* development in an urban area. There are practical differences in each type of development. Make sure the attorney knows how to handle your developer no matter where you're buying. As a bonus, if you hire an attorney who has done a lot of work for buyers in the development in which you're purchasing a home, you'll get someone who already knows the legal lay of the land, has already seen and read through the condo declaration, and knows where the developer may be willing to kick in a few extra upgrades or items. It could make the deal go much more smoothly.

When Complications Arise

If a deal is really complicated, you will almost certainly need an attorney, no matter where you live. Sam once worked on a house closing that seemed pretty ordinary until he found out there were 10 lenders. He had to negotiate a separate deal with each lender until they were all satisfied. The extremely complicated closing took 10 hours. Someone at the closing called it the "hour per lender" deal.

20/20 hindsight

Once again, hiring a real estate lawyer is *not* the same thing as having your uncle Harry, the tax attorney, do your real estate closing. Real estate law is specialized. Uncle Harry may be a whiz at writing wills, or leasing airplanes, or finding creative places to put your money, but he may get you nailed to the wall in two minutes if he doesn't truly understand the finer points of real estate law.

Once you hire the attorney, let him or her do the job. If the attorney advises you on certain points, believe him or her. If he or she tells you to do something, do it. The attorney knows the ins and outs of real estate law much better than you do.

SHOULD I CLOSE AT THE BEGINNING, MIDDLE, OR END OF THE MONTH? WHY DOES IT MATTER?

QUESTION 46

When you choose to schedule your closing will be a point of negotiation between you and the seller. The issues you need to consider are personal timing and money. Here are some points to help you clarify why timing is everything.

- Set the closing date according to when your current lease ends. If you're living in an apartment, it's foolish to close when you still have six months left on your lease, unless you can easily sublet your apartment or you have an escape clause. If you close at the beginning of a month and your lease expires at the end of the month, and you don't need to do any work in your new home, you'll be paying double rent for one month, which can be costly. Poor timing is one of the biggest mistakes a home buyer can make (see Appendix I for a list of other common mistakes a home buyer makes).

- If you close at the beginning of a month, the lender will require you to prepay the interest on your loan from the day of closing to the end of the month. Therefore, the cash you would need at closing will be more than what you would need if you chose to close at the end of the month. For example, if you close April 15, you'll have to prepay your mortgage from April 15 to April 30. If you close April 30, you only pay one day's mortgage interest.

- If you're trying to decide whether to close December 31 or January 2, remember that you get to take deductions for your house in the year that it closes, even if it's on the last day of the year. If you close December 31, the points you pay at the closing on a purchase, plus any prepaid interest, are deductible on your income tax statement for that year. If you choose to close on December 31, make sure that your deductible costs will be greater than the standard deduction allowed to you by the IRS. Talk to your accountant or someone familiar with these real estate tax issues to find out how they might affect your situation.

Paying in Arrears—Except for Sub-Par (Sub-Prime) Loans

Mortgage interest and principal payments are paid in arrears—that is, you pay on July 1 for money you've borrowed in June. If you close April 15, you would pay a half month's mortgage interest in cash at closing. You would then pay nothing until June 1, when you would pay the interest for the month of May. On July 1, you pay interest for the month of June. And so on.

The reason for this is that loan payments are computed at a certain rate, and that rate remains constant, like a fixed-rate loan. The lender must manually compute the amount of interest from the day of closing to the end of the month.

The only time this would change is if you're getting a *sub-par* loan. Most home buyers will fall in the excellent or good credit category; lenders will grade these borrowers "A" or possibly "A−," which means they have a few problem on their credit history, but nothing serious.

The last week of the month is the busiest time for title companies (not to mention moving companies). If you decide to close at the end of the month, be sure your attorney schedules the closing well in advance. Otherwise, you might find that the title company is booked up and can't accommodate your closing.

If you have serious credit problems, but still have enough credit to get a loan, you might fall into the B, C, or D category of sub-par lending. You may then have to prepay the interest on your loan before you even borrow it. So if you close on June 15, you'd have to prepay your interest through the end of the month. Then instead of waiting until August 1 to make your next mortgage payment, you might be required to pay it on July 1. That way, you stay a month ahead.

If a lender is going to require this on your loan, it should be fully explained to you and written into your loan documentation. If you get a sub-par loan, ask your lender to fully explain your payment schedule.

If your lease expires the same day as your closing, be sure you have a backup place to live just in case you don't close on the property—even if it means moving to a hotel or back home with the folks for a few nights. Sometimes properties just don't close. In new construction, the house might flunk its final inspection. Or, more likely, it just isn't done yet and doesn't have its Certificate of Occupancy (also called "C of O" in real estate jargon). Either way, make sure you're protected, even if it means paying for an additional month of rent.

WHAT IS SELLER DISCLOSURE?
HOW DOES IT AFFECT ME?

At the beginning of the 1990s, the term *seller disclosure* was virtually unknown. By the end of the decade, it had become a buzzword.

Essentially, seller disclosure requires the home seller to disclose any known *material latent defects* in his or her property. That bit of jargon means the seller must disclose whether the property has any hidden or unseen defects, or problems, that could adversely affect its value.

Buyers like seller disclosure because it tells them, up front, about the condition of the property. Some sellers like disclosing the defects because it protects them from buyers' discovering the defects during an inspection and then asking for money to fix the problems. Other sellers don't. They feel uncomfortable with this formal process of baring their home's soul, so to speak.

As a buyer, you want to find out everything you can, in advance, about the condition of the home. If you run into a seller disclosure form (and it is increasingly likely that you will), the form will ask detailed—or not so detailed—questions about the condition of the home. If the seller answers the questions honestly (there usually is an option for "don't know," which is completely useless to a home buyer), the form may list such problems as water in the basement. The seller, of course, will say the price of the house takes into account these problems. You will then have to decide if the house is worth the asking price if it also needs a new roof and a new furnace or air-conditioning system.

> Remember, anything about the purchase and sale can be negotiated. Whether you get it depends on how desperately the seller wants to sell, and current market conditions.

20/20

hindsight

The History

Here's a little bit of history to explain the hoopla over seller disclosure. Although it seems as though state law should automatically cover seller disclosure, in many cases, it did not—at least, not specifically.

In 1987, California passed a law that codified the questions the seller must answer. In addition, the agent for the seller, the buyer, and the seller himself or herself must sign off that they have reasonably inspected the property and disclosed any defect.

By 1992, only California and Maine had some sort of formal regulation requiring sellers to disclose any hidden material latent defects in the property. In Maine, the broker is required to ask specific questions that the state has designated. The broker must gather this information at the time the property is listed and provide this information in writing to the buyer prior to, or during, the preparation of an offer.

In 1992, Coldwell Banker, a national real estate company, announced a new policy that required all sellers listing property with the company to fill out and sign disclosure forms. Although some sellers weren't thrilled with the prospect of having to fill out a form that asks specific questions about the house, land, and neighborhood, buyers are generally glad to have it.

State law in Illinois prior to 1993 was silent on the issue. In effect, that meant if the house had a hidden defect and the seller knew about it but didn't say anything to anyone about it, then the buyer was stuck with the problem. Caveat emptor: Buyer beware. If, however, the seller told his or her broker about the hidden defect, the broker was obligated to inform the buyer.

Although seller disclosure forms cause consternation for both home buyers and sellers, wouldn't you rather know what's going on before you buy rather than after you move in? Each state requires a slightly different form of disclosure, but all states require that sellers answer questions truthfully about the physical state of their home. You should ask very specific questions about any problems or defects the home might have or have had.

For example, you might ask if there has ever been leaking or moisture or flooding in the basement. If the answer is "yes," ask what caused these problems and whether they were fixed. You can ask the real estate agent, but chances are he or she won't know the real answers. The agent might say "Not to the best of my knowledge," which doesn't help you at all. To protect yourself, you'll need to ask the seller these questions directly. Don't be shy about asking for copies of the proof of payment if the seller indicates the problem has been fixed. That way, you'll have the name of the contractor or vendor should you have a similar problem in the future.

To see a sample seller disclosure form, look in Appendix IV.

By the mid-1990s, things were changing nationwide. Since then nearly every state has enacted laws requiring sellers to make a full, and in most cases written, disclosure about any material latent defects in their property. In Illinois, sellers must now fill out a 22-question seller disclosure form.

According to the NAR's legal counsel, one of the largest areas of controversy in the process of buying and selling homes is the failure to disclose defects in property. The majority of lawsuits after closing, where buyers are unhappy, involve the alleged failure to disclose some condition affecting value or desirability.

The finger is usually pointed in the direction of the broker first, and then to the seller. Because the NAR protects the interests of brokers, it feels sellers, rather than brokers, should shoulder the responsibility for disclosing defects in their house. As the NAR's attorney has said: "The agent has the duty to disclose factors that he can observe with a reasonably diligent inspection. The broker doesn't live there. Seller disclosure forces those issues to be addressed."

Ask your broker whether your state requires seller disclosure, and whether the seller needs to make that disclosure in writing. Also ask the seller to answer specific questions about the condition of the property *before* you make an offer to purchase.

DO I NEED A HOME INSPECTION? HOW DO I FIND A REPUTABLE HOME INSPECTOR?

The quick answer is YES! Except in the rare situation—for example, you're buying a home from your parents that you have lived in and know intimately—savvy brokers always advise their buyers to have the home inspected by a professional inspector or someone you know is knowledgeable about construction matters and issues involved in residential properties.

But hiring an expert doesn't excuse you from looking at the home carefully before you get to the inspection stage. Remember, the inspector will charge you between $300 and $700 or more for each inspection. By keeping a sharp eye out for the following, you may be able to spot some major problems and eliminate a potential property *before* paying an inspector.

The Home Buyer's Watch List

When you start visiting homes, watch out for:

- **Wet, clammy, sticky, smelly basements.** A damp feel to a basement can hint at water seepage caused by improperly graded soil, or an improperly laid foundation.

- **Cracks in the basement.** A visible crack line in the interior of the basement or on the exterior foundation could point to more-than-normal settling. Or the house may have been built on a new landfill, a hill, or an improperly graded site. It could also point to an area prone to earthquakes or earth movement during heavy rains.

- **Bad smells.** If a house smells bad, it may have a biological problem, like mold growing in the ductwork, or behind vinyl wallpaper. Mold can be scrubbed away with bleach and water, or other cleaners, but you may have to rip out ductwork to get at it.

- **Poorly fitted ductwork.** Heating and cooling systems can be problematic, especially if the original work was done in a slipshod way. Check the duct lines to see that they fit snugly and securely.

- **Discolored spots on walls and ceilings.** Discoloration could be the result of a water problem—a leak from the roof, the walls, or the pipes. Beware of a fresh paint job, particularly in the top floor of the house or the basement. It may be covering up a problem.

- **Improperly fitted skylights.** Skylights, which are now extremely popular, are usually one-piece preassembled units that are popped into a hole in the roof. Check for discoloration, peeling paint, or other signs that the skylights were improperly fitted or may be leaking.

- **Damp attic.** Poor attic ventilation can lead to moisture being trapped in the upper recesses, causing dry rot or condensation. The underside of the roof should never be wet.

- **Insulation.** Does the house have adequate insulation? If not, you could be looking at a fortune in heating and cooling expenses. If the home has insulation, ask about the R factor (the higher the number, the better) and be sure the insulation is facing the correct way.

- **Sloppy masonry work.** Has the homeowner tried to personally patch up the masonry? Are there holes in the mortar? It could be a sign of a larger problem. If you're looking at new construction, sloppy masonry and detail work can mean that other work was also done in a slipshod way.

- **Do-it-yourself electrical work.** Proper electrical wiring is a must to avoid future problems that could be costly to fix as well as a serious safety concern. If the electrical box is a mess, it could mean trouble for you.

- **Poorly graded landscaping.** Does the landscaping slope away from the house (the high point should be against the house)? If so, great. If the landscaping is sloping toward the point where the house connects with the ground, or if the walk around the side of the home is pitched toward the home, it's a good bet there has been or will be a leakage problem into the basement. Water is a very damaging substance (think about the Grand Canyon), and the constant pressure of water (and snow melting) moving toward the house can cause tremendous damage to the foundation.

- **Fuzzy windows.** If the home has double-paned or thermal-paned windows, and the windows appear to be fuzzy or full of condensation, the seal has been broken. The windows are no longer working properly and will ultimately have to be replaced—and that can cost quite a chunk of money.

- **Spotty windows.** Look closely at the windowpanes and woodwork. Black spots could be a sign of mold.

There are thousands of potential hazards when purchasing a home, and most buyers have no idea where to begin to look for problems. That's why it's so important to have the proper inspections completed before the expiration of the inspection contingency. First, you never know a home unless you've lived in it. Second, most people aren't particularly familiar with the structure and mechanicals of a house, town house, or condo. The roof may look fine to your eyes, but a house inspector may see peeling shingles and notice water marks from leaks on the ceiling. A house inspector can be yet another voice helping you to distance your emotions from the purchase of the home.

Consider hiring a professional home inspector even if you're buying a new home. Why? Because even though the house may be new it doesn't guarantee that it was built correctly. Inspectors have shared stories with me about new construction projects that have had outlets wired incorrectly, and ground fault interrupters that aren't connected at all. They've seen balconies that are not fully bolted into the side of the building, hot water faucets that only feed cold water, and dishwashers that aren't bolted into the cabinet (so they rock side to side and the water pipes get loosened and leak).

For new construction buyers, if you're going to hire a home inspector at the end of the project, consider, instead, hiring an inspector at the four critical junctures of the home building process: (1) after the foundation is poured; (2) after the house is framed; (3) after the house has been wired and plumbed (before the walls get finished); and (4) before you close. Coordinate with the builder or developer to make sure you can bring through the home inspector and that someone from the development company will be available to answer any questions. When interviewing an inspector for this task, make sure he or she has done *new construction* inspections before.

Finding an Excellent Home Inspector

Once you've received the right to have the home inspected (through the inspection clause attached to the contract), you have to hire your home inspector or put together your home inspection team (to conduct multiple inspections for pests, toxic substances, and the general condition of the home).

If you look in your local telephone book, you'll find dozens, if not hundreds, of people calling themselves "professional home inspectors." Some of them are, some of them aren't.

Some of the most qualified home inspectors are members of the American Society of Home Inspectors (ASHI), a nationwide, nonprofit professional association founded in 1976. ASHI only admits as members those home inspectors who have performed at least 750 home inspections according to the ASHI Standards of Practice, or 250 inspections in addition to other licenses and experience. Applicants must also pass a written exam, receive approval on at least three sample inspection reports, and perform a satisfactory home inspection before a peer review committee. In fact, ASHI is now consulting with many state legislatures that are thinking of passing laws to license home inspectors (currently just a handful of states, including Texas and Illinois, license home inspectors).

Where can you find a good inspector? Ask your real estate broker for a list of suggestions. When you call inspectors, keep the following in mind:

• **Compare fees.** Fees should range from $300 to $700, or more, depending on the size of the home. Ask what's included in the fee and how long the inspection should take. Be prepared to allow at least two hours for a thorough inspection of a moderately sized property.

- **Compare telephone manner.** The inspector should be courteous and knowledgeable. Ask for a list of specialized inspectors you might call (for radon, asbestos, electromagnetic power, water quality, pest control, etc.). Ask whether the inspector is bonded, licensed, and insured. Ask whether the inspector is a member of ASHI or another professional inspection association. Ask for references, and then call them.

- **Make sure you'll receive a written report.** You should receive the report either on-site (many inspectors now do their reports on handheld computers that plug into printers in the car) or by fax or e-mail that day or within 24 hours. Be clear on when you'll receive the report, and what kind of report it is. Will it be a checklist only, or will the inspector write his or her overall view?

These days, many inspectors carry a handheld computer and keep a printer in their car. They can hand you a report right after finishing the job, allowing you time to review the report and ask questions while the inspection is still fresh in your mind.

Once you've found your inspector, have him or her come out before the expiration of the right-to-inspection clause in your contract. You will usually have about five days from the time you sign the contract to have your inspection. Don't wait until the last day, in case it's raining or the inspection needs to be rescheduled.

When interviewing the home inspector, make sure he or she will be inspecting the entire house, top to bottom, inside and out. If the inspector balks at inspecting the basement, crawl space, attic, garage, or anything else, find someone else. If the inspector tells you these places will be inspected and then balks when actually at your home, call his or her supervisor, or consider ending the home inspection at that point. The home inspector clearly isn't doing his or her job, nor is he or she giving you what you're paying for.

For home buyers living in the northern half of the country, snow can pose huge problems for home inspectors. If a big snow occurs the night before your home inspection, the inspector will be limited in what he or she can do. The inspector may be able to brush off the snow from the roof to see a small piece of it, but he or she will not be able to make a thorough assessment, nor will he or she be able to ascertain the condition of the landscaping. A heavy rain can also make it difficult to properly inspect the home. Also, an inspector can't properly test out an air-conditioning system in the winter, or a heating system in the summer. Finally, try not to have the inspector come after dark because you want him or her to inspect the entire property's exterior and interior spaces. Daylight makes the process easier.

The Inspection Report

At the end of the inspection, or perhaps the next day, the inspector will give you a report of what's wrong with the house. The report should be complete, and it should be written. Ideally, the report should include the inspector's written remarks as well.

Be Sure to Tag Along

If you're smart, you'll go to the inspection and walk around with the inspector. Ask a lot of questions as you go along. The inspector should be happy to explain everything to you. It's an excellent opportunity to learn about the home you're buying and what to watch out for in the future.

Watch Out for This Trick

If a qualified, licensed, and bonded house inspector tells you the property may need $20,000 worth of repairs within the first five years, it should change the way you think about it. Is the property still a bargain? Should you look elsewhere? Can you afford to buy a home that will need such a substantial cash outlay within such a short period of time? Is the house a great deal anyway? (If your contract has an inspection contingency, you should be able to terminate the contract and get your earnest money back. Then you can search for another home.)

If the home inspector offers to complete any work he or she recommends to you, politely decline the offer. It doesn't happen too often, but the inspector could be suggesting there is trouble where there is none, simply to drum up more business.

20/20

hindsight

The Inside Skinny on Home Inspectors

Over the years, I've received loads of mail from disgruntled home buyers who believe they hired lousy inspectors who did a lousy job. And I've also received loads of mail from disgruntled home inspectors who feel they are being picked on for no good reason.

I believe the truth lies somewhere in the middle. Sometimes home inspectors miss things they should not. Sometimes home buyers have unrealistic expectations about the home they're buying. All home buyers have to understand this truism: *Old houses have old problems. The older the house, the more problems it will have.*

Brand-new and newer homes have problems, too, but once a house passes its 15th birthday, unless it has been flawlessly maintained, you'll need to address and correct problems as the years go on. That's just part and parcel of homeownership. If you're not ready for that responsibility, either buy a new house or continue to rent for a while.

You need to find a qualified home inspector who won't scare you needlessly. (Some home inspectors make old grout sound like the roof is caving in.) But you also need one who will tell you the truth and not kowtow to agents who refer them business. If that sounds like a conflict of interest waiting to happen, pat yourself on the back. That's exactly how it works in many places.

I believe that a home inspector should stand behind the reports he or she has written for clients. Many don't. Many written inspector forms are nothing more than checklists where the options are "Good," "Fair," "Poor," and "Recommend Specialist for Further Inspection." Too many referrals to specialists and you may find yourself wondering what added value the home inspector provides. (If the inspector only recommends you to specialists without identifying a real problem, it's a diminishing value that may ultimately not be worth the fee you paid.) Not only that, when you sign the agreement for your professional house inspection, you're basically signing away your rights to sue the inspector if he or she has missed something or made an incorrect assessment.

I find that to be outrageous. Home inspectors should stand behind what they write. If they can't, they should have insurance to cover their mistakes. Every home buyer should ask the home inspector whether or not he or she carries an errors and omissions (E&O) policy, and for how much. Better home inspectors have these policies.

Home inspectors are not the only individuals who do professional home inspections. Some contractors and structural engineers also do home inspections and can give you an opinion as to the structural integrity of your home. Both contractors and engineers are typically licensed by your state, and they carry insurance.

Although I recommend you contact the American Society of Home Inspectors (ashi.com) for a referral to an ASHI-certified inspector in your neighborhood, you should know that ASHI doesn't appear to police its wayward members, police its ethics code, or step in to mediate trouble between its member inspectors and homeowners who have had problems. Also, some home inspection companies appear to hire anyone off the street to work for the ASHI-trained owner. You may think you're hiring an ASHI-certified inspector when, in fact, you're not getting what you paid for.

Other national organizations claim to certify home inspectors. Before you hire such an inspector, check out the requirements for membership and certification. If they don't at least meet ASHI's standards, you have to wonder if the home inspector really knows what he or she is doing.

The Bottom Line

Despite these caveats, I do think almost every home buyer should have his or her home inspected. Just make sure you're getting what you pay for.

SHOULD I TEST FOR TOXIC SUBSTANCES AND CONTAMINATED WATER?

You've already asked for the right to have a professional inspector inspect your house. And you've asked for the right to have your home inspected for pests. Have you thought about having an inspector test for toxic substances?

Once a rare addition to contracts, toxic substance inspections—including radon, lead, water, and asbestos—have become a regular part of most real estate contracts. Unfortunately, most home inspectors are not qualified to do specialized tests for toxic substances. You must therefore find separate inspectors who specialize, or purchase the appropriate test in your local hardware store.

Here are the major toxic substances for which home buyers are inspecting these days:

- **Radon.** A study by the Environmental Protection Agency stated that 22,000 deaths a year are attributed to radon, a gas that seeps through cracks in the house or foundation from the earth. According to an EPA pamphlet, "Radon is the second leading cause of lung cancer in the U.S., after cigarette smoking. As you breathe it in, its decay products become trapped inside your lungs. As these products continue to decay, they release small bursts of energy that can damage lung tissue and lead to lung cancer. It's like exposing your family to hundreds of chest X-rays each year." Of the home buyers and homeowners who actually check for radon, the EPA estimates around 20 percent will find an unacceptable level. Although you can purchase an EPA-listed radon gas test kit in your local hardware store, it may be better to have a professional inspector perform the test, which requires two to four days of exposure in the home. (Or start with a store-bought test and hire a professional should the test indicate higher than acceptable levels.) Radon emissions can be fixed, either by sealing the cracks in the basement or crawl space or installing an air system that sucks out the gas from beneath the home. **For more information:** Call the EPA's hotline at (800) SOS-RADO.

- **Asbestos.** If you're buying new construction or anything built since the mid-1970s, you probably don't have to worry about asbestos. If you are buying an older home, some asbestos is likely in the house to insulate pipes or boilers. Asbestos, in its friable state, is a microscopic airborne fiber that is ingested through the nose or mouth; it lodges in the lung and can cause lung cancer. If not disturbed, the threat from asbestos is minimal, if any. You can hire an asbestos specialist to determine whether the home has asbestos and how much it will cost to have it wrapped or removed (the two ways to abate the threat). Lori, a first-time buyer in Chicago, said she wasn't deterred from buying her home because of asbestos. The seller agreed to give her a cash credit (a payment to the buyer at closing) equal to the price of removing the asbestos. **For more information:** Contact your local OSHA (Occupational Safety and

Health Administration) office of the federal government, or your local office of the federal Consumer Product Safety Commission.

- **Lead paint.** High levels of lead in paint and water (see below) have been connected with mental and physical development problems, particularly in young children. Lead is usually only a problem when ingested or inhaled. Lead paint is most often found in older homes (its use has been banned for more than 20 years) and can simply be covered up. In HUD homes, or those financed with an FHA mortgage, lead paint must be removed or covered over. A test by an outside agency can run between $100 and $300, depending on the number of samples tested. The federal government recently passed a lead paint law that requires home sellers of homes built before 1978 (the year lead paint was removed from the shelves) to disclose that there may be lead paint in the house. You can purchase lead tests that look like short, white swabs at your local hardware store. You simply swab the painted surfaces; if the swab turns red, there is lead present. Again, the problem with lead paint is only serious if you ingest lead paint chips or dust (if, for example, during renovation of your home). **For more information:** Call your local office of the federal Consumer Product Safety Commission or check out the EPA lead website (epa.gov/opptintr/lead/).

- **Lead in water.** High levels of lead in water is another problem, particularly in old homes and apartment buildings. If pipes soldered together with lead begin to corrode, lead particles can be released into your water supply. If the water is contaminated at the source (from your local city or municipal water supply), you may want to consider buying a filtering system or bottled water, or looking for another home in a different area. Inexpensive water filtering systems that can be purchased at your local hardware store claim to take out at least 93 percent of all lead in water. **For more information:** Call your local office of the Federal Consumer Product Safety Commission.

- **Electromagnetic radiation.** One of the most recently discovered hazards is electromagnetic radiation from high-voltage power lines. Only a few studies have been done, and the results are mixed. Some seem to show an increased rate of cancer and other unusual diseases in people who live in homes that are located directly underneath high-voltage power lines. Other studies show no increase of cancer or other diseases. Power companies deny the link, but you may want to avoid the risk that there may be a problem or that other problems will be discovered later. There's another risk: Property prices may not rise as quickly because of the perception that there is a problem—whether or not one actually exists. Since there is no way to shield yourself from the electromagnetic radiation, you must simply find another house to buy. There is a test for electromagnetic radiation, which can cost between $100 to $250, depending on the house.

Mold

When we gutted our home four years ago, the house was basically open to the humid Chicago summer air for about three or four months.

In the fall, while we were cleaning up from the renovation, we noticed that mold had begun to grow on an old wood door in the old part of our basement. So we hired someone to simply wash it away with bleach and water.

"That's not a bad way to go as long as you don't have a really large spot of mold, say an area no bigger than 10′ × 10′," says Josh Appleman, a certified environmental health specialist based in Ft. Wayne, Indiana. "But I wouldn't advise doing it yourself if the area is any bigger."

Since the second edition of this book was published, mold has surpassed all other toxic substances, except for asbestos, in terms of dollars spent for its removal. But it ranks much higher on a home buyer and homeowner's list of concerns. The problem has become so severe in the past few years that mold removal (or remediation, as it is known) has become a very big business. So big, not to mention expensive, that many insurance policies have excluded mold removal from the items that are covered if a pipe breaks and your home is flooded.

Let's back up a bit. Every house contains mold spores. You'll find mold on dogs and kids, in the yard, in the bathroom, and in the basement. But most often, you'll find that mold spores cling to wet or damp spaces, like a wet basement wall, the windows of a house that has too much humidity and too little fresh, cool air moving around, or inside the walls, where a roof leak has no chance of drying out.

According to the Centers for Disease Control (cdc.gov) and the Environmental Protection Agency (epa.gov) websites, mold starts growing within 24 to 48 hours of being exposed to water or an extremely humid environment.

197

"If a house has a history of water problems, it could have a mold problem as well. If building materials (at a new construction site) stay damp and conditions are right, mold could start to grow. If the relative humidity of a home is above 60 percent, or if the house is closed up with no air-conditioning, mold can begin to grow," Appleman explains.

Julie and Adam's Story

Julie and Adam bought a lot across the street from where they lived and built a new house. When it was done, they moved in and put their house up on the market for sale. A couple made an offer for the house, and the deal closed.

After the house sold, the couple didn't move in right away. It was summer, and the house was closed up, and the air-conditioning was turned off. Mold grew like crazy.

When the couple finally moved in, their kids began getting sick. They finally realized mold was the cause and moved out of the house. The house had grown so moldy it was uninhabitable. The couple sued Julie and Adam for selling them a house that contained mold, but they lost the case.

In the meantime, the house basically had to be torn apart, board by board, and rebuilt. But that still didn't do enough to solve the mold issue. As we went to press, the house had been torn down and a new house was being built on the property.

Harmless Mold, Killer Mold

Most mold spores are relatively harmless, but some forms of mold are extremely dangerous or even toxic, including *stachybotrys chartarum*, also known as black mold. If you have allergies or asthma, you may be more sensitive to mold.

Michael's Story

Michael was renting an apartment with his girlfriend when he developed a cough. Being 26, he thought he had a cold; it didn't occur to him that something could be terribly wrong. Several months later, it was much worse. He finally went to the emergency room, but it was too late. His aunt told me that after Michael died, an autopsy concluded he was allergic to mold. The apartment in which he had been living was filled with it.

"Mold today is like asbestos was 20 years ago," says Lawrence, a professional home inspector based in Chicago. "In the property inspection business there is always the problem de jour. And consumers are being taken advantage of because of it."

Lawrence says some cases of mold are life threatening, but most aren't: "Mold remediation companies are in the business of scaring consumers into doing more (and spending more) than they need to.

"With asbestos, removal caused more problems than good. But asbestos and mold are very emotional (buzzwords) today," Lawrence says. "If you think you have a problem and someone scares you enough, you will sign a contract for remediation services."

When you shop around for your first home, be on the lookout for obvious signs of mold. If the house has a damp, musty smell, that could be mold. If you see spores clinging to the walls (which might look like a black, gray, or green shadow on the walls) or the ceiling in the basement, that could be a sign of mold. If you see spores on the inside of the window, and you still decide to make an offer, then you should tell the professional home inspector to keep a sharp outlook for a possible mold problem.

"In one case I just evaluated, a gentleman was living in the basement and thought there was spray paint on the walls. It turned out to be mold. He had to cover his nose and mouth with his shirt when we went down. I had on a respirator," Appleman recalls.

Marya's Story

Marya went looking to buy a house. She came across what she thought was the perfect home. The home inspector discovered the house was covered in mold. Apparently, the owners had moved away and locked up the house during the summer without leaving the air-conditioning on.

She asked her attorney what she should do. He advised her to back out of the deal. "No matter how clean you get this house, there could always be a mold problem. There's no reason to stay when there are so many other homes for sale out there."

Marya ended up backing out of the deal and buying a different house.

What You Can Do

Whether you own or rent, if you have a leak, if your home floods, or if you get water in your basement, you can expect mold to grow unless you dry things up quickly. Don't worry about saving money. Control the humidity in your house by using your air conditioner or dehumidifier in the summer or on humid days.

As Appleman points out, it's far less expensive to keep mold at bay than do any remediation work. Although his company does not do remediation at all, he estimates that it would cost a homeowner at least $1,000 to start with mold removal. Remediation costs can run as high as several hundred thousand dollars.

> Real estate attorneys advise that the language you use in your contract should state that the "sale is contingent upon satisfactory results of the environmental tests." If you don't include this kind of language, you could find yourself having the right to have the tests done, but not the right to back out of the deal if the house fails to pass the tests to your satisfaction. For more details about legal language that would be appropriate in your area, consult a real estate attorney.

The News on Synthetic Stucco and Mold

Since the late 1990s one of the biggest sources of mold problems has been with homes made with synthetic stucco, also known as EIFS. There are many different trade names for synthetic stucco, including Dryvit.

The problem seems to be that synthetic stucco is a polymer, which is like plastic. When you coat the exterior of your house in synthetic stucco, it's difficult for air to circulate. If water infiltrates the house between the synthetic stucco and the wood frame or plywood holding the house together, mold can grow because of the lack of air circulating. In other words, the wood gets wet and then can't dry out.

Millions of dollars have been awarded to homeowners whose synthetic stucco homes became uninhabitable. You can check out current litigation at various class action websites (ClassActionsOnline.com, ClassActionAmerica.com and http://securities/stanford.edu, which is run by Stanford University).

If you're buying new construction that contains synthetic stucco, you may want to read up on what kind of synthetic stucco has been applied, who applied it, and where current litigation is with the company that manufactured it. Although there are homes made with synthetic stucco that do not have a water infiltration problem, many do. One study suggests that a majority of homes made with synthetic stucco either have, or will have, a problem with water infiltration over time.

If you buy a home with synthetic stucco, hire a home inspector who specializes in EIFS systems to check your home for moisture infiltration every six months. If holes or cracks develop in the home, fix them quickly to avoid causing permanent damage to your home. To find a home inspector who specializes in EIFS, start with the American Society of Home Inspectors (ashi.com).

One of the big questions is, why is mold becoming an issue now? One answer appears to be that the new homes being built are much more "airtight" than homes built 20 or 30 years ago.

Windows are double-paned (making them more energy efficient), caulks that seal joints have improved, house wraps have become more impervious to moisture, roofing materials are stronger, and so on.

Also, the huge demand for new construction has put pressure on builders to turn out houses faster than ever. A newspaper investigation published in 2003 found that *80 percent of some 800 new homes built in a particular metropolitan area in Florida had some sort of problem.*

To ensure your new home is being built correctly, you should have a professional home inspector on the premises at least four times during construction. Once the house is built, you may miss the signs of future problems, like a roof vent that was installed incorrectly.

For more information on all of these toxins and more, check out the EPA toxin link at epa.gov. Also, local home improvement and hardware stores offer inexpensive tests for most toxic substances. You can spend around $10 to get a reasonably accurate test that will indicate the presence of mold, lead, and other toxic substances.

WHAT IF THE INSPECTORS FIND SOMETHING WRONG WITH THE HOME I WANT TO BUY?

It's likely that your home inspector or your toxic substance and pest inspectors *will* find something wrong with the property you want to buy. Remember, that's their job. Once a problem is found, and it might

QUESTION

50

be a small problem or a big problem, you have to ask yourself two questions:

1. Is the problem fixable or unfixable?
2. At what price is the problem fixable?

Here are some examples of *unfixable* problems:

- The house sits on a fault line.
- The house is in a floodplain.
- The home's foundation is severely cracked (a major crack is one that is larger than one-eighth inch).
- The house's water supply has been contaminated by the local dump.
- The house is located under electromagnetic power lines.

Almost everything else is fixable—even most kinds of earthquake damage.

Often, sellers assume that home buyers *want* an inspection to find problems so they can negotiate a lower price. If this is your strategy to buy the house at a lower price, don't be surprised if the seller refuses to do anything and you're stuck taking the house in "as is" condition. Also, in a hot market, many sellers may be unwilling to do more than the bare minimum, if anything at all. That's a symptom of a strong seller's market. In a buyer's market (where there are more homes for sale than qualified buyers), you'll have more leverage. You should find, however, that most sellers are happy to do what's reasonable and fair. If that's all you ask for, you shouldn't have too much of a problem.

But is it affordable or smart to try and fix every problem? Is the house worth it? You can fix a leaky roof or replace it entirely, but is the house worth its $100,000 price plus $5,000 for a new roof? What if the house also needs a new furnace and hot water heater? What if it needs upgraded electricity for a clothes dryer? What if the pipes are old and leaking?

If your inspectors find something wrong with the house, you have two options: (1) withdraw from the contract (provided you have the right inspection contingency) or (2) renegotiate the purchase price to reflect the cost of fixing the items marked on the inspection list. If you decide to withdraw from the contract, have your attorney write the letter. If you decide to go ahead but want to renegotiate the purchase price, talk to your broker and your attorney about what may be customary for your area.

WHAT DO I DO IF THE SELLER OR BROKER HAS MISREPRESENTED THE CONDITION OF THE HOME?

If you find out from the inspection that the seller or broker has misrepresented the condition of the home, and you have a properly written inspection contingency, you have the option of walking away from the deal. You may also report the broker's conduct to the state agency that regulates real estate professionals. (See Appendix VI for a list of agencies that regulate brokers in all 50 states.)

> You may be upset and frustrated, but you have to consider yourself lucky not to have bought what could easily have turned out to be a lemon of a house. Nothing is more frustrating than living through one home crisis after another.

If you find out after you close on the home that the seller or broker has clearly misrepresented the condition of the home, or did not disclose everything they knew about the property or should have known about the property, you can take them to court. But be prepared to prove that they did have knowledge of the problem or should have had knowledge.

Ilyce and Sam's Story

When we bought our co-op, the seller and the seller broker told us that everything was working in the unit. We forgot to test the dishwasher before closing. (Rule No. 1: Always run all the appliances in an inspection.)

The first night we were in the apartment, we decided to turn on the dishwasher. Nothing happened. Sam reached down under the sink and turned the water back on (the sellers had apparently turned off the water to the dishwasher). The next morning we found out why. The dish washer leaked all over our new downstairs neighbors' kitchen, ruining their window shade.

We were furious. Obviously, the sellers knew that their dishwasher leaked, which is why they turned off the water. Would we have not bought the unit if we'd known about the dishwasher? Of course not. It cost us only $150 to replace the window shade plus $60 to replace the faulty hose.

But were we steamed! We wrote a nasty letter to the sellers and felt much better.

first time buyer tip

Make sure your inspection contingency allows you to withdraw from the deal if the home inspector gives you an unsatisfactory report on the property. But remember, all homes, even new ones, have problems. And old homes often have older and more difficult problems. Keep your expectations in line with what you're buying. If you're buying an older home, don't assume it will be in perfect condition or that the seller will pay to upgrade the house with next-century technology. If that's your assumption, you may be better off renting.

7

Possession and Other Parts of the Offer to Purchase

WHAT IS POSSESSION?

You've heard the cliché: Possession is nine-tenths of the law.

In real estate, *possession* is when you actually take physical control of the home. Most buyers take possession of the home at the closing. The keys, garage door openers, and other security devices are handed to the buyer from the seller, who has moved all of his or her belongings from the home. At that moment, you have the right to do anything you want with *your* house.

Sometimes possession is given either before the closing or after. Let's say you need a place to live or want to renovate the home prior to the closing. The seller might let you take possession early by a few days so that you can move in or get started on your remodeling. Many real estate attorneys advise sellers not to allow a preclosing possession by the buyer. It's very risky. The buyer might move in and then decide not to close. At that point, the seller becomes a landlord and may have to pursue an eviction proceeding against the buyer.

Usually possession issues in a residential real estate transaction involve a seller who wants to stay in the house after closing (see Question 53).

Possession and the closing date are closely linked. Sometimes they're used as negotiation points when money isn't the primary issue. In one case in California, a first-time buyer made a full-price offer for

205

a woman's house, but the woman was having trouble accepting the offer. She hadn't found a place to move her family and was worried. The buyer stretched out the date of the closing, in exchange for a few thousand dollars off the sales price, and the deal went through.

With new construction, you can't close on your new house and move in until the builder has obtained a Certificate of Occupancy (also known as the "C of O"). This certificate is issued by the local municipality and certifies that the house meets code and that basic necessities (such as the walls, roof, electricity, plumbing and other mechanicals) are in place and are working. If you're concerned about the condition of the home and the builder says he's received the "C of O", ask to see it. If you have any questions, call the local building or planning department that issued the "C of O". "C of Os" are only issued once the house is virtually complete, even though punch list items (small details that haven't yet been installed or need to be fixed) may remain.

WHAT IF THE SELLER WANTS TO STAY IN THE HOUSE AFTER THE CLOSING?

QUESTION 53

When the seller indicates he or she would like to stay on after closing for a few days or weeks, it's called a *post-closing possession*. There are two issues to consider:

1. **Charging a reasonable daily rate.** If you've got a few weeks to go on your lease or if Mom and Dad are gracious about letting you camp out for a few more nights, you might want to grant the post-closing possession. If you do, you'll want to charge the sellers a reasonable rate for the extra time they stay in what will now be your house. This "reasonable" rate should cover your daily expenses, including the daily cost of your mortgage, homeowner's insurance, and taxes.

2. **Overstaying the welcome.** The risk with letting the sellers stay after the closing is that they might never leave. And if the sellers don't leave, you'll have to force them out. At that point, you'll want to make them pay dearly for each extra day they stay, so the seller realizes it will be much cheaper to leave.

If the sellers do not indicate, during the contract negotiations, a wish to stay past closing, but then announce at closing their intent to stay for a while, you may have a problem. Real estate attorneys generally advise buyers to refuse to close unless the sellers have moved out. Usually, the threat of not closing is enough to get the sellers motivated to leave.

If you schedule your final walk-through after the sellers have moved out, or while they are moving, you'll know that they're really going to be, or are, gone. The ideal situation is to walk through the property and then go directly to the closing.

In cases where the seller asks to stay in the home after closing (either because the seller's purchase of another home is a couple of days later, or the seller is arranging a move to another city), you can give them the couple of days (a set number) for a modest fee that will cover all of your expenses of ownership. But when those days are up, the sellers should pay a fee that encourages them to move out *fast*. An amount of money large enough to convince the sellers it's time to move should be held back at closing, in an escrow account, in addition to the daily fees they will owe you.

If the money is held in escrow, and your seller turns out to be a deadbeat, it's much more likely you'll see that cash.

Calculating a Daily Fee That Will Motivate the Seller

There are several ways to calculate a daily fee that will motivate your sellers:

1. Charge the same prices as an expensive, local hotel.
2. Find out the going rent for the home like yours, then divide by 30 (days of the month) and multiply by two or three.

In either case, you want the sellers to understand that staying in the home will be a very expensive proposition. If all else fails, and the sellers continue to stay in your new home, you may have to take legal action. Consult your attorney for advice.

In some areas of the country, it's customary for the seller to retain possession *at no cost* for three to five days after closing. Your broker or attorney should be able to advise you on local closing customs.

WHEN IS THE RIGHT TIME TO TERMINATE THE CONTRACT? HOW DO I DO IT?

The question you should ask yourself is: Why do I want to terminate the contract to purchase?

If you want to terminate the contract because you're feeling buyer's remorse (see Question 55), you can't. That's the tough part about the real estate game. The rules say, when you sign and present the offer, and seller accepts it, you have a deal. Unless your inspector finds something wrong with the home, or your attorney rejects the contract, or your lender won't grant you a mortgage, you're pretty much stuck.

Some unscrupulous buyers will tell their attorneys to summarily "reject" a contract if they get cold feet. That's not really fair to the seller, who has allowed the prospective buyer to tie up the property during the negotiation process. In addition, the sellers may be able to sue you for specific performance, making you live up to the deal to which you signed your name.

You may be able to walk away from the contract at other times, if you are willing to forfeit your deposit or earnest money. Most first-time buyers have little cash, so the idea of giving up 5, 10, or 20 percent of the purchase price, or even $1,000, seems a little steep. But it has been done many times before. In this case, the earnest money is either split between the seller and the broker, or the seller gets to keep it all.

Returning the Earnest Money

When you put down a good faith deposit, also known as the earnest money, it's usually deposited in the escrow account of the seller broker. The seller broker may not release that money to you without the seller's permission.

I frequently receive letters from buyers telling me that a seller broker refuses to release their cash deposit. If you terminate the contract for valid reasons, the seller should sign off on the release of the earnest money. But sometimes sellers don't—just out of spite.

If this happens to you, your next step will likely be to explore your legal options. Talk to your real estate attorney. You may have to file suit in order to shake your money loose.

WHAT IS "BUYER'S REMORSE" AND HOW DO I COPE WITH IT?

QUESTION 55

"Buyer's remorse" is the sinking feeling in the pit of your stomach that you've made a terrible mistake. It usually occurs the minute, day, or week after your broker presents your offer to purchase or you sign the purchase and sale agreement. It keeps you awake at night, tossing and turning in a cold sweat, as you wonder how you're going to make the payments and you agonize over your choice. Did you make the right one?

Pam, a broker in Rock Hill, South Carolina, says if a first-time buyer has buyer's remorse, the only person to blame is the real estate agent. "If the agent has truly done her job and qualified those people, and found out what they really wanted in their first home, then they should be happy," she says. "But if the agent turns a blind eye to their insecurity about buying a home and doesn't try to help them understand the process, it can be very tough."

Susanne's Story

No one is exempt from buyer's remorse—even an industry player like my mother.

My mother, Susanne, is one of the top real estate agents in the Chicago area. In some years, she has sold in excess of $20 million in property.

Until recently, the only home she'd ever bought is the one she bought nearly 40 years ago. She'd never even had a mortgage.

Even though she's helped thousands of people successfully buy and sell homes throughout her career, when the time came to buy a condo in a new construction development, she came down with a bad case of buyer's remorse.

It was the perfect investment: All of her expenses were covered for the time she owned it. But she couldn't wait to get rid of it. Even though she made a good investment, she's never quite gotten over it.

On the other hand, three years ago, Susanne decided she was ready to move out of the 1920s apartment she lived in. She bought a new condo that was about to be built just west of Michigan Avenue in downtown Chicago. When the time came to move, she was ready. It took a little longer to sell her co-op than she had planned, but she had no qualms at all about leaving—and no more buyer's remorse.

Fighting Your Emotions

Buying a home is such an emotional process that first-timers often get overwhelmed. Real estate agent Pam says brokers should be understanding and help clients *know* whether they are making the right decision for the right reason. Brokers should be able to read the personality of that buyer and make sure that the decision is not 100 percent emotion and zero percent common sense.

Pam says that she often helps her distraught first-time buyers with something she calls "The Ben Franklin Close." She advises her buyers to make a list of everything you like about the house and then everything you would change. This, she says, will help you make a rational decision by seeing the pluses and minuses of a home.

Curing Buyer's Remorse

What's the cure for buyer's remorse? As the sages say, "Time heals all wounds." Give yourself six months in your new home. If you still hate it, you can always turn around and try to sell it. Chances are, after six months to a year, you'll be settled in and feeling a whole lot better.

first time buyer tip

Your best defense against a bad case of buyer's remorse is preparation. If you haven't already created your wish list and reality check, you should do so. Knowing the difference between what you want in a home and what you can't live without will help you understand the important compromises that have to be made when you purchase your first home. And that's what it is—your *first* home, not your last one.

8

Financing Your Home

HOW MUCH CAN I AFFORD TO SPEND ON A HOME?

Although I covered some of this information in Chapter 4, it's worth taking a closer look. Once you've found a home, or once you've decided to get preapproved so that you can seriously shop for a property to buy, you're going to want to think about mortgages and housing affordability in greater detail. The good news is that many websites, including ThinkGlink.com, have calculators and tools that can make it a lot easier and faster to calculate the numbers.

Most Americans simply guess at the amount they can spend: "Let's see, I earn $50,000 a year, and I've been told I can spend two and a half times my annual income on a house, so that means I can spend $125,000. Right?"

Perhaps. If interest rates are 10 percent for a 30-year fixed-rate loan, *and* you have no debt, *and* you have 20 percent to put down on a home, then you can probably spend $125,000 for every $50,000 in income. But if interest rates are 8 percent for that 30-year loan, and you don't carry much, if any, debt, and you still have down payment cash, you might be able to spend $150,000 or more on a house. And if interest rates are at 6.5 percent, you might be able to spend $200,000 or more for every $50,000 in income.

Confused? You're not alone here, either. But it's not that tough to use the formulas that mortgage lenders use to calculate how much house you can afford. Or you can call a local lender and get prequalified or preapproved for your loan. Even easier is to go online at any number of sites and use the calculators. Many sites will do virtually

211

instantaneous loan approvals. (I'll give you some web addresses at the end of this section, but first I think you should understand how the calculations work.)

> The worst thing about guessing how much you can afford to spend is that you might be wrong—but you start looking at homes that are out of your price range anyway. That can only lead to one thing—heartbreak. Once you start looking at homes that are too rich for your budget, it's awfully hard to settle for what you can afford.

Assets and Debts

Every discussion about how much you can afford should start with assets and debts—how much you have versus how much you owe.

The amount of debt you carry is very important. Conventional loan programs will allow you to spend up to 28 percent of your gross monthly income (GMI) on your mortgage payment and up to 36 percent on total debt, including your mortgage, car payment, school loan payment, credit card payment, and other consumer debt. If you carry no other debt besides your mortgage, you'll be allowed to spend the full 36 percent of your GMI on your mortgage payment. If, however, you spend 10 percent of your GMI on debt, that will reduce the amount of money you have available for your mortgage each month.

> Gross monthly income is different from take-home pay. You might spend 36 percent of your GMI on your total debt, but it may feel like 50 percent or more of your take-home pay, after taxes and your 401(k) contribution have been deducted.

For example, Susie and Don earn $75,000 per year. Their gross monthly income is $6,250 per month. If they have no debt, a lender will allow them to spend up to 36 percent of their GMI, or $2,250 on their mortgage, real estate property taxes, and insurance. But if they pay $250 per month on their car loan, and $200 on a graduate school loan, and $100 on their credit card debt, that will reduce the amount they can spend on their mortgage by $550, leaving them with only $1,700 per month to spend on their loan.

That $550 may not seem like a lot, but as you'll see, it can translate into a huge amount of purchasing power.

When it comes to applying for a mortgage, the two best things you can do are (1) pay off all of your debt or as much as possible, and (2) make sure your credit is as good as gold. Home buyers who have the best credit get the best rates and terms for their mortgage. The difference in the interest rate you'll get if you have a high credit score and a low credit score is shockingly huge.

Take a look at this chart from MyFico.com, a joint venture between Equifax (one of the three leading credit reporting bureaus) and Fair Isaacs (the company that created the credit score). To calculate where your score is, and how raising it would change the amount of interest you'll pay over the life of your loan, visit the credit score calculator at MyFico.com.

How Your Credit Score Affects What You'll Pay for a $200,000 Loan

FICO SCORE	APR* (%)	Monthly Payment	Total Interest Paid
720–850	6.167	$1,221	$239,437
700–719	6.292	$1,237	$245,285
675–699	6.830	$1,308	$327,307
620–674	7.980	$1,465	$327,307
560–619	8.531	$1,542	$355,200
500–559	9.289	$1,651	$394,362

*APR is the Annual Percentage Rate on your loan. Total interest paid is the amount of interest you'll pay on a $200,000 loan over 30 years plus certain other lender fees and charges.

If the highest credit scores (anything over 720 is considered the highest group of scores) will receive a 30-year mortgage at 6.167 percent, the worst credit score will get an interest rate that is more than 3 percentage points higher. Worst, the homeowner with bad credit will pay more than $160,000 in interest than someone who has great credit.

Prequalification vs. Preapproval

When you get *prequalified* for a loan, you're essentially asking the lender to eyeball your numbers and tell you what he or she thinks you can afford to spend on a home. The guess means more than your guess because the lender does this every day.

When you get *preapproved* for a loan, the lender looks at how much you earn, owe, and have in the bank. Then, the lender commits in writing to funding your loan, pending a successful appraisal of the property. It used to take days or weeks to get preapproved for a loan, but today most loans can be preapproved in minutes.

Being preapproved for your loan means the lender has committed in writing to fund your loan, no matter which house you buy. The only caveat is that the house must appraise out in value. It makes you an exceptionally strong buyer because the seller knows going in that a lender has approved you and you are qualified financially to buy the house.

20/20 hindsight

Sellers and their agent will perceive a preapproved home buyer to be "stronger" financially than one who is simply prequalified (although many real estate agents use the terms interchangeably). In a seller's market, where there are more home buyers than homes available for sale, you should get preapproved for your loan, rather than prequalified. Being preapproved will allow you to move much faster through the lending process, and time may be critical.

First Time Buyer Tip

For some sellers, being "preapproved" isn't good enough. A new trend among home sellers is to require the buyer to submit their credit history *and* credit score along with their offer to purchase.

The World Wide Web of Home Loans

Mortgage lending websites have exploded since 1994. You can go to hundreds of thousands of places to get information about improving your credit history and credit score, apply for a loan, or get more information. Today, you can bank online, get approved for your loan online, and pay your mortgage electronically (and save the postage).

The following are different types of electronic lenders:

• Big national lenders, like Countrywide Home Loans, Bank of America, and Chase Manhattan

• Small local mortgage brokers

- Aggregators, which bring together dozens or even hundreds of mortgage lenders and use technology to automatically sort through which loan program is right for you (priceline.com and lendingtree.com are two of the bigger aggregators)
- Portals, like HouseandHome.com (Microsoft's home portal) and Yahoo.com
- Auction sites, like eBay.com

Other Internet lending models may spring up in the future, so continue to stay plugged in even after you buy a home. If you don't wind up selling your home in five to seven years, you may well need a lender to help you refinance or get a home equity loan. For more information about applying online, see Question 60.

First Things First

Before you call a lender, or go online and start playing around with Internet calculators, you ought to know how lenders go about qualifying you for your loan. The worksheet on the following page should help you figure it out.

20/20 hindsight

Lenders will require you to have enough cash on hand (i.e., in a savings account) to pay at least 2 months' worth of mortgage payments and the tax and insurance escrow payments. This is called your *reserve*. Lenders will not allow you to spend literally everything you have to buy your first home. So if your monthly mortgage payment is $1,000, you'll need at least $2,000 in reserves plus closing costs (if any) to close on your home. Subtract that amount from the down payment you've accumulated. For more information on how much you can expect to pay for closing costs, see Questions 63 and 65.

Playing the Interest Rate Game

As I said earlier, interest rates have a significant effect on how much you can afford to spend on a home. At 10 percent, you might be able to afford twice your income. At 6.5 percent, it might be nearly four times your income.

Everyone wants to buy or refinance when rates are at their lowest. But hardly anyone ever gets that super-low rate. Home buyers and

1. Gross Monthly Income (GMI)
      from all sources: _____

2. Multiply by:
      .25 (25%), a conservative number
      .28 (28%), the conventional amount
      .33 (33%), allows you some debt payments
      .36 (36%), if you have no debt
      For the loan-to-income ratio   × _____

3. Subtract your current monthly debt service:
      Credit cards   _____
      Car loan(s)/leases   _____
      Charge accounts   _____
      School loan(s)   _____
      Other personal debt   _____
      Total Debt Service   − _____

4. Subtract monthly or semimonthly condominium or co-op
      assessments, or homeowner association fees,
      if applicable   − _____

5. Maximum monthly mortgage payment   = _____

6. Subtract real estate property and tax monthly
      escrow   − _____

7. Net monthly mortgage payment   = _____

8. Multiply by 12 (months of the year)   × ___12___

9. Annual mortgage payment   = _____

10. Divide by the current interest rate   ÷ _____

11. Total amount of mortgage   = _____

12. Plus cash you have available for the down payment
       (save some for closing costs and 2 months' reserve)   = _____

13. Approximate amount you can spend on a home   = _____

homeowners sit on the fence waiting for rates to drop further and are surprised (and a little hurt) when they realize rates have gone back up and they've missed the trough.

The truth is this: A quarter-point change in interest rates doesn't mean much over the life of your loan. On a $100,000 loan, the difference in interest paid if the loan carries a 7.5 percent versus 8.5 percent interest rate is only about $70 per month, although it adds up to $25,000 over the life of the loan. But you're probably not going to stay in your first house for the next 30 years. Chances are you'll sell or refinance within five to seven years. In that period of time, the difference in what you'll pay is negligible, and you can negate it by either prepaying your mortgage or going with an adjustable-rate mortgage (ARM) rather than a fixed-rate loan, which will carry a lower interest rate. (See Question 77 for information on ARMs.)

In the next few questions, I'll talk about different types of loans, how to choose the right one for you, and the loan application process.

WHAT IS A MORTGAGE?

QUESTION 57

If a person agrees to lend you money, he or she likely will ask you to put up something to collateralize the loan. The collateral must be something of equal or greater worth than the amount of the loan so that the lender feels secure in giving you the money.

Here's a formal definition: A *mortgage* is a document in which you pledge the title to your home as the collateral. The lender agrees to hold the title (or agrees, in some states, to place a lien on your title) until you have paid back the loan plus interest. The lender gives you the money; in exchange, you agree to make monthly installments of principal and interest, home insurance premiums, and real estate taxes. Most people somewhat mistakenly call this collective amount their "mortgage payment."

A Brief History of Home Loans

The history of mortgages in the United States is interesting. Before the Great Depression in the 1930s, we didn't have mortgages the way we know them today. Back then, people paid cash for their homes. Or they would take out very short "balloon" mortgages, on which they would pay interest for maybe five years, and then owe the entire balance in one huge "balloon" payment.

When the stock market crashed in 1929, most people lost their life savings and were unable to pay back their mortgages. So they lost their homes. Many other people were unable to pay their real estate taxes and they, too, lost their homes. In 1930, so many people in Cook County (the county in Illinois that includes Chicago) couldn't afford to pay their real estate taxes (less than 50 percent paid) that the city canceled the year's real estate tax collection. That's why Cook County collects its real estate taxes a year in arrears. In other words, Cook County homeowners pay last year's taxes in the current year; taxes paid in 2006 will be for taxes owed from 2005.

The War Ends

At the end of World War II, many returning veterans had money to spend. The U.S. government decided U.S. soldiers were good risks and helped design a plan to lend them money to buy homes. The plan allowed them to borrow money for 30 years and pay it back slowly, with interest. The program was such a huge success that commercial lenders soon followed suit.

That was the beginning of the modern mortgage industry. Today, trillions of dollars in mortgages are made every year and are sold on the secondary market. They are such a stable source of income (less than 4 percent of all mortgages fail or go into default) that investors—huge pension funds, for example—buy mortgages from banks, savings and loans, and mortgage brokers. This puts money back into the system, where it can be lent again.

Because almost all loans are resold on the secondary market, you can expect your loan to be among them. In fact, don't be surprised if your loan is sold over and over again. But don't worry. Even if your loan is sold, it doesn't mean you have to pay back the loan all at once. What the new lender is buying is either the right to service your loan (meaning, to collect the funds) or to hold your mortgage note—or both. If your loan is sold, there will be a period of 60 to 90 days where records get transferred or merged and there may be some confusion. Be vigilant and keep calling for more information if you're not sure about your mortgage balance or account. It's up to you to make sure you're paying the right lender.

Some lenders do keep a small percentage of loans in-house. Called *portfolio* loans, they typically have more relaxed qualifications for approval. To find out if your mortgage will be kept or sold, ask the person taking your application what percentage of loans are kept or sold. Remember to ask if *your* loan in particular will be sold. Don't be surprised if the answer is yes. The vast majority of home loans are resold into something called the *secondary market*. If your loan is sold, another company may be hired to "service" the loan for the new investor. If your loan is not sold, you will continue to pay and deal with the local folks who gave you your loan.

A Big, Scary Scam

One of the more common scams is the mortgage sale scam. Here's what happens: You receive a notice that your loan is being sold and a new company, XYZ Capital, will now collect your monthly mortgage check. You're instructed on official-looking letterhead to send your mortgage payments to the new company.

What you don't realize is that there is no new company. It's a scam. So you send in one, two, or even three months' worth of payments. And go on with your life.

Out of the blue, you get a call from your old mortgage company wondering why you're 60 or 90 days late in paying your loan. Your credit has been damaged, and even though you've already paid out to XYZ Capital, you still owe your regular monthly payment to your real mortgage company.

Of course, you can go to the Federal Trade Commission (www. ftc.org) and file a complaint. But what could you have done to protect yourself ahead of time?

If you receive a letter like this announcing that your mortgage has been sold, be sure to call up your original lender to confirm that the loan has indeed been sold. Get the name, and the toll-free telephone number of the new lender from your original lender. The new lender is required by law to provide a toll-free number that you can call to check on the status of your account.

That's all it takes. If you do find out the letter you've received is a fake, call the FTC immediately. With any luck, they'll be able to put the scam artist out of business permanently.

HOW DO I GET INFORMATION ON MORTGAGES?

Getting the information is easy. Sorting it all out and choosing the best home loan for you is a little tougher.

Here are some good sources of information:

1. Newspapers. The real estate section of your local newspaper probably has something like a "mortgage watch" column. This column gives you a list of maybe 5 or 10 local mortgage companies and the loans and rates they are currently offering. As you peruse this list each week, remember that those rates are anywhere from 4 to 10 days old, and the interest rate may have shifted up or down. If you call one of those companies, don't ask for the rate you saw in the newspaper. Instead, ask for their lowest rate on a 30-year or 15-year or 1-year ARM. Mortgage companies also advertise heavily in the real estate section. You can call several of those companies to inquire about rates and programs as well. If you go online to the newspaper's website (most newspapers have their own websites, like ChicagoTribune.com and LATimes.com), you can click on the real estate section and find more current rates.

2. Real estate agents and brokers. Real estate agents usually know which local mortgage companies offer good rates. Your agent's firm probably owns its own mortgage company (not to mention title or escrow company, alarm system company, and perhaps even appraisal company). Your agent should be prepared to give you a list of at least three different mortgage companies he or she knows are good and responsive, including the one the agent's firm owns.

3. Local lenders. Walk into your local bank, savings and loan, or credit union (credit unions typically have really inexpensive mortgages for their members) and ask for their free information (they should have gobs of it).

4. Local housing authority. Your local housing authority is an excellent place for free information. It may also have special programs for first-time buyers. These programs could include down payment assistance or extra-low interest rate loans for families who meet certain income or location requirements. If you qualify, you may be able to get a loan that carries an interest rate that's well below the market rate.

5. The federal government. Write to Consumer Publications, Pueblo, Colorado 81003, and ask for their free information guide. Or go online to Pueblo.gsa.gov. A word of warning, however. These federal publications talk about mortgages in general. They're good as far as they go, which isn't nearly far enough. If you have questions after reading through one of these little booklets, call your local mortgage company and get answers.

6. Online. Almost everything you can get in person is now available on the Web. Fannie Mae (homepath.com or fanniemae.com) and Freddie Mac (freddiemac.com), the two secondary mortgage market (which trade on the New York Stock Exchange), have excellent websites chock-full of information on buying a home and getting a mortgage. Bank Rate Monitor's website (bankrate.com) is devoted to providing the latest interest rate information for mortgages, as well as car loans and credit cards. Aggregators like Microsoft's House and Home, Lending Tree, Priceline Mortgage, and E-Loan all provide helpful information, in addition to allowing you to play with calculators and apply online. Large national mortgage companies like Countrywide Home Loans (countrywide.com) and Bank of America (bankofamerica.com) also have excellent information, typically in several languages. These companies' sites offer good, time-tested information. In fact, information from several of my books and years of columns runs on several of these sites. But new sites are always emerging. To stay on top of it, try the International Real Estate Digest (ired.com), which ranks sites and attempts to list and categorize many of the real estate sites out there in Webland.

WHAT IS THE DIFFERENCE BETWEEN A MORTGAGE BANKER AND A MORTGAGE BROKER? HOW DO I FIND A GOOD LENDER? WHO ARE THE PEOPLE INVOLVED WITH MAKING THE LOAN?

The essential ingredient to a successful purchase is finding a lender you can trust to walk you through the process. Where do you find such a person? To begin with, it's important to understand that lenders come in all shapes and sizes, and they're called by different names.

- **Mortgage brokers** are involved with the origination side of the business. They take loan applications, process the papers, and then submit the files to an institutional investor, typically an S&L or a bank or a mortgage banker, who underwrites and closes the loan. Mortgage brokers usually work with a wide variety of investors who buy loans on the secondary market, which provides mortgage bankers and brokers with an almost inexhaustible supply of money with which to make new mortgages—and to offer a wide variety of loan packages. Some mortgage brokers seem to have more lending flexibility and can work with those folks who might otherwise have a tough time getting a mortgage.

- **Mortgage bankers** go a step further. They, too, work within the origination side of the business, but they also get involved with servicing and closing the loan in their own name with their own funds. If you go to a bank for a loan, the mortgage banker takes the loan application and lends you the money from the bank's own coffers. Once you close on the loan, the same company might service your account, collect payments, and make sure your real estate taxes are being paid. Or the company might sell your loan on the secondary market (to institutional investors) and then re-lend the money. Mortgage bankers make their money on underwriting the loan. You pay fees and points, which the banker pockets. Mortgage bankers might make additional money on the spread between the rate on your loan and the going rate of loans in the secondary market, which is called the *service fee premium*.

Be sure to ask your loan officer if your loan carries a service fee premium. The service fee premium should be disclosed. The higher the fee, the greater the chance that your loan's interest rate is actually above the going market rate.

Qualities to Look for in a Mortgage Company

How should you select a mortgage company? Pick a company based on experience, customer service, and recommendations. The one thing you *shouldn't* do is to make the decision based solely on which lender is offering the lowest rates. Rates are extremely important, but there is a tremendous amount of competition in today's mortgage market. That means all mortgage brokers and bankers should be offering mortgages at competitive prices. If a company is offering a mortgage package that's well below market rates, beware. (Remember the old cliché: If it sounds too good to be true, it probably is.)

All mortgage companies generally choose from the same pool of institutional investors. A company offering abnormally low rates might make up the difference by increasing closing costs or tacking on additional settlement fees.

Richard, president of a mortgage brokerage in Evanston, Illinois, reminds borrowers that the lowest rates do not necessarily mean you automatically get good service (in a perfect world, they might), and fast, efficient service is essential for a smooth closing.

Make sure the lender you choose will be able to deliver the funds to close on your new home. Most lenders offer free preprinted pamphlets and booklets on the mortgage process. The federal government also offers free (or nearly free) booklets from the aforementioned Consumer Publications Office, Pueblo, Colorado 81003, or pueblo.gsa.gov. (See Appendix V, General Resources, for additional places to call or write.)

Choosing the Right Lender for You

Choosing the right lender will take some time, effort, and lots of telephone calls, because lenders today offer a plethora of mortgage options that are individually tailored to each borrower's financing needs. In major metropolitan areas, there are dozens, if not hundreds, of mortgage brokers and bankers; in smaller communities, the numbers fall proportionately. Still, there should be ample choices and fairly stiff competition among lenders for your business.

> Remember, when going to apply for a loan, you're in the driver's seat. You're giving them *your* business, not the other way around. If a lender seems condescending or doesn't treat you fairly or with civility, take your business elsewhere.

Starting Out

The first thing to do when starting to look for your loan is to *find out the current mortgage interest rate*. You want to know the following information:

- The current interest rate lenders are charging for their most common mortgages
- How many points (a point is 1 percent of the loan amount) they are charging to make the loan

- The annual percentage rate (APR) of the loan (which adds up all the extra costs and fees and amortizes the cost over the life of the loan)
- What lengths of loans the mortgage company offers (7/23, 5/25, 30-year fixed, 15-year fixed, 5-year balloon, etc.; for more information on various mortgage types, see Questions 73–78)

As we discussed in the previous question, the easy way to get this information is to look in your local newspaper for the mortgage watch column, or go online.

Newspapers often track current lending rates because they know many of their readers either own a home or are interested in buying or selling. The mortgage watch column lists a handful of lenders (anywhere from five to more than a dozen) and their current mortgage offerings. Telephone numbers and addresses are usually provided.

Clip the mortgage watch column for several weeks, compare the prices quoted for various loans, and call up the lenders that seem to have the best deals. At this point, there is no way for you to tell which mortgage banker or broker will be able to give you the best service. All you can go on are price and product.

If you choose to go online, you'll either have to go to an aggregator, like eloan.com, houseandhome.com, or lendingtree.com, or to an individual lender's website, or to my current favorite independent site for interest rate information, BankRate.com. Each of these sites should give you the current interest rate. The mortgage sites will allow you to apply online.

The Good, the Bad, and the Ugly

How do you find a good mortgage banker or broker? As with finding a good real estate broker, seek out recommendations from friends and family. Your real estate broker may have excellent suggestions, so be sure to ask for a list of lenders. If you have a real estate attorney, ask him or her for a few names. Once you receive several names, go to their offices and talk to the manager in charge. Look around—some new mortgage brokers actually work out of their home—and investigate with whom you'll be doing business. Find out how long the company has been in business. Ask them how many mortgages they have closed and for around how much money. It's important to work with a company that has a track record.

You should feel entirely comfortable with your lender and your loan officer. If you get a funny feeling at the office, leave and find another mortgage company. If you're concerned about its track record, or the way it deals with its customers, don't be afraid to approach your local Better Business Bureau (bbbonline.org), chamber of commerce, or your state attorney general. You can also call the Mortgage Bankers Association (MBA) of America (201-861-6554, 1125 15th Street, NW, Washington, DC 20005-2766) to see if any claims have been filed. Finally, feel free to ask for references, and then call them.

If you feel you are being unfairly treated by a lender, or are being charged outrageous fees, or if the lender has made promises that are not kept when you show up at the closing, you may be in the grip of a predatory lender. For more information on predatory lenders, see Question 85.

One you've interviewed lenders, go back online to compare rates and fees. You may find it easier and faster to apply online with a lender. Although you can't do your entire closing electronically yet, I'm guessing that by the time I next update this book, you might very well be able to have an electronic settlement.

Loan Officers and Others

Once you've begun to compare rates and mortgage products (see Question 73 on mortgage types), it's time to meet the people who will be guiding your loan through the approval process.

The loan officer is the person you'll be dealing with, your primary contact. This person should be with you all the way through the process, from application to closing.

Typically, the loan officer will take down all the information and create a file for your application. Then the loan processor (the loan officer's partner) will order the appraisal, credit report, and title. After that information is obtained, the loan is packaged up and sent to the investor, who makes the decision on whether to approve your loan. All the way through, your contact should be with the loan officer, the person you've dealt with from the very beginning.

These days, lenders can approve your loan virtually instantaneously. It takes just a few minutes once they've electronically entered your information and credit report into the computer. In a fast market, it's great to be able to be approved so quickly, but don't think you'll get your loan right then and there. If an electronic appraisal is done on your property (i.e., instead of the lender sending someone out to physically appraise the home, it's done via electronic databases), that can be done quickly as well. In a hot market, however, appraisers who survey the home on-site get backed up, and there may be a two- or three-week delay until they can actually get out to see the home and do the requisite research. Still, over the past five years, the time it takes to apply for and get approved for a loan has dropped dramatically. Once you apply, you should know almost immediately if you'll qualify to buy your home.

Beware of hand-offs. Some companies use a loan officer to take your application, but then other people you have never met continue the process. Make it clear you don't want a *loan processor*. You want to have confidence that the loan officer will handle the application through to the end, will care about your needs, and will make sure the deal gets done.

How Do You Know Whether the Loan Officer Is Doing His or Her Job?

Generally (and this includes extremely busy periods of low-interest-rate refinancing), approval of a loan application shouldn't take more than a week. It's the appraisal process that takes much longer than expected. Through the late 1990s and early 2000s, getting a bank to complete the appraisal process was taking as long as six weeks! Closing on a loan was taking upward of two months, and in some cases as long as three or four months.

When you're applying for your loan, ask the loan officer how long it is taking to complete each part of loan process, from applying to approval to appraisals to close. If you're hearing about delays in mortgage processing, or if you're getting numerous requests for additional information, then you should start to get concerned. There's nothing wrong with a loan officer calling to say that four pieces of documentation are still needed for your file. But if you're getting multiple requests for documentation, including repeat requests for the same documents, then the loan officer didn't do his or her job in the beginning.

Unless you have special circumstances—for example, you're self-employed or you trade commodities—the loan officer should ask for everything right up front. And you should make every effort to give the loan officer all that is needed to get your application approved and the loan closed before your loan lock runs out. It is wise to discuss any particular issues affecting your financial picture early in the process and preferably before you put down any money. Some of these issues might include credit problems, previous bankruptcies, divorces, recent job changes, and so on.

Remember, you're the customer. If you're not happy with the service you're receiving from your loan officer, speak up! Ask to talk to the supervisor or the head of the office. If that doesn't get you anywhere, ask to have your application fee refunded and find another lender. Even if the lender doesn't refund your application fee, you should switch lenders if you feel uncomfortable or aren't getting the proper service. After all, buying a house is the biggest single investment you'll probably ever make. You want to have a team of professionals around you that you can count on.

HOW DO I APPLY FOR A LOAN? SHOULD I APPLY ONLINE FOR A MORTGAGE?

Applying for a loan is different from getting prequalified. Getting prequalified before you buy property involves going to a lender and having the lender analyze your assets, liabilities, and income stream. From these items (which the lender may just take your word on), the lender comes up with a dollar amount you can borrow.

You'll need to actually apply for your loan when you get *preapproved*. And that's when things change. The lender will want to see documentation and proof that you actually have the assets and debts you say you have. You will sit down with the loan officer, who will ask you questions and write down the answers. Or you will sit down at your computer, log on to a website, and fill out your own application.

Handy Information

Having the following information can speed up the process significantly:

- Copies of all bank statements for the last three months
- Copies of all account statements, including stock brokerage accounts
- Most recent pay stub for you and your spouse or partner
- W2 form for the past two years
- If you're self-employed, the past two years of tax returns plus a profit-and-loss statement for the year to date
- A gift letter, if part of the money you're using to buy the house has come as a gift from your parents, friends, or other relatives

Important Decisions

You'll have to make some important decisions at the time of application.

1. What type of mortgage should you choose? At the time of application, you'll have to decide which mortgage type is right for you. (See Question 73 for a discussion of different mortgage types.) The type of mortgage you choose depends on two factors: (1) how long you plan to stay in the house, and (2) how much risk you are willing to take.

You'll have to decide if you're the type of person who likes little risk (a fixed loan would probably work well for you), some risk (a two-step loan like a 7/23 or 5/25 might be the ticket), or a lot of risk (ARMs—adjustable-rate mortgages—are a good choice, and they even have built-in caps on how high the interest rate can jump each year and over the entire life of the loan). The loan officer should be happy to go over the different mortgage products offered by his or her firm, and to counsel you on which one might be right for your situation.

2. Should you float the rate or lock in? When the lender asks you this question, he or she is really asking you if you want to lock in at the current rate or take a gamble that the rates will drop a bit before you close on the loan.

Here's how the float option works: Let's say you go in on Monday and fill out an application. The rate for a 30-year fixed loan is 8 percent. You're scheduled to close in two months. You think interest rates are going to drop in the next 60 days, so you opt to float your loan, meaning that at any point in the next 60 days you can call to lock in the rate. If rates drop, you'll get the lower rate. But if rates go up, you'll have to pay the higher rate. If, however, you think that mortgage rates can't possibly go lower than they are before you're scheduled to close, then it's in your best interest to lock in the rate of your mortgage. Locking in means that the interest rate you pay on your mortgage will be whatever the mortgage rate is on the day you make the application.

Locking in or floating the interest rate has nothing to do with what type of mortgage you choose. You can choose to float the rate or lock in on all types of mortgages, including a fixed-rate or an adjustable-rate mortgage (ARM).

3. How long should the lock be? This sounds like the same question as above, but it's not. When you apply for a loan, the mortgage rate offered by the lender is only good for a specific amount of time. You have to choose how long you want the rate to last, while remembering that *the longer the rate lock, the higher the interest rate.*

Lenders usually offer to hold the rate for 30, 45, or 60 days. You should base the length of the lock on when you're supposed to close on the loan. For example, if you apply for a loan 28 days before you want to close, you might choose to hold the rate for 30 days. If you're going to close in 38 days, you might choose to lock in for 45 days.

Lenders will rarely offer to hold a lock for longer than 60 days, but if you need to close quickly, they might manage to approve your mortgage and lock a rate for 7 days. The shorter the lock, the more important it is to furnish your lender with everything he or she needs to get your loan going.

The reason lenders don't like to lock in rates for extended periods of time is that interest rates fluctuate daily and often change several times each day. With that much activity, it's difficult for lenders and investors to predict how much interest rates will change over the course of two months. To protect themselves, they limit the length of lock-ins. Just remember, the longer you want the lender to hold the lock, the more you'll pay for that privilege.

If you're buying new construction, it's likely that you're buying off of a blueprint, unless you're buying a developer's spec house. It could take anywhere from four months to two years (in the case of some loft or condo conversions) for the property to be ready. If you've got to wait nine months or longer until closing, don't try to lock in a rate now— you'll pay way too much. You're far better off waiting until you're only 60 days out from closing, and then watching mortgage interest rates rise and fall until you decide it's a good time to lock in the rate.

4. How many points, if any, do you want to pay? Another decision you'll have to make is how many points you want to pay at the closing. Most first-time borrowers don't realize there is an inverse relationship between the *points* (a point is one percentage point of the loan amount) you pay and the interest rate you receive. You may have to pay some points or fees, but the more points you pay, the lower the interest rate. If you pay no points up front, you'll have a slightly higher interest rate, and pay more over the life of the loan.

Points are paid in cash (usually tough for first-time buyers to come by) at the closing, but the federal government allows you to deduct them from your income taxes during the year of the closing. Or you can amortize your points (pay them over the life of the loan), which will ultimately increase your rate.

I'm often asked whether points paid for a refinance can be deducted for tax purposes. The answer is, unfortunately, no. You must amortize the points over the life of the loan and deduct a portion of points each year. However, if you refinance your loan, say, in five years, you may deduct any remaining points on your old loan in the year you refinance.

Why might you want to pay additional points? Let's say you decide to close on your home in November. That means you might only have one month's worth of mortgage interest to deduct in that year. However, if you decide to pay three or four points in cash at closing, you would have more to deduct for the year, and can maximize your deductions. If you decide to pay five points, the lender might lower your rate by a point and a half. That's called "buying down" the loan.

Some developers use a different buydown to entice first-time buyers to purchase new construction. They'll "buy down" the interest rate for the first two or three years with cash. This doesn't have anything to do with you paying more points up front in exchange for a lower interest rate, though they're both called the same name. You receive two significant benefits from buying down your interest rate: (1) a larger deduction, and (2) a lower interest rate for the life of the loan.

Here's how points work: If you need a $100,000 mortgage, each point is $1,000. If you decide to buy down your loan with five points, you will need $5,000 in cash at closing just to cover the points paid to the lender.

Good Faith Estimate of Closing Costs

Every time you put in an application for a loan, the lender is required by the federal Real Estate Settlement Procedures Act (RESPA) to give you a good faith estimate of your closing costs. That sheet of paper should detail every fee you'll likely pay, and add it all up for you. You may even be asked to sign the document, to prove that you've seen it.

Many first-time home buyers feel somewhat deceived by the good faith estimate because the actual costs at closing may be slightly or significantly different from the costs originally listed. A good lender should get very close to the actual closing cost numbers in the estimate. However, an estimate is an estimate. Last-minute costs may come up at closing. If you feel that the charges are unusually high, you or your real estate attorney can talk to the lender and renegotiate. If a charge seems unfair or completely outrageous, and it was not on the good faith estimate, you should refuse to pay it.

NEVER walk away from an application without getting a copy of every document you've signed. It is extremely important to be able to document in writing every step in the application process. If your lender ever gives you trouble, you'll have to prove what was said and what was signed. Also, signing a document signifies that you've actually read it. Take the time to read all documents in the application, and don't be afraid to ask questions of the loan officer. Remember, you're not the first first-time buyer the loan officer has dealt with. And you won't be the last.

QUESTION 61

WHAT KIND OF DOCUMENTATION WILL I NEED FOR MY APPLICATION?

If you've spent months searching for the perfect home, the last thing you want are delays in the mortgage approval process. Unfortunately, a delay in getting approved for your mortgage can push back the closing or be a viable reason for the seller to cancel the purchase contract.

One problem that can cause a delay is faulty or missing documentation. Even after going through pounds of paperwork during the mortgage application process, lenders often request more documentation.

According to one loan officer, most borrowers don't understand exactly how much detailed information the lender will need to approve their loans. Here is a list of documents your loan officer may ask for. You should be prepared to provide these documents, or copies of them, at a moment's notice.

1. All W2 forms for each person who will be a coborrower on the loan.
2. Copies of completed tax forms for the last three years; include any schedules or attachments.
3. Copies of one month's worth of pay stubs.
4. Copies of the last three bank statements for every bank account, IRA, 401(k), or stock account the coborrowers have. Bring a copy of your most recent statement for any assets you have.
5. A copy of the back and front of your canceled earnest money check. Contact the bank if this has not yet come through.

6. A copy of the sales contract and all riders. You'll also need both brokers' names, addresses, and phone numbers, and the same information for both your attorney and the seller's attorney.

7. If you are selling a current residence, a copy of the listing agreement and, if the home is under contract, a copy of the sales contract.

8. If gift funds are involved, the giver must provide proof that he or she had that money to give, such as a copy of the giver's recent bank statement. You must then show the paper trail for the money, including a deposit slip. The giver will have to fill out a gift letter affidavit, available from the loan officer, indicating that the funds were a gift and the gift giver does not expect repayment.

9. Complete copies of all divorce decrees.

10. Copies of an old survey or title policy for the home you are buying, if available when you apply for the mortgage, or when it becomes available during the purchase process.

11. If you are self-employed, complete copies of the last two years' business tax returns and a year-to-date profit-and-loss statement and balance sheet with original signatures.

12. A list of your addresses in the last seven years.

13. If you have made any large deposits (i.e., larger than your monthly income) into your bank accounts in the last three months, an explanation, with proof, as to where the funds came from.

14. If you have opened a new bank account in the last six months, a letter explaining where the money came from to open this new account.

15. Addresses and account numbers for every form of credit you have.

16. Documentation to verify additional income, such as Social Security, child support, and alimony.

17. If you have had a previous bankruptcy, bring a complete copy of the bankruptcy proceedings, including all schedules and a letter explaining the circumstances for the bankruptcy.

18. For a Federal Housing Administration (FHA) or Veterans Administration (VA) loan, bring a photocopy of a picture ID and a copy of your Social Security card. Also, bring proof of enlistment for a VA loan. (See Question 79.)

19. If you have any judgments against you, a copy of recorded satisfaction of judgment, and copies of documents describing any lawsuits with which you are currently involved.

No-Doc Loans

A loan that requires almost no documentation is commonly referred to as a *no-doc* loan. No-doc loans are for people who either can't, or don't want to, provide the documentation lenders need to process a conventional loan.

If you don't want to produce documentation, you can get a no-doc loan. But be prepared to pay extra for it. Depending on what kind of documentation you do or do not produce, your loan could carry an interest rate that's several percentage points higher than a conventional loan.

Carie and John's Story

Carie and John recently decided to leave their jobs in the New York publishing world and move to Denver to be near Carie's family. Like many New Yorkers, they paid relatively cheap rent for more than a dozen years and had decided long ago not to buy into the Manhattan housing market.

After they resigned from their jobs, they got in touch with a Denver-based mortgage company and a friend who sells real estate. Even though neither Carie nor John has any idea now what they'll do once they get to Denver, they were approved for a reasonably priced no-doc loan.

"I know *I* wouldn't be comfortable lending to me," Carie said with a laugh. "But I'm glad they said yes."

She and John moved west, found a house, and by the time you read this, they'll have closed on it.

QUESTION 62

WHAT TYPES OF CIRCUMSTANCES MIGHT FOUL UP MY LOAN APPLICATION? HOW CAN I FIX THEM?

Lower rates have led to a crush of business at mortgage lenders' offices and, as a result, the application process may take longer than usual. The real problem is that a delay can force you to the wall on the occupancy of your new home and even threaten the terms of your loan, such as the interest rate and the fees the lender charges.

It's vital that you, the buyer, stay on top of things from the day you apply for your loan through the closing. Often you can do some things to help speed the mortgage loan process and meet that pressing deadline.

Any number of things can go wrong during the mortgage approval process: You or the lender can lose documents; the lender may demand more documentation; appraisals may run late; or verification from banks or your employer may not be processed quickly enough. Mortgage experts agree that problems can surface with interest rates, points, or the up-front fees a lender charges to make a mortgage loan. In fact, they estimate that as many as 30 percent of all mortgage applications will face some problem with the interest rate or points.

The Rate Lock and Yet Another Scam

To eliminate the uncertainty of changeable interest rates, borrowers may pay their prospective lender for the privilege of locking in a specific interest rate and number of points (a point is equal to 1 percent of the loan amount). The lock is good for a predefined time, usually 30 to 60 days. When you lock in your rate, you must close on your mortgage before the lock expires, or you lose the preset interest rate.

But the mortgage loan process can easily go awry, particularly when interest rates start to fluctuate. Lenders, nervous about their investments and eager to charge the highest interest rate possible, are not as eager to close on their loans as when interest rates are dropping. According to the former director of consumer affairs for the Office of Banks and Real Estate, which regulates and monitors mortgage brokers, mortgage bankers, and financial institutions in Illinois, there are many ways for the lender to give you trouble.

"The lender may give you a lock on the interest rate that is intentionally too short given the current market conditions," she says.

A reasonable lock period is 60 days. Lenders rarely agree to extend a lock to 90 days because of market volatility. But the director says lenders often *play the float* with your mortgage. Although you think you've locked in at a certain interest rate with a certain number of points, lenders will, in essence, gamble with the rate rather than actually lock it in, hoping that interest rates will slip further. If they do go down, the loan officer and the mortgage company will then split the excess between the current interest rate and the rate you locked into.

If Rates Go Up

The fun starts when interest rates begin to rise. If the loan officer has been playing the float with your loan, and the rate goes up, he or she will have to pay the difference between your locked-in interest rate and the current market rate out of his or her pocket to close on the loan. And because loan officers are loath to pay out, they will often find something "wrong" with your application at the last minute, forcing you to accept a higher interest rate or more points, says one loan officer.

There are a few things you can do to guard against such situations and to ensure you get the mortgage loan you applied for within the time frame allotted in your application contract.

- **Two can be better than one.** Some experts recommend that buyers apply for two different mortgages at two different companies. Float the rate with one application and lock in the other. "If you have trouble with one of the lenders, you can always play each against the other," says one loan officer. Of course, this method of safeguarding will cost you an additional application fee of $200 to $500, unless you can get the lender to waive the fee until the closing.

- **Get the lock commitment in writing.** Never accept a verbal lock. "That way you'll have proof that the lender went against the bargain," suggests the Illinois attorney general's office.

- **Get hard copies of everything.** Make sure you receive copies of anything you sign during the mortgage application process before you walk out the door. Don't let the lender mail the papers to you.

- **Secure a good faith estimate.** Make sure the lender hands you a good faith estimate of closing costs before you sign anything or pay anything.

- **Keep your lifestyle intact.** Don't make major lifestyle changes after the application has been made and before you close on the property. Don't buy a car. Don't increase your indebtedness in any way. Don't change jobs. It's likely that the lender will pull a second credit report just before closing, and those lifestyle changes could sink your loan application.

- **Keep in touch.** Keep in direct and close contact, at least weekly, with your loan officer throughout the process. Experts say that if you aren't going to be approved for a loan, the lender should know within days—certainly within two to four weeks (four is an extreme case). Typically, lenders can tell you almost instantaneously if you're approved. Credit reports can be pulled up while you're sitting there. If you aren't approved while you're sitting in the lender's office, you'll want to call almost daily to see if the loan officer needs any additional information.

- **Create a paper trail.** Once your loan officer tells you he or she has all the documentation required for your loan, immediately send a letter by certified mail which states that per your conversation, the loan officer requires no additional information. Keep a copy for yourself as part of your paper trail. You'll also want to keep a copy of every bit of paperwork and correspondence between you and the lender.

If, after all this, the loan officer tries to back out of your locked-in rate agreement and force you to take higher rates and points than you originally agreed to, experts suggest you start yelling. Literally. The squeaky wheel gets the grease. If the loan officer tries to make you take a higher rate, contact the manager of the office. Have your attorney yell for a while, and drag out the closing. A few threats about sending letters to the attorney general's office, the Better Business Bureau, and other consumer-action organizations should get the loan officer to back down.

Of course, sometimes the problem isn't the lender.

Bennett's Story

Bennett wasn't really interested in selling his house until he was contacted by an eager real estate agent one day. The phone call came in 1999, in the midst of a super-hot seller's market, and the agent wanted to know how much Bennett wanted for his house.

Bennett named a sky-high price, and much to his surprise, the buyers accepted. But then the appraisal came back, indicating that the house was actually worth about $50,000 more than Bennett had asked. So, much to the buyers' chagrin, Bennett changed his mind.

A week or so later, the agent showed him the appraisal sheet, and Bennett could see that the appraiser had actually located his house in the midst of a much hotter neighborhood, and used comps (the sales prices of comparable property in the same neighborhood) from a different neighborhood.

So the deal was on again. But then the buyers didn't have enough money for the down payment. Bennett agreed to lend them $10,000, but structure it as a loan to one of the buyers' mothers. The mother, in turn, would gift the money back to the buyers. After the closing, the money would be repaid to the seller.

Bennett's attorney got wind of the deal, and it smelled bad. Sellers are not supposed to give the down payment (or any extra cash) to the buyers "under the table," so to speak. And if a wacky transaction is structured, like this one, the lender has to be notified in advance and approve the deal. By not informing the lender, Bennett and the buyers were on the verge of committing mortgage fraud—which the federal government takes quite seriously.

Bennett's attorney ended up saving the deal, but it took quite a while to sort everything out. The closing was delayed for several weeks.

HOW MUCH OF A DOWN PAYMENT WILL I NEED TO BUY MY HOME? SHOULD I PUT DOWN THE LARGEST OR SMALLEST DOWN PAYMENT POSSIBLE?

These days, the answer starts at zero—actually, less than zero. You can get loans with nothing down; loans where the down payment is a gift from friends, relatives, or a grant; or loans where you actually put down some cash. But you can also get loans for more than the purchase price of the home, either because your loan allows you to fold in the closing costs on the loan or because you've got a special FHA loan to help you improve the property.

Zero-down and very low down payment loans (where the amount you put down is 3 percent or less) are a relatively new phenomenon. As lenders get more comfortable with the idea that the vast majority of people who have no equity in their homes are still good risks, the zero-down mortgage programs will continue to expand.

What You Should Put Down

The standard down payment is 20 percent of the sales price of the home. If the home costs $100,000, a conventional lender would require that you have $20,000 in cash for a down payment plus closing costs. Lenders ask for 20 percent down because homeowners with a larger equity stake in the home are less likely to default on the mortgage than those homeowners with a smaller equity stake. If you put down at least 20 percent on your home, you will not need to pay for private mortgage insurance (PMI), which can cost between $45 and $60 per month per $100,000 of loan value.

But lenders today recognize that 20 percent of the sales price is a huge amount of cash for most first-time buyers. In San Francisco, a first-time buyer house might cost as much as $500,000. If you're putting down 20 percent on that house, you'll need to come up with $100,000 in cash for the down payment plus another $20,000 or more in closing costs, fees, and reserves.

As a result, several widely available mortgage options will allow you to put down significantly less. For example, first-time buyers commonly put down 10 or 15 percent of the sales price. Conventional lenders will allow a smaller down payment (anything less than 20 percent) as long as the borrower purchases private mortgage insurance (PMI). PMI is paid monthly, along with your mortgage, until you have about 20 percent equity in the home. The law requires lenders to automatically cancel PMI once your loan-to-value ratio reaches 22 percent. (For more information on PMI, see Question 75.)

If you choose an FHA loan, you can put down as little as 3 percent, of which 2 percent may be a gift from a friend, relative, or a grant from a nonprofit housing organization. (You'll need mortgage insurance, however.) As we went to press, President Bush announced that the FHA would soon begin offering zero-down loans. Legislation is now working its way through Congress to begin making that statement a reality for first-time buyers.

VA loans, which are backed and administered by the Veterans Administration and are available only to qualified veterans of the Armed Services, have a zero-down option. But these loans tend to be more expensive than conventional zero-down options. Very low down payment loan options (3 or 5 percent down) from the VA are more reasonably priced.

A new development is that other nontraditional lenders are jumping into the mortgage game. Merrill Lynch, the brokerage company, offers a loan that allows you to borrow your down payment on a margin account against assets that you hold in brokerage accounts with the company. Fidelity offers a similar program. The idea is that you borrow 100 percent of the cost of the home and pay the going mortgage rate. If you have retirement accounts, or investment assets you don't wish to sell in order to come up with down payment cash, you may wish to investigate these programs. If your accounts are with other financial companies, talk to an account representative about what kinds of similar programs are offered. Many of the larger financial companies also offer nontraditional loan programs for their clients who are buying or refinancing their homes.

Borrowing on margin means that you're essentially using your brokerage account (and the stocks, bonds, and mutual funds it contains) as collateral for whatever it is that you're buying. Sophisticated investors have used margin accounts for years, to fully leverage their holdings and invest money they don't necessarily have readily available. The danger with borrowing on margin is that if your assets in the margin account suddenly drop dramatically in value, there is a risk that you'll be called upon to sell them at a disadvantageous time, in order to maintain a certain loan-to-value ratio in the margin account. Be sure you fully investigate how these accounts—and their mortgage margin account options—work before you sign on the dotted line.

Putting Down More, Not Less

When might you be required to put down more, rather than less?

In special circumstances, a higher down payment may be required. Some co-ops may require a 30 or 40 percent cash down payment to prove that the resident has the financial means to cover any capital expenses that may be required in the future. Co-ops may even require a much higher down payment than that, if they permit financing at all. Requiring a high cash down payment is another way for the co-op to filter out those individuals whom the residents choose not to have in their building. Fortunately, most co-ops have done away with the higher down payment requirement in order to make the units more affordable.

Some cash-rich folks (or first-time buyers with trust accounts) just don't like the idea that they owe anyone, and can't get used to it. These folks should put down as much as they can.

In the next section, we talk about how to figure out whether you should put down the smallest or largest down payment you can afford.

Small Down Payment vs. Large Down Payment

Whether you put down a small or large down payment depends on the following things:

1. How much cash you have lying around
2. How nervous you are about leveraging your finances
3. What you plan to do with your cash instead of putting it down on a house

There is no right answer when it comes to the question of down payments. Some people can borrow 100 percent of their home's purchase price and invest the rest in obscure technology stocks and still get eight hours of sleep a night. Other people get the jitters just thinking about their 80 percent loan-to-value ratio. And for some folks, the question isn't how much to put down (they have trouble scraping together the down payment) but whether to put extra cash they receive after the closing toward paying down their mortgage or to invest it monthly in the stock market.

Generally, first-time buyers are squeezed to the hilt. If they can scrape up a 10 percent cash down payment, they consider themselves lucky. But if you have more cash available, there are two schools of thought on the size of the down payment. Some experts feel that you should purchase your home with the smallest down payment possible. This will leave you with some cash for emergencies, decorating, and any renovation work you may want to schedule. By taking out the biggest loan possible, you'll have cash to invest the money elsewhere.

On the other hand, you may want to put down a larger down payment to cut down the size of your monthly mortgage payments—and save yourself the monthly cost of private mortgage insurance (PMI), which can run $45 to $60 for each $100,000 in purchase price.

The more dollars you put down, the lower the cost of owning the home. Why? You pay less interest over the life of the loan. If you put down 20 percent versus 15 percent, and the difference is $5,000, you should strongly consider putting down the 20 percent because you'll also be saving the PMI cost, which can really add up.

Making the Decision

The real question you need to ask yourself is this: What am I going to do with the money if I don't put it down on the house?

Over the past 70 years, the stock market has returned an average of about 10 percent (about 30 percent of that return came from dividends and the rest from stock price appreciation). Housing prices, during the same period, rose about 3 percent a year, although during the decade from 1994 to 2004, home prices nationally rose more than 5 percent for several years running. But that doesn't tell the whole story. In 2004, home prices rose nationally an eye-popping 13 percent. Homes in Las Vegas rose 41 percent in value in 2004! In some parts of the country, prices rose more than 100 percent during some of those years. Henry, a home buyer in Manhattan, bought a two-bedroom, two-bath condo for $439,000. Eight years later, his property had tripled in value. "A condo on a lower floor, in not as good condition, recently sold for $1.5 million," he reported. That's a hefty return—but one you can't count on.

Let's stick with traditional housing appreciation numbers (and consider anything you earn in excess of that to be a bonus). If you can put down 20 percent and save the cost of PMI, and you get a $100,000 loan, you'll have about $50 per month to invest in the stock market that you wouldn't otherwise have had. You might even have a larger initial investment to make in the market. Once again, it comes down to how you feel about leveraging your financing, and whether you'll be able to sleep at night. I recommend putting down 20 percent, if you can.

Should You Prepay Your Loan?

The question of prepaying your loan versus investing that extra cash each month in the market is a bit easier to answer.

Every dollar you use to prepay your loan actually earns you the net rate of interest you're paying on your mortgage. For example, if your loan rate is 8 percent, and you don't itemize (you take the standard deduction on your federal income tax form), every dollar you prepay earns 8 percent, a pretty darned good rate. If you were to invest that same dollar in the stock market (either in mutual funds or individual stocks or bonds), you'd need to earn at least enough to meet that return plus pay taxes. So if you're in the 15 percent bracket, you'd need to earn about 10 percent on your money. If you're in the 28 percent bracket, you'd need to earn about 11.5 percent on your cash.

I believe in diversification, and a real estate investment (even if it is your own home) is a pretty good counterpoint to the stock market. So I recommend you do a little of each.

If you get a 30-year fixed-rate loan, and you make one additional payment per year, you'll cut your 30-year loan to anywhere between 18 and 21 years. If you make two extra payments per year, you'll cut your loan to less than 15 years. (Of course, you could just get a 15-year loan and save even more money because you'll get a lower rate of interest.) Or you can get a 5/1 adjustable-rate mortgage and plow the difference between what you would have paid with a conventional 30-year loan and what you owe each month into prepaying your mortgage.

The rest of your extra cash should be used for regular investments in the stock market, either through your company retirement account, a Roth IRA, a 529 College Savings Plan, or other brokerage account.

I firmly believe that buying a house isn't just a decision about where to live. It's a decision about your financial future. Studies show that the younger you are when you buy your first house, the wealthier you'll likely be in your lifetime. When you're buying your first home, or your second, or your third, you should keep your personal finances in mind. If you buy the right house in the right neighborhood, and it goes up in value over time, you've not only made money, you've enhanced your net worth. And that, in turn, enhances your ability to leverage your wealth. Finally, when the average American retires, more than 70 percent of his or her wealth is tied up in his home. Investing in your own home makes a lot of good financial sense. I talk a lot about all of these financial concepts and more in my book *100 Questions You Should Ask About Your Personal Finances*.

SHOULD I BORROW FROM MY 401(k) OR OTHER RETIREMENT ACCOUNTS TO FUND MY DOWN PAYMENT?

Here's the ideal scenario for a first-time buyer: You've been working hard and saving every penny you can in the years before you buy a home; you've accumulated a small pot of cash that you can use as your down payment; you've either paid off your credit cards or avoided going into debt at all; your school loans are small and manageable.

Generally, first-time buyers don't have perfect credit scores or large bank accounts. When it comes time to figure out where your down payment cash is coming from, many home buyers turn to their 401(k) accounts.

Borrowing from a 401(k), an IRA, or a different retirement account seems like the perfect solution. The cash is just sitting there, accumulating, and you're *years* away from retirement.

The first question to answer is "Can you borrow from your 401(k)?" That depends on the individual plan your company has set up. Some companies permit you to borrow from a 401(k), but you may be limited as to how long you can keep that cash out of your retirement account. For some companies, you may be limited to only five years before the loan would have to be paid back, with interest. If you don't reimburse your account within the prescribed time, the IRS could look at the loan as a distribution, which would require you to pay a 10 percent penalty plus income taxes. Other companies will allow you to borrow the money for a down payment without a set period of time to pay back the loan. Check with your plan administrator to see if your company does permit you to borrow, and under what circumstances.

You could withdraw up to $10,000 to use as a down payment from either a conventional IRA or a Roth IRA. You would have to pay regular income tax on the cash but would not be subject to the 10 percent penalty.

The real question is, *should* you borrow from your retirement accounts to fund your down payment? I have mixed feelings on the issue. I understand the desperation many first-time buyers have when they're scraping together the funds for a down payment, but the practical side of the equation can't be ignored: You can borrow every dollar you need to buy a house, but no one will lend you a dime for retirement. (I often use this line with regard to paying for a child's college tuition. You can borrow cash to pay tuition bills, but not retirement bills.)

On the other hand, there is that pot of cash just sitting there. If you need to borrow only a small percentage of what you have, and will pay it back within a few years (with interest) and will still be able to put away 401(k) money, then borrowing from your future retirement to pay for your down payment probably won't damage your long-term retirement prospects.

But if the home loan will empty the coffers, you might want to think again. Also, if you leave your job before the loan comes due, you may have to pay it all back within a couple of months or risk paying a penalty to the IRS.

The Bottom Line

Look elsewhere for cash before you tap your retirement accounts. A better bet is to use a very low down, or zero-down, payment option now available through conventional lenders and the FHA.

WHAT FEES ARE ASSOCIATED WITH A MORTGAGE APPLICATION? WHAT LENDER'S FEES WILL BE CHARGED FOR MY MORTGAGE?

QUESTION
65

There are usually three fees you may be required to pay at the time of your mortgage application:

1. **The application fee,** which can range from zero to $500.
2. **The appraisal fee,** which can range from $200 to $300, depending on where you live.
3. **The credit report fee,** which ranges in price from $25 to $100, per person.

These fees might be grouped together under the application fee. Many times the lender will apply part of the application fee toward the appraisal and credit report fees. If you're planning to apply for two mortgages (one fixed, one floating), it's best to try to negotiate the lowest up-front fee possible, or find a lender that has no application or up-front fees.

Online Lending

If you apply online, you may pay just one, smaller fee—say, $200—which will cover your initial application and credit report. Or the fee will be applied toward all of your lender fees. You'll usually be asked to give your credit card on a secured site.

But that's not all. Next I'll talk about the entire range of lender's fees you'll have to pay in order to close on your loan.

Lender's Fees

Way back when times were simpler, lenders often charged home buyers a flat fee to close on a loan. But as interest rates have fallen and some banks have experienced financial troubles, most lenders have begun charging for many different services that were formerly covered by the flat fee. Some mortgage experts say lenders have sought to make up their lost profits by nickel-and-diming buyers to death.

There has been a push, both from the federal government and from Fannie Mae and Freddie Mac, the two secondary market lenders, to lower the costs associated with homeownership. By adopting technology and lowering the cost of making a loan, Fannie Mae and Freddie Mac hope to make homeownership even more widely available to more Americans.

The Name Game

Not every bank calls every charge by the same name, which can make comparing lenders as tough as comparing apples and station wagons.

Lenders are supposed to make it easy for you to know and understand their costs of doing business. At the time of the application, the lender is required by the federal Truth-in-Lending Law to provide a written, good faith estimate of all closing costs. And it's supposed to *accurately* reflect your closing costs. Mortgage brokers recommend that you shop around for the best deals before actually applying for a mortgage. You should also not be afraid to negotiate lower fees, and to ask for detailed explanations for each one.

The time to negotiate fees with the lender is *before* you sign your application. Once you've signed the application, it's too late. You've made your deal and will have to live with it.

Here are some of the fees that lenders may try to charge you for the privilege of lending you money. The fees cited reflect ranges given by real estate experts across the country, though actual charges may be higher or lower, depending on your individual situation and location:

1. Lender's points, loan origination, or loan service fees. The lender's points—a point equals 1 percent of the loan amount—may also be referred to as the service charge. The points are the largest fees paid to the lender and usually run between 1 and 3 percent of the loan amount. Occasionally, the points will run more than 3 percent, particularly if the borrower chooses to buy down the loan rate. **COST:** Usually zero to 3 percent of the loan or more. If you're paying more than 5 points, shop around. You could be working with a predatory lender.

2. Loan application fee. The money charged by the lender to apply for the loan. The application fee is almost never refundable, which means you'd better be pretty darned sure you want a loan from a particular lender and will actually be approved for it. **COST:** Usually between $0 and $500.

3. Lender's credit report. The lender may actually pull up two credit reports on you. The first will come just after you have filled out the application and paid the fee; if a second report is ordered, it will be pulled just before closing, to make sure you haven't made any enormous purchases or gotten into credit trouble during the elapsed time. Most first-time borrowers don't realize there may be two credit checks. However, you only pay once. **COST:** Usually between $25 and $75, per person. If two people are purchasing the property, the cost will be, say, $50 each, or $100. Sometimes the charge for the credit report has been known to run as high as $75 each, which is ridiculous, given that it costs the lender a fraction of that for each report.

4. Lender's processing fee. With this fee, the lender is trying to pass onto you some of the cost of doing business. The processing fee is the fee for processing the loan application. **COST:** Usually between $75 and $450.

5. Lender's document preparation fee. The cost of preparing the loan documents for the closing. **COST:** $0 to $250.

6. Lender's appraisal fee. This is the fee lenders charge you to have the home you want to purchase appraised. Lenders supposedly charge you exactly what they're being charged for the service, which is provided by an outside contractor. *Electronic appraisals* present a new wrinkle to this equation. Lenders search a huge database for comps (the sales price of homes similar to yours that have sold recently) to come up with an approximate appraisal. Electronic appraisals haven't yet been perfected, but this is the future of the industry, except for unusual or extremely expensive homes. **COST:** Usually from $225 to $400. If the lender does an electronic appraisal, you might only be charged $100, though the lender might pay just a fraction of that.

7. Lender's tax escrow service fee. This is a onetime charge to set up and service your real estate property tax escrow (see Question

70). The unfortunate part is you'll still pay even if you decide to pay your own taxes out of your own account. **COST:** From $40 to $85.

8. Title insurance cost for the lender's policy. Most times, the title insurer will have a flat fee for the loan policy that will be given to the lender. If you want a title insurance policy that will pay you if there is a problem (called an "Owner's" policy), that will be an additional, though very worthwhile, fee. **COST:** Between $150 and $350 for the lender's policy only.

9. Special endorsements to title. If the lender requires extra title endorsements, the buyer must pick up the cost. Some of these might include a condo endorsement, if you're buying a condo; a PUD (planned unit development) endorsement, if you're purchasing a home in a development having specific zoning characteristics; an environmental lien endorsement (a statement to the lender that the lender's mortgage on the property won't be affected if the government finds an environmental hazard on the property and files a lien against it so that the owners clean it up); a location endorsement (proves the home is located where the documents say it is); and an adjustable-rate mortgage endorsement. **COST:** $75 to $100 each.

10. Prepaid interest on the loan. The per-day interest charge on the loan from the day of closing until the last day of the month in which you close. This is paid at closing because the lender has to calculate it by hand. After you pay, you then skip a month and begin to pay your regular monthly balance. This is because the loan is paid in arrears. **COST:** A separate calculation is required for each borrower, but your lender should calculate it for you and put it on your good faith estimate.

NOTE: The above charges are only the lender's charges for doing business with you. For a list of all the closing costs you can expect, see Question 90.

WHAT ARE JUNK FEES? HOW DO I AVOID THEM?

QUESTION 66

Mortgage brokers say that some of the lender's costs are legitimate. For example, it costs at least $250 to send someone out to do an appraisal almost anywhere in the country.

But some lenders create "junk fees" purely to increase profits. True junk fees are often difficult to identify because the lender has given them legitimate-sounding names, which can confuse borrowers. As one mortgage banker puts it: "When I see names like 'underwriting fee' and 'commitment fee,' I can tell that these types of fees are being beefed up. When you have an appraisal fee or a credit report fee, you know the lender is being charged by different agencies or companies to do actual things. Those agencies or companies charge the bank and the customer pays it at the closing. But what is an underwriting fee? If you don't underwrite the loan, you have nothing. Buyers should have the lender explain charges they don't understand, and negotiate to exclude certain extra charges. For example, it's ridiculous to pay for an underwriting fee."

It's even sillier when you realize that with technology, the lender's time and costs have dropped. The idea is to pass those savings onto the customer, something that the federal government and secondary mortgage market leaders Fannie Mae and Freddie Mac are actively pushing for. Unfortunately, passing along the savings to the consumer means someone else's profits are being shaved.

Be sure to negotiate lender's fees before you pay the application fee. Once you've completed the application, it's too late to renegotiate. You've structured the deal, and both you and the lender must live up to the application contract.

If you've got the moxie, it's not a bad idea to call several lenders and ask them to submit bids to you on a particular type of loan listing *all* fees. If you ask 10 lenders to do this, 5 might actually do it. Then you can go back to the lenders and pit one bid against another, knocking out those lenders who can't match the lowest terms. Using this method, you should end up with the best possible mortgage with the fewest possible points and fees. Online aggregators, like Lending Tree, claim to do this work for you. But through the nearly 20 years I've been reporting on real estate, I've found there is no substitute for good, old-fashioned shopping around.

Fair Fees vs. Junk Fees

Over the years, several lenders have complained about my views about junk fees. "It isn't fair that lenders can't make any profit" is a common complaint I've heard.

According to Brian Jessen, a top loan officer for Chicago-based Harris Bank, you can expect your lender to pocket about 1 percent of the loan amount. When you add up the fees—not including things like prepaid interest on the loan, which you can control by when you set the closing date—they should come to about 1 percent of the loan amount, if you're getting a market-rate loan. If the fees are more than 1 percent, and your loan isn't below the market rate, something could be wrong. You should take a closer look at the numbers, and perhaps do some more shopping around, before you sign your loan documents.

WHAT IS TRUTH IN LENDING?

Under the 1974 Real Estate Settlement Procedures Act (RESPA), the lender is required, in most circumstances, within three days of receiving your application, to give or mail to you a Truth-in-Lending statement that will disclose the *annual percentage rate* (APR) of your loan. (See Question 68.)

In many cases, the APR will be higher than the interest rate stated in your mortgage or deed of trust note because the APR includes all fees and costs associated with making the loan. In addition to interest, points, and fees, other credit costs are calculated into the total cost of the loan. The Truth-in-Lending statement also discloses other pieces of useful information, such as the finance charge, schedule of payments, late payment charges, and whether additional charges will be assessed if you pay off the balance of your loan before it is due. This is known as the *prepayment penalty*.

A Quick Word About Prepayment Penalties

Many states do not permit lenders to charge a prepayment penalty. But national lenders and federally chartered banks may be able to attach one even if prepayment penalties are illegal in your state.

Prepayment penalties prohibit you from paying off your loan for the first two to four years. *Just so we're clear, this also means you cannot sell your home or refinance your loan within the first two to four years without getting penalized.* You can still make extra payments toward the balance of the loan. If you do refinance or sell your home, you'll be subject to a penalty of anywhere from 2 to 4 percent of the entire loan amount. The lender will not waive the penalty even if you are just one month shy of the expiration of the penalty period.

On the other hand, the lender will give you a somewhat reduced interest rate if you accept a prepayment penalty. That's the trade-off you're making.

Another reason to avoid prepayment penalties is that they are sometimes associated with predatory lenders. Predatory lenders want to lock you into an ultra-high interest rate loan for as long as possible. (For more information on predatory loans and how to spot a predatory lender, see Question 85.)

Frankly, I'd rather see you do almost anything than get a loan with a prepayment penalty. If you or your spouse or partner lose your job, or get sick, or get transferred, you will be limited in what you can do with your property without triggering the prepayment penalty. If interest rates drop—too bad! You can't take advantage of that situation either.

And Now, Back to Our Regularly Scheduled Truth-in-Lending Statement

Some of the information that the lender is required to disclose may not have been finalized by the time the Truth-in-Lending statement is sent. In that case, the lender's statement will say it is an estimate. The lender will *always* provide you with a new Truth-in-Lending statement at the closing. If you want to know about the charges you'll be paying before the closing, you can call the lender and ask if all the estimates on the statement were correct.

WHAT IS THE ANNUAL PERCENTAGE RATE (APR)?

Under the Truth-in-Lending law, the lender must tally up all the costs involved in making the loan and amortize them over the life of the loan. The APR is what the loan is actually going to cost you if you keep the loan until the end of the loan term. It includes the interest rate, points, fees, and any other costs the lender charges for doing business. If you go to a bank and look at its percentage rate of interest, it will also have the APR for that loan listed. The difference might be

considerable: If the interest rate a bank will charge you for your mortgage is 8 percent, the APR might be 8.75 percent or even higher.

The APR is one tool for helping you compare various loans. For example, if Lender A and Lender B each offers you an 8 percent, 30-year fixed-rate loan with one point, you'll be able to use the APR for each loan to see which loan will cost more.

But keep in mind that a loan that has the higher APR may be better for you than the loan with the lower APR, depending on how long you're going to hold the loan. Also, APR has absolutely no meaning, once you close on your loan.

When you're comparing loans, you're actually better off stripping down the loan to its essential components (basic loan with interest rate, and then costs and fees) rather than using the APR.

WHAT IS A GOOD FAITH ESTIMATE?

Under the terms of the Real Estate Settlement Procedures Act (RESPA) of 1974, when you file your application for a loan, the lender must provide you with a good faith estimate (GFE) of closing costs.

Usually the lender will give you the estimate before you leave the office after completing your application, but your loan officer may also legally send it to you within three business days. (If you do not receive your GFE within three business days, your lender has violated federal law. Find a new lender.)

The GFE is based on the lender's experience of the local costs involved with making a mortgage in your area. Any cost the lender anticipates must be stated—except for a paid-in-advance hazard insurance premium (if any), or other reserves deposited with the lender (hazard and mortgage insurance, city property taxes, county property taxes, and annual assessments). The estimate may be stated as a flat dollar amount or a range. The GFE form must be clear and concise, and the estimates must actually reflect the costs you will incur. It is your right to question any estimate of any cost that is provided in a dollar range rather than a flat fee.

If the lender does keep some funds in reserve, they may or may not be included in the estimate. Be sure to add them into your calculations of closing costs. And remember, closing costs can change. It's a good idea to check with the lender a few days before closing to determine the accurate closing cost for each item.

WHAT IS A REAL ESTATE TAX ESCROW?
WHAT IS AN INSURANCE ESCROW?
HOW CAN I AVOID SETTING THEM UP?

QUESTION 70

A real estate tax escrow is an account set up by a lender. Into it goes the amount of money your lender tacks onto your monthly principal and interest payment to cover your real estate taxes. When the tax bill comes up, the lender takes the money out of the escrow account and sends it to the tax collector. A lender will also collect for your home-owner's insurance policy (for noncondo and non-co-op properties), which are included in the fees you pay to the lender to hold in escrow for payment of your real estate taxes and insurance premiums.

Paying It Yourself

Why don't most owners pay their own taxes and insurance? Histori-cally, government institutions that developed the concept of the 30-year fixed-rate mortgage collected additional money for real estate taxes and homeowner's insurance. The default rate due to unpaid real estate taxes was low. As private lenders moved into the market, they followed suit.

Today, every state has passed legislation that says that lenders may require real estate tax and homeowner's insurance escrows. Real estate taxes are a priority item for lenders, as the lien for real estate taxes comes before the lender's mortgage lien. That means if you default on your loan, and the home is sold to pay your bills, your real estate tax bill is paid before anything else, including the lender's mortgage (com-monly called the first mortgage). Therefore, it's in the lender's best in-terest to make sure that property taxes are always paid.

Skeptics will tell you that lenders require escrows because they're a large source of free money. Currently, only a dozen states require lend-ers to pay interest on escrow accounts, although there is national legisla-tion pending that will force lenders to pay interest on all escrow accounts.

Lenders will tell you tax and insurance escrows help them protect their investment. They also make the argument that borrowers like being budgeted so they aren't surprised with a huge tax bill once or twice a year. Both arguments have some merit.

Federal legislation regarding escrows is worded to allow the lender the authority to withhold or impound money to cover taxes and insur-ance. Some limitations, however, went into effect in the early 1990s.

Lenders are limited to withholding no more than two months' worth of cushion. And they must provide an itemized statement of money coming into your account and bills that are paid, similar to a checking account statement.

In other words, if you pay $100 per month to cover your real estate taxes and insurance, your lender may only hold an extra $200—or two months' worth—in escrow.

Fine. So why doesn't your lender pay you interest on that money? Because many states and the federal government don't require lenders to do so.

Lenders argue that escrows are complicated and an extra burden to them. They say it's an expense to them to keep in touch with each homeowner's bills, all of which are due at different times. However, these services are computerized, and lenders do charge a onetime escrow service fee that should offset some of these costs.

Many lenders insist on a tax escrow, no matter how much equity you have in a house. They may tell you if you are using an FHA or VA loan that an escrow is required under the terms of that mortgage agreement. That isn't quite true. Although both FHA and VA loans contain provisions for real estate property and insurance escrows, the lender has the option to waive it.

According to industry professionals, some lenders will not demand an escrow account if you have a low loan-to-value ratio. For example, if you put more than 30 percent down in cash, most lenders will cancel the mandatory real estate tax escrow clause. In many states, lenders must waive the escrow requirement if you pledge a savings account with an amount that would be sufficient to pay your real estate taxes. By pledging the account, you can maintain control over payment of your taxes and receive interest on your money.

first time buyer tip

Not all lenders charge for the privilege of paying your own real estate taxes and homeowner's insurance premium. And you may want to find one that doesn't.

254

If you suggest this option and the lender balks, do not hesitate to say you'll be happy to call the state's attorney to check on the legality of the issue. Faced with that threat, the lender should back down. The exceptions are federally chartered savings banks, which claim they are not required to comply with state laws regulating this part of the lending process.

If you are successful in getting your lender to agree not to require an escrow account, you might find yourself hit with a onetime fee not to have one. That fee can run as high as 1 to 2 percent of the loan amount. In some states, charging this onetime fee may violate state law. Ask your real estate attorney for clarification.

When Something Goes Wrong

It's important to realize that escrow accounts can easily go awry. Some lenders have collected enormous sums of money from individual homeowners. One attorney said a lender tried to collect two years' worth of real estate taxes from his client up front. This is, of course, against the law.

Sara's Story

When I was writing the first edition of this book, I interviewed Sara, who at that time was a first-time buyer who had recently moved to the East Coast. She told me that the lender to whom her bank sold her mortgage increased her tax escrow by 46 percent. She was told the lender needed several months' cushion. At first she refused to pay the overage, instead sending 8 percent over her normal payment.

"I heard from everybody, from the computer people all the way to the president of the company. Finally they started returning my checks. After a few months they make it hard for you. I finally paid it," Sara said, adding that she had almost 30 percent in equity in her property.

Today, the lender couldn't get away with what it did to Sara. The law clearly states that lenders may hold no more than the equivalent of one year's worth of property taxes plus two months extra or less based on when the taxes are due on your home.

One thing a lender has is the ability to ruin your credit quickly. Even if you're having trouble getting your message through to the lender, don't stop paying your mortgage. Pay everything the lender asks of you while you fight the battle. If you prevail, you'll not only receive your money back, but you'll have kept your credit intact. And in today's electronic market, our ability to get a mortgage is almost solely based on our credit history.

Insurance Escrows

Federal law allows mortgage lenders to require you to buy enough homeowner's insurance to cover the mortgage amount in case of fire, earthquake, tornado, or other catastrophe. Of course, you'll want to get additional coverage that will also protect your equity in the home plus the cost of replacing your personal possessions and rebuilding your home to today's standards.

To ensure that the homeowner's policy insurance premium is paid, lenders often will require homeowners to pay the insurance premiums in the form of monthly payments that are tacked onto the regular mortgage payments of interest and principal. The money goes into an insurance escrow. Once a year, the lender will dip into that fund and pay the insurance premium. Insurance is one of the four parts of PITI—principal, interest, taxes, and insurance—and is one of the basic costs of homeownership. Overall, the insurance escrow works like the real estate tax escrow, except that you never get rid of it.

Mistakes Home Buyers and Homeowners Make

One of the biggest mistakes home buyers and homeowners make is not getting enough homeowner's or hazard insurance. While getting the right kind and amount of coverage may be expensive, it could be the best investment you ever make.

Arnie and Penny's Story

Arnie and Penny lived in their south Florida ranch home for many years. It had a red tiled roof, stucco walls, and a swimming pool. Palm trees towered over the property, and a neighbor's century-old mango tree dropped buckets of sweet fruit onto their lawn once a year.

It was a quiet, peaceful neighborhood, until Hurricane Andrew struck in the mid-1990s, leaving a path of bleak destruction in its wake.

Arnie and Penny's house was badly damaged. The pool was destroyed, a portion of the house collapsed, water flooded everything, and tiles were popping up everywhere.

Fortunately, Arnie and Penny had chosen a type of homeowner's insurance that guaranteed that the insurer would rebuild the home to modern-day standards and building codes. Although it was significantly more expensive than ordinary homeowner's insurance, the policy paid not only for the nearly complete rebuilding of their home, but also for the family to live in a rental town home while the work was being completed.

Arnie and Penny had to go to court to force the insurer to pay up, but in the end, it was worth it: Their claim was paid in full.

As your home appreciates in value, it will become more expensive to rebuild should something happen to it. Make sure your homeowner's policy keeps up with not only your home's increase in value, but also the increase in the number and value of your personal possessions, including furniture, clothing, artwork, and jewelry.

Avoiding Real Estate Tax and Insurance Escrows

Lenders will generally forgo the real estate tax escrow requirement if you meet the following criteria:

1. Put down 30 percent or more in cash. Most lenders use a 30 percent cash down payment as the benchmark for deciding whether or not to forgo the requirement for a real estate tax or insurance escrow.

2. Pledge an interest-bearing account. If you promise to keep a certain amount of money (enough to cover a year's worth of taxes) in an account at the lending institution, your lender should allow that instead of an escrow account. But you will likely have to use additional funds outside of the pledged account to pay your real estate tax bill.

If you don't meet either of these criteria, you'll probably have to have an escrow account for real estate taxes. However, once you've built up the required 30 percent equity in your home, you can try to end your real estate tax escrow the next time you refinance (if your lender doesn't offer a procedure for terminating the escrow).

Insurance escrows work almost the same way. Lenders almost always require an escrow account for insurance, and they are allowed to by law. Still, you can make this a point of negotiation. Ask your lender what you would have to do to have this escrow waived.

Fees, Fees, and More Fees

Even if you meet the criterion for avoiding a real estate and insurance escrow, don't imagine you won't still have to pay something. Lenders typically charge a onetime fee to automatically check that you're paying your tax bill.

WHAT SHOULD I DO TO MAKE SURE THE MORTGAGE APPLICATION PROCESS GOES SMOOTHLY? WHAT DO I DO IF THERE ARE PROBLEMS?

Sometimes, the mortgage process seems to have been set up just to bring out the beast in all of us. It can be a brutal, ego-shattering experience—one that not too many people enjoy. The idea is to make the entire process go as smoothly as possible. You don't want to raise the hackles of your loan officer, but at the same time, you want to remind him or her that you're in control of the situation.

Here are some specific things you can do to make the process go more smoothly.

1. Straighten out your finances. If you don't have a grip on what's coming in and what's going out (and where, and why), you may be in for a rough time when you apply for a home loan.

David and Denise's Story

David was a doctor and Denise was a second-year resident at a Boston hospital when they decided it was time to buy a house. David was making nearly $100,000 and Denise was pulling in close to $35,000. They figured together they had a decent salary and should stop wasting money on rent and start taking advantage of some of the deductions of homeownership.

When they went to get prequalified, however, they were in for a rude shock: Together, David and Denise had a *negative* net worth! They had around $80,000 worth of school loans to prepay, plus they had a car loan and credit card payments. The loan officer told them it would be very difficult for them to be approved.

Realizing the loan officer was probably right, David and Denise went about paying off some of their loans. They made it a priority to pay off their credit card debt and their car loan. They consolidated their school loans and refinanced them at lower rates. They made sure their payments were made on time. They put off buying that second car and canceled their planned vacation to Europe and instead chose to drive around New England.

When they went back to the loan officer six months later, their financial portfolio was much improved. The loan officer gave his approval, and David and Denise started looking for a home. When they found one four months later, they sailed through the mortgage application process.

2. Give your credit record a checkup. Everyone's heard the horror stories: Your mother, sister, neighbor, or friend goes to buy a home only to discover that the credit report contains negative or inaccurate credit information. Somewhere along the line his or her credit history has been tampered with. Instead of having a clean record, he or she has an $80,000 outstanding bill for a liver transplant (or a lease on a Mercedes, a student loan, or something equally improbable). The loan officer looks at the outstanding bill and gives you a choice: Clean up the credit problem or no loan. Some choice. And you've probably heard how difficult it is going to be to get your credit history cleaned up. Maybe so, but it's important to try nonetheless.

Here's what to do: First, order a credit report on yourself. Three major national credit companies do this: (1) Trans-Union (transunion.com, 800-888-4213), (2) Equifax (equifax.com, 800-685-1111), and (3) Experian (experian.com, 888-EXPERIAN). For less than $10, each credit bureau will send you your credit report. Starting December 1, 2004, you are entitled to get a free copy of your credit report each year. (To get your free copy, go to AnnualCreditReport.com). If you want to order a combined report from all three credit reporting bureaus, you can purchase one through MyFico.com, which is the result of the partnership between Equifax and Fair Isaacs, the corporation that invented the credit score.

This is the same information lenders will receive. By getting a copy of your credit report before you apply for a loan, you'll get a first look at any problems or discrepancies that have sprung up.

Let's backpedal a moment and talk about credit bureaus. In this computerized, big-brother-like world we live in, credit bureaus generally have exchange agreements with companies that provide credit, like credit card companies (Visa, MasterCard, American Express, and others) and department or retail stores (including Bloomingdale's, Target, Kohl's, Marshall Field's, Spiegel), as well as banks, credit unions, and savings and loans.

On a daily, weekly, monthly, or semiannual basis, these companies electronically send all the information they have on their customers (and how they are paying their bills) to the credit bureau, which stores it in a mammoth database and updates the records of each person on file. When you go to a store like Limited Express and sign up for its credit card, it calls the credit bureau (to do a credit check) to be sure you have enough funds to pay your bills. Banks do it the same way. When you go to apply for a mortgage, the lender wants to know how many debts are outstanding, and what your track record is in paying them. Credit bureaus provide that information.

They can even tell if you've been paying your taxes or if you have court judgments against you.

Mark and Marlene's Story

Mark and Marlene were first-time buyers in the Seattle area. They had been looking for a home for several months and finally found the house of their dreams. Since they had been prequalified (as opposed to preapproved) for their loan, they knew they could afford the property, and they had the cash for the down payment.

But when they went to apply, they were rejected by the lender. The lender pulled a credit report on the couple and discovered that they had "forgotten" to file their taxes in the two previous years. When he went back to the couple to inform them that they had been rejected for the loan, they were shocked at the news. The lender simply didn't want to have anything to do with them. After all, if they could forget something as significant as their federal taxes, how would they deal with a monthly mortgage payment?

So let's say you've ordered your credit report from Trans-Union and it turns up an erroneous $80 bill from a hospital you've never been to. You realize that this isn't your bill. What do you do? You could go to the credit bureau, but since they didn't originate the information (remember, all the information is sent to the credit bureau from the companies giving credit), they probably won't be able to help you. In fact, you may find the credit bureau's response (or lack thereof) to be particularly distressing and frustrating, although a new law administered by the Federal Trade Commission requires credit bureaus to respond to such complaints within 30 days.

Any correspondence you send to a credit bureau should be typewritten and sent via registered or certified mail, return receipt requested. That way, you'll be able to develop a paper trail of what you sent, when you sent it, and who received it.

According to a recent study, as many as 79 percent of credit reports contain at least one error. One-quarter of all credit reports contain inaccurate information serious enough to derail your application for credit. In other words, if you don't get rid of the inaccurate information, you could be turned down for your home loan!

Go to the Source

Go directly to the source of the problem—in this case, the hospital. Ask them to pull up the payment record and try to work out whose bill it actually is. (Or if it turns out to be yours, pay it.) There should be some identification other than name that can easily solve the problem, like a Social Security number, the male/female check box, age, race, and so on.

Once you prove that the bill is not yours, the hospital (or other credit originator) should correct its computers. (This happened to a Chicago woman whose name was the same as her mother's. Even though the Social Security numbers were different, she had a heck of a time getting the report cleared up because the credit bureau computer kept confusing the names.)

It may take some time for a correction to work its way through the company's computers to your credit bureau. If you've started the process before you've found a home, you shouldn't have too much trouble. On the other hand, if you've gone to a lender because you've found the house of your dreams and then discover your credit is in jeopardy, you may want to get a letter from the credit originator that explains there has been a mistake and it has been corrected. Get your name cleared as quickly as possible.

If you discover that someone else has been using your credit to purchase property, cars, furs, jewels, and so on, you will probably have a big problem. This may be a case of identity theft, which is the most frequent crime committed in the United States. If this is the case, consult your attorney, the state attorney's office, or the local office of the Federal Trade Commission.

3. Gather the information you need ahead of time. It's a very good idea to gather needed information ahead of time and organize it so that it's easily accessible. If you know ahead of time that you'll need complete copies of your past two or three tax returns plus a current pay stub, or a current profit and loss if you're self-employed, you'll be able to have that information on hand when the lender comes calling. I recommend you buy a file holder to hold all of the relevant documents to ensure you have *what* you need *when* you need it.

4. Know the current lending guidelines. Get a current copy of the lending guidelines for Fannie Mae (homepath.com or fanniemae.com), Freddie Mac (freddiemac.com), Federal Housing Authority (fha.gov), and, if applicable, the Veterans Administration (va.gov, for VA loans only). You can get this information at your local Housing Authority or on the Web.

Although it may seem that the loan officer's primary job is disqualifying mortgage applicants, the reverse is true. The loan officer wants to qualify as many applicants as possible (lenders make their money by approving loans) but is restricted by the rules and regulations of a larger, more powerful body—the secondary mortgage market, of which Fannie Mae and Freddie Mac are the leaders.

If you understand that the secondary mortgage market (which will ultimately buy your loan and repay the lender, who will then make another loan) actually controls the lender, it's easier to understand why the lender must ask you again and again for more documentation. Usually, repeated requests for more documentation mean that the lender wants to approve your loan but there are obstacles (like creditworthiness) that must be cleared up.

If you understand up front what your lender is going through, it may help smooth the process.

5. Qualify your lender. Just as you shop for a broker and a new home, it's very important to shop for a lender. Not all lenders are created equal. Loan products, services, style, and personal attention vary greatly. Look for a lender that is best qualified to meet your needs. Look for someone exceptionally well trained and thoroughly knowledgeable in the mortgage type you want to use. Look for someone who is seasoned in the business and can guide you through with a practiced hand.

For example, if you're self-employed, and you've only been self-employed for a year, you may be considered to have sub-par credit, even though you may have paid every bill on time in your life. The reason: Lenders need to see that you've been self-employed, maintaining an income for at least two years, and have the tax returns to prove it. At this point, your choices would be to wait until you've been self-employed for two years, or go with a sub-par loan (also known as a B or C loan in the lending industry). Sub-par lending can mean that a piece of your credit is missing, or you have bad credit. You may pay a little more for this loan, but a lender who works frequently with loans like yours knows where to go to get your loan funded.

For more information on choosing the right lender, see Question 59.

> Most first-time buyers don't know that if they receive money from their parents as a gift toward the down payment, they need a letter from their parents stating that the money is a gift and does not need to be repaid. In addition, if your parents or relatives are going to give you money, it's a good idea to have that money in your account six months before you actually go to apply for a loan. Banks will look at your monthly balances for the past six months. The higher the balance, the more likely it is that you'll be approved for your loan.

HOW DO I GET THE BEST LOAN AT THE BEST RATE ON THE BEST TERMS?

The most important thing to remember is that the best loan for you may not be the cheapest loan you're being offered.

Your loan should work for *your* personal financial situation; that may mean paying a bit more up front for a lower long-term rate, or paying nothing up front for a higher rate. Either way, lenders now offer so many different financial products that it's easy to find the creative solution that's best for you.

After you find it, there are some things you can do to get that loan at the best price possible.

- **Know what you want.** The mortgage market is extremely competitive for *conventional* loans, which in 2005 meant loans under $359,650. (The amount usually adjusts upward every year.) Look at the real estate section of your local paper and identify the "mortgage watch" column. Call a few of the lenders who appear to offer the lowest rates and have them bid on your business. You can also go online to Bank Rate Monitor's site (bankrate.com) and check out the daily mortgage rate (plus the daily rate on auto loans, credit cards, and a host of other credit products).

- **Stay on top of interest rates.** Interest rates change at least once each day, and sometimes even more frequently. If you decide to float your loan, watch the bond market activity closely. If rates seem to be dropping, react quickly and call in your lock. Then get the confirmation in writing.

- **Watch the points and fees.** The number of points and fees also changes frequently. Martha and Ken watched as the number of points required on their loan rose to four and a half and then fell back to two. They locked in at two and a half points. You might also choose a no-point, no-fee (non-recurring fees, like title cost, not an insurance premium) loan, but be prepared to carry a higher interest rate over the life of the loan.

- **Consider using a mortgage broker.** Brokers usually have access to more than a dozen investors, and their job is to do the shopping around for you. Mortgage brokers can offer a wide variety of choices, but don't be afraid to tell them about other mortgage packages you've discovered elsewhere. Let them offer you a better deal. You'll also want to stay on your guard, since end lenders (known as investors) pay mortgage brokers a fee for every loan they buy (call it a finder's fee). The only problem is that the lender gets a higher fee for every loan that's above the market rate. So the lender has a real incentive to sell you a loan that's more expensive than you'd otherwise have to pay. This practice is called *service fee premiums*. Ask your mortgage broker to disclose the service fee premium he or she is being paid by the end lender to do your loan. If it's more than 1 percent of the loan amount, look elsewhere for a loan.

- **Don't be afraid to negotiate for lower fees.** Ask for detailed explanations of fees and speak up if you don't like something. Once you have a detailed listing of fees and charges from each lender, you can compare apples to apples, then go back to the lender and ask for the elimination of specific fees.

- **Consult with your real estate attorney** *before* **you apply for a mortgage.** Some first-time buyers believe a real estate attorney should be called in only if a problem arises. Others call the attorney *after* the deal has been negotiated. The truth is, your real estate attorney should probably be the first call you make after having your offer to purchase accepted, or maybe even before. Real estate attorneys who do a lot of house closings know the people at the title companies, the brokers, and the mortgage players. They can give you resources, point you in the right direction, and guide you toward a successful house closing. If you're living in a state where real estate attorneys are not commonly used (like California), you should know your stuff even more thoroughly before you meet with the lender.

20/20 hindsight

When the first edition of this book was published in 1994, loans over $203,000 were considered to be jumbo loans. As we went to press at the beginning of 2005, jumbo loans ranged from $359,650 to about $750,000. Loans from around $750,000 to a million fall into the "super-jumbo" category, and home loans over a million dollars are in a separate category altogether. The conventional mortgage amount, $359,650 in 2005, changes every year or so. How much it changes depends on how fast home prices are rising. What's the difference between getting a conventional loan and a jumbo loan? You'll have to pay more fees and a higher interest rate. How much? The difference can be up to a point (a point is 1 percent of the loan amount) in additional fees, plus the loan will carry an interest rate that is up to a half point higher than a conventional loan. You can add another 1¼ to 1½ percent to the interest rate for super-jumbo loans. That's why you should try to get a conventional loan. It'll save you loads of money down the road.

9

Playing the Mortgage Game

In this chapter you'll find answers to your questions about what types of loans exist, how private mortgage insurance helps home buyers to purchase their homes, and what to do if a lender isn't treating you the right way.

WHAT ARE THE DIFFERENT TYPES OF MORTGAGES AVAILABLE? HOW DO I CHOOSE THE RIGHT TYPE FOR ME?

Mortgage lenders around the country currently offer literally dozens of different mortgage products. In fact, most lenders can tailor a loan that's exactly right for you.

So many options, so little time. It seems overwhelming, but if you start to ask a few questions, you'll soon figure out that your lender is actually offering only six or seven basic mortgage types. It's just that in today's world of personalized banking, lenders say, everyone wants something made to order for his or her specific financial situation.

Making the Right Choice

The right mortgage for you will depend on several factors, including your monthly income today and what you expect it will be in the future, the assets you currently hold, and how much debt you're carrying. Other factors can influence your mortgage decision as well. Do you want to pay points (a point is 1 percent of the loan amount) up front, or do you prefer to pay them over the life of the loan? Do you want to gamble that interest rates will stay low and get an adjustable-rate mortgage (ARM)? Or would you feel more comfortable paying a fixed amount each month?

Lenders offer a variety of financing options simply because today's home buyers want a cure for every ill. For example, if you plan to live in your house for only three to five years, you might consider a two-step loan, also known as a 5/25 (pronounced "five twenty-five") or a 7/23 ("seven twenty-three") mortgage, or a one-year adjustable-rate rather than a fixed-interest-rate mortgage.

Here is a quick description of the basic types of mortgages available in the marketplace. The following questions offer an in-depth explanation of these mortgages, along with suggestions as to which type of buyer might actually benefit from which type of mortgage.

- **Fixed-rate mortgage.** The original and most popular type of loan when interest rates are low, a fixed-rate mortgage charges the same percentage rate of interest over the life of the loan. Home-owners repay the loan with a fixed, monthly installment of principal and interest. Fixed-rate loans can be taken out in a variety of lengths, including 10-year, 15-year, 20-year, and the ever popular 30-year loan. In the mid-1990s, a 40-year version of the fixed-rate loan was introduced. With a 40-year fixed-rate mortgage, you won't start building up any appreciable equity in your home until somewhere near the 20th year of the loan. But lenders are finding that consumers like 40-year mortgages because they can buy a more expensive house.

- **Adjustable-rate mortgage (ARM).** Adjustable-rate mortgages have interest rates that fluctuate and are pegged to one-year Treasury bills or a specific index. The initial rate of interest is usually quite low, and then the rate bumps up between one and two points per year. There is usually a yearly cap of one or two percentage points, and the loan also has a lifetime ceiling cap, usually around five or six points. The interest rate can also go down. In the late 1980s and early 1990s, ARMs proved to be the best deal around because interest rates sank and then stayed low. Homeowners whose initial interest rate was around 5 percent now have loans at 6.5 to 7 percent and have saved thousands of dollars on their loans.

- **Two-step mortgages.** Also known as 5/25s and 7/23s, these mortgages come in two different flavors: convertible (which converts the loan to a fixed loan for the remaining 25 or 23 years, respectively) and nonconvertible (which converts the loan to an ARM). They are similar loans with different numbers attached. The 5/25 is a 30-year loan that has a fixed-interest rate for the first five years and then adjusts into a convertible or nonconvertible loan. The 7/23 is a similar 30-year loan but adjusts after seven years instead of five. Both of these loans can be amortized over the entire 30-year period. They are considered more risky than fixed-rate loans, but they are significantly less risky than ARMs during the first five or seven years. As a result, the interest rate is lower than a standard 30-year fixed-rate loan but slightly higher than a 1-year adjustable.

- **FHA mortgage.** Preset spending limits are the hallmark of an FHA mortgage. The loan amounts are set by the median prices of different cities within a particular area. The difference in loan amounts between rural and densely populated areas can vary by as much as $25,000 or more. The best part about an FHA loan is the low down payment required; very little needs to come out of your pocket. With some special government-backed loan products, you need only put up 2 percent of the loan amount, although I expect this to fall further as mortgage companies become more sophisticated with super-low-down-payment loans. However, be prepared: If you put down less than 20 percent, you'll pay a steep mortgage insurance premium. Other up-front costs are part of the bargain and must be considered when choosing an FHA loan. FHA loans are assumable, which means you could simply take over the payments from your seller (provided you qualify), saving a lot of cost and hassle.

- **VA loan.** A VA loan is administered by the Department of Veterans Affairs in Washington, DC, and is designed to help qualified veterans of the U.S. Armed Forces buy homes with no down payment. In addition, veterans are not allowed to pay points to the lender, although they are responsible for some loan fees. That prohibition sometimes causes a problem because the seller usually gets stuck for the extra bucks. Only veterans who have served a specified number of days and who get a certificate of eligibility from the Department of Veterans Affairs can qualify for a VA loan.

- **Balloon mortgage.** This type of mortgage can be any length at all. Some balloon mortgages require monthly payments of principal and interest; others only require interest. In either case, when the loan comes due (after, say, five or seven years), the loan balance must be repaid in full. Balloon mortgages can be paid in one of two ways: (1) the mortgage can be amortized over 15 or 30 years, and the homeowner just pays the first five or ten years of the loan before paying it off or refinancing; or (2) the homeowner pays only the interest on the loan (as opposed to interest and principal, as when a loan is amortized) until the end of the loan period. For example, if you borrow $100,000 on a five-year interest-only balloon, the $100,000 is due on the last day of the five-year period. Throughout the five years, you pay interest only on the money.

- **Graduated-payment mortgage (GPM), also known as the negative amortization loan.** The GPM was originally designed for first-time buyers because it offers reduced monthly payments early on in the life of the loan. The payments become larger as the loan progresses and, hopefully, the finances of the borrower improve. Most lenders have steered away from the GPM in recent years as two-step mortgages have become more popular. In fact, the FHA eliminated its GPM in 1988, but GPMs seem to be making a comeback as first-time buyers look for ways to get more house for their cash. Interest-only loans can be a form of negative amortization loans. GPMs are complicated loans that require a tremendous amount of paperwork, whereas 5/25s and 7/23s are relatively easy to package.

- **Shared-appreciation mortgage.** A shared-appreciation mortgage is a financial concept borrowed from commercial property transfers. The lender offers a below-market rate in exchange for a share in the profits of the home when it is sold. There are significant benefits to this. As the buyer, you get all the tax benefits, and the lender doesn't make any money unless you do. On the other hand, if the home appreciates greatly, you could end up paying a lot of that profit to the lender. Shared-appreciation mortgages are most commonly coordinated by nonprofit associations seeking to help low-income first-time buyers become first-time homeowners. They use community development block grant (CDBG) funds to help make up the difference between what low- to moderate-income families can afford and what the competitively priced commercial products want to see on a borrower's balance sheet.

- **Biweekly mortgage.** The name for this mortgage product comes from the number of payments you make per month: two. Each payment represents half of what a regular monthly payment might be, but because you pay every other week, that adds up to 26 payments, or a 13th month. *Making that 13th payment, no matter what form it takes, will significantly cut down the amount of interest you'll pay over the life of the loan.* The trouble with biweeklies is that, although they are easier payments to make (particularly if you get paid biweekly), the obligation to pay twice a month can be onerous, particularly if money is tight. And with some lenders you'll get charged a hefty sum (as much as several hundred dollars) to set up a biweekly loan. You can achieve the same effect on your loan by simply making an extra payment a year, or dividing that extra payment into 12 pieces and paying a little extra each month.

QUESTION 74

HOW SMALL A DOWN PAYMENT CAN I MAKE? WHERE CAN I FIND A ZERO-DOWN LOAN?

Not so long ago, if you wanted to buy a house, you had to come up with 20 percent in cash for the down payment. So if you were buying a $100,000 house, you needed $20,000 in cash.

Study after study has shown that coming up with the down payment has been one of the toughest obstacles for first-time home buyers to overcome. Scraping together that extra cash each month, on top of rent, utilities, child care, and credit card payments, excluded those whose finances were more marginal from the benefits of homeownership.

Things began to change when the FHA started permitting home buyers to purchase homes with 10 percent down, and then 5 percent down. Studies showed that defaults did increase as home buyers put less and less down on their homes, but the actual number was tiny. Apparently, there was a profitable market to tap. Conventional mortgages followed suit and began offering 95 percent loan-to-value ratio mortgages. Soon, the FHA dropped its down payment requirement to just 3 percent. Conventional lenders followed, introducing 97 percent loan-to-value ratio loans.

While the down payments were decreasing, lenders (led again by the FHA) were increasing their debt-to-income ratios. Instead of allowing borrowers to spend only 28 percent of their gross monthly income on the mortgage and up to 36 percent on their total debt, home buyers were permitted to spend up to 41 percent (or more, in some cases). Industry experts saw that these marginal home buyers (made up of significant numbers of minority and immigrant families) were already spending as much as 50 percent of their gross monthly income on rent—and were making it work.

The FHA decided home buyers only needed to put down 2 percent on a house. The rest of the down payment could be a gift from a family member, or a grant. In response, conventional lenders went a step further. The Veterans Administration had always offered qualified veterans a true zero-down loan, but the loan was expensive. In the late 1990s, conventional lenders began offering true zero-down loans to ordinary home buyers. Some of the programs were either restricted by income or area. Some continue to be available to all home buyers.

Let's be clear about one thing: Any time you put down less than 20 percent in cash on your home, you'll either pay private mortgage insurance (PMI) or FHA mortgage insurance (if you get an FHA loan), unless you opt for an 80/10/10 or an 80/15/5 loan. I'll talk more about PMI in Question 75. PMI can be expensive, although the cost fell throughout the past decade. And although PMI must be canceled automatically by your lender once you've reached a certain level of equity, it could take you 10 years or more to get there. You'll pay more in PMI premiums the lower the down payment. It gets particularly expensive when the down payment is below 5 percent. But if paying PMI is the only way you can buy a home, it's generally worth it. (Legislation has been proposed that would allow a homeowner to write off the PMI premium paid each year much the same way you're allowed to deduct the interest you pay on your mortgage and your real estate taxes. So far, this legislation hasn't gone anywhere, but be sure to keep your ears open, just in case.)

Finding a Low-Down-Payment Loan

Almost any major mortgage banker or broker can do a low-down-payment loan. If you need the extra lending ratios, you may need to go with an FHA loan. Almost all lenders can and will do an FHA loan (although it requires a bit more paperwork). Simply ask which loan options require that you put 5 percent down, or less.

Finding a Zero-Down Loan

As we go to press, legislation has been proposed that would permit the FHA to back zero-down loans. This legislation has a fairly good chance of passing, at which time zero-down loans will be available at your neighborhood lender's office. Until then, here are just a few of the true zero-down loans, and where you might find them:

1. Merrill Lynch 100 Home Loan. This loan can be used if the borrower has assets being held in a Merrill Lynch brokerage account. To get the 20 percent down payment, you'd have to tap into these assets (which may include retirement accounts, stocks, or bonds) and sell them. If you don't want to sell these assets but still want to buy a house, the Merrill Lynch program allows you to borrow the 20 percent you need for the down payment, using these assets as collateral. The nice thing is that you'll pay the going 30-year interest rate on the whole 100 percent loan, instead of a much higher interest rate. The danger to this program, and others like it, is that you're essentially borrowing the 20 percent on margin. If your assets suddenly fall in value, the 20 percent part of the loan could be called, and you'll have to come up with the money all at once. The Merrill Lynch program tries to guard against this by only allowing you to borrow against a small portion of your assets. Before you decide on this loan, read the brochures thoroughly and ask plenty of questions.

2. Fidelity Home Loan program and others. Fidelity, which owns some of the largest mutual funds in the country (including Magellan, its flagship fund), has set up a program similar to the Merrill Lynch program. I wouldn't be surprised if in the next few years other financial companies start developing other different sorts of lending guidelines to meet the needs of their customers.

3. Individual bank programs. Several years ago, Bank of America introduced a 100 percent loan that was available to people who met certain income criteria. The loan was specifically designed for the first-time buyer market. The loan may or may not be available when you're in the mortgage market, but other lending institutions may offer special 100 percent loan programs. As lenders begin to understand how these loans work and where consumers who take these loans are most vulnerable financially, I predict that more of these 100 percent loan programs will pop up.

4. Nonprofit organizations. Traditionally, nonprofit organizations and housing authorities have used Community Development Block Grant (CDBG) funds to help first-time home buyers with either down payment funds or by lowering the interest rate on the loans. Start your search for these programs at your local housing authority and see what programs are being offered. The programs change frequently, so be prepared to call several times.

The higher your loan-to-value ratio, the higher your monthly costs will be. Sometimes it's better to not stretch yourself too thin financially. I call this concept *underbuying*. When you underbuy, you spend less than you can afford because you choose to make your financial life a bit easier. Brokers will often encourage you to *overbuy*; that is, spend as much or even more than you can comfortably afford today, on the theory that soon you'll be earning more money and will be in a house that is the right size for you and your growing family. Whichever way you go, make sure you think it through first. You'll be using your leverage if you overbuy, but that financial risk won't be worth anything if you can't sleep at night.

WHAT IS PRIVATE MORTGAGE INSURANCE (PMI)? HOW CAN I AVOID PAYING IT? HOW DO I GET RID OF IT? HOW DOES IT DIFFER FROM FHA'S MORTGAGE INSURANCE AND MORTGAGE/CREDIT INSURANCE?

Private mortgage insurance (PMI) is an often necessary expense that accompanies buying a house with less than 20 percent down in cash. Although it's expensive, PMI allows you to purchase a home with a small down payment, and it helps the lender resell your mortgage on the secondary market to an institutional investor.

By definition, PMI is additional insurance designed to protect the lender from individuals who default on their loans and who have less than 20 percent equity in their property. Mortgage experts say that, compared with home buyers who put down the traditional 20 percent of the purchase price, those who make small down payments are more likely to default on their home loans. Therefore, lenders require those riskier buyers to purchase PMI to insure the lender against the extra risk—and ensuing cost—of foreclosure.

Fannie Mae and Freddie Mac have regulations prohibiting lenders from making a loan in excess of 80 percent of the purchase price without PMI. The difference between putting down 20 percent and, say, 15 percent or even 10 percent, wouldn't seem to make a substantial difference on the surface, but a spokesperson for the Mortgage Bankers

Association of America (MBA), a nonprofit organization serving the needs of lenders nationwide, says that 20 percent provides a necessary cushion for both home buyers and lenders: "If I put down 20 percent and lose my job, and the house has declined in value, I can still sell it and pay off the mortgage and come out even or with a little bit of cash. But if I've only put down 5 percent in the same set of circumstances, then I'll come out of the deal owing money."

Although it is expensive, PMI has its upside for buyers, too. About 30 percent of home buyers, most of them first-timers, can't put together enough cash for a 20 percent down payment. PMI allows many people to purchase property years earlier than they otherwise would have been able to. Buyers who are required to purchase PMI have to pay for that additional security, but they gain from being able to get a mortgage with much less cash up front. This is considered a plus by many real estate experts, who argue that you should buy a home with as little cash as possible.

First-time buyers often wonder whether every lender charges PMI. (Not all lenders advertise it.) "If a customer calls me and says a lender doesn't charge PMI, I ask them to check the interest rate," says Ray, a mortgage banker. "It's always one quarter or three-eighths of a percent higher than ours. And you'll be paying it for the life of the loan."

PMI Is Getting Cheaper and Easier to Cancel

Since I wrote the first edition of this book, several important things have occurred that will ultimately make it less expensive for home buyers who have PMI.

First, a new law was passed. The Homeowner's Protection Act of 1998 requires all lenders who closed on loans after July 29, 1999, to provide consumers with an explanation of how the homeowner can cancel his or her PMI policy. There are three ways to do it:

1. If you believe your home has reached the 20 percent equity threshold, you may hire an appraiser to appraise the value of your home. If indeed you have passed the 20 percent equity market, your lender must cancel your PMI payments.

2. Each monthly mortgage payment consists of both principal and interest. Each bit of principal you repay goes to build up your equity. Starting with loans that are originated after July 31, 1999, lenders must inform borrowers annually that they may cancel their PMI once they've reached the 20 percent equity threshold. On a 30-year loan, you might

hit the 20 percent threshold somewhere around the tenth year. If you prepay your loan, you'll cross the equity threshold a lot faster.

3. If you do not request a cancellation of your PMI premium once you've hit the 20 percent equity, the lender is now required to automatically cancel your PMI once you hit the 22 percent equity threshold. This will be done whether or not you request it.

You don't have to wait for 10 years if the value of homes in your neighborhood has risen more quickly. If home prices rise an average of 3 percent a year, you may reach the 20 percent level in 6 to 7 years, rather than waiting until 10 years. If you bought a house in certain neighborhoods in Chicago in 2003, for example, your house might have doubled in value by the spring of 2004. If you bought in Las Vegas in 2003, your home might have appreciated 41 percent by October 2004. If you buy a fixer-upper and make the right improvements, your home could reach the 20 percent equity threshold in months, not years. It all depends on what you buy and what you do to your property after the purchase. Stay on top of local housing values if you have PMI—the savings will be worth it!

Canceling PMI as soon as possible can save you hundreds of dollars per year and even thousands of dollars over the life of your loan. If you use the money you save each year (which could amount to $300 to $500 per $100,000 in loan amount) to prepay your loan, you'll save not only a few thousand dollars but perhaps tens of thousands of dollars in interest. But lenders will not cancel PMI in the first two years you have your loan, even if the property has doubled in value. To get rid of PMI on a new loan you have had for less than 24 months, you'll have to refinance.

The Cost of PMI

The premium price depends on the purchase price of the home and the type of mortgage you've selected (fixed 30-year, fixed 15-year, ARM, 7/23, or balloon). You can expect to pay anywhere from $45 to $60 per month for every $100,000 of loan amount.

Canceling Your PMI Premiums

As we discussed, you don't have to pay PMI throughout the whole life of the loan, unless you've opted to put the cost of PMI into the interest rate of your loan. If that's the case, you'll have to refinance to get rid of it.

When you close on your loan, the lender is required to give you information on how to cancel your PMI payments when you've reached the magic 20 percent equity threshold. Once you've reached the threshold (either by reaching that point in your loan term or because your home has increased in value), you may request (and pay for) an appraisal of your home. If the appraisal shows your home's value, in combination with the equity you've built up with your regular mortgage payments plus any prepayments, puts you at the 20 percent equity level, the lender must cancel your PMI payments.

If you do nothing, the lender is now required to cancel your PMI once your loan-to-value ratio has reached 22 percent. But the lender will not cancel PMI within the first two years (and somtimes up to five years) that you've had your loan.

FHA Loans

Frequently, home buyers wonder if they have to pay private mortgage insurance if they get an FHA loan. The answer is no. But that doesn't mean you're not paying for some form of mortgage insurance.

All government loans require mortgage insurance, which they refer to as MI or MIP. But because you're getting a government loan, you get the government version of PMI. Unlike PMI, however, you can never cancel your mortgage insurance on an FHA loan, even if you reach 50 percent in loan-to-value ratio. *The only way to cancel MI on your FHA loan is to refinance into a conventional loan.*

first time

buyer tip

276

Lenders must tell you at the closing exactly how many years and months it will take for you to pay off enough of your loan to cancel PMI. This doesn't include any rise in your home's equity, which could shorten the time frame considerably. Plus, your mortgage servicer must provide you with a phone number each year that you can call for information about canceling your PMI.

If your lender balks at canceling your PMI, contact the department or agency that regulates mortgage lenders in your state. If your lender is federally chartered, you can call the Treasury's Office of Thrift Supervision or the Federal Deposit Insurance Corporation. Check Appendix V, General Resources, for more details.

How to Get a Low-Down-Payment Loan Without PMI

There is one way to get a low-down-payment loan without paying for PMI. It's called an 80/10/10 ("eighty-ten-ten") or an 80/15/5 ("eighty-fifteen-five") loan.

The concept here is that you're essentially getting two loans simultaneously, a regular 80 percent loan-to-value ratio first mortgage, and a home equity loan. With an 80/10/10, the first mortgage is for 80 percent of the sales price of the home, the home equity loan is for an additional 10 percent of the cost, and the final 10 percent represents your down payment. With an 80/15/5, the home equity loan is for an additional 15 percent of the cost of the home, and you put down 5 percent.

There are pluses and minuses to the 80/10/10 loans. The good thing is that you don't pay PMI. And, because home equity loans up to $100,000 are tax-deductible, you can deduct the interest you pay. Private mortgage insurance is never tax-deductible.

(The 80/10/10 and 80/15/5 loans, also known as "piggyback loans," have caught on so quickly and become such a big profit drain for the private mortgage insurance companies, that private mortgage insurers have lobbied Capitol Hill to pass legislation that would allow homeowners to deduct their PMI premiums. As we went to press, the legislation had not passed.)

Unfortunately, the interest on the home equity loan tends to be higher than on a regular loan, which means you'll pay more in interest. But since it's tax-deductible, the numbers work out almost even between a PMI low-down-payment loan and an 80/10/10. (And when interest rates are at 30- or 40-year lows, an 80/10/10 tends to be the better deal.)

Who's a good candidate for an 80/10/10? If you work for a company that pays a good bonus once a year, and you know that the size of your next bonus will allow you to entirely pay off the home equity portion of the loan, you may want to go this way. That's because you'll be able to get to a conventional-size mortgage a lot faster and save yourself the cost of PMI.

Talk to your lender, think about how long you'll have this loan, and work out the numbers before you make this important decision.

Comparing PMI, MI, and Mortgage/Credit Insurance

As we've just discussed, PMI is required by all lenders whenever you put down less than 20 percent on a house. The lower your down payment, the higher your PMI premium.

FHA mortgage insurance (also referred to as MI) is the government version of PMI. It is required on all FHA loans no matter how much you put down in cash. In addition, you can never cancel it. The only way to get rid of MI on an FHA loan is to refinance out of that loan into a conventional loan.

Credit insurance, also referred to as mortgage insurance, is an entirely different matter. This is insurance designed to pay off your bills in case something should happen to you. Depending on the kind of insurance you get, it will either pay off your credit card bills or your entire mortgage.

Sound good? It isn't. Credit insurance and mortgage insurance are extremely expensive. And you're paying a lot of money for something that is a declining liability. That means, every month when you write a check to the credit card company or to your mortgage lender, your check includes principal and interest. So, each month, your principal balance due falls a bit.

Suppose you take out mortgage insurance that will pay off a $100,000 loan if you die before the loan is paid. If it's a 30-year loan, and you don't die for 30 years, you'll have paid off your mortgage before taking advantage of the policy. If you then let the policy lapse, you've paid out for 30 years for nothing. If you die 15 years into your $100,000 mortgage, the balance due may only be $70,000, and yet you're still paying for $100,000 in coverage. After the insurance pays off the balance of the $100,000 mortgage, you might expect that your survivor will get the extra $30,000 in cash, right?

Not likely. You've forfeited that $30,000. If you're worried about how your spouse or partner will manage the bills after you're gone, consider buying term life insurance. It's a heck of a lot less expensive than mortgage or credit insurance, and you'll get everything you're paying for. Also, your spouse or partner will have the option to use the funds in any way he or she wants to. Perhaps paying off the mortgage at that time wouldn't be in his or her best interest. Term life insurance provides options that aren't available with mortgage or credit insurance.

20/20

hindsight

One of the things we do to show our family and friends how much we love them is to plan ahead in case the unthinkable happens. Planning for how your loved one will live and be able to stay in the home you're buying (if that's what you feel is best) is something for which you should carefully consider and prepare.

WHAT IS AN ASSUMABLE MORTGAGE? ARE THESE LOANS STILL AVAILABLE?

QUESTION 76

Sometimes a broker will show you a property, then lean over and say, "And it's got an assumable mortgage to boot." You nod, knowingly, but inside you're wondering what's up. The broker is obviously trying to tip you off to something, but you're not exactly sure what's going on.

Here's the answer: With an *assumable mortgage*, the buyer takes over from the seller the legal obligation to make monthly payments of principal and interest to the lender. There is no change to the terms of the loan, which is attractive to buyers in a high interest rate environment. The lender, assured of getting repaid on the loan, then releases the seller from his or her liability.

How do you find out if a mortgage is assumable? Most conventional mortgages are not assumable; that is, a *due-on-sale* clause is built into the verbiage of the loan. A due-on-sale clause means that if you sell the home, you may immediately owe all of the money to the lender. FHA mortgages are assumable, which is one reason brokers like to show first-time buyers FHA properties.

Another reason you might like an assumable mortgage is that it can be cheaper and easier to assume a loan than take out a new loan. If you, the buyer, decide to assume the mortgage of the seller, and if you qualify for the loan, you may pay fewer closing costs and fees, and less paperwork needs to be completed.

If you purchase property that is *subject to* an existing mortgage, you take over the loan payments, but the seller remains liable for the mortgage amount. There is no formal transfer of obligation or liability, as with an assumable mortgage. If someone tries to convince you to buy a property subject to a mortgage, make sure the lender can't call in the loan as a result of the transfer of title. If you purchase property subject to an existing mortgage, and the lender, upon receiving notice of the transfer of title, calls in the loan, you could be forced to pay off the entire loan immediately.

Since interest rates dropped in the early 1990s assumable mortgages have fallen out of favor. FHA loans are still assumable, but if interest rates are lower than the rate of the assumable mortgage, you're better off getting a new loan than taking over the older, more expensive mortgage. Also, frequently, you'll pay more for the property (because the home has appreciated in value) than whatever balance remains on the mortgage. Unless you have the cash to make up the difference (between the mortgage balance and the price the seller wants for the house), you'll need a new, larger loan. Some agents and brokers still tout "assumable loans" as being something you need to pay attention to, but in reality, you're better off shopping around to find the right mortgage program for you.

WHAT IS A FIXED-RATE MORTGAGE? WHAT IS AN ADJUSTABLE-RATE MORTGAGE (ARM)?

The original and most popular type of mortgage is the fixed-interest-rate mortgage. The amount of the interest and principal repayment is amortized in equal amounts over the life of the loan. Many homeowners like the financial security of knowing that they will pay exactly the same amount of money each month (excluding property tax or insurance payments to an escrow account) until the loan has been paid off in full.

Although the concept of fixed-interest mortgages hasn't changed much, most lenders now offer borrowers a choice in how long a loan they want. A 30-year mortgage was, and is, the most popular length, but 10-, 15-, and 20-year fixed mortgages have recently become more popular as interest rates have continued to stay relatively low.

Recently, a 40-year loan was introduced. On a $100,000 mortgage, you might save an additional $50 per month if you went with a 40-year loan instead of a 30-year loan. But for that savings, you have an additional 10 years of interest payments. It's just not worth it. The rising popularity of interest-only loans has basically eliminated any interest in 40-year mortgages.

When interest rates are low, borrowers find that the shorter loan length offers a significant financial advantage over a regular 30-year mortgage. Homeowners can save thousands of dollars in interest payments if they shorten the length of the loan by up to 15 years. Of course, the shorter the amortization period, the higher the monthly payment. But the loan is amortized faster, so you pay less interest over the life of the loan.

For example, if you take out a $100,000 30-year mortgage at 8 percent interest, your monthly payments toward principal and interest would be around $730. If that same mortgage was 15 years in length, your monthly payment would be around $940.

You'd end up paying $262,800 in principal and interest over the life of the 30-year loan. You'd pay only $169,200—nearly $100,000 less—over the life of a 15-year loan.

	15-Year Loan	*30-Year Loan*
Monthly payment	$940	$730
Total payments	$169,200	$262,800

When you get a 15-year loan, the interest rate is usually lower than the rate for a 30-year loan. Even if you prepay your 30-year loan down to the point where it will terminate in 15 years, you'll save more money by going with a 15-year loan because the interest rate on the whole loan is less.

Who Would Benefit from a Fixed-Rate Mortgage?

Buyers on a limited or fixed income and those who do not like to gamble with interest rates are usually best served by a fixed-rate mortgage. Those buyers who can handle the higher payments and want to pay down their mortgage as fast as possible are best served by a 10-, 15-, or 20-year fixed-rate mortgage. Still, people who choose a 30-year mortgage for the initial lower payments and want to pay it off faster can make an additional mortgage payment per year—a 13th payment—and direct the lender to use that money to repay the principal (write it on the check). This is called *prepaying your mortgage.* An extra payment a year will significantly lessen the amount of interest you pay over the life of the loan.

There are several ways to successfully prepay your mortgage: (1) You can make a lump-sum payment if you happen to come into some cash, perhaps through an inheritance; (2) you can divide your regular mortgage payment by 12 and add $\frac{1}{12}$ to each monthly mortgage payment you make, directing the lender in writing to apply the difference to the principal balance (you may even have something on your mortgage coupon that you can check off for that purpose); or (3) you can make one complete extra payment per year, on its own, at any time.

If you make a 13th payment every year, beginning the first year, on a 30-year mortgage, you'll effectively cut your mortgage from 30 years to between 18 and 21 years, depending on when you pay the extra amount. For example, you'll shave more time off the length of your loan if you make your extra payment on January 1, than if you pay it on December 31.

If you want to pay off your 30-year loan in 15 years (or 12 years, etc.) you can go online to any number of sites, including ThinkGlink.com and Eloan.com. The amortization calculators can help you readjust your amortization schedule so you know how many years you'll cut off your loan if you prepay a certain amount each month. You can also play around with this if you use Quicken, QuickBooks, or Microsoft Money financial software to keep track of your expenses.

Be aware, however, that an extra payment per year does not relieve you of the obligation to meet your monthly payments. Even if you pay twice the amount owed one month, you still must make your regular mortgage payment the next month. Moreover, on 30-year fixed-rate loans, the 13th payment does not lessen future monthly payments. It does alter the end balance on your account, and shortens your loan term.

Adjustable-Rate Mortgages (ARMs)

An ARM is a mortgage with an interest rate that adjusts at specific times over the life of the loan—usually yearly, every three years, or every five years. But there is even a 10-year ARM, which adjusts once every 10 years.

Adjustable-rate mortgages are attractive to a variety of buyers because the initial interest rate is much lower than those on almost any other type of loan. Interest rates on one-year ARMs tend to start out very low—sometimes as low as 4 or 5 percent—and increases in the rate are generally tied to an economic index, such as one-, three-, or five-year Treasury securities. When the time comes for your loan to adjust—either yearly, every three years, or every five years—a margin of between one and three percentage points is tacked onto whatever index the loan is tied to. This is how the lender comes up with your next interest rate.

National Cost of Funds Index

As an example, let's look at one index, the National Cost of Funds, which is based on the average cost of funds for savings and loans. Let's say the National Cost of Funds index is at 6.25 percent. If your lender charges 2.5 percentage points as a margin, your new mortgage interest rate based on that index would be 8.75 percent when the loan adjusts.

ARMs are likely to fluctuate with the economy, though you can get an idea of how much your mortgage will adjust by keeping an eye on economic indicators, such as the prime interest rate and the interest rate the Federal Reserve charges banks. Even if the prime rate soars in the next few years, ARM holders are somewhat protected by a lifetime cap on their loan's interest rate. This cap, usually five or six percentage points over the lifetime of the loan, limits how much the interest rate can go up. With a six-point cap, an ARM starting at 5.25 percent could never go higher than 11.25 percent. *Make sure your loan has an interest-rate lifetime cap, and that the loan can only go up only 1 or 2 percentage points per year.*

Going Down

ARMs, the lender likes to point out, can also readjust downward after the first adjustment period. In that case, the borrower could reap the benefit of his or her gamble for years to come. Let's say you need a $100,000 loan. You decide on a three-year ARM that has a starting interest rate of 6 percent, a two-point cap per year (the loan can only go up two points a year), and a margin of two and a half points over the Treasury bill to which it is tied.

For the first three years, your interest payment is $6,000, or $500 per month. At the end of the three years, let's assume the rate rises to 7 percent (just because the interest rate *can* go up two percentage points doesn't always mean it will). You will then pay $7,000 per year, or $583.33 monthly. (This example isn't exactly precise because I haven't amortized the numbers, but it works for straight interest loans. To create your own comparisons using amortized numbers, try Eloan.com's online amortization calculator, or my amortization calculator at ThinkGlink.com.)

ARMs vs. Fixed-Interest Rate Loans

Let's compare the $100,000 ARM we've just discussed with a $100,000 30-year fixed-rate mortgage at 8 percent:

Year	ARM	Fixed-Rate Loan
1	$6,000	$8,000
2	6,000	8,000
3	6,000	8,000
4	7,000	8,000
5	7,000	8,000
6	7,000	8,000
Total	$39,000	$48,000

If you were the borrower in this example, and you had chosen an ARM over a fixed-rate mortgage, you would have saved yourself $9,000 over six years. But what if the ARM had increased over and above the interest rate of the fixed-rate mortgage? If you consider that most folks move or refinance their mortgages every five to seven years, it's unlikely that the interest rate would have risen in that period of time to overcome the savings gained by using an ARM.

But let's say it does: You have a $100,000 ARM that adjusts every year and has a two-point annual readjustment cap with a lifetime cap of 6 percent:

Year	Interest Rate	ARM
1	5 percent	$5,000
2	7 percent	7,000
3	9 percent	9,000
4	11 percent	11,000
5	11 percent	11,000
6	11 percent	11,000
Total		$54,000

The ARM would cost $54,000 versus $48,000 for a fixed-rate loan. Assuming that the ARM readjusted upward at the maximum cap every year, it would have cost $6,000 more than the fixed-rate mortgage.

The truth of the matter is: It's impossible to predict long-term interest rates. No one has a crystal ball. In fact, if you bought your home in 1990, your ARM interest rate would have dropped the first year and held steady somewhere around 6 to 7 percent for the rest of the decade, saving you thousands of dollars over a fixed-rate mortgage.

As interest rates fall, the spread between ARMs and fixed-rate mortgages drops. As we closed out the 1990s, the spread between a 1-year ARM and a 30-year fixed-interest-rate mortgage was just 1 percent. That has continued as we head into 2005. But because rates were so low (at one point in time you could have locked in on a 30-year fixed-rate loan for as little as 5.5 percent), more people chose to get a fixed-rate loan than an ARM. That choice is, in fact, the home buyer's greatest opportunity. If interest rates rise when it comes time to buy your first home, you can simply choose an adjustable loan. If rates then drop after you've owned your home for a while, you can turn around and refinance into a fixed-rate mortgage. From 1999 to 2004, I refinanced my home about six times, each time using a 5/1 ARM. Our current 5/1 ARM carries an interest rate of around 4.25 percent, which will remain fixed until 2009. (And by that time, I hope to have my home loan paid off in full.)

Who Could Benefit from an ARM?

Buyers who carry more personal debt (in the form of credit cards, school loans, or a car loan) might benefit from the lower interest rates associated with an ARM, particularly if they can show that they have a good job and salary prospects for the future. Lenders generally will allow a housing expense—that is, mortgage principal and interest, private mortgage insurance, and property taxes—to equal no more than 28 percent of the borrowers' monthly gross income (income before taxes), unless they get a higher debt-to-income loan.

For example, if your gross monthly income is $4,000, you could afford monthly mortgage and property tax payments of up to $1,120. All debt, including installment and revolving loans (credit cards, car payments), should not exceed 36 percent of gross income, most lenders say. Conventional lenders have recently begun stretching the upper limit of the debt to income to around 40; only FHA goes above that. Lenders never calculate a loan on the basis of future earnings, but they might be willing to stretch the needed qualifications beyond normal parameters if, for example, you are a fourth-year medical student with a guaranteed residency in the near future, or a third-year law student with a job offer.

(When lenders stretch the requirements for prospective borrowers, they usually keep the loan within the institution's portfolio, meaning they don't resell the loan on the secondary mortgage market. That way, they needn't worry about Fannie Mae and Freddie Mac's requirements, and they have additional lending flexibility.)

Ask Yourself: How Long Do You Plan to Stay?

How long you plan to stay in your new home will have an effect on what you buy, where you buy it, and how you plan to pay for it.

If you know you're going to stay in a home for only five to seven years, you may want to get an ARM. Lenders acknowledge the strong probability that, compared with a fixed-rate mortgage, an ARM will end up with a lower interest rate over the entire term of the loan.

Ilyce and Sam's Story

When we bought the 1880s farmhouse in which we've lived for the past decade or so, we decided to use a 5/1 ARM rather than a 30-year fixed-rate mortgage.

It might have seemed a strange choice. We had found the house in which we wanted to spend the next 20 or 30 years. We were going to settle down and raise our family here. So why use a 5/1 ARM?

We guessed, correctly, that within five years of buying the property we would need to refinance our mortgage to pay for a "gut-job" renovation of our home. We asked ourselves: "Why get a 30-year mortgage when we were going to refinance in 5 years?"

So we went with the 5/1 ARM. The interest rate, as I remember it, was at least one percentage point or more less than the going 30-year fixed mortgage interest rate.

When we refinanced five years later in 1999, interest rates were beginning to go down. From 1999 to 2004, we refinanced our mortgage no less than six times. Each time, we used a 5/1 ARM.

286

I've never been one to try and "time" the mortgage market (or the stock market for that matter). But when you refinance so often, you're bound to get lucky once in a while. The 5/1 ARM we now have is at 4.25 percent. We agreed to lock in our refinance just before rates started to rise from their 46-year lows.

Our payments have dropped precipitously. To borrow a cliché, we're making hay while the sun shines. We not only use our "savings" each month (the difference between what we would be paying for our loan and what we are now paying) to prepay our mortgage, but we have started to add more each month as our income has improved.

The net result? In five years, thanks to the savings we have generated by using the 5/1 ARM, we have managed to pay down more than 25 percent of our mortgage. We expect that within the next four to five years, we will be able to pay off the loan entirely.

The Bottom Line

Just because you've found the house of your dreams doesn't mean you have to commit to a 30-year mortgage.

WHAT IS A TWO-STEP MORTGAGE? WHAT IS A BALLOON MORTGAGE?

A two-step mortgage is a hybrid cousin of the adjustable-rate mortgage (ARM) and fixed-rate mortgages. Also known as a 5/25 (pronounced "five twenty-five") or a 7/23 ("seven twenty-three"), a two-step mortgage combines the relative steadiness of a fixed-rate mortgage with some of the risks and rewards of an ARM.

Two-step mortgages come in two varieties: convertible and non-convertible. A convertible two-step mortgage means that a 5/25 or 7/23 loan has a fixed interest rate for the first 5 or 7 years, then converts into a fixed-rate mortgage for the remaining 25 or 23 years, respectively. A nonconvertible two-step mortgage means that the 5/25 or 7/23 has a fixed interest rate for the first 5 or 7 years, and then converts into a 1-year adjustable-rate mortgage (ARM), which adjusts each year for the remaining 25 or 23 years of loan term.

Let's look at the convertible version in a little more detail. The 5/25, for example, is a 30-year loan that has a fixed interest rate for the first 5 years and then has a onetime adjustment that determines what the rate will be for the remaining 25 years of the loan. As with other

30-year loans, it's amortized over 30 years. The 7/23 works the same way but is set at a fixed-interest rate for 7 years, and then adjusts once for the remaining 23 years of the loan.

Clearly, lenders have been keeping their eyes on the trends of homeownership. If the average homeowner sells or refinances his or her home every 5 to 7 years, there is not as much need for 30-year loans. Instead, these hybrid loans allow the homeowner to start off at a much lower interest rate, which will then adjust once during the life of the loan. If you choose a 7/23, it's more than likely you'll move before the rate adjusts—or soon thereafter—which will allow you to take full advantage of the first 7 years of lower-than-average interest rates.

As with ARMs, the onetime adjustment for both of these loans is tied to an economic index. The increase would be based on the status of the index at the end of the five- or seven-year term. Above the index rate, the lender often tacks on a margin, usually in the neighborhood of one to three points. If the index is at 5 percent at the end of seven years, and you have a three-point margin on your loan, your new rate would be 8 percent.

Let's compare the savings between a 5/25, a 7/23, and a 30-year fixed loan. Assume the loan amount is $100,000, and the interest rate is 7 percent (5/25), 7.5 percent (7/23), and 8 percent (30-year fixed). After five years, you would have paid $35,000 for the 5/25, $37,500 for the 7/23, and $40,000 for the 30-year fixed. If you move or refinance within five years and had a 5/25 mortgage, you would have saved yourself $5,000. Even if you stayed through the sixth year and the rate went up to 8 percent, you would still have saved $5,000 for the first five years.

Who Could Benefit from a 5/25 or 7/23?

First-time buyers who do not plan to stay in their homes for more than five or seven years would save thousands of dollars in interest by going with this type of loan, which has a lower initial rate than fixed-rate loans.

Ideally, you'll sell your home or refinance your mortgage either before or just after the rate adjusts upward. (The rate can also adjust downward, as those buyers who opted for an ARM in recent years have happily discovered.) But even if you stay in your home 10 years with a 7/23, the overall loan rate you pay may be far less than if you had chosen a fixed-rate loan. The rate on a two-step mortgage can be a full percentage point or more below the rate on a 30-year fixed.

Two-step mortgages have become extremely popular, as homeowners (particularly first-time buyers) have begun to realize they don't

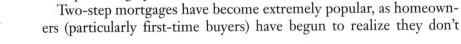

288

need the long-term steadiness of a fixed-rate mortgage because, unlike their parents, they most likely won't spend 30 years in the same home.

Balloon Mortgages

Before 30-year fixed-interest-rate mortgages were invented (we're talking about the pre-Depression era), everyone who bought a home and didn't pay cash had a balloon mortgage. Essentially, the buyer would borrow money at the exorbitant interest rate of about 3 or 4 percent for a short period of time, anywhere from one to five years. During the loan term, only the interest on the loan was paid, in monthly or semiannual installments or as one annual payment of interest. At the end of the loan term, the borrower owed the entire principal in full.

So if you had borrowed $10,000 at 4 percent interest for five years (remember, a brand-new car cost less than $2,000 in those days), you would have owed only $400 in interest per year, or $2,000 in interest over the life of the loan (the interest was paid separately). At the end of five years, you would still have owed the $10,000 in principal. It was simple and easy, and usually everyone paid off the balance. The concept of a balloon mortgage allowed you to buy a little bit of time to scrape together the cash to actually purchase the property.

As I explained earlier, balloon mortgages worked fine until the Great Depression, when folks lost all their savings and couldn't pay the interest on the money they borrowed, let alone meet the balloon payments. After World War II, the federal government began a program that offered returning veterans an opportunity to purchase a home and pay it off over 30 years. That was the beginning of the 30-year fixed mortgage. When the 30-year mortgage was successful and took off, the balloon mortgage became an infrequently used financial vehicle.

Who Could Benefit from a Balloon Mortgage?

With so many financing tools available today, only a few people choose to purchase a home with a balloon mortgage. Sometimes co-ops (remember, you don't buy a co-op, you buy shares in a corporation that owns the building and then lease your unit) may be purchased with a balloon mortgage, or other special financing tool, because the shares held are personal property (like a refrigerator, clothes, or a typewriter), not real property (like real estate).

In addition, the interest rate on a 5-year balloon (some banks offer a 10-year or 15-year balloon mortgage) might be less than some other financing options. A few buyers will choose it, especially if they know they might sell within that time period.

WHAT IS AN FHA LOAN? WHAT IS A VA LOAN?

An FHA loan is often called "the first-time buyer's mortgage." The reason is clear: FHA loans require a much smaller down payment than conventional loans. It's common to have an FHA loan with only 5 percent down (or less), whereas conventional lenders prefer to see a 20 percent cash down payment, which is often too steep for most first-time buyers. (Conventional lenders will allow you to purchase a home for less than 20 percent down, but you'll have to pay private mortgage insurance. You'll pay the FHA's version of mortgage insurance if you get an FHA loan with less than 20 percent down.)

Everyone Qualifies for FHA Loans

Some mortgage seekers wrongly assume that an FHA loan is a government-sponsored handout; that is, you have to be of a certain income level to qualify. That's not true. There are no income requirements for obtaining an FHA loan, and you don't have to be a first-time buyer.

Instead, the only restriction is the amount of money you can borrow. Here is a chart with the current loan limits, as we went to press. Be advised that these numbers change frequently. You can check out the latest loan limits by going online to the website of the Department of Housing and Urban Development (www.hud.gov) and clicking through to "Buying a Home."

2004 FHA Loan Limits

Size of Unit	Standard Limits	High-Cost Areas
Single family	$160,176	$290,319
Two family	205,032	371,621
Three family	247,824	449,181
Four family*	307,992	558,236

*Loans for properties that contain more than four units are considered to be investment properties. As an investor (even if you plan to live in one of the units), you'll pay a higher interest rate if you purchase, say, a six-unit building than if you purchase a four-unit building.

FHA Loan Limits

FHA loan limits are not fixed by metropolitan area. A metro area that covers several counties might encompass various FHA loan limits. Generally, expensive suburbs have higher loan amounts, while more rural areas (where prices are assumed to be lower) are allowed smaller loan amounts.

High-Cost Areas

Several years ago, Congress authorized HUD to increase the FHA loan limits for Alaska, Guam, and Hawaii to as much as 150 percent of the high-cost area limit. In 2004, legislation was introduced to include other high-cost areas, including Boston, New Jersey, New York, and Los Angeles, among others, since the median cost of homes there exceeds even the high-cost FHA loan limits.

web resources

To find out the specific FHA loan limits for your county, log on to this website: https://entp.hud.gov/idapp/html/hicostlook.cfm. This page of the HUD website appears to be updated annually, so you will always be able to find out what the FHA loan limit is for anywhere you want to live.

Best Feature of an FHA Loan

The most attractive feature of FHAs is that the borrower needs only as little as 2 percent of the loan amount as a down payment. If the property is a single-family house (which includes condos, co-ops, town homes, and multiunit buildings with four or fewer units), however, the loan comes with a steep mortgage insurance premium. Just because these government-backed loans are available to all homeowners doesn't mean an FHA loan is a freebie. *An FHA loan can be more expensive than a conventional loan.* FHA lenders require the same debt-to-income ratio as for a fixed-interest loan or an ARM. The big difference is the size of the down payment. If a house costs $100,000, an FHA loan would require the buyer to come up with perhaps just $2,000 in cash—far less than conventional lenders would require.

Who Could Benefit from an FHA Loan?

Cash-strapped first-time buyers are the logical beneficiaries. Another advantage is that FHA loans are assumable, which allows the next buyer to have lower costs in purchasing the property because he or she isn't taking out a new loan. When buyers assume an FHA loan, lenders are allowed by law to charge a few hundred dollars, plus regular loan origination points and fees, such as for a credit report.

FHA loans are also a good choice for people who have had credit problems or bankruptcies in their past. The government does not regard these past financial problems in the same light as a private lender would. As long as the loan-to-income ratios are met, and the borrower can pay the mortgage insurance premium (which can be steep), even former bankruptees can qualify. As one lender puts it, an FHA loan is a good way to begin to rebuild a credit history. The idea behind the FHA loan is to provide an outlet for people who do not have access to other financial outlets.

If you have severe negative information on your credit history, including a bankruptcy, court judgments, or charge-offs, and you have been slowly rebuilding your credit history, an FHA loan may be the only option available to you. Although some lenders will try to entice you with offers of getting a loan within one year of bankruptcy, what you won't be told is that the interest rate you'll pay is about the same as charging your house on a credit card! FHA loans can fill in the gaps until your credit is considered good enough for a conventional lender.

VA Loans

One of the many benefits that comes along with joining a branch of the armed forces is the helping hand Uncle Sam offers when it comes time to buy your house. The Department of Veterans Affairs in Washington, DC, guarantees loans for veterans, allowing them to purchase homes at favorable lending terms with no down payment.

The VA started the program at the end of World War II, and since the program began in 1945, more than 13 million veterans have obtained loans worth more than $360 billion. A spokesman for the

VA estimates that more than 4 million VA loans are currently out-standing. Although the program has changed some since its inception, VA loans generally restrict the amount of money the veteran is obliged to pay for his or her loan. However, the veteran is required to pay some closing costs, including a VA appraisal, a credit report, a survey title, recording fees, a 1 percent loan-origination fee, and a VA funding fee.

The VA funding fee is the expensive part. Except for a brief period during the 1960s, when it was used to distinguish cold war veterans from those who had put in wartime service, there used to be no funding fee for obtaining a VA loan. However, in 1981, a .5 percent funding fee was reinstated. (Disabled veterans who receive compensation were, and continue to be, exempt from the fee.) In 1984, the funding fee was increased to 1 percent; in 1990, it was raised to 1.25 percent. As of November 1, 2004, veterans taking out their first no-down-payment loan were required to pay a 2.15 percent funding fee to the Department of Veterans Affairs. Veterans taking out subsequent no-down-payment loans are required to pay a funding fee of 3.3 percent. If the veteran puts down 5 or 10 percent of the sales price, the funding fee is reduced.

(The VA says it charges a higher no-down-payment funding fee to discourage veterans from using the program. For my money, none of this makes much sense. The whole point of getting a zero-down-payment loan is because you don't have the cash for a down payment. Requiring a 2.15 percent or 3.3 percent funding fee is like asking someone to come up with that amount in cash. If you had the cash, you might as well go to a conventional lender or FHA and put 2 or 3 percent down on a house.)

Reserves and National Guard Veterans Pay Even More

If you're in the reserves or the National Guard, the cost of getting a VA loan is even more expensive.

If you fall into either of these categories, and want a no-down-payment loan, you'll pay a 2.4 percent funding fee for your first loan and 3.3 percent for subsequent loans. If you put down 5 to 10 percent, you'll pay a 1.75 percent funding fee for your first or subsequent VA loan, compared with the 1.5 percent that regular military personnel pay.

293

Bottom-Line VA Loan Benefits

For a long time, a VA loan was the only zero-down option available. Another plus of the program was that the VA worked closely with veterans who had trouble with their finances subsequent to getting a VA loan. In many cases, the VA took over these loans and homes, which is why the VA loan default rate was so high. But the loan was only available to qualified veterans of the armed services, which didn't help the rest of the home-buying population.

The recent introduction of super-low down payment loans and the new zero-down loans reduces the need for the VA loan, which has grown to be far more expensive than conventional financing. But there are other benefits: The loans are assumable (a buyer can take it over from the seller for very little money—an added incentive for the veteran-as-seller), and the VA has a policy of "forbearance," which means "worthy" veterans experiencing a temporary economic setback are somewhat protected against foreclosure. In rare instances, where a lender has decided to foreclose on such a "worthy" veteran, the VA has stepped in and paid off the lender, putting the loan in its portfolio. Today, you can choose from several VA loan programs, including fixed- and adjustable-rate mortgages. Lenders, buyers (the veteran), and sellers may openly negotiate who will pay the loan's discount points. In the past, the veteran was not allowed to pay any points to the lender.

Here are the various types of loan programs approved by the VA:

- **Traditional fixed-rate mortgage.** A standard fixed-rate loan. Each payment is fixed over the life of the loan and is made up of principal and interest.

- **Adjustable-rate mortgage.** A standard ARM. The interest rate adjusts at various points over the life of the loan.

- **Graduated-payment mortgage (GPM).** This loan requires borrowers to make smaller than normal payments for the first few years (typically five years). These payments gradually increase each year and then level off after the end of the "graduation period" to larger-than-normal payments for the remaining term of the loan.

- **Buydowns.** The builder of a new home, or the seller of an existing home, may "buy down" the veteran's mortgage payments by making a large lump sum payment up front at closing. The lump sum is used to pay off a percentage of the payment due each month for the first few years of the loan (typically one to three years).

- **Growing equity mortgage (GEM).** This little-used repayment plan provides for a gradual annual increase in the monthly payments with all of the increase applied to the principal balance. The annual increases in the monthly payment may be fixed (for example, 3 percent per year) or tied to an appropriate index. The increases to the monthly payment result in an early payoff of the loan (11 to 16 years for a typical 30-year mortgage). Most home buyers who can afford a GEM opt for a 15-year loan with the lower interest rate.

Who Might Benefit from a VA Loan?

They are expensive, but a VA loan might be just the ticket for veterans who are short on cash. VA loans are often sold on the secondary market, and so the upper loan limit usually matches the Fannie Mae and Freddie Mac upper loan limits ($330,700 in 2004). If you're a reservist with six years of duty behind you, you're now eligible for a VA loan. The catch is, you'll pay a funding fee that's three-quarters of a percent higher than your active-duty compatriots.

To apply for a VA loan, simply take your eligibility certificate to a lender. You're eligible for a VA loan if you served 90 days of wartime service in World War II, the Korean conflict, the Vietnam era, the Persian Gulf War, or the war in Iraq and were not dishonorably discharged. You are also eligible if you served between 6 and 24 months of continuous active duty from 1981 through today and were not dishonorably discharged. Check with your VA loan office for more details on eligibility.

WHAT IS AN INTEREST-ONLY LOAN?
SHOULD I GET ONE?

Everyone seems to be getting the same message from mortgage lenders these days: Pay less for your home loan.

It's a good message—if you know what you're currently paying and understand what you're being offered.

Most lenders want borrowers to refinance and believe they can lower the interest rate loan holders are paying. Perhaps that's true. If

you had bad credit and have spent years paying down a 10 percent loan, you might be able to refinance if you've improved your credit. Or if you financed your home and got an 8 percent rate on your loan, now you might be able to do better.

If your time frame has changed, you may be able to switch from a 30-year fixed-rate mortgage to a 5/1 adjustable-rate mortgage, which could substantially lower your interest rate.

In the past few years, however, a different kind of loan has once again been gaining mass appeal—the interest-only loan.

Roaring Twenties Redux

Interest-only loans were fairly commonplace during the Roaring Twenties. When the interest-only period expired, homeowners typically refinanced the loans to new interest-only loans. This worked out fabulously, unless the borrower's house lost value or he or she became unemployed and couldn't make the payments.

Such a scenario happened en masse when the stock market crashed in 1929 and the Great Depression began. At that time, American banks stopped making interest-only mortgages (and most mortgages in general). Mortgage companies and banks began making new interest-only loans at the start of the millennium, some 70 years later.

How They Work

Unlike conventional loans, where every payment consists of interest *and* principal, every monthly payment you make with an interest-only loan is 100 percent interest.

The biggest problem with an interest-only loan is that you never build up any equity in your home by paying down the principal. The only way to build up equity is if your home appreciates in value.

Interest-only proponents say that isn't an issue. Typically, the interest rate on an interest-only loan is below that of a 30-year fixed-rate mortgage. As I was updating this edition of the book, I was finding interest-only rates as low as 2.875 percent, compared with the 6.3 percent lenders were charting on a 30-year mortgage. That's a huge difference. If you compare the cost of those two mortgages side by side, it's easy to see why interest-only loans would be of interest to home buyers.

Most interest-only loans have interest-only periods for 5, 10, or 15 years out of a 30-year loan. At that point, the loan adjusts to whatever the current market interest rate is, and your payment skyrockets. Why? Because you have to start paying back the principal of the loan. Instead of having the principal payments spread out over 30 years, you have them spread out over 15 (with a 15-year interest-only period), 20 (with a 10-year interest-only period), or 25 years (with a 5-year interest-only period).

Interest-only loans typically carry a variable rate of interest, for at least part of the time. Some of these loans are tied to the London InterBank Offered Rate (known as LIBOR), which is the interest rate international banks charge each other. The LIBOR adjusts every six months. Other interest-only loans carry rates that adjust monthly. (Loans that adjust every month tend to offer the lowest rates because they are the riskiest kind of loan to get.)

On a conventional adjustable-rate mortgage, the interest rate cannot adjust upward more than one or two percentage points per year. These mortgages have a lifetime interest rate cap of 5 to 6 percent. But interest-only mortgages are a different breed. One interest-only mortgage starts at 3.75 percent and is capped at 12 percent. The rate adjusts monthly. That's a huge risk to take.

Why think about the future when the interest-only period will last 10 to 15 years? Clearly, the up-front cost savings are wooing customers nationwide.

"Interest-only mortgages are currently being presented to consumers as a way to buy more home for the money," explains Keith Gumbinger, HSH Associates spokesperson. "In reality, this is probably the most dangerous method of marketing these products, [because] you're encouraging people to stretch themselves to the limit."

And beyond. As Gumbinger notes, although it's true that borrowers can purchase homes they might otherwise not have qualified for, there is no free lunch. The costs of selling a home can exceed 7 percent, so you could end up owing money to your lender at the closing if the price of your home falls below the amount of your mortgage. When you're not adding to your equity each month, the odds of that are more likely.

Holden Lewis, a writer for Bankrate.com, has compared interest-only loans to leasing that BMW or Mercedes that you can't quite afford to buy. The only difference is you're not leasing your home. You're buying it and will benefit from any price appreciation.

How the Numbers Work

Instead of paying $1,000 per month on a $150,000 mortgage with a 7 percent, 30-year conventional loan, you'd pay just $695 per month during the interest-only period of a 30-year, interest-only loan. (Remember, the interest-only period on these loans is just 5, 10, or 15 years out of a 30-year loan.)

You could take your $305 per month savings and use that to prepay your home loan. Many savvy homeowners use that strategy when they choose a 5/1 ARM over a 30-year conventional mortgage—they save on the interest rate and use those savings to prepay the principal.

According to The Banker's Secret, a software program written by financial authors Marc Eisenson and Nancy Castleman, if you added $305 to each $695 payment, you'd shave 13 years off of your 30-year mortgage, paying the loan off in just 17 years. You'd save $47,357 in interest.

If people wanted to prepay the principal, however, they'd probably get 15-year fixed-rate loans, currently available at about a half point less than the conventional 30-year rate. The folks who instead are getting interest-only loans in droves are first-time buyers seeking to stretch their purchasing power as far as it will go.

According to lenders like Countrywide, Washington Mutual, and Wells Fargo, and secondary market leader Fannie Mae, which expects to purchase $2 billion worth of interest-only mortgages this year, it's the lower monthly cost of these mortgages (during the interest-only period) that is proving attractive to so many home buyers and homeowners.

After all, if you don't spend an extra $305 per month building up equity in your home, you'll have more money to pay down debt, or add to it.

Is an Interest-Only Loan Right for You?

If you know you're moving in a year or so, and you can get an exceptionally low rate on an interest-only loan, and you have something important to do with the extra cash, then perhaps this is a good loan to consider.

But many homeowners use their home equity as a kind of a piggy bank or a checkbook. They use it to provide a cushion against everything from college expenses to catastrophic illness coverage. If you don't start to build up equity when you first own your home, this nest egg might not be as large as it should be—or may not be there at all—when you really need it.

In other words, don't rob your financial future just so you can live in a bigger house today.

Another Reason to Use an Interest-Only Loan

If you're selling your first house and buying another and have to carry both mortgages for a short period of time, you may want to refinance your first mortgage into an interest-only loan, to lower the costs of carrying the property.

If you're a sophisticated investor, you might believe in leveraging your investments to the maximum. The thinking goes like this: Put as little down on your property and pay only the interest on the loan. Use the savings to prepay the mortgage or invest elsewhere.

These are two legitimate uses for an interest-only loan, but I like the security of knowing that every payment I make puts at least a few dollars toward the principal.

Shopping for an Interest-Only Loan

Although some lenders do offer interest-only loans, and Bankrate.com does feature them on its site, you may do better by working with a reputable mortgage broker who can tap into all of the interest-only loan programs for which you qualify.

SHOULD I AUTOMATICALLY GET A HOME EQUITY LOAN OR HOME EQUITY LINE OF CREDIT (HELOC) WHEN I CLOSE?

The last time Sam and I refinanced, we were offered a free home equity line of credit (HELOC) at a fantastic rate: one point below the prime rate. In other words, a HELOC is a variable-rate loan, but we don't pay anything unless we tap it.

More home buyers are getting a home equity loan or HELOC when they close on their mortgage. There are several reasons to do this:

299

1. You can avoid paying private mortgage insurance (PMI). As we discussed earlier, 80/10/10 loans, also known as "piggyback" mortgages, allow you to get an 80 percent first loan and a 10 percent or even 15 percent second loan. This second loan is actually a home equity loan. Doing this will allow you to avoid paying PMI.

2. You get a great deal. A free HELOC won't raise the rate you get on your primary home loan, so you should take it, even if you have no plans for the cash. You never know when a medical emergency, job loss, untimely death, or other tragedy will cause a cash crunch in your budget. This can be your rainy-day backup if you've already run through your emergency fund.

3. You want to make improvements to your property someday. This way, the cash will be ready when you need it.

Don't use this cash as a checkbook and blow it on something frivolous. But having a home equity loan or HELOC can give you options in various situations.

ARE THERE OTHER LOAN PROGRAMS I SHOULD KNOW ABOUT?

Although you won't see the following loan programs too frequently, from time to time they do appear in the guise of "special first-time buyer" loans. Negative equity mortgages and graduated-payment mortgages do have some limited value, but you'll be much better served going with other, more conventional, financing options.

Negative Amortization Mortgages and Graduated-Payment Mortgages

Demand for complicated, expensive mortgages like negative amortization and the graduated-payment mortgage has fallen as interest rates have declined. Some of the newly invented mortgages—like the two-step loans and ARMs—are easier to work with and require far less paperwork and attention.

Just in case these loans ever come back into fashion, here's the scoop: Negative amortization mortgages and graduated-payment mortgages are loan programs that allow you to pay less than you would normally owe if the loan was amortized conventionally.

For example, if your payment should be $1,000 per month, on a negative amortization mortgage, you might pay just $800 per month.

The extra $200 per month that you would have owed gets tacked onto the back of the loan. So if you borrow $150,000, at the end of the first month you'd owe $150,200. At some point in time, you'll either have to refinance the larger amount you now owe, or start paying much more than you would owe, say, $1,200 per month, to catch up.

A graduated-payment mortgage works almost the same way. It is a step-payment mortgage that starts out with a low interest rate that increases a certain number of percentage points each year until the loan levels out at a higher, fixed rate. If the going interest rate is 6 percent for a 30-year fixed-rate loan, you'll start out at an artificially low level—maybe 4 percent for the first couple of years—before bumping up to 5 percent, then 6 percent, and then perhaps leveling off at 7 percent for the remaining loan term.

The problem with GPMs is that they require a lot of individual calculations, and each loan must be structured to the specifics of each borrower. That's not cost-effective. Mountains of paperwork make these loans expensive to maintain and adjust. They have essentially been replaced by the 5/25, 7/23, and one-year ARMs, which are easier to use and more fair to home buyers.

Who Could Benefit from a Negative Amortization Mortgage or a GPM?

With affordability at fairly high levels (due to super-low interest rates), there is hardly any interest for these mortgages, a trend that real estate banking experts believe will continue. People used to want a GPM because it meant that they could qualify for the loan at the lower interest rate. The problems started when the loan would readjust upward. Essentially, borrowers were locking themselves into higher payments down the road. If their projected income didn't match the actual increase in interest payments, the borrowers had trouble.

The worst part about either of these loans is that the borrower ends up paying interest on interest in a potentially never-ending cycle. Unfortunately, predatory lenders have picked up on these two loans and have been reeling in victims who get locked into mortgage hell. (See Question 85 for more information on predatory lenders.)

A Buydown Mortgage

A buydown is a financing technique that lets someone other than the buyer pay cash up front to the lender so the first few years of the loan will be less costly. As buydowns have become more popular through the years, more lenders across the country have begun to offer their own tailor-made versions of this loan.

The principle is simple. Typically the seller (or the developer if you're buying new construction, or a relative) buys down the mortgage rate, allowing the buyer to qualify for a below-market mortgage. With a 3-2-1 buydown mortgage, the first year would be assessed at three percentage points below the note rate, although that rate is good only for the first year. The second year, the buyer pays interest at a mortgage rate two points below the note rate; in the third year, the mortgage rate is one point below the note rate. Thereafter, the mortgage interest rate is set at the original note rate.

The concept of buydowns is similar to both the ARM and the two-step mortgages, in that the interest rate starts lower and goes higher. Unlike those mortgages, the buydown is artificially deflated by the seller or another third-party source. The seller makes up the discount that is given to the buyer. This type of mortgage does offer another option. A first-time buyer can often combine the buydown with an option like the ARM for a super-cheap rate the first few years. If you get a buydown and combine it with a 5/25, it can put you significantly ahead of the market and increase affordability.

Here's how it works in terms of the interest owed (with no principal payment): If the buyer takes out a $100,000 loan at 8 percent interest, the annual interest payment would be $8,000, or $666.67 per month. But with a 3-2-1 mortgage, the buyer would pay only 5 percent interest the first year ($5,000 per year or $416.67 per month), 6 percent interest the second year ($6,000 or $500 per month), and 7 percent interest the third year ($7,000 or $583.33 per month). The total savings would be $6,000 for the buyer. The seller picks up that additional mortgage cost, which is generally paid in cash to the lender at closing. Then, every month for the first three years, the lender takes a portion of the money and adds it to the amount the buyer sends in.

The buydown is still primarily used by developers. In buyer's markets (more homes available than qualified buyers), however, sellers use this financing option to entice first-time buyers, who will likely earn more money down the road and will be able to afford larger mortgage payments.

You might also see buydown mortgages coming from your local housing authority or local nonprofit housing agency. Municipalities will often offer below-market interest rates on programs for first-time buyers. Either the reduced interest rate is good for the entire loan term, or for a set period of time, say the first two to five years. To find special first-time buyer programs, contact your city, county, or state housing agency. (See Appendix VI for resources.)

The Buydown's Effect on a $100,000 Loan

Year	Your Interest Rate	Your Payment	Regular Interest Rate	Regular Payment
1	5 percent	$416.67/month	8 percent	$666.67/month
2	6	500.00	8	666.67
3	7	583.33	8	666.67
4	8	666.67	8	666.67

Total interest savings for the buyer: $6,000 over the first three years of the loan.

20/20

hindsight

As I've traveled the country speaking to first-time buyers, I've noticed some are confused about whether they are better off paying the most interest they can (to increase their mortgage interest deduction) or the least amount possible. My feeling is that you should never do anything simply because you're going to get a bigger tax deduction. Instead, concentrate on the cash that goes out of your pocket every day.

Why? If you're in the 28 percent bracket, the net interest rate you pay may drop from 6 percent to 4 percent. But you're still paying 4 percent. If you put the cash into an investment earning 7 percent, after the taxes you pay on that earning, you're about even with the 4 percent you paid to borrow that cash. You'd have to earn about 10 percent on your money to pull significantly ahead. Depending on the stock market, that's tough to do, even for top money managers. Even worse, most Americans don't itemize on their federal income tax form. If you don't itemize, you can't take advantage of the mortgage interest deduction.

If you want to save yourself tens of thousands of dollars, or more, concentrate on paying off your mortgage early. Every dollar you prepay earns you your net rate of interest—guaranteed! If your loan carries an interest rate of 7 percent, then every dollar you prepay effectively earns 7 percent by decreasing your loan term (and saving you interest on the back end).

Eric's Story

When Eric, a certified public accountant, and his wife put up their home for sale, they offered to buy down the mortgage of whoever bought the property.

Steve, a first-time buyer, ended up making the winning bid on the property. Unfortunately, Steve didn't understand the concept of a buydown mortgage. At first, he refused Eric's offer for the buydown, but he later saw the benefit and accepted.

The buydown ended up saving Steve approximately $4,500 on his loan.

A Purchase Money Mortgage

A purchase money mortgage is a form of seller-provided financing. With a purchase money mortgage, the seller offers to give a first mortgage to you, the buyer. In taking over the role normally played by a bank or savings and loan, the seller would secure the loan with a down payment, and you would pay the seller monthly installments of principal and interest. Although you get title to the property, the seller has a lien on the property.

If you default on the mortgage, the seller can reclaim the property. A purchase money mortgage can work well for buyers because they don't pay any points or other costs to obtain the loan. The seller enjoys an excellent return on his or her funds.

See Question 83 for more information on seller financing.

Articles of Agreement

With the articles of agreement, you enter into an installment agreement to buy the home over a specified period of time. The seller keeps legal title, and you receive equitable title, which means you receive an interest in the property but do not own it. The benefit to you, the first-time buyer, is that the seller will usually accept a much smaller down payment (perhaps 5 percent of the sales price of the home) and yet will still feel comfortable with the arrangement.

Remember: With articles of agreement, the seller retains title to the property until you've paid off the loan. If you default on the property, the seller may need only evict you to reclaim possession of the home, and you could lose all of the equity you've built up until then.

Howard and Emily's Story

Howard and Emily had owned a condo for years, but when they wanted to sell, they couldn't get anyone interested in their neighborhood, which had fallen on hard times. So they put an ad in the newspaper, offering to sell their property for $3,000 down.

Sally saw the ad, checked her bankbook, and realized she had enough cash to buy the apartment. She moved in and paid Howard and Emily as if they were the bank. Over time, she was able to afford a regular loan and paid off the loan held by Howard and Emily. Until then, Sally got a tax deduction, which helped her save more money.

Although the articles-of-agreement purchase seems similar to a lease with an option to buy, the two methods of buying a home are completely different. With the articles of agreement, Sally does not own the home but since she is paying the real estate taxes and making payments to the seller with interest, she gains the tax benefits. (Real estate taxes and interest are tax-deductible.) If Sally leased the home with an option to buy, Howard and Emily would also have retained ownership of the home until Sally had exercised her option. But because they would have paid the taxes, they would have had the tax benefits, not Sally.

Purchasing a home through articles of agreement can work very well for some home buyers. But it is extremely important that the buyer consult with an attorney who will look after his or her interests. Documents will need to be recorded to protect the buyer's *ownership interest* in the property that he or she is building up through regular principal and interest payments.

WHAT IS SELLER FINANCING? WHAT IS A LEASE WITH AN OPTION TO BUY?

QUESTION 83

One of the most flexible sources of real estate financing can be the seller of the property you want to buy. Why are sellers interested in providing financing? For many sellers, the return on their investment (in your mortgage) will be far greater than the amount they can get in the open marketplace. In addition, sellers who provide financing sometimes sell their property more quickly.

As a home buyer, you should be interested in seller financing because (1) by eliminating any potential red tape that could slow down or mar the closing, you can close more quickly, and (2) you might get financing at a below-market interest rate. Not every seller will help you purchase his or her home. Look for a seller who is ready to trade down to a smaller property or, perhaps, retire to a rental community. Otherwise, it's likely the seller will need your cash to purchase his or her other home.

Judith and Scott's Story

First-time buyers Judith and Scott fell in love with a house. Unfortunately, with their combined salaries (at the time, she sold advertising for a magazine and he was a second-year medical resident), they couldn't qualify for a large enough mortgage to quite make ends meet.

Although Judith and Scott knew it meant scrimping and saving, they were sure they could afford the payments. So they went to their seller and asked her to take back a second mortgage. She agreed and offered them a rate that was a half point cheaper than the rate they got for their first mortgage. They closed on the house. A year and a half later, when interest rates dropped, Judith and Scott refinanced and paid off the seller.

When it works, seller financing works beautifully. But consider the experience of Karen, a regular reader of my column, "Real Estate Matters."

Karen's Story

Karen was eager to sell her California bungalow. She took the advice of her real estate agent and took back the mortgage for the buyers.

That was the beginning of four years of problems with the buyers. They missed several loan payments (and finally stopped paying them altogether). They twice failed to pay their property taxes. They went through bankruptcy to avoid foreclosure. They refused to pay the cost of Karen's bankruptcy attorney plus courts costs. And finally, they committed homeowner's insurance fraud—twice!

They finally left, and Karen reclaimed possession of the house. It was a disaster inside. She spent thousands of dollars fixing up the place.

In the course of the last four years, the housing market in her neighborhood skyrocketed. Karen was able to resell the house at a tidy profit. But even that money, she says, wasn't worth the agony of dealing with a pair of irresponsible buyers.

Seller financing isn't for everyone. And, even though it's touted as being a win-win situation for everyone (buyer, seller, agent), it doesn't always work out that way. Home buyers should recognize that sellers have to protect themselves. If you're seeking seller financing, be ready to allow the seller access to your credit history via a credit report. A savvy seller will also request financial references, such as the name of your superior at work, and perhaps will do a background check.

Here's a letter from another reader of my "Real Estate Matters" column. For her, seller financing didn't work out exactly as she expected.

Nancy's Story

"Twenty-two months ago we purchased a home with owner financing. I paid my mortgage on time each month and also put $15,000 down on the house.

"Two weeks ago I found out that the home was going into foreclosure and that the owner had not made any mortgage payments in 12 months on the property. There is a lien on the property for the 2001 property taxes of $1,960, and a lien on the house for $2,100 for nonpayment of federal income taxes from the owner. Property taxes for 2002 are also due ($1,600).

"The home appraised for $182,500 and the principal balance was $156,199. I was able to get preapproved for $164,000, so I had no problem buying the house. But this is where everything goes downhill.

"The mortgage company was not willing to work with me. They wanted $24,952 in late payments and interest, for a grand total of $181,151 or $5,000 now and $3,000 a month for 12 months, or I was told to buy the house on the courthouse steps.

"With the $6,000 in liens on the property, the cost of the home is near $190,000—way above its appraised value. The existing mortgage company refused our lender's offer for a short sale of $157,000.

"I have since moved out of the house, and it sold for back taxes on September 3. I had invested about $10,000 in remodeling in the home as well, so I lost a total of about $44,000.

"Can I apply a lien on the property for this huge amount I am out of pocket?"

My answer to Nancy: I believe you're completely out of luck when it comes to recovering your money, but let me go through what I believe happened here and how it could have been prevented.

First, you didn't purchase this property outright. You bought it on a land contract, also known as the installment plan.

For buyers, there is no benefit in purchasing property this way. All you're doing is putting yourself at great risk. The only benefit to a seller is that he or she controls the property in case the buyer fails to make the payments. The seller is still the owner and can kick out the buyer much as he or she would kick out a renter. It doesn't require foreclosing on a loan gone bad.

Your first mistake was not having a real estate attorney assist you with the purchase of this home, even though you live in a state where attorneys are not normally used to close residential transactions. When you purchase by installment contract or do owner financing, you must have someone who represents your interests.

Your second mistake was not learning what liens were filed against the title to the property. Title insurance would not necessarily have protected you in this situation, but would have told you that your seller had a mortgage and may have revealed other liens.

Your third mistake was that you didn't record your installment contract with the recorder of deeds. That would have put the world on notice that someone else had an interest in the property.

Your fourth mistake was paying good money after bad. Buying on a land contract is similar to being a renter. As a renter, you would never have put $10,000 in improvements into that property.

Clearly, your seller defrauded you. He basically said, "I'll sell to you and you pay me and I'll pay my lender." But he didn't hold up his end of the deal.

What could you have done to prevent this situation?

You should have bought this home outright with a mortgage from the seller. This would have required the seller to pay off his loan, and any other liens, and put the title in your name.

Barring that, you should have paid the seller's lender directly, with any extra being paid to the seller. That way, at least you would have known that the mortgage was being paid and that the lender had enough cash to pay the real estate taxes.

Clearly, you could have afforded conventional financing. I'm unclear why you didn't get it. You put your trust in the wrong guy.

You can try and sue the seller, but more likely than not, you're out $44,000 in cash. If the seller authorized you to complete the improvements, you may be able to file a mechanic's lien against the property. But more likely than not, it will get wiped out when the lender sells the property.

Consult with an attorney regarding any legal options that may be available to you.

Seller Financing Options

Seller financing comes in many forms. The seller can:

- **Provide all the financing and take a straight first mortgage** (eliminating the need for a commercial lender). This is called a *purchase money mortgage.*
- **Take back a second mortgage, to help you scrape together the down payment.**
- **Buy down your mortgage, to enable you to qualify for more house.**
- **Arrange a purchase by articles of agreement.** Also known as an installment purchase, you'll receive an interest in the home, which becomes yours after you pay off the seller in full.

Whatever form the seller financing takes, it's in your best interest to explore this possibility. However, beware the difficult seller who will constantly call you for his or her money. That kind of overbearing behavior is difficult to stomach. If you do opt for seller financing, keep the transaction at arm's-length.

Lease with an Option to Buy

A lease with an option to buy, also known as a lease/option or rent-to-own, allows home buyers to build up a down payment while they're living in the house they think they want to own. Why would you lease an option instead of buying it outright?

- You're short on cash for the down payment and closing costs.
- Your credit history and credit score aren't good enough for you to qualify for zero-down payment options.

- You don't have at least one year of work history or at least two years if you're self-employed.

- You're not sure if you like the area and want to "test" it out.

- Your company may transfer you within two years and you're not sure the property will appreciate enough in value to cover future closing costs. If you wind up staying, you can buy the house at a later date.

Lease options can help out if you just need a little extra time to get your financial history in order.

Jennifer and David's Story

When Jennifer and David were 23, they started to prepare for buying their first home. Jennifer wrote to me for advice.

"In a year, we'll have enough for about a 5 percent down payment, and enough income to support a loan of about $170,000," she wrote. "The problem is that I've heard that two or even three years of tax returns are required by lenders to get approved for a loan. I'm only 10 months into my first real job, and my boyfriend starts his first job this month. We have not filed our taxes in the last two years. As student dependents of our parents with very little income to speak of until recently, we never filed, which now seems like a mistake."

In her e-mail, Jennifer acknowledged she sounded immature and financially naïve, but said she and her boyfriend were responsible citizens, if a bit misguided.

"We both have good credit and are now turning our attention to establishing some investment potential. Do we need to worry about our lack of tax returns getting in the way of a successful loan application?" she asked.

My answer to Jennifer was simple: (1) get caught up on your last two years of tax returns, (2) start talking to lenders about what kind of loan you would qualify for and how long you'd have to wait to get it, and (3) consider leasing a condominium that you like with an option to purchase it in another year.

That way, Jennifer and David would be able to more quickly "accumulate" their down payment but would know what to do to get their financing in place.

How Lease/Options Work

The buyer purchases a one-year (or multiyear) option on a home by giving the seller a nonrefundable option fee, which is usually a small percentage of the house price. Then, the buyer moves into the home and pays rent each month, a portion of which the seller credits back to the buyer as a future down payment for the home.

For example, if you were to pay $1,000 per month in rent, with 33 percent of the rent credited toward the down payment, you'd accumulate $333 each month, or nearly $4,000 per year, toward the down payment for the home. In addition, your nonrefundable option fee may be credited toward the down payment.

There are no hard and fast rules about how much of the rent can be credited toward the down payment. It's up to you to negotiate. Some sellers will give you credit for 100 percent of your rent payment. Others won't give you anything. Typically, the seller will give you somewhere between 25 and 40 percent.

It isn't just the rent credit that needs to be negotiated in a lease with an option to buy situation. You've also got to negotiate the price and terms of the sale of the house, just as if you were buying it outright. Once you and the seller have reached an agreement, the price of the home can never vary, even if it appreciates in value.

Buyers should remember that even though they have an option to purchase the home at a later date, the seller remains the sole owner of the property until the buyer exercises his or her option. This is different from other forms of seller financing, such as a purchase mortgage or articles of agreement, where the buyer has some claim to the property. Since the seller owns the home, the seller retains the tax benefits of homeownership and can deduct mortgage interest and property taxes from the federal income tax form.

One of the nice things about doing a lease/option is that the option is typically renewable—although you may be asked to pay another nonrefundable fee, which you can negotiate to be applied toward your down payment. A home investor at a California home buyers' fair once told me she had been renewing her option on a particular home for 23 years. During that time, the house tripled in value. Now, she knows what she is buying, and she has nearly paid off the house in rent credits.

Here's the best part about a lease/option: If you decide, at the end of the year, that you don't like the home or the neighborhood, or if you

discover the home has a hidden material defect (like a cracked foundation) that will cost thousands of dollars to repair that you don't have,
you can pay your last month's rent and walk away.

Finding a Lease/Option

Some sellers advertise their homes as lease/option in the classified section of the local newspaper, under "houses for rent." The rest of the
time, it's up to you to ask. You're looking for a seller who doesn't need
the cash from the sale to purchase something else. Try sellers who
have had their home on the market for a long time, or who have already purchased another home and are paying two mortgages. (Your
rent could cover the costs of their former home.)

WHAT LOANS EXIST FOR BUYERS WITH MEDIOCRE OR POOR CREDIT? WHERE DO I GET ONE?

Almost all home buyers who apply for a loan will be graded A or A−.
Grade A borrowers are those who have perfect or very good credit
reports, who have been in their jobs for at least two years, and who always pay their bills on time. Lenders estimate as many as 90 to 95 percent of all borrowers will fall into the Grade A or A− category.

So who is a B or a C borrower?

"It could be anyone walking down the street," says Joe, president of
a B-C lending company. He likes to share the story of Ed and Vivian as
an example of how anyone, including you, your parents, or your next-
door neighbor, could fall on hard times quite unexpectedly.

Ed and Vivian's Story

Ed and Vivian were just three years away from paying off the mortgage
on their home when the Northridge, California, earthquake hit in 1994.
Although their home was not badly damaged, Ed's printing business almost collapsed.

Due to severe damage sustained in the earthquake, three of his
largest clients closed up shop, virtually overnight, and moved out of
state. Without the income from these three clients, Ed's once-profitable
business started running in the red. With the business unable to sustain
itself, the couple eventually filed for bankruptcy.

> But this story has a relatively happy ending. Ed and Vivian went to see a sub-par lender, also known as a B-C lender. This lender helped them refinance their home and use the equity to pay off their debts and get their business going again. Within two years, Ed and Vivian were back on their feet. Their business was once again thriving, and they were able to refinance their higher-interest rate loan for a conventional mortgage.

Ed and Vivian are the typical B-C loan customer, says Harvey, a sub-par lender. "It's someone who, through no fault of their own, got downsized and lost their job. It's someone who went from a decent income to unemployment and couldn't make their credit card payments. Or they've been 30 days late, twice in the past year."

Good people who have a bad credit problem is how Rick, another mortgage banker, describes B-C applicants. "If you've had a bankruptcy any time within the past 7 to 10 years, or if you've had medical bill problems, or other situations where your credit score is so low you can't get a mortgage through the regular channel," then you may be right for a B-C loan.

You may also be a B-C borrower if you own too many pieces of investment property, need a "no-document" loan because you don't wish to disclose all of your income, you've been self-employed for too short a period of time, or you're purchasing a unique piece of property that doesn't fit into the secondary lending market's A-borrower mold.

There have always been small mom-and-pop lending shops that catered to folks who had major problems with their credit, but the B-C industry has only really come into its own in the past three years, as credit scoring has evolved into a fine art, Rick says.

Credit scoring drives the entire sub-par market. Rick adds that the credit scoring model has improved to the point where a lender can pull up a credit report and guess with at least an 85 percent accuracy rate whether the borrower should get the loan.

B-C lending depends on different criteria than if a buyer has good or only slightly tarnished credit.

If you have cash, but lousy credit, a B-C lender might be able to help you because the most important component of a B-C loan is the loan-to-value ratio. If you're hardly putting down anything, it will be difficult to find a legitimate B-C lender who can help you.

The types of late payments you've made are important, too. You get a much heavier ding for a late payment on a mortgage than if you've been late on your student loan or on a local department store charge card. (The order of importance for late pays is mortgage, car loans, credit cards, student loans, and charge cards.) Other important components are your credit score, any collection accounts you have, and whether you've gone bankrupt.

Surprisingly, neither your income (other than making sure you can afford the monthly payments) nor your job history counts for much.

Mortgage experts say that the B-C lending business is all about risk-based pricing. The bigger risk the bank takes, the more you pay.

For example, while an A borrower might get a $240,000 loan for zero points at 7.5 percent from a conventional lender, a B borrower would pay zero points and 10.5 percent for the same loan. A C borrower would pay zero points and 12.5 percent.

Almost every B-C loan is tailor-made. For example, on these loans, you can pay additional points and lower your rate. Five points (a point is 1 percent of the loan amount and fully deductible in the year you purchase your house) could lower your interest rate from 10.5 percent to 8.5 percent.

Your loan-to-value ratio also has an impact on the interest rate your loan carries and the points and fees you'll pay. If you get a loan that has an 80 percent loan-to-value ratio, meaning you only have 20 percent equity, you'll pay more than if you get a 60 percent loan-to-value ratio loan and have 40 percent equity.

Bad Apple Lending

Because B-C lending has been a small-time business up to this time, unacceptable practices have become commonplace. In a typical setup, a home buyer with fairly good credit who doesn't understand the process, doesn't speak the language, or hasn't been through a mortgage process before will sit down with a lender. The buyer's credit report will get pulled up and the lender will see two or three late payments over the course of the past few years.

The lender will make a big deal about these late payments and tell the borrower he or she no longer qualifies as an A borrower. But wait—the lender does have a loan for which he or she can qualify.

The only catch? The loan carries a much higher interest rate. But if the borrower makes good and keeps the loan for six months, the broker will be able to refinance it into a lower-rate loan.

According to lenders, what's happening is that an A or even an A– borrower is getting shoved into a B loan, which is hugely profitable to the broker. Then, in six months, the broker refinances the loan into another loan slightly above market rate, which is so much lower than the first rate that the customer feels like he or she is getting a great deal with good service. The bad apple lender could pocket $10,000 or more on such a transaction.

Legitimate mortgage bankers and sub-par lenders can't pull that scam because their companies require them to try and *raise* the borrower's grade. "If they're an A, they go to the regular side of the table. If they're a B, or any of the fine gradations of B or C, they get moved over to the B-C side of the table," Rick says.

"We view our loans as credit repair loans because we tell the customer, 'You've had challenges in the past, so we'll take your debts, consolidate them for you, reduce your monthly payments, give you a fixed rate for 24 to 36 months, and the opportunity to get back on your feet.' In 12 to 36 months, their credit is repaired by their hard work and they can go elsewhere," Harvey explains.

Many lenders believe that soon all loans, no matter whether the borrower is classified A, A–, B, C, or D, will move to risk-based pricing. This means that borrowers who have the best credit scores will get the best deals on loans. Right now, if you have had, say, two late payments, you'll still get the same mortgage deal as someone who has never been late with a payment. Because credit score modeling continues to be refined and the technology continues to improve, soon every borrower will pay exactly what he or she should, depending on an individual credit report. If nothing else, it's an added incentive to keep your credit as clean as possible.

WHAT IS A PREDATORY LENDER? HOW DO I SPOT ONE?

A lender who charges excessive fees; a lender who tells you your loan application won't be approved if you don't buy high-priced credit insurance; a lender who tells you your credit isn't good, when it is— these are some of the characteristics of predatory lenders.

They are the bad apple lenders who prey on unsuspecting or unsophisticated borrowers. And plenty of borrowers are turning into victims. One report estimates that homeowners lose more than $9 billion dollars to predatory lenders each year.

As Biata found out, the dangers include not just losing all the equity you've built up in your home, but losing the house itself and destroying your credit score in the process.

Biata's Story

A polish immigrant, Biata came to the United States more than 15 years ago. She married, got a job, had a daughter, and bought a three-flat in Chicago. One day, her husband simply walked out. Biata found she couldn't quite make the mortgage payments on her single salary. So she went to the lender, a reputable bank.

The loan agent said, "We can't help you, but I know someone who can," and steered her toward a predatory lender.

Biata refinanced her home loan with the predatory lender. The loan was supposed to be for $200,000. Within four years, she owed—according to the lender—more than $500,000 in interest and principal, even though she had paid the lender more than $300,000 in those four years (and had the receipts from Western Union to back up her claim).

The last time I spoke with Biata, she was on the verge of losing her home. Her credit history had been tarnished; her credit score was sunk. She was sick with worry over her situation and couldn't figure out a way to get out.

What was even worse about Biata's situation is that she did everything right. By going to her original, legitimate lender to refinance, she should have been given a good deal. Instead, she was falsely told the bank couldn't help her and was served up as a victim to a particularly awful predatory lender.

Warning Signs

It's difficult to even define what a predatory lender is. In some states, a lender is considered "predatory" by the interest rate charged or by the points and fees tacked onto the loan. In other states, a lender is defined as predatory if it continues to remortgage the same house over and over again with no benefit to the homeowner.

Several branches of the federal government, including the Department of Housing and Urban Development and the Federal Trade Commission have been working in tandem with the Mortgage Bankers Association of America, national and local mortgage and real estate companies, and trade organizations to highlight the financial dangers associated with getting a loan from a predatory lender. The Mortgage Bankers Association has published a website (StopMortgageFraud.com) which highlights the following as some important warning signs of predatory lending:

1. False information. Predatory lenders will often encourage you to include false or misleading information on your mortgage application, in direct violation of federal law.

2. Blank spaces on your application. Were you asked to leave spaces or signature lines blank on your application? Take a look at your "final" application. Was information changed?

3. Missing information. Did the lender give you a good faith estimate, a truth-in-lending disclosure, a HUD-1 settlement statement (at closing), or a special information booklet on lending about borrower's rights?

4. Payments going up. Has your lender suggested refinancing your home loan several times, ostensibly to take advantage of lower rates, but you find each time you "refinance" your payment and interest rate rise? Has the total amount you owe on the home risen as well? This is called "serial refinancing."

5. Daily interest rate penalty. Do your loan documents reveal that your interest rate calculation will change to require you to pay "daily interest" in instances when your payments are late?

6. Loan amount is too high. Is the loan amount higher than the sales price of the home? Is it more than you asked for? Did you do a "cash out refinance" but never got the cash?

7. Unexpected costs. Were you charged additional costs and fees at your closing that were not disclosed previously on your good faith estimate or your HUD-1?

8. Credit insurance tacked onto the loan. Were you required to buy credit insurance as a condition for getting your loan approved? It is illegal to tell a borrower that purchasing credit insurance is a condition for approval. Credit insurance itself is not illegal, but it is generally a waste of money and can significantly raise the cost of your loan.

9. Hefty prepayment penalties that lock you in for years. Predatory lenders love prepayment penalties, because they lock in a borrower to a super-high interest rate for a long, long time.

317

Although knowing the warning signs of predatory lending can help, each borrower (including you) must be vigilant to make sure he or she is not caught in a predatory lender's web. A spokesperson from the MBA explained, "It's up to each borrower to stand on the front lines and fight predatory lending with knowledge."

In other words, know your stuff, and you won't get duped.

The Borrower's Bill of Rights

Many borrowers are confused about what information they're entitled to ask for, and what information the lender is required to deliver.

According to the Stop Mortgage Fraud website, the borrower has the right to a "clear and forthright explanation of the terms and conditions of the loan" and has the right to "truthful disclosures regarding the rates and costs of the loan."

The lender should disclose to you the final annual percentage rate (APR) and the amount of the regular payments in the good faith estimate within three business days of applying for your loan. A borrower has the right to not be subject to deceptive marketing tactics (like "bait and switch" loans, where you think you're getting one thing, but end up with quite another), and to obtain credit counseling prior to closing on the loan.

Borrowers cannot be forced to finance any portion of fees or points, and they cannot be forced to buy credit insurance as a condition of getting their loan approved. Finally, borrowers have the right to have a mortgage lender report favorable (as well as unfavorable) information to the three major credit reporting bureaus on a timely basis.

Predatory lenders frequently force borrowers to finance hefty fees and points in conjunction with making a loan, padding the lender's pocket with thousands of dollars in extra profit. On top of that, predatory lenders will collect a hefty commission for selling a credit insurance policy, which pays off your mortgage in case of death. But credit insurance offers an increasingly limited benefit (your mortgage amount declines with every monthly payment) for an extremely high premium.

(You're much better off buying term life insurance, which will do exactly the same thing but gives you added flexibility for much less money.)

One of the big problems with predatory lenders is that borrowers who truly have poor credit find they can't get out of that hole because a bad lender will not report their history of on-time payments. Instead, they'll only report payments missed (if they report the loan at all). When you apply for a loan, you should directly ask the lender if your on-time payments will be reported to a credit reporting bureau. If they won't, immediately withdraw your application from this lender.

> For more information on predatory lending, check out the StopMortgageFraud.com website. Your state attorney general's offices, and your state department of consumer affairs may also have websites that contain useful information about predatory lenders. If you are unsure if your lender is legitimate, call the state attorney general's office and ask whether any complaints have been filed against the company.

WHY ARE SOME LENDERS WILLING TO GIVE ME A MORTGAGE FOR 125 PERCENT OR 130 PERCENT OF THE HOME'S SALES PRICE?

As competition continues to shake out the mortgage industry (and bring down costs for consumers), lenders are under pressure to develop new loans and new products that will satisfy consumers' demands.

Two relatively new entries to the product mix are 125 percent and 130 percent home loans.

How can you borrow more than a home is worth? Good question. There is one legitimate way to do this, and several other ways you should avoid.

The Good 125 Percent Loan

If you are purchasing and renovating a house, you may borrow up to 125 percent of the value of the house, as long as the home will appreciate in value to at least the cost of the complete renovation.

You'll need to jump through several additional hoops to get this loan, which is offered by FHA. You'll have to submit your plans, plus a contractor's estimate, for review and approval by the lender before your loan can be funded. But it's a nice way to finance your home improvement costs at your regular mortgage rate.

New Construction

What if you already own a piece of land and want to finance the construction of your home? You'll have a couple of options here. You can do a construction-to-own loan, in which the lender will give you a loan based on appraisals of how much the house will be worth once it is complete. If you paid cash for the land, or inherited the property, you may be able to take out a loan against the vacant lot and use that to build your home. Consult with your local lender for details.

But Stay Away from These Loans

The much more common 125 and 130 percent loans are those created to entice those consumers with severe cash and credit problems who want to purchase or refinance their home.

Here, the lender will give you a loan that's in several stages. You'll pay the going mortgage rate for the first part of the loan, which will be the standard 80 percent loan-to-value ratio (as if you had 20 percent to put down in cash). The next 20 percent will be financed at a slightly higher rate, perhaps with more points and fees, and private mortgage insurance. The next 25 or 30 percent will be like charging the money on your credit card. You can expect to pay anywhere from 12 to 18 percent interest (or more) for this part of the loan.

Essentially, you're getting three loans, and when you average the loan together, you'll see you're paying through the nose for the privilege.

Who should get these loans? No one. They're inherently risky, particularly for someone who's in a precarious financial position. More often than not, it isn't the quality lenders who are offering them; the shady, bad apple lenders offer these loans as a supposed panacea for whatever credit problems are affecting your credit report.

WHAT IF I'M REJECTED FOR MY LOAN?

QUESTION 87

After all the hours spent searching for the perfect home, negotiating the purchase price, working with your attorney to perfect the contract, and applying for a mortgage, it's extremely disappointing and frustrating to be rejected for a loan. But before you give up and decide you'll never be able to afford a home, you should know that hundreds of people get rejected for loans every day. Sometimes it's their fault, and sometimes lenders reject them for reasons that seem to defy logic or comprehension.

Sam once had a client who was rejected for a loan by several lenders. Her ex-husband had declared bankruptcy, but because her name was on some of the credit card accounts, her credit was tarnished along with his. Another first-time buyer was rejected because she had just bought a new car, and the lender decided her debt-to-income ratios were out of whack. A third first-time buyer couple was rejected by a handful of lenders because the husband truthfully stated that his business was being sued for $100,000. Because the lawsuit was ongoing, the lenders decided it was too big a risk.

Let's look at the reasons why you might be rejected for a loan.

1. Credit Report Problems

When you apply for a mortgage, or any other type of loan, the bank or mortgage broker will pull up your credit report. This report includes all of your financial information, including every credit card account you have, the balances due, and your payment record; current and past addresses; any bankruptcies or other credit problems; bank and money market accounts; any outstanding loans; and a host of other credit information. The credit report is used to determine whether you're a good credit risk.

A recent study showed that as many as 79 percent of all credit histories contain at least one factual error, and 25 percent contain errors bad enough to influence your credit score. Fixing credit report errors can raise your score.

Numerous types of credit report problems (which may or may not be your fault) would cause a lender to reject your application for a loan. First, if you've ever missed a credit card payment, or been late with a credit card payment, or defaulted on a prior mortgage or school or car loan, it will probably show up on your credit report. If you've filed for bankruptcy within the past seven years, that will show up on your credit report. If you haven't paid your taxes, or a judgment has been filed against you (perhaps for nonpayment of spousal or child support), it will also show up. Failure to pay your landlord, doctor, or hospital may turn into a black spot on your credit report.

Credit report companies get their information about you from companies that extend credit, like department stores, lenders, banks, and credit card companies. The information is updated on a periodic basis—sometimes daily, sometimes annually. Since people actually enter in the information into the company computer, there is a good chance that a mistake has been made somewhere along the line.

If you feel that your credit report is wrong, experts say it's best to take it up with the organization or company that is claiming you owe them money. Try to find documentation that proves the mistake and have it corrected as quickly as possible. If there is a more serious problem, such as a bankruptcy filing or a judgment against you, or if you've not filed your income taxes or have "forgotten" to pay back a school loan, you may have a more difficult time getting the lender to approve your loan application. If you've been late paying your bills, regroup by paying in full and on time for six months to a year to prove to the lender that the late payments were an aberration. Be sure all your taxes are paid in full and on time.

If the credit report contains errors, you should contact the credit bureau immediately. A recent law requires the credit bureau to deal with your written request to correct errors within 30 days.

2. Inconsistencies in Information

Sometimes lenders will find inconsistencies between what you've told them on the application and information the loan officer discovers. If you say your income is $45,000 annually and the lender calls your employer for verification and finds out that it's only $30,000, that's probably grounds for rejection. The lender figures if you've lied about something as basic and easily checkable as your income, you may have lied about something more important.

Most lenders, upon discovering minor inconsistencies (if you say your income is $45,000 and it's really $44,500), will ask you about them and give you a chance to explain. Others won't. The bottom line is: Be straight with the lender. Answer his or her questions honestly and if you don't know the answer to a question, say so. Don't make anything up. If you get rejected for providing false or misleading information, consider the lost application fee a cheap lesson. Honesty is always the best policy.

3. Employed Less Than Two Years

Lenders like to see that you're earning a stable income. They like consistency. They like knowing that someone has been employing you and will continue to employ you. That's why most lenders will generally reject you for a loan if you've been employed less than two years.

As with most rules, however, there are exceptions. If you're a secretary making $25,000 and the company across the hall offers you a job as an executive secretary for $35,000, most lenders will be delighted to see you take the job and earn the extra income, even if it's a couple of weeks before closing. Why? Because lenders like lateral moves (that is, the same job for better pay at a competing company) or a step up the corporate ladder (from vice president to president). Although you're changing jobs, you're changing for the better, and the lender should be understanding.

If, however, you spend a year as a mechanic, then become a short-order chef for six months, then move into used-car sales, the lender may reject your application, even if you've moved up in income—too much movement, not enough consistency.

4. Being Self-Employed

What if you're self-employed? Being self-employed adds an extra twist to the process of getting a mortgage because lenders don't view self-employed workers as being as stable as those who are employed by others. (Although the good news is, you can't be fired!)

Lenders will rarely approve a mortgage unless you have been self-employed for at least two years. When you apply for the mortgage, you'll have to bring profit-and-loss statements, as well as your last two tax returns. The lender won't look at your gross income. Net income (that is, gross income minus expenses) is what's important. Remember this when looking for a home, because you may be over-estimating the amount of money you'll be able to borrow. For example, if you have gross earnings of $75,000 and expenses of $50,000, a lender will consider your income to be $25,000, even though you may feel you can spend more. Some mortgage brokers specialize in getting loans for self-employed people. They work with lenders who keep these loans in their portfolio and therefore have more relaxed lending policies.

If you're self-employed for less than two years, back away from the application and wait until you have been running your own business for at least two years. Or find a lender who specializes in placing loans of this type. If you're employed but all or most of your salary is from commission, you may also be a good candidate for rejection, especially if you've been at it less than two years. Try to speak to your mortgage lender before you apply. Also, avoid paying any fees up front, so that if you aren't approved, you won't lose any money.

Sam once represented a man who had taken a new commission-only sales job about six months before making an offer on a home. Although the man was pulling in an excellent salary, he couldn't find a lender who would approve a mortgage. After several weeks of making the rounds to no avail, the man was offered a better job for even more money, in Boston. Thanks to his mortgage contingency, he backed out of the purchase (without penalty) and decided to move his family to Boston.

5. Losing Your Job

If you lose your job before the closing, it can mean an instant rejection of your loan application. If you're married, and your spouse earns enough money to support the mortgage payments, then the lender may approve the loan anyway. If your application is denied based on job loss, wait until your job prospects change and you've found a new job. Try to find something in the same field, for about the same (or more) money; otherwise, you may be subjected to the two-year employment rule.

6. Unapproved Condo Building or New Development

Sometimes you'll get rejected for a loan and you won't even be the problem. Institutions that buy loans on the secondary market have a specific set of guidelines that lenders must follow. One of these rules is the *70 percent rule* for condominiums. Lenders like their home buyers to purchase condos in buildings in which owners occupy at least 70 percent of the building. Why? For stability. Lenders believe that homeowners will take better care of property than renters. This makes sense, as owners have more of a stake in a property than renters.

Historically, condo buildings that have a high percentage of renters can lose their value. If you're rejected because of the 70 percent rule, you may want to seek out other lenders who will keep your loan in their own portfolio (instead of reselling it on the secondary market to Fannie Mae or Freddie Mac), and who may be more flexible on this rule.

If the building is less than 50 percent owner-occupied, you may want to rethink your purchase. Or you may want to seek out a lender that has made loans to homeowners in that building.

Buyers who purchase new construction town houses and condominiums may also have a tough time finding a lender who will approve their loan. Conventional lenders like to see development projects that have been in existence for more than two years. They like to see a new construction project more than 50 percent owner-occupied before they'll grant a loan; otherwise, the project could go into default and the properties might drop in value (an anathema to a lender, who wants to protect the investment). If you get rejected for a loan for your new town house or condo purchase, check with the developer. A developer will usually arrange for some sort of financing package from a lender who will keep the loans in-house for one to two years, and then resell them on the secondary market.

7. Low Appraisal

Another reason people get rejected for loans is that the property doesn't "appraise out." When lenders say a home doesn't appraise out, they mean that the bank's appraiser has determined that the home is worth less than the buyer is ready to pay for it. Let's say you offered $150,000 for a home, with 20 percent ($30,000) as a cash down payment, which is all the savings you have in the world. You're counting on the bank lending you the additional $120,000 to purchase the home. But when the bank actually sends in the appraiser, the home is appraised at $120,000, and the bank will only lend you 80 percent (or $96,000). You need to come up with an additional $24,000 in cash to close on the home.

If you can't come up with the $24,000 to close on the house, the lender will reject your loan application.

8. Adding New Debt

Sometimes buyers think they'll be able to get away with making a large purchase after they've been approved for a mortgage. For example, if you get approved for your loan and then two weeks before closing you go out and buy a new Corvette, with hefty monthly installments, the lender's going to know. How? What few people realize is that lenders may do two credit checks: before they approve your loan and before you close on it. Lenders are increasingly watching out for folks who incur large new debts that may interfere with their repayment of the mortgage. Don't buy a new car just before closing. Wait until after you close.

9. Refusal to Provide New Documentation

If the loan officer calls you up and asks for additional documentation, by all means provide it. Refusal to provide information is grounds for loan application rejection. If the loan officer continually asks for additional information, or asks you to send material you've already sent, this may be indicative of an extremely disorganized and pressured office. Or you may have another problem.

10. The Gambling Game

As I discussed earlier, this isn't an official scam, but it happens often enough that first-time buyers, repeat buyers, and homeowners looking to refinance their loans should be aware of it. As you have now seen, there are plenty of reasons why a loan application might not be approved. One problem that doesn't get much media attention is this: Some loan officers gamble with your locked-in interest rates, hoping to put more money in their own pockets.

Although that sounds surprising (it is) and perhaps illegal (technically it is, but it isn't enforced as long as the lender lives up to the lock agreement), a little explanation might help you understand why some loan officers might gamble with your rate.

To eliminate the uncertainty of changeable interest rates, borrowers may pay their prospective lender for the privilege of locking in a specific interest rate and number of points (a point is equal to 1 percent of the loan amount). The lock is good for a predefined time, usually 30 to 60 days. When you lock in your rate, you must close on your mortgage before the lock expires, or you lose the preset interest rate. Experts say that the mortgage loan process can easily go awry, particularly when interest rates are headed up. Lenders, nervous about their investments and eager to charge the highest interest rate possible, are not as eager to close on their loans as when interest rates are dropping.

According to the Office of Banks and Real Estate, which regulates and monitors mortgage brokers, mortgage bankers, and financial institutions in Illinois, lenders often "play the float" with your mortgage interest rate. Although you think you've locked in at a certain rate with a certain number of points, lenders will, in essence, gamble with the rate rather than actually lock it in, hoping that interest rates will slip further. The loan officer and the mortgage company will then pocket the difference between the new current interest rate and the rate you locked into.

The problems start when interest rates begin to go up instead of down. If the loan officer has been playing the float with your loan, and the rate goes up, he or she will have to pay, out-of-pocket, the difference between your locked-in interest rate and the current market rate to close on the loan. And because loan officers are loath to pay out, they will often find something "wrong" with your application at the last minute (such as new documentation that's needed, etc.), forcing you to accept a higher interest rate or more points, says one loan officer.

If you feel that your loan rejection is without merit, and can prove that you sent all the information required, you may want to complain to your state regulatory body. Remember, the squeaky wheel gets the grease. Make sure you are heard loud and clear.

11. Racial Rejection

Recent investigations and surveys of the mortgage banking industry seem to prove that minorities, specifically African Americans, are twice as likely to be rejected for a loan as Caucasians. And that makes people very angry. If you feel you've been rejected for a loan simply because you're African American, file a complaint with your state attorney general's office, the state office that regulates the mortgage banking industry, and other regulatory agencies, including the Department of Housing and Urban Development (HUD). If the rejection is for an FHA loan, notify your local housing authority office.

In Appendix VI, you'll find contact information for the departments and commissions that regulate mortgage lenders and real estate brokers in all 50 states.

10

Before You Close

WHEN SHOULD I SCHEDULE MY PRECLOSING
INSPECTION? WHAT DO I DO IF I DISCOVER
SOMETHING IS DAMAGED OR MISSING?
WHEN SHOULD THE SELLER MOVE OUT?

When it comes to buying or selling a house, the cliché holds true: No
good deed goes unpunished.

Patty and Frank's Story

Patty and Frank agreed to buy a $300,000 condominium from David
and Marla. When they negotiated the contract, David and Marla agreed
to leave all the fixtures, including light fixtures, refrigerator, sconces,
and bookcases that were attached to the wall. Everything was so
friendly that Patty and Frank decided to forgo the preclosing inspection.
They didn't need to walk through the condo because David and Marla
assured them that everything was in order.

   After the closing, everyone shook hands, and David and Marla handed
over the keys. Patty and Frank went over to their new condo, opened the
door, and discovered that it had been stripped bare: no light fixtures, no
refrigerator, no sconces, and huge holes in the wall where the bookcases
had been ripped out. They were, understandably, heartbroken.

   Although David and Marla certainly should have lived up to the contract (they could be sued), Patty and Frank should have taken it upon
themselves to have a final walk-through of the condo before closing.

Never Leave Anything to Chance (or Goodwill)

Most first-time buyers don't realize that they should ask for a preclosing inspection. Just about everyone understands that they can ask for an initial inspection, and bring a licensed house inspector along to point out what's wrong with the home. But too many first-time buyers aren't told that *they should request the right to a second, preclosing inspection.*

To avoid getting burned, schedule the walk-through as close to the actual closing as possible, certainly within the 24 to 48 hours prior to closing. *If possible, the sellers should have already moved out.* The whole point of the walk-through is to protect yourself and your future property from sellers who aren't as nice as they seem to be, or who are actually as nasty as they appear. By inspecting the premises, you're ensuring the seller has lived up to his or her agreements in the sales contract. And if he or she hasn't, you want to know about it in advance of the closing so remedies (both monetary and otherwise) can be agreed upon before money changes hands.

Look for the Details

What should you look for in a preclosing inspection? To start with, make sure that the condition of the home hasn't changed since you signed the contract several months earlier. Remember, you probably negotiated for the home some 60 to 90 days ago and have spent the past weeks arranging for your mortgage, packing, and preparing to move. As Patty and Frank discovered, a lot can change in 60 days—or afterward.

Here is a general checklist for your walk-through:

- Turn on every appliance.
- Open every door.
- Make sure nothing is broken.
- Be certain everything the seller agreed to leave is actually there, and in good shape.
- Be certain that when the sellers moved out, they did no damage to the home.

It's vital that you turn on every appliance that's being left in the home, including the dishwasher. As you may recall from an earlier question, Sam and I learned the hard way. Our story bears repeating.

Sam and Ilyce's Story

When Sam and I were closing on our prewar vintage co-op, we decided to have a final walk-through. We had been in the unit several times and knew that we were going to make some significant cosmetic improvements, so we weren't too worried about the condition of the walls and wallpaper, flooring, and so on.

But when we walked in, the apartment was a mess. Our sellers were a retired couple who had lived in the unit for 25 years and had a huge accumulation of stuff. Boxes were stacked everywhere. Clothes had been taken from closets and laid down. Furniture had been moved. It was difficult to actually walk through the apartment and look at things. But we plodded along.

When we got to the kitchen, we opened the fridge. It seemed cold and relatively clean, though at least 20 years old. When we got to the dishwasher, we said to ourselves, "Well, we'll probably replace this soon after closing, so why bother testing it out?" Our sellers, hovering over us, assured us everything worked. We felt as if we were in the way, so we left.

We closed on the unit and moved our stuff in that afternoon. That night, after unwrapping a stack of dishes, Sam suggested we test out the dishwasher. We put a load in, started to run it, and nothing happened. Sam reached under the sink and found the water valve. Sure enough, it had been shut off. ("Now why would they shut off the water?" Sam said to himself.) Sam turned on the water and started the dishwasher. Then, we went to sleep. It was about 3:00 A.M.

We woke up around 7:00 A.M. to banging on the door. In our bathrobes, we opened the door to find one of the co-op's engineers and our new downstairs neighbor complaining that we'd ruined her ceiling and window shade, and who knows what else, all because our dishwasher leaked.

It cost us around $150 to replace our neighbor's window treatment, and another $70 or so to have someone come out and replace the dishwasher's hose. (We never had another problem with the dishwasher, but I can tell you that I never used it without some sense of concern.)

Years later, Sam and I still discuss whether our old sellers actually knew that the dishwasher leaked. Regardless, we know we should have tested the dishwasher while we were there, and let it run a full cycle.

Don't Be Shy

It's equally important to open every door. Don't be afraid to poke your head into your seller's messy closets to look for anything unusual or broken. Finally, be certain that everything the seller agreed to leave is actually in place and in the apartment. Check your contract if you're not sure whether that window air conditioner was part of the agreement. Are the window shades or curtains supposed to be left? Or did the seller want to take them? If the seller asks you at the preclosing inspection if he or she can take additional items, simply say, "I have to check with my attorney." That will give you time to think about whether you want to keep or give away that chandelier.

Another Sam and Ilyce Story

When we went for our preclosing inspection before closing on our house, our sellers were in the process of moving out. There were boxes everywhere, and it was extremely difficult to move through the house.

Our seller looked out onto the backyard and motioned toward the swing set. "My son built that," he said.

We looked out and nodded. "It's a fine piece of work," Sam said.

"My grandchildren just love playing on it," our seller said.

"I can imagine they do," I said, looking over the fine construction, two swings, sandbox, and long, blue slide. The top of the slide was built like a small fort, with straight sides. I imagined little children climbing up to the top and hiding out, then escaping down the slide.

"If you're not going to use it, would you mind if we took it with us?" our seller asked.

Sam and I looked at each other and smiled. Although it was true that we didn't have children at the time (we now have two), we were planning to put that swing set to great use over the next few years.

"I'm sorry," I told our seller. "But we do plan to use it. It stays."

To replace that set with one of the same quality would have cost us, at the time, more than $700. I wasn't ready to ante up that kind of cash so that our seller could have a ready-made play area for his grandchildren in his new home.

New-Construction Walk-Through

If you're buying new construction, you'll be looking for different things on your walk-through. You want to be sure that everything the developer promised would be done and put in is actually there (and working) before closing. This includes any sod or plantings, doorknobs, doorbell, window screens, fixtures, appliances, and so on.

Be sure that everything works in every room. Take a hair dryer or radio with you and test out the electrical sockets in each room. You can buy a simple device that will tell you if a socket has been wired correctly. Make sure everything has been painted and is in working condition. Turn on the water in the showers and sinks, and flush the toilets. If there is a garage, make sure the electric door opener works.

With new construction, there are always a few last-minute items that need to be finished, and it may not be possible for the contractor or developer to get them finished before closing. That's why you need a *punch list*—a list of all items that need to be fixed in the home before you consider it completely finished.

During your preclosing inspection, write down all of the items that need attention: that loose tile in the master bath; the wall that wasn't painted; the electrical outlet that doesn't work; the tree that should have been planted in the side yard. Have your attorney or broker present the punch list to the developer at closing, or before closing, and have the developer agree to fix these items (in writing) before you actually close. Most developers should be happy to comply with any reasonable request.

Attendance Is Mandatory

Who should go to your walk-through? My mother, Susanne, makes it a point to go to almost all of her clients' walk-throughs. She says she helps the buyer remember what was where, amid the mess and muck of moving. It goes without saying that you, the buyer (or buyers, if you're buying with someone else), should attend the walk-through. You should ask your broker to be there. Beyond that, the seller or the seller broker may attend. Sometimes, if the buyer is out of town, the buyer's attorney will attend.

If the seller attends and you notice that certain things are missing, try to avoid a confrontation. Have your broker speak to the seller or seller broker to confirm what was written in the contract.

Some buyers like to have a professional house inspector attend the preclosing inspection. I think that's overkill in most cases. The preclosing inspection isn't about finding a leaky oil tank. You should be looking for things like a gash in the wall caused by the L-shaped sofa as it was moved out of the home. That gash is something you could ask the sellers to fix before closing, or they could give you a credit for the damage at closing.

333

Missing in Action

What should you do if you discover during the preclosing inspection that something's missing or damaged? Make a list of anything that doesn't seem right to you and call your attorney immediately after you leave the home. You can also call your broker. Your attorney may telephone the seller's attorney before closing or may present a list of items at closing. Either way, the list will have to be resolved before you'll agree to close on the house.

The list gives you some leverage, because as anxious as you are to move, the sellers are equally anxious and have most likely found another place to live. Perhaps they are scheduled to close on a new home shortly after you buy theirs. At this point, most sellers, and the attorneys, will find a way to make everyone happy. The seller may offer you $45 instead of fixing the back door. He or she might offer you $600 for the washer and dryer their movers took "by accident." Or the seller might say, "Forget it, I'm not fixing the east window screen."

The preclosing inspection or walk-through gives you your last opportunity to make sure that the property is in the same condition (except for normal wear and tear) as the day you bought it. It's important that you take full advantage of that opportunity.

Make Sure Your Sellers Move Out

Unless there are some extraordinary circumstances, make sure the seller is completely out of the home before you close on the home. That doesn't mean the end of the business day, as in, you close at 10:00 A.M. and the seller's out by 5:00 P.M. Your new home isn't a business. Getting the seller out by the closing means that if you're scheduled to close at 10:00 A.M., the seller is packed and gone by 9:59 A.M.

After closing (and getting all of his or her money), the seller has little, if any, incentive to move out. If you close and pay money to the seller, and then the seller decides not to leave, you might have a real problem getting the seller out. Also, the seller no longer has any interest in the property once the deed changes hands. An unscrupulous seller might be inclined to inflict damage (if the transaction has been a bit hostile), or may be less than careful when moving his or her items out of the home. You want to protect your property, and the best way to do that is to make sure the seller is out before money changes hands.

Sometimes buyers and sellers make other arrangements. For example, suppose the seller has had the home on the market for a long time—say, a year—and within the year, the seller went out and bought another home and moved. The house you're buying is vacant and perhaps empty of furniture. The seller, unless he or she is in a high income bracket, will want to close as quickly as possible to end the burden of paying two mortgages (on your house and the new house). You don't want to close until your apartment lease is up (to avoid paying both rent and mortgage), but you do want to get in a little early to do some painting. Would the seller mind? It doesn't hurt to ask. If the seller seems to hesitate, offer to "rent the house for a few days before closing," for a nominal daily fee.

The earliest the seller would probably want to let you into a house would be two to three weeks before closing. Still, there's not much risk for a seller in this situation. Time marches forward quickly to the closing.

There's greater risk for you, the buyer, if the seller wants to stay in the house *after* closing. Let's look at why a seller might want to do this:

1. No place to go. The seller may not have found anywhere to live. This is the most dangerous for you, because there is no end in sight for when the seller might leave. It could be in a few days, a few months, or never. Also, you're going to be coming from somewhere and will want to—or have to—move into your house.

2. Bad timing. The seller isn't scheduled to close on his or her new home until a few days after closing. Most sellers are going to turn around and buy something new. In a perfect world, the sellers would attend your closing while they simultaneously closed on their new house. However, this isn't a perfect world, and the sellers will usually want to close first on your home (because then they'll be able to use the funds to purchase the new home). So you might be scheduled to close on your house on a Friday, and the seller is scheduled to close on his new place on Monday and may ask to "rent" your house for the weekend. If you can spend a few extra days in your current place of abode, and if the seller will pay you the daily rate you want, then that's fine. (Just so you know, the seller could close on his or her new place a few days ahead of your closing by using a financial product known as a "bridge loan." A bridge loan is a short-term loan that allows the seller to borrow enough money to close on his new home before he sells his old home. Some sellers get into trouble, however, by buying a new home before trying to sell their original home. If that happens, and they use a bridge loan to fund the new purchase, they could end up paying the equivalent of three mortgages simultaneously: their original home mortgage, the new home mortgage, and their bridge loan.)

3. Change of heart. Sometimes, after fixing up a house for sale, the seller decides he or she doesn't really want to move after all. Ideally, this change of heart will come before the seller has accepted an offer. But it has been known to happen a day or so before closing.

Paying the Piper

How much should you charge for each extra day the seller stays in the home? First, calculate exactly how much the home costs per day.

Add up your monthly mortgage (principal and interest), taxes, and insurance premiums, then divide by 30 or 31 (unless it's February). That number is your average minimum out-of-pocket cost to own and maintain the home each day. Let's say you have a $100,000 mortgage that costs you $666.67 per month. And let's say your real estate tax bill is $3,000 per year or $250 per month. Your insurance premium is $35 per month.

$$\$666.67 + \$250 + \$35 = \$951.67 \text{ (monthly cost of the home)}$$

$$\$951.67 \div 30 = \$31.72 \text{ (daily cost of the home)}$$

The daily fee and the length of the after-closing stay should be negotiated before the closing. There should also be a stiff daily penalty for each day the seller stays in the house past the agreed-upon deadline. You, or your attorney, should make it completely clear to the seller and his or her attorney that the seller will not receive all the proceeds from the closing until he or she has moved out of the house and you've had a chance to walk through the house to verify that the house is still in good condition and the appliances and plumbing are still in working order.

It would cost you $31.72 per day for PITI (principal, interest, taxes, and insurance), which is generally the most expensive part of homeownership. If you think that $31.72 is too cheap for a daily fee to adequately encourage the seller to make his or her after-closing stay a short one, increase the daily fee by as much as you think is necessary. A few dollars more per day for electricity, heat, gas, water, sewer, and garbage pickup wouldn't be out of line. Also, if there are any assessments (for condos, co-ops, and town houses), those fees should also be included. A fee of $50 or $75 per day starts to add up pretty quickly.

When to Hold Back Money at Closing

How much money should be held back at closing? It's a good idea to retain enough cash to cover the payment due for the after-closing stay, plus at least another 10 days' worth. *Usually, this amount is equal to 2 to 3 percent of the purchase price of the home,* although it may be subject to local custom and, in some cases, state law. If you give the seller all the money at closing and the seller remains in the house, you may have to sue to collect your daily fee from the seller. The money should be given to your real estate broker, the title company, or an unassociated third party and held in an escrow account.

WHAT EXACTLY IS THE CLOSING?
WHERE IS IT HELD?

By now you've probably heard about "The Closing," which is also called "The Settlement," depending on where you live in the country. (For purposes of this book, I'll refer to it as the closing, but if you're hearing "settlement," rest assured that we're talking about the same thing.)

Real estate industry professionals talk about The Closing as if it were (1) a big show on Broadway, or (2) some huge black hole in outer space, sucking buyers, sellers, brokers, lawyers, inspectors, money, and mortgages into a netherworld blender, out of which pops a deed that now has your name on it. Those are the two extremes. After it's over, you and your broker will either describe your closing as a dream or a nightmare. Rarely have I heard closings described as being somewhere in the middle.

Let's start at the top. Why do we have the closing? One attorney put it this way: If you were the seller, would you take the buyer's personal check, fold it up, and put it in your pocket, and then hand the buyer the deed to your house? Of course not. You would want some security that that check was really going to clear. Conversely, you, the buyer, want some reassurance that the deed you're being given is actually the seller's to give. Your lender, worried that you will take bad title to the home, which could mean trouble down the pike for your loan, also wants that same reassurance. The broker wants some security that he or she will actually get paid the commission. The attorney wants to know his or her fee will be paid.

Everyone wants to be protected. It is from this point that today's closing or settlement evolved. "Closing a transaction" has always described the point in time when the deal is completed. One party has paid another for certain rights, privileges, property, or other goods and services. When the passing of money or other consideration has occurred, and the goods and services have been received, a deal is deemed closed. Kaput. Finished.

Around the country, closings are generally held at the office of the title or escrow company, which issues title insurance for the buyer and the lender. The title company researches the chain of title to the home. Your attorney reviews the information furnished by the title company to make sure you will get "good" title to the home when you close. Once the title issues have been resolved (if they need to be resolved), then the title company will insure the title in your name—with any exception shown on the policy—in the amount of the purchase price. But remember, lender's title insurance covers the *lender's* losses on the property, if some outside claim to the title is eventually upheld. If you want to protect *your* interests, you will have to purchase a separate title policy that insures your losses, known as an "owner's" policy.

A title or escrow company facilitates the closing by providing a forum for the free exchange of documents and releasing of funds. Generally, the title company acts as an agent for the lender to protect the lender's best interest. However, the seller usually selects which title company will be used, because he or she is the party that generally pays for title insurance. (Who pays for the title policy is dictated by local custom.) If the title company can act as agent for the lender, and close the transaction, the closing will take place at the offices of the title company. Otherwise, the closing may take place at the office of the lender, or another location acceptable to the lender.

In several states, including California and New York, it's more common to have what's known as an escrow closing. In this case, the title company acts for the benefit of both parties, using a document called an "escrow agreement." The title company will only disburse money after certain steps take place. For example, in an escrow closing, the title company will send someone to the recorder's office (where deeds are recorded). Once the name on the deed has been verified as being that of the sellers, and the transfer of title has been accomplished, the title company will allow the closing to take place. If there are any problems along the way, the title company returns the closing funds to the buyer and seller and records a deed from the buyer back to the seller.

In states that have escrow closings, typically no one attends a "closing" the way folks in the northern and eastern parts of the country think about it. In other words, don't expect to go to one place and sign a lot of documents. Instead, you provide the escrow company with your set of instructions, paperwork, and money, as does the other side. Once the instructions from both parties are carried out, monies are collected, checks are cut, and monies are disbursed, the deal is considered closed. It may happen when you expect it, or it may take some extra time.

The Closing

From the buyer's perspective, the closing can be generally broken into three pieces:

1. Review and signing of loan documents. In the first phase of the closing, you, the buyer, must review and sign all the loan documents provided by the lender. There may be 7 to 20 documents or more, including the actual mortgage, note, affidavits, Truth-in-Lending statements, estimate of closing costs, and the escrow statement letter that outlines how much will be paid in to the real estate tax and insurance escrows.

2. Exchange of documents between buyer and seller and title (or escrow) company. The second phase of the closing deals with the relationship between you (the buyer), the seller, and the title company. There is an exchange of documents that must be signed by you and the seller, and of other documents that require the additional signature of the title company's representative. Depending on your local customs, the seller will provide certain documents for your inspection to verify that they are correct:

- The deed
- The bill of sale
- An affidavit of title
- Any documentation that may have been required in the contract, including paid water bills, certificates of compliance with laws pertaining to smoke-detection equipment, lead paint, termite or radon inspection (these items will vary from state to state, and even county to county)
- Condo assessment full-payment certificate
- Co-op assessment full-payment certificate
- Insurance certificate
- Property survey (except for condos and co-ops)

You may have anywhere from a handful of documents to a dozen or more that will require both your signature (and your spouse's or partner's) and the seller's signature. After you have finished with these documents, the title company will have more papers for you to sign. These documents generally relate to the title or are papers the title company must send to the Internal Revenue Service regarding the purchase and sale of the home. Your documentation may include these:

- The RESPA (Real Estate Settlement Procedures Act) "HUD-1" statement outlines who provides the money, and from which sources, and details how the money gets paid out. This document is signed by you, the seller, and the title company.
- Disclosure statements about construction contracts or any agreements entered into within the past three to six months for work to be done on the property. This is to ensure that no outstanding mechanics' liens could be placed on the property.
- Disclosure statement about any tenants who have access to the property other than the buyer or seller.
- Statements about any other matters that could ultimately affect the title to the property, such as lawsuits.
- If the sales price of the home exceeds $250,000 if you're single, or $500,000 if you're married, IRS form 1099, which relates the sales price of the home. Once signed by the seller, it will be used to cross-check the seller's IRS form with documentation signed by the title company regarding the purchase and sale of the home.

Many of these documents are signed and notarized. (Each state and county has little particular quirks regarding documentation. For example, any document that will be recorded in Hawaii must be typed and signed in black ink only. Otherwise, it will not be accepted. In other parts of the country, the notary stamp must be embossed.) Once the documents are notarized, the closing can proceed to the final step: disbursement.

3. Disbursement of funds. Once all the documents have been signed, dated, and notarized, the title company can proceed with the disbursement of funds. It will take the money from you, the buyer, and cut checks to the seller, the seller's lender (if applicable), the brokers, the title company, and the attorneys. Since everyone usually gets paid out of the closing proceeds, it's easy to see why the title company doesn't accept personal checks, even for a few pennies. Title companies accept only cashier's or certified checks, or a wire transfer, because they are equivalent to cash.

And If No Lender Is Involved?

Good question. Almost all first-time buyers will have some sort of financing involved with their purchase simply because it's expensive to buy a home (even a home that costs $30,000), and most first-time buyers don't have that kind of cash stuffed inside their mattresses. If there's no lender, or if the seller is acting as lender through seller financing, the buyer and seller can sit down together and exchange and sign documents. Or they can have the title company act as intermediary between seller and buyer in an escrow closing. The closing may take less time (most closings that involve financing generally take between 30 minutes and two hours) and will certainly have fewer steps overall.

In the next few questions, I'll dissect some of the more complicated pieces of the closing and explain in a bit more detail why they're important.

WHAT ARE MY CLOSING COSTS LIKELY TO BE?

As I explained in Question 65, lenders charge certain fees for giving you a mortgage. Every lender won't require you to pay every fee, but charges can add up quickly.

QUESTION
90

In addition to the lender's fees, the other closing costs to be added up include: title fees, recording fees, city and state transfer taxes, and so on. The lion's share of the buyer's closing costs is generated by the mortgage. The lender's points (a point equals 1 percent of the loan amount), which may also be referred to as the service charge, the discount points, or the origination fee, are the largest single fee paid to the lender and it usually runs between 1 and 3 percent of the loan amount. Occasionally, the points will total more than 3 percent, although some loans are available with zero points.

(Remember that for every extra point you pay up front, the lender will decrease the interest rate of the loan. If you have the cash and are planning to stay in the home for a long time, you might want to pay three points to get the lowest interest rate possible. The points are fully deductible on your income tax return in the year you buy your home. On the other hand, if you're strapped for cash today but know that down the line your prospects for a higher income are good, you may want to go with zero points and a slightly higher interest rate, then refinance down the line.)

If you've been reading this book start to finish, you know that when it comes to calculating closing costs, your lender is supposed to make it easier for you by giving you a written *good faith estimate* of all closing costs. This estimate is supposed to accurately reflect the buyer's closing costs. "But a lot of times, people are surprised when they actually get to the closing," says Neil, a real estate attorney. "The Truth-in-Lending law is supposed to take the surprise away, but it doesn't require that the lender explain what the costs are used for and where they are going."

If the loan officer taking your application doesn't do a good job of explaining what happens at the closing and what the charges are going to be, you might not feel so good when the big day arrives.

Here's a list of your closing cost responsibilities. Remember, not every charge will apply to your loan, and your actual fee may be higher or lower depending on your specific situation. Ask your real estate attorney or broker to help you go over this list and identify how much each item might cost. On page 345 is a worksheet that you can fill in when you get your own finalized closing costs.

1. Lender's points, loan origination, or loan service fees— Usually 0 to 3 percent of the loan, or more.

2. Loan application fee—$0 to $500.

3. Lender's credit report—$25 to $65.

4. **Lender's processing fee**—$75 to $350.

5. **Lender's document preparation fee**—$50 to $250.

6. **Lender's appraisal fee**—$225 to $400.

7. **Prepaid interest on the loan**—Paid per day until the end of the month in which the closing occurs.

8. **Lender's insurance escrow**—About 15 to 20 percent of the cost of the homeowner's insurance policy for one year.

9. **Lender's tax escrow**—If you have one, it will cost about 33 to 50 percent of annual property taxes, depending on the time of year you close. (This is just at closing. After closing, you will begin to make regular real estate tax and insurance escrow payments as part of your monthly mortgage payment.)

10. **Lender's tax escrow service fee, a fee to set up the tax escrow**—$40 to $95.

11. **Title insurance cost for the lender's policy**—$150 to $500 or more, based on the dollar amount of the home you buy. The cost to the buyer for title insurance may be relatively small because the seller may have paid a basic fee to the title company, and the lender's policy is issued simultaneously. In many parts of the country, the seller must ensure that the home is owned free and clear, so the seller picks up most of the cost of title insurance. When you refinance, you'll find that the cost for title insurance goes up substantially. If you purchase a $100,000 house, your title insurance cost might be a flat $150. If you refinance that house, your title insurance may skyrocket to $415 or more. That reflects the additional $265 that the seller paid to ensure that you received good title to his or her home.

12. **Special endorsements to the title**—$100 each, or more. Depending on the type of property you are buying, your lender may require that special endorsements be added to the title. If the lender requires an environmental lien endorsement, it may cost $100. A location endorsement proves the house is located where the documents say it is. If you choose an adjustable-rate mortgage, that may be another $100 endorsement, depending on the title company. If the property is a condominium, there may be a condo endorsement. For a town house, there may be a PUD (planned-unit development) endorsement. As you can see, three or four extra endorsements can really add to your closing cost tab.

13. **Unpaid house inspection fees**—$250 to $400.

14. **Title company closing fee**—Runs from $200 to $500 or more.

15. **Recording fees, of deed or mortgage**—$25 to $75.

16. **Local city, town, or village property transfer tax; county transfer tax; state transfer tax**—The charges that you, the buyer, will pay vary from city to city, and state to state. In Illinois, for example, the seller picks up the county tax ($.50 per $1,000 of sales price) and the state tax ($1.00 per $1,000 of sales price). In Chicago, the buyer picks up the city transfer tax (a hefty $3.75 per $500 of sales price). There may be other special taxes on high-end property. And certain kinds of property, such as co-ops, may, under certain circumstances, be exempt from property transfer taxes. In general, property transfer taxes can range from nothing to $5.00 per $1,000 of sales price, or you may be assessed a flat fee of $25 or $50 per transaction.

17. **Flood certification fee**—$10 to $50. A fee you'll pay to determine whether the home you're buying is in a floodplain.

18. **Attorney's fee**—If you need an attorney to help you close your deal, flat fees generally start at $300. Although some attorneys in large firms work solely on an hourly rate, loads of real estate attorneys do house closings for a flat fee, and then may charge a small amount extra depending on whether your deal turns out to be particularly complicated or difficult. NOTE: If you live in an escrow closing state, like California, you won't be paying an attorney's fee because you won't be using an attorney. But you will be paying an escrow closing fee, which would be similar to a title company charging you for the space it takes to close the deal—except that they don't charge for it.

19. **Condo move-in fee**—A building charge that can run from nothing to more than $400.

20. **Association transfer fee**—Often required for condominium and town house buyers. This fee can range from nothing to more than $200.

21. **Co-op apartment fees**—Sometimes, small fees are required by co-op associations for transferring shares of stock (remember, with a co-op you're not buying an apartment, you're buying shares in a corporation that owns the building in which your apartment is located), or doing name searches. These fees can range from $50 to more than $200 or may be based on a percentage of the purchase price.

WORKSHEET
Closing Costs

Name _____

Property Address _____

Closing Date _____

1. Lender's points, loan origination, or loan service fees _____
2. Loan application fee _____
3. Lender's credit report _____
4. Lender's processing fee _____
5. Lender's document preparation fee _____
6. Lender's appraisal fee _____
   a. Second appraisal (if required) _____
7. Prepaid interest on the loan _____
8. Lender's insurance escrow _____
9. Lender's tax escrow _____
10. Lender's tax escrow service fee _____
11. Title insurance cost for lender's policy _____
12. Special endorsements to the title _____
13. House inspection fee(s) (unpaid) _____
    a. House reinspection fee (if needed) _____
14. Title/escrow company closing fee _____
    a. Special endorsements to the title _____
15. Recording fees, of deed or mortgage _____
16. Local city, town, or village transfer tax _____
    a. County transfer tax _____
    b. State transfer tax _____
17. Your attorney's fee _____
    a. Lender's attorney's fee (if any) _____
    b. Other fee _____
    c. Other fee _____
    d. Other fee _____
    e. Other fee _____

Total Closing Costs _____

22. Credit checks for condo and co-op buildings by the board—Variable.

(Just so you don't think the seller gets off scot-free, he or she will also pay a long list of closing costs, including: survey, $150 to $1,500; title insurance, $300 to $1,500 (in some areas of the country, the buyer may pay this fee, too); recording release charges for the mortgage, $23 to $70; broker's commission, usually 5 to 7 percent of the sales price; state, county, and city transfer taxes; paid utility bills, including water, sewer, or electricity, $10 to $25; credit to the buyer of unpaid real estate taxes for prior year or current year, depending on the way your state collects property taxes; attorney's fee, $250 and up; and FHA fees and costs, depending on the loan amount.)

Current tax law states that as long as you have lived in your primary residence for at least two of the past five years, when you sell that home, your profit will only be subject to capital gains tax if it exceeds $250,000 (if you're single) or $500,000 (if you're married). And you no longer need tell the IRS about the sale of your home unless it exceeds these levels. Any tax that you would owe on the sale of your home would be due the April 15 following the year in which you sold your home. So if you close on July 1, 2005, you would pay any capital gains tax owed on April 15, 2006.

QUESTION 91

WHAT IS A TITLE SEARCH? WHAT IS TITLE INSURANCE? WHY DO I NEED THEM?

How do you prove you own something? Generally, you have a bill of sale, or the certificate of title to the item—let's say it's a car—that's registered in your name with the state. If anyone inquires who owns that cherry red Ford Mustang, the state can tell them it's you. Proving that a seller owns a particular home, however, is a little more difficult. Lenders will not allow you to purchase a home without knowing it actually belongs to the person who is selling it. How do you prove the seller owns the home you want to buy? You conduct a title search.

During a title search, the examiner looks at the chain of title of a home, working backward from owner to owner until it reaches the point where the land was originally granted or sold from the government to the original owners or developers. If the title has been recorded correctly, you should be able to trace the lineage of a piece of land all the way back to when that area of the country was settled. (As with many of our laws, we derive our methods of recording title from the English system, in which some records of property ownership stretch back a thousand years or more.)

How the title search is carried out varies from city to city and depends on what kinds of records have been kept. Public records that may affect a property's title include records of deaths, divorces, court judgments, liens, taxes, and wills. Public records in a wide variety of county and city offices must be examined, including those in the recorders of deeds, county courts, tax assessors, and surveyors. Since many local governments have not yet computerized their records, the majority of title searches are performed manually. Someone may spend hours poring over different documents in various offices. If the municipality in which you are buying has computerized this information, title searches can be done in a matter of minutes.

Title searches are conducted by lawyers, title companies, or title specialists, to discover whether there are any problems—called "clouds" in the industry—with the title. The lender wants to know if any liens (claims made against a property by a person or tax assessor for payment of a debt) or judgments (by a court of law) or easements (known or unknown rights) have been filed against the property, which might prevent you from receiving good title.

Top 20 Things Title Insurance Protects You From

There are more than 100 reasons you should have title insurance. I've included the top 20 things here, courtesy of First American Title Company.

1. Forged deeds, mortgages, satisfactions, or releases
2. Deed by person who is insane or mentally incompetent
3. Deed by minor (may be disavowed)
4. Deed from corporation, unauthorized under corporate bylaws or given under falsified corporate resolution
5. Deed from partnership, unauthorized under partnership agreement
6. Deed from purported trustee, unauthorized under trust agreement

347

7. Deed to or from a "corporation" before incorporation, or after loss of corporate charter

8. Deed from a legal nonentity (styled, for example, as a church, charity or club)

9. Deed by person in a foreign country, vulnerable to challenge as incompetent, unauthorized, or defective under foreign laws

10. Claims resulting from use of "alias" or fictitious name by a predecessor in title

11. Deed challenged as being given under fraud, undue influence, or duress

12. Deed following nonjudicial foreclosure, where required procedure was not followed

13. Deed affecting land in judicial proceedings (bankruptcy, receivership, probate, conservatorship, dissolution of marriage), unauthorized by court

14. Deed following judicial proceedings, subject to appeal or further court order

15. Deed following judicial proceedings, where all necessary parties were not joined

16. Lack of jurisdiction over persons or property in judicial proceedings

17. Deed signed by mistake (grantor did not know what was signed)

18. Deed executed under falsified power of attorney

19. Deed executed under expired power of attorney (death, disability, or insanity of principal)

20. Deed apparently valid, but actually delivered after death of grantor or grantee, or without consent of grantor

It doesn't seem possible any of these items could ever happen to you, right? That's what Roberta and Dave thought.

Roberta and Dave's Story

Roberta and Dave bought a house in a suburb of Chicago. They had the land surveyed. When they actually moved into the house, they discovered that years earlier a neighbor had built a garage that took about 10 feet off the back end of their property.

> The survey should have noted that the garage encroached on their property. The title Roberta and Dave received to the land wasn't "good" title because the encroachment created a defect on their property. In other words, someone was making use of their land without their permission. If Roberta and Dave had bought title insurance, their insurer (if it failed to catch the encroachment) would have reimbursed them for the portion of land that they paid for but to which they didn't receive good title.

Title problems don't often come up, but when they do come up, they can blindside you. One Texas home buyer purchased a single-family house with a swimming pool in the backyard. After a few heavy rainstorms, his neighbor filed a complaint with the local municipality, complaining of flooding. It turns out that there was an easement between the two properties designed to keep the land open specifically for drainage. When the seller had built the pool, he had filled in the land and altered the water flow. Because the title search didn't turn up the easement, and the survey didn't catch that the property had changed, the title company paid hundreds of thousands of dollars to buy the property, fix the problem (which included removing the pool), and resell the home to someone else.

If the insurer notes the encroachment, you, the buyer, are considered to have been notified of the defect and must approach the seller about it before the closing. A title search looks for any clouds on the title to the home. Title insurance protects you and the lender against any mistakes or errors or omissions made by the individual performing the search. If you buy a home from Dan and Shelly, and a long-lost relative turns up with irrefutable evidence (say, a recorded deed from the property's original owner) that she actually owns the home, you'll have to turn over the home to the long-lost relative. Now, the title search should have turned up this information, but whoever conducted the search missed this important piece of evidence. What happens in a case like this is the lender finds it has lent you money to purchase a property from someone who didn't really own it. An owner's title insurance policy protects you, the buyer, from any losses associated with the cost of any errors made. The lender's title policy protects the lender's interest.

Paying the Premium

Title insurance is paid as a onetime premium; the cost is based entirely on the sales price of the home. In many communities, the seller pays for the cost of the title search, since he or she wants to guarantee that you, the buyer, will receive good title to the home. The lender will insist that you pay for, or obtain from the title company, title insurance that covers the lender. The lender may not insist that you get an owner's policy, which will compensate you if there is an error (title insurance insures the lender against errors), but it's an excellent idea. If you purchase the owner's policy at the same place you buy title insurance for the lender, you may be able to get a discounted rate. In addition, ask your real estate attorney if he or she works regularly with a title company. Attorney's may be able to flex their economic muscle (they may do a lot of house closings and the title company may be eager to encourage their business) to get you a discounted rate.

Finally, if the seller has owned the home for only a short period of time—say, a few years—you may be able to get a discounted policy by checking with the seller's original title company. It may be able to give you a "reissue" rate, at a significantly lower premium.

I'm often asked whether a homeowner can buy title insurance. The answer is no. The only time you can buy an owner's title insurance policy is when you close on the home and in very limited cases thereafter. Many first-time buyers are confused by the purchase of title insurance and mistakenly believe they have already purchased their own *owner's* policy when in fact they have only purchased a lender's policy. If you have a lender's policy, it's the *mortgage lender* who will be reimbursed for a loss—not you!

WHAT IS RESPA? WHAT DOES THE HUD-1 STATEMENT LOOK LIKE?

In 1974, Congress decided Americans were suffering from abuses in the title industry. Title companies were giving kickbacks to real estate agents and brokers who referred buyers to settlement agencies. Mortgage lenders were paying fees to real estate agents who steered them business. And the consumer was being bartered like pork bellies.

Congress decided buyers should be free to choose their own title company or settlement agency and should have more power in the entire transaction. The Real Estate Settlement Procedures Act (RESPA) was passed to address these issues.

Section 8 in the RESPA code is the kickback provision, according to the Mortgage Bankers Association of America (MBA). It makes it a crime to pay or receive any money, or give or receive anything of value, to another person for the referral of any real estate settlement services, which includes making a mortgage loan. (Your broker cannot legally receive money for referring you to Jones Mortgage Company down the street.)

Sections 4 and 5 of the RESPA code deal with disclosure. Mortgage companies must tell you how many loans they resell on the secondary market before you take their mortgage. They also are required to tell you when they are actually selling your mortgage. Finally, the company that buys your mortgage must disclose all sorts of information, including a telephone number and a name of a person you can contact if there is trouble with your loan. (These disclosures form the basis of the stack of documents you must sign, sometimes in quadruplicate, before you can close on the property.)

RESPA, which is regulated by the department of Housing and Urban Development (HUD), also requires that lenders give their prospective borrowers a copy of a HUD information booklet within three days of receiving the loan application. Lenders must also, within three days, give the good faith estimate (GFE) of what the buyer's closing costs will be. (As I mentioned earlier in the book, if your lender does not give you a GFE within three days, the lender is in violation of federal law. Take your business elsewhere.) Mortgage companies are required to make another disclosure: the HUD-1 settlement statement, which outlines exactly what monies come in and how they are distributed. This is a closing document that you will have to sign. It is filled out by the title company once all the numbers have been called in.

The HUD-1 statement is instructive for both buyers and sellers because it shows exactly where the money comes from and where it is going. The buyer's and seller's costs are itemized side by side. It also neatly wraps up a lot of the issues we've been talking about.

The first line of the "Summary of Borrower's Transaction" indicates the contract sales price. The settlement charges, or closing costs, are on the next line. On the middle of the page, there is a line for the deposit or earnest money, and another line detailing the principal amount of the new loan. Your application fee will also be listed. Finally, any extra city, county, and perhaps real estate taxes will be listed. Everything is totaled up at the bottom, where you'll see the amount of cash you'll need to close the deal.

On the seller's side, the contract sales price is at the top. Then comes his or her settlement charges, or closing costs. Another line details the payoff of the seller's first mortgage loan (including who holds that loan). The earnest money is listed next (it's been paid to the seller, sometimes with the interest), and the title charge (title insurance). Finally, adjustments for items unpaid by seller, including any city, county, or real estate property taxes, are recorded. The bottom line indicates how much cash the seller will receive from the deal.

Page two details exactly what settlement charges, or closing costs, the buyer and seller are paying and to whom. For example, a $225 charge may be paid to ABC Appraisal Company for a home appraisal. You may have paid $60 for a credit report and $300 for a mortgage application. (The problem with finding all of this out at the closing is that it's a little too late to start shopping around for another mortgage company if you find yours has added onerous charges that it didn't disclose on the good faith estimate. "Of course," wonders one first-time buyer, "once you go through all the work and actually get to the closing, who's going to quash the deal for an extra $100 here or there?")

Keep handy a file that contains a copy of all the information you've given to your lender, plus all of the documentation you've received in return, especially the good faith estimate. If you get to the closing, or the day before the closing, and you see that the lender has added all sorts of charges and fees above and beyond what was quoted in the good faith estimate, you (or your attorney, if you're in a state that uses attorneys) should have an immediate conversation with the lender about these extra charges, and why they've been added to your account. Feel free to whip out the initial good faith estimate and compare the two statements. The lender shouldn't be more than $25 over the good faith estimate. If the numbers come in over that, there could be a problem.

A separate page, which isn't part of the HUD-1 but is given out by some title companies, looks at disbursements (who gets what money, whose name is on the check). Ten to 15 checks may be written at the closing, including ones for title insurance, for city or county stamp taxes, for inspections, to the real estate broker, for the mortgage insurance premium, to the real estate attorney, to pay off any other mortgages or liens, to the seller, and others. Usually within 30 days of closing, the bank releases the real estate tax and insurance escrow proceeds (if any) to the sellers. They no longer need real estate tax and insurance escrow for a property they've sold.

Some folks feel that RESPA is a waste of time. Others find the disclosures and HUD-1 statement to be useful to consumers. Once you get to the closing, you can decide for yourself.

Lunchbox Loan Deals

As the number of homeowners in the United States hit an all-time high in 2004, there was talk in the real estate industry about pushing costs for home buyers even lower than they are—which is pretty low.

But the buzz around Washington, DC, seems to mostly concern the costs of buying a home—title charges, lender charges, and closing costs. We've discussed all these things in this book.

Right now, many of these costs are state regulated. In those states where the costs are regulated, they tend to be a lot higher than in states where the costs are unregulated. For example, I pay less for my title insurance in Illinois, where that cost is unregulated, than I would in a state that regulates title insurance. The economic principle behind that savings is that competition drives down price. (Why don't all states deregulate costs? Because various lobbying organizations are stronger in some places.)

The next bright idea that's being tossed around is lowering all of the costs associated with buying a home by packaging them all together. For example, when choosing a title company or an escrow company, you'd get a preselected group of closing costs, which would ostensibly be less expensive than costs you could get by shopping around. I've decided to refer to this phenomenon as the Lunchbox Loan. Why? Because when you buy a lunchbox for a charity, or at a sporting event, it typically has everything you need inside it: sandwich, vegetable, chips of some sort, fruit, dessert, a drink, a napkin, and plastic silverware. That's what the government is talking about doing—packaging together everything you need to close.

I can't tell you if, or when, this is going to come to pass—my crystal ball cracked years ago!—but the federal government wants to continue to increase homeownership. Decreasing costs is one way to help more people buy homes. Every dollar a home buyer saves, however, means a dollar lost in profit to a company providing the service, which is why this Lunchbox Loan idea isn't quite cooked yet.

QUESTION 93

DO I NEED HOMEOWNER'S INSURANCE? WHAT SHOULD IT COVER?

If you need a loan to buy your home, you will be required to purchase homeowner's, or hazard, insurance. The reason is simple: Lenders want to know that you're protecting their investment from harm. When you take out a mortgage, you're pledging your home as collateral for the loan. The papers you sign say that if you default on the mortgage, the lender may begin foreclosure proceedings and take over the home. The lender's primary goal is protecting the value of the home. Issues of concern to the lender are damage by fire, water, tornado, flood, or a tree crashing in through the roof. Let's say you have no insurance, you have a $100,000 loan, and there's a fire. In a few hours, the lender's $100,000 has disappeared in a puff of smoke.

There's almost no way (unless you have seller financing and the seller either foolishly or unwittingly fails to insist on it) that you'll get a mortgage without having to purchase enough home or hazard insurance to cover at least the amount of money the lender has given you. (You'll have to bring to the closing a piece of paper that says you've purchased a policy for at least a year, and that it's effective on the day of closing or earlier.)

Even without the mortgage requirement, you should carry homeowner's insurance. In addition to the mortgage, you likely have a significant personal investment in your home. On a $100,000 property, you may have put down $10,000 to $20,000 in cash. You may have paid between $3,000 to $5,000 in closing costs. Plus, you may have decorated the interior of the home, or renovated, or built an addition. You have personal possessions. What goes up in flames can be worth double or triple what you actually owe the lender.

20/20 hindsight

The amount of homeowner's insurance you carry should cover the cost of replacing your home *today*, not when you bought it 5, 10, 20, or even 35 years ago. If you are doing a lease with an option to buy, carry renter's insurance that would cover the cost of replacing your personal possessions if they become damaged, stolen, or destroyed in some kind of catastrophe. As part of the option agreement, require the owner to carry enough homeowner's insurance to rebuild the house to current building code should it burn to the ground before you pick up your option. Make sure you see a copy of the policy and paid premium before you move into the property.

Condos and co-ops have different types of insurance because the property's common elements—a hallway, an interior staircase, the elevators, the roof, a laundry room, or landscaping in common areas—must be covered separately. Typically, co-op or condo associations will hold a building insurance policy that covers the common elements of the property and will satisfy your lender's desire for a "building policy." But don't be confused. This policy does not cover you. You will still need a separate policy that meets your lender's requirements as well as your own.

What Kind of Insurance Is Available?

The insurance industry offers this assortment for homeowners:

Type	Coverage
HO2	Most perils, except floods, earthquakes, war, and nuclear accidents
HO3	All known perils (with a few exclusions)
HO4	Renter's insurance. Similar in scope to HO2, but geared toward renters, not homeowners
HO6	Homeowner's insurance for condos and co-ops
HO8	Special insurance for older homes, but rarely used

Why haven't I included HO1, HO5, and HO7 coverage? According to the Insurance Information Institute, they are no longer used. HO1 provided limited, bare-bones coverage and is no longer being offered in most states. HO2 is also quite limited. HO3 is the most popular type of coverage for homeowners.

Choosing the Best Kind of Coverage

In some ways, homeowner's insurance is the easiest type of insurance to purchase. You basically decide (1) what you want to cover and (2) how much you're willing to pay as the deductible amount on any claim. These items will dovetail into a policy that's right for you.

What kind of coverage should you get? Most people purchase a general policy that covers the house and its contents. Condominium and co-op owners need their own unique policies, but they still cover the unit and its contents.

Homeowner's Insurance Perils

According to the Insurance Information Institute (III.org), a nonprofit information group for the property/casualty insurance industry, your homeowner's policy should cover the following 16 listed perils (a *peril* is the calamity from which you're trying to protect yourself):

1. Fire or lightning
2. Windstorm or hail
3. Explosion
4. Riot or civil commotion
5. Damage by aircraft
6. Damage by car
7. Smoke
8. Vandalism and malicious mischief
9. Theft
10. Volcanic eruption
11. Falling objects
12. Weight of ice, snow, or sleet
13. Accidental discharge or overflow of water or steam from within a plumbing, heating, air-conditioning, or automatic fire-protective sprinkler system, or from a household appliance
14. Sudden and accidental tearing apart, cracking, burning, or bulging of a steam or hot water heating system, an air-conditioning system, or an automatic fire-protection system
15. Freezing of a plumbing, heating, air-conditioning, or automatic fire-protection sprinkler system, or of a household appliance
16. Sudden and accidental damage from artificially generated electrical current (does not include loss of a tube, transistor, or similar electronic component)

Floods, earthquakes, and mud slides are never covered on a regular homeowner's policy. A "riot of civil commotion" may or may not be covered. Since the September 11, 2001, terrorist attacks, terrorism insurance has become an issue in some places. If you want coverage, you'll have to purchase separate insurance to cover each of these risks. A "land disturbance" may or may not be covered. What about a chemical or paint spill? Damage from wild animals? Backed-up sewers and drains? Bloodstains? Scorching without fire? What about the additional living expenses you'll have to pay if your home is demolished and must be rebuilt? Be sure to ask. And be sure to get the answer in writing.

Comparing Policies

When comparing policies, look at the deductible, what's covered, and what type of coverage you're buying. *Replacement insurance* guarantees that the insurer will pay for the cost of replacing the home as it stands today, up to the amount of your coverage. *Guaranteed cost replacement* coverage guarantees to rebuild your home no matter what the cost and has a rider built in to take care of inflation. A *cash-value* policy will reimburse you based only on your property's current market value—not what it would cost to build it new. Today, guaranteed cost replacement has been somewhat limited. Insurers might only pay to rebuild your home up to 120 to 125 percent of your policy amount. It's up to you to stay on top of how much it will cost to rebuild your home.

Replacement cost insurance for contents may only reimburse you for the actual, depreciated value of the items. If you paid $2,000 for a sofa 10 years ago, and the insurance company says it's only worth $1,000 today, but it will cost $3,000 to purchase another one just like it, you'll have to cough up the extra cash to buy a new one.

Pay attention to the cost-per-square-foot calculations your insurance company uses. They might estimate replacing your home will cost only $60 per square foot. In reality, only the cheapest of construction costs that little. Replacing your home the way it is, with all the tile, hardwood floors, wallpaper, marble, and granite you may have will cost far more. A more realistic estimate is $125 to $200 per square foot, depending on where you live. For a high-end home, expect to pay upward of $225 per square foot.

Other Types of Coverage

Some places call it *code-and-contention* coverage, and others call it *building code* coverage. Still others call it an *ordinance-and-law* rider. Either way, the intent is to cover the cost of meeting new building codes that may have gone into effect after your home was built and that apply to any new homes. If you lack code coverage, your insurer will probably only pay what it would cost to rebuild your old home in its original condition. Because you can't do that, you'll pay the rest to bring the house up to code. Some companies include code coverage in their basic policies, but if you don't ask, you won't know.

If changes in zoning have occurred, you may be out of luck—unless you have zoning coverage. For example, if you live in a beach house and the zoning law was changed to restrict any new development on the beach, and your home burns down, you might find yourself unable to rebuild on your site. That's where zoning insurance kicks in. It ensures you can rebuild where you want to go. The policy should state that you can build your exact house, no matter what the cost, on a different lot. If it doesn't, choose another policy.

You should also have a policy that covers the cost of replacing your foundation. (Seems obvious, but some insurance companies don't include it.) A *personal articles rider* is the official name for extra coverage of your expensive jewelry and fine art. Make sure you have current appraisals to support your claim. And don't forget home office coverage. If you run a business out of your home, you'll need a rider to cover that business.

20/20 hindsight

If you have a home office, you may also need special liability coverage for your home-based business. Check with your insurance agent about adding an umbrella rider to your homeowner's policy for additional liability coverage.

first time buyer tip

Pictures speak louder than words. If your home is destroyed, the last thing you'll want to do is try to prove what you owned and when you bought it. Take a video camera and record everything in your home. Make sure you date it with a current newspaper in the screen, and then go around your home, inside and out. Back up the video with close-ups of jewelry, furs, rugs, and fine art. Put the tape, the photos, and any appraisals in a safe-deposit box outside your home.

They Want to Know *What?*

When you contact an insurance agent to get a homeowner's insurance policy (or if you do it via the Web), you'll need to provide the insurer with some basic information about your home. Here are some of the questions you'll be asked:

1. What is the complete address of your home (or the home you'll be buying)?

2. What is your home made of? (Homes made of aluminum siding or shingles are typically considered to be made of wood.)

3. Is your home one story? Two stories? Split level? Other?

4. How many rooms are there?

5. What is the listing price of your home? What was the purchase price?

6. How old is your home? When was it built? What kinds of major improvements does it have (like a new roof, or new mechanicals)?

7. What is the square footage of your home? (Multiply the length by the width and then multiply that number by the number of livable stories. Typically attics and basements don't count.)

8. How far away is the nearest fire department? How about the nearest fire hydrant?

9. Does the home have security devices, including smoke detectors, alarm systems, security lighting, dead-bolt locks, or carbon monoxide detectors?

10. Is your home located on a floodplain?

11. Are there other structures on the property (like a garage, guest house, or cabana)?

12. Do you own a dog?

13. Do you have any valuable jewelry, fine art, furs, antiques, or silverware? Do you typically keep large amounts of cash in the house? (You may need special insurance riders to protect these items.)

14. What kind of deductible do you want to pay? (The higher the deductible, the lower your premium.)

15. Do you have a business on the premises? (Typically, homeowner's insurance policies either don't include a home-based

business or have extremely low coverage. If you have a business based at home, you may want to purchase a home business rider or a rider for your computers and other electronic devices.)

16. How much liability insurance do you want? (Typically, home-owner's policies include a certain amount of liability coverage. But in these litigious times, you may prefer increased coverage.)

By knowing the answers to these questions ahead of time, you'll speed up the time it takes to find the best deal.

Discounts and Deductions

Although homeowner's insurance is getting more expensive (a direct result of a spate of disasters in recent years where insurance companies took huge losses), there are ways to cut down on your costs. If you move or refinance, you might be tempted to poke around and see what else is out there. If you've got a good record, you should find plenty of options. You might even cut your premium by up to 35 to 50 percent. Here are some ideas:

1. Shop around. Once you have insurance, you'll be tempted to stay the course unless something happens, but you may be able to lower your premiums simply by shopping around. If you can't lower them, at least you'll feel good knowing you got the best deal. Direct writers of homeowner's insurance include American Express (800-535-2001), Amica (800-242-6422), GEICO (for auto, home, or boat insurance, 800-841-3000), and USAA (800-531-8100). They do their selling over the phone and if you qualify, you'll save, big time, on the commissions. Even with a great policy, you might be able to drop your premium further with one of the ideas given here.

2. Raise your deductible. Some insurance companies will drop you if you make more than two claims in a year. Make sure your insurance covers you for the catastrophes and plan on picking up the cost of the everyday expenses. Raising your deductible from $250 to $500 might enable you to shave 12 percent off your premiums. Raise your deductible to $1,000 and your savings may double.

3. Tout your improvements. If you've put on a new roof, and it's made of a flame-repellent material, you might've earned yourself a discount. A new plumbing system, new wiring, or a new heating system might also qualify.

4. Get connected. A home security system might qualify for a small discount of 3 to 5 percent. But connect it to the local police and fire station, and you might lower your premium by up to 15 percent annually. If you put in a sprinkler system or smoke detectors, you might get smaller discounts.

5. Grow old. If you're over the age of 55, you can probably get a discount.

6. Educate yourself. Your insurance company may offer an education program or brochures that will allow you to lower your premium once you've attended or read the material.

7. Buy your home and auto policy from the same insurer. Some companies that sell homeowner's, auto, and liability coverage will take 5 to 15 percent off your premium if you buy two or more policies from them.*

8. Insure your home, not the land it sits on. If a tree falls in your backyard, chances are it won't hurt anything except the grass. Don't include the value of your land when figuring out how much homeowner's insurance you need.

9. Stop smoking. The Insurance Information Institute says smoking accounts for more than 23,000 residential fires a year. Quit. Not only will you save on your homeowner's insurance, but you'll probably save a bundle on health insurance (and health-related costs, not to mention the cost of the tobacco products you won't have to buy over your lifetime).

10. Is group coverage an option? Professional, nonprofit, and alumni organizations often offer discounts for association members.

11. Stick around. If you've kept your coverage with the same insurer for years, you should ask for special consideration. Some companies will give discounts of up to 6 percent if you've been a policyholder for six years or more.

12. Look around. Your home is an appreciating asset; some items in your home are depreciating as the years go by. If you've purchased special riders for certain items, you may be able to reduce your coverage if they've lost their value. If you've sold items covered by riders, instruct your insurance company to remove the rider from your policy.

---

*Some states don't allow discounts on premiums. Why? Most likely it's because the state insurance lobby is strong, and deductions lower the insurers' profits. Ah, politics.

13. If all else fails, move. According to a study by the nonprofit Insurance Research Council, it costs insurers 42 percent more to cover losses in the city than it does to settle claims for those who live five miles outside the city limits. City dwellers may be paying double the amount that nearby suburbanites pay for their insurance. Before you put your home up for sale, however, consider this: The 6 percent sales commission you'll likely pay to sell your home would more than make up the difference in city-vs.-suburb insurance premiums for a long, long time.

web

resources

The Insurance Information Institute publishes a small book called "How to Get Your Money's Worth in Auto and Home Insurance," which describes the process of buying the proper insurance coverage. Contact them online at iii.org.

Floods and Earthquakes

If you live in a floodplain (check with the local municipality for floodplain information), your lender will require you to have flood insurance. You can only buy basic flood insurance from the government, although most agents sell the policies. The average cost is about $300 for $100,000 worth of coverage, and the maximum limit as this book went to press is $250,000 for the structure of your home and $100,000 for the contents. Finished basements are not covered by federal flood insurance policies, except for basics like the washer, dryer, furnace, and air-conditioning units. You'll take the loss on any carpeting and wood paneling, not to mention items you may have stored, in your basement. The cost of your policy depends on the value of your home, construction costs, and where your home is located. (If it's close to a shoreline, you'll pay a lot more for your policy.)

Frankly, flood insurance is about the cheapest kind of insurance you can purchase, and it's well worth the few hundred bucks you'll spend, since your regular homeowner's insurance won't cover anything if you get flooded because of a rising body of water, and that includes an 18-inch rainstorm. (If your basement floods because your sump pump failed, your regular insurance company will probably pay, though you'll want to ask your insurance agent to be sure.) Still, only 20 percent of folks who live in a floodplain have flood insurance.

For details about flood insurance and referrals to agents, call the Federal Emergency Management Agency (FEMA) at 800-427-4661, or check out its website at fema.gov.

Earthquakes

Earthquake insurance, unlike flood insurance, is offered through private insurers, typically as added coverage (called an *endorsement*). But the recent spate of earthquakes has made this insurance very difficult to buy and relatively expensive. This helps to explain why only about 10 percent of homeowners living in earthquake areas actually have earthquake insurance. You can purchase earthquake insurance through your insurance agent, though it is not available everywhere (by law, insurers in California must offer earthquake insurance). The cost depends on where you live (whether you are close to a fault line), what type of home you have, and whether the structure incorporates modern anti-earthquake technology. In some areas that are highly seismic (except California), earthquake coverage may not be available at any price.

Some Final Thoughts

When you put together your final homeowner's policy, don't forget these items:

- **College may not be covered.** Some policies cover your kid's stuff when he or she is away at school. Some don't. Be sure to ask. For a few extra dollars, you can get a rider that will fully cover Junior, plus all the hotshot computer equipment he's bringing with him, against things that happen in a college environment.

- **Make sure your stuff is fully insured.** Most policies will reimburse you up to half the face value of your policy. If you have a $300,000 homeowner's policy, most insurers will pay up to $150,000 for you to replace your personal belongings. If that's not enough, investigate additional coverage to fill the gap.

- **Under the umbrella.** The general liability portion of a regular homeowner's policy is pretty small. Consider getting additional coverage that will give you an overriding umbrella liability policy—just in case.

• **Don't make this mistake.** As the years go on, make sure you continue to update your policy to reflect the true cost of rebuilding your home. For a regular house that doesn't include perks like granite countertops in the kitchen and limestone bathroom tile, you should expect to spend $100 to $175 per square foot to rebuild and refurnish your home. That means, if you buy a 2,500-square-foot house today, and it burns to the ground tomorrow, the cost to rebuild your home, to current building standards, could range from $250,000 to over $430,000—even if you paid less than that to purchase it. If your home does have the granite countertops, four or five bathrooms, or a fancy kitchen, you can expect to pay $200 to $400 per square foot, or $500,000 to $1 million. Will it always be this much? If you live in a small town, or in a condominium or co-op, you may pay less. Live in an expensive city, and you can expect to pay more.

HOW SHOULD I HOLD TITLE TO MY NEW HOME?

When Janet and Scott bought a house in a suburb north of Chicago, they wondered how they should hold title. Scott, a pediatrician just starting his own practice, was well aware of the litigious nature of society. Industry statistics tell him that he is likely to be targeted in a medical malpractice suit over the course of his career as a doctor. Scott was worried someone could sue him and take away their home.

Other homeowners have the same concerns. Whatever business you're in, there may come a time when your home may be in jeopardy. If you declare bankruptcy, your creditors may be able to attach a lien against your house, possibly even forcing you to sell it. There may be a judgment against you. *The time to think about how to protect your home, your largest investment to date, is now, before you buy it.*

How you *hold title*—that is, the ownership of your real estate—is important. Often, the way in which you hold title is an afterthought. In many cases, buyers aren't even asked what their preference is.

If you're married, you often get joint tenancy with rights of survivorship. If you're single, you hold property in your own name.

But there are other ways of holding title that might help you in certain situations.

For example, should something go wrong, and one spouse or partner gets sued professionally, how you and your spouse or partner own your home can mean the difference between the house's being sold to pay off a judgment, and you being allowed to live there until you choose to sell.

Your ownership of your home and other assets can have important estate considerations as well.

When it comes to holding title, all things aren't equal for married spouses and those partners who are unmarried. In many situations, unmarried partners will need to consult with an estate planner or real estate attorney to make sure their interests are protected under state law.

Here are some ways you may hold title to your home and the effect it may have on your estate.

Individuals

If you're a single person, your options for holding title to your home are rather limited. You may hold title to your property as an individual, or you may hold it in one of a variety of trusts.

If you hold the property in your own name and a creditor comes after you, the creditor may be able to force the sale of your home to pay off your debt. If you die while holding property in your own name, even if you name your heir in your will, your will (and the property you own) will go through probate and be subject to probate fees.

If you're an individual, the best way to avoid probate is to put your property in a trust. You might also ask your tax or estate attorney if a corporation or limited liability company might be a good choice.

Joint Tenancy

Joint tenancy with rights of survivorship is the most common way married couples hold property, but two nonrelated individuals may also own a piece of property as joint tenants.

The nice thing about joint tenancy is that it allows you and the co-owner to each own the property as a whole. If you own property as joint tenants with rights of survivorship, your share in the property is immediately transferred to your surviving spouse or partner upon your death. Your share is subject, however, to any debts, claims, and expenses you've left behind.

You should also consider the estate planning issues of how your surviving partner will inherit your half of the property. Depending on state law, your spouse would inherit your half (married couples are usually assumed to own property equally) at a stepped-up basis. Your half of the property would be revalued on the day you die, and your spouse would inherit it at its current value.

If you and your surviving partner are not married, the property would be divided based on how much each partner contributed to the purchase of the property. For example, if you each contributed 50 percent of the cost, then your surviving partner would inherit your half of the property and get the stepped-up basis.

If you can't prove how much each of you contributed, state law may attribute total ownership to the partner who dies first. That may have serious estate implications. Consult an estate or tax attorney for more details.

The key words to look for when considering joint tenancy are "with rights of survivorship."

Tenancy in Common

Tenancy in common allows each person to own his or her piece of the same property separately.

For example, you may own 40 percent, your spouse or partner may own 40 percent, and your parents may own 20 percent, but each co-owner may use and enjoy the whole property. You can't be restricted to using just the 40 percent of the property that you own. And you may sell your share of the property to anyone you choose, just like you might sell stock in a corporation.

Tenancy in common is available to married couples or to two or more individuals, although it's not usually used for property purchased by married couples. When you die, your share of the property goes through probate before it is distributed according to your will.

Tenancy by the Entirety

Tenancy by the entirety is similar to joint tenancy in that it has rights of survivorship. However, it is only available to married couples.

The key difference between tenancy by the entirety and joint tenancy is this: If you own property as tenants by the entirety, both spouses must agree before the property becomes subject to one spouse's creditors.

Neither spouse alone can do anything that would create a claim or lien on the marital property. As long as the couple is married, and owns the property, tenancy by the entirety protects the interest of each spouse in the marital home.

For example, if your spouse gets sued, the creditors could not force the sale of the residence, because you and your spouse each own the whole property. The creditors would have to wait until the marriage is severed, or the other spouse consents to the claim, or the property is sold. Once the property is sold, a claim can be attached to the proceeds.

Tenancy by the entirety is not available in every state. Again, it is only for married couples.

Think About a Trust

The only way you can avoid probate is to put your property into a trust. Here are some alternative ways to hold title that may also affect important estate planning issues.

Land Trust   A land trust is a legal creation. The sole asset in the trust is the property you are buying, and you are the beneficiary of the trust.

At one time, a land trust might have been used to obscure the identity of the beneficiary. Today, that veil has largely been lifted. Individuals, two or more buyers, married couples, and children may be the beneficiaries of a land trust.

There are no estate tax advantages to a land trust, and it is not available in every state, but if there is a successor beneficiary, the property will pass directly to that individual, avoiding probate.

Qualified Personal Residence Trust (QPRT)   This is another type of trust that allows you to discount the future value of your home and possibly save on the gift and estate taxes you'd otherwise owe.

Here's how it works. You set the term of the trust, and place your home into it. You're allowed to live in the home for the term of the trust. The beneficiaries of the trust (your heirs) will receive the home when the term of the trust expires.

If you put your house in a QPRT for five years, your beneficiaries will own your house at the end of the five years. If you're still living, and want to stay in your home, you'll have to rent it.

The benefit of a QPRT is that the IRS allows you to discount the future value of the house according to a preset schedule. You'll pay gift tax on a much lower amount, which will cost you less than the estate tax.

If, however, you die before the QPRT term expires, the property reverts back to you. You'll be credited for any gift taxes you've paid, but you will have lost the fee you paid to an attorney to set up the QPRT.

If you survive the term, however, a QPRT can be helpful in planning your estate. Typically, you are allowed to set up only two QPRTs, one for your primary residence and a second for a vacation home.

Living Trust   A revocable living trust is another way to pass assets from one generation to another and avoid probate.

You set up a trust, and then transfer assets, such as your home or stocks, into the trust. You may name beneficiaries and leave a list of instructions for the trustee who will administer the trust.

For many people, trusts take the place of wills. Also, living trusts aren't public documents, so the privacy aspect is appealing.

But because you retain complete control of the assets in a living trust, it does nothing to lower the estate taxes you may eventually owe.

Family Limited Partnership

By creating a family limited partnership, parents can pass along pieces of their property to their children (or anyone else) by making them small limited partners of a partnership that owns the property.

Limited partners traditionally don't manage the property or have an active role in it. This limited role (hence the name) allows you to discount their share of ownership, which results in lower estate and gift taxes when the property is transferred.

Another value to a family limited partnership is that it allows individuals to give property to their heirs over time, in small amounts, which is less expensive than deeding over small pieces of a particular property.

Unless you own a large ranch, plantation, or other significant residential property, you probably wouldn't use a family limited partnership. Traditionally, they're used to pass down commercial, industrial, or other types of real estate.

Estate Considerations

If you're unsure about the best way to hold title to your property, consult with a real estate attorney, estate planning attorney, or accountant, who can explain the ins and outs of each type of ownership. There may be some very real reasons to go one way or another, and you should be thoroughly informed before you close on your home. One reason might be the amount of total assets you and your spouse or partner own. Although you may want to share title equally with your spouse, if you have joint assets that exceed $1.25 million (going to $2 million in 2006), holding property as joint tenants may not be the economically savvy choice. Tax-wise, or estate-wise, it may be better for you to own the property on your own, or to place it into a trust. Emotionally, it may be difficult for you and your spouse to accept an unequal ownership of assets. For detailed explanations, your financial planner can help you work through the various options.

Community Property States

Finally, community property states are Arizona, California, Idaho, Louisiana, Nevada, New Mexico, Texas, Washington, and Wisconsin. If you live in a community property state, and are married, every asset you purchase during the marriage is assumed to be owned equally between you and your spouse.

Let's say you purchase a house as an investment during the course of your marriage. Only your name is on the deed. When you die, your spouse is assumed to own half of that property. The ownership of the property is divided equally between your spouse and your estate.

Very special issues are involved with community property, especially if you move to a state that doesn't allow it. Check with your estate attorney or estate planner for details.

11

The Closing

WHO SHOULD ATTEND THE CLOSING?
WHAT SHOULD I DO IF I CAN'T BE THERE?

The closing contains some of the most important legal contracts you'll sign. You're promising to pay thousands of dollars for a place to call home. I'm willing to bet that this will be the largest single investment of your life, which is why it's probably a good idea for you to attend the closing.

(If you live in an escrow state, like California, you may not have a "closing" the way it is described here. You may give a list of instructions to the escrow company, and then go in and sign all of the documents described here. The seller will also go in, usually separately, to the escrow company with a list of instructions and sign the documents. When the lists of instructions have been completed, the escrow company will conduct the actual closing, then call you to come and pick up the keys to the house. Usually this happens on a preset day, but it could happen at any time within a two- to three-week period.)

For a buyer, a closing is like a command performance. All of the buyers—that means you, your spouse if you have one, or any partners who are going into the transaction with you—must attend. There are two compelling reasons for you to attend: (1) you have to sign your name a dozen or more times on various documents, and (2) you have to read those documents to make sure everything is in order.

Who else generally attends the closing? If you're in a state where attorneys are involved, your attorney and the seller's attorney will generally be there. Also, the seller broker and the subagent or buyer broker (who are very interested in making sure everything goes smoothly up until the final papers are signed and the final checks—including theirs—are cut) will often attend. There will generally be a title officer (if you are closing at a title company) or other closing agent, and there may be a representative from the lender. Sometimes the lender will bring along an attorney. Whether the sellers attend is up to them. You need to be present to sign documents, but sellers' documents can be signed ahead of time.

Even when you mark your calendar two to three months in advance, there can be a last-minute scheduling conflict with the closing. An important business trip comes up, or someone gets sick, or perhaps a family member passes away and you want to attend the funeral in another state. Whatever comes up, call your attorney and see if you can juggle the closing date. It may be possible, especially if the seller already owns another home, or the seller is taking back financing or moving to an interim home before going to a permanent residence. Moving the closing up or back a few days is the least onerous way to deal with a scheduling conflict.

If you cannot change the date of closing—if, for example, the seller is closing on his or her new property that same day and requires the proceeds from the sale—then consider assigning a *power of attorney* to someone who can step into your shoes and sign your name legally at the closing. A power of attorney is the legal right you give someone (usually your attorney) to act on your behalf. Usually it is limited to a single transaction, but an elderly parent or relative may give a power of attorney when he or she is no longer able to manage his or her affairs.

When you are purchasing your home, you're better off giving the power of attorney to someone who is familiar with the transaction. If the only person who knows the details is your attorney, and he or she is willing to accept that designation, then that's who should have it. If a friend or family member is familiar with the transaction, then that person should be designated.

In most cases, it's not smart to give your real estate broker the power of attorney. Many brokers work for and represent the seller, so there's a potential conflict of interest. You wouldn't give power of attorney to the seller, but if you gave it to the seller broker, in effect you would be doing just that. If your broker is a buyer broker, then you may want to discuss power of attorney. But remember, no matter who the broker represents, he or she is not a disinterested third party. In most cases, the broker has a significant amount of money riding on the outcome of the closing. If something comes up at closing (see Question 97), you want the person with power of attorney to look out for your best interests, not his or her own.

Find out ahead of time whether your lender will allow your documents to be signed with a power of attorney. Ask what power-of-attorney form is required. Many lenders will not accept power-of-attorney signatures on their documents. In that case, you'll need to presign your document if, for whatever reason, you can't attend the closing.

WHAT ARE PRORATIONS?

Let's say that Ginny makes an offer to purchase Maureen and Mike's home. In the two months up until the closing, some bills come due that must be paid. Maureen and Mike pay the water bill (which comes every six months), the second installment of real estate taxes (they're due in March and September), and the gas bill (which comes once every two months). On the day of closing, Maureen and Mike's attorney tells Ginny the dollar amount on her share of these prorated expenses.

Almost every closing has some costs prorated, simply because we don't pay for our housing needs on a daily basis. Can you imagine trucking on down to the county clerk's office to pay your real estate taxes *every day*? What about your electric bills? Water bill? Association dues? Many of these costs are spread out over a long period of time. Depending on where you live, you pay your real estate taxes once or twice a year. It isn't fair for Maureen and Mike to have paid an entire year's worth of property taxes, if they live in the house for only nine months of that year before selling to Ginny. Likewise, if Ginny bought the home just before the second installment of taxes was due, it wouldn't be fair for her to pay for six months of taxes, when she would only have three months in the home.

A little bit of math evens things out for everyone. How do you calculate prorations? Identify the number of days covered by the bill and then divide the bill by that number of days. That gives you a daily fee. Then multiply by the number of days up to and including the closing.

For example, let's say Maureen and Mike's property taxes are $2,000 for the year, broken into two installments of $1,000 each, half due on March 15 and the other half due on September 15. Each $1,000 represents 183 days per year (it's actually 182.5, but we'll round up).

$$\$1,000 \div 183 = \$5.46 \text{ per day}$$

If the closing is on September 16, Maureen and Mike have already paid the real estate property taxes for the rest of the year. At closing, Ginny would have to reimburse them each day, to year-end, that she's going to live in the house. From September 17 to the end of the year is 106 days. Multiply 106 by the $5.46 daily fee:

$$106 \text{ days} \times \$5.46 \text{ daily fee} = \$578.76$$

Ginny would owe Maureen and Mike $578.76 at closing. The calculation can work in reverse also. Let's say the closing is on September 14. On September 15, Ginny pays the $1,000 real estate tax bill. From July 1 to September 14 is 76 days. Multiply 76 by the $5.46 daily fee:

$$76 \text{ days} \times \$5.46 \text{ daily fee} = \$414.96$$

If the closing was on September 14, Maureen and Mike would owe Ginny $414.96 for their share of property taxes.

Asking for a Bit More

In some states, it's common to ask the previous owners to pay a little extra in real estate taxes above the daily fee, because in many areas property taxes rise each year and the exact amount for the next bill may not be known. Instead of asking for the daily fee multiplied by the number of days, the buyer may ask the seller to put up 110 percent of the daily fee to cover any increases. In our example, the daily fee of $5.46 would be increased to $6.01 to cover any increase in taxes.

Your real estate attorney (or your broker, if you're in a state where attorneys are not used for house closings) will calculate prorations for every bill that has some sort of shared time arrangement, including gas bills, water bills, assessments to homeowners' associations, and real estate taxes. This also includes any insurance policies (above and beyond hazard insurance required by the lender) or service agreements the buyer will have to pay for. Any bill can be prorated using basic math.

(Generally, telephone service is shut off when an owner vacates a home, and the new owners must start their own account. The local electric company will generally change the name on the service the day of closing and then begin billing the new owners.)

Some attorneys draw up a reproration agreement. If the sellers reimburse the buyer for more than the actual bill, sometimes the buyer and seller agree to recalculate the bill to reflect the actual amount paid. Here's how it works: If you thought the bill was going to be $100 and the seller's share was 25 percent, the seller would have paid you $25. But if the actual bill ends up being only $80, the seller's share is only $20, so you would owe the seller $5 (which is paid after closing when the recalculation is done.)

Local custom dictates who pays for, and who receives the benefit for, the day of closing. Your attorney, broker, or closing agent should be able to advise you on local customs.

Yet Another Escrow Account

Sometimes proration money is kept in escrow (by a disinterested third party), but this usually happens only with substantial amounts of money. The escrow manager then makes payments to the buyer based on the bills that come in and will return any extra money to the seller. The important thing with prorations is that the seller must pay all of his or her costs before closing is complete. Otherwise, you may have to chase the seller to get your fair share.

QUESTION 97

WHAT DO I NEED TO BRING WITH ME TO THE CLOSING? WHAT IF SOMETHING GOES WRONG AT THE CLOSING?

The simple answer, "Bring yourself," won't quite do here. You also need to bring money. You could bring cash, but the preferred methods are a cashier's or certified check. You must also bring your homeowner's insurance certificate (to prove you have it) and any documents the lender requires (these should have been spelled out in the commitment for the loan).

On the day before the closing, check with your attorney to see how much money you should have the check made out for. It's not a disaster if you bring too much, as the title company can cut a check to you for the difference. The problem comes if you have too little. In that case, you may find the closing stretched out as you run all over town trying to convert a personal check into a cashier's check. You may also wire transfer funds, but you'll need to get the proper information to know where, and to what account, to wire the money. And bring a favorite pen. You'll be signing your name quite a few times.

> Usually the check you bring to the closing can be made out to your name and endorsed to the title company at closing.

What If Something Goes Wrong at the Closing?

Just when you think you've crossed the finish line, it seems to move farther away. That's what closing feels like sometimes. You solve one problem and another crops up. And another. And another.

When Janet bought her condo, she discovered that the loan amount on the loan document was incorrect. And then she noticed some of the documentation didn't have her correct address! Leo and Genna's loan agreement also had an incorrect amount. At the last minute, the developer who built Bart and Michelle's town house refused to put $1,500 into escrow to cover the sod and landscaping that was supposed to be part of the deal. One buyer refused to close on a condo for 24 hours because the sellers—who didn't live there anymore—couldn't find their mailbox key.

There are at least 10 reasons why a closing doesn't happen, is delayed for a few days, or is stretched out:

1. Money problems. Money problems are one of the most frequent reasons home sales may not close on time. For example, if you're transferring money by wire, it's always a possibility that the money will get tied up, or there will be a delay in the processing of the wire transfer. Sometimes the numbers don't add up and a buyer will find that he or she is short. Lenders and title companies don't take personal checks, so you may have to run across town to get that personal check converted into a certified or cashier's check.

375

2. Missing loan package. If the lender's documents aren't there, you're not closing. If the loan package has to come from out of state, and it's shipped via overnight delivery, it's always possible that the package will be lost or delayed. If the loan package is missing documents, they may have to be sent by messenger or faxed over to the closing. In addition to adding more time, the lender may try to charge you for the messenger service or even for use of the fax. You should vigorously deny these charges, particularly if it was the lender who made the mistake.

3. Disagreement about documents. Read all of the documents carefully. The loan company may try to slip something in or make changes to the documents you didn't agree to.

4. Incorrect loan documents. Nothing can create problems like incorrect information on loan documents. Check to be sure that you're actually getting the amount of money you agreed to and that your address, phone number, and other personal information are correct. Be certain the interest rate is correct. Bring inconsistencies and wrong information to the lender's attention. New documents may have to be drawn up, or the lender may try to get by with correction fluid.

5. Last-minute requests. Sometimes the lender will make a last-minute request for documentation at the closing. At Leo and Genna's closing, the lender requested a copy of the canceled deposit check. To safeguard against time-wrenching delays, it's a good idea to bring everything with you to the closing.

6. Walk-through problems. If you do the final walk-through (ideally, after the seller has moved out) and find that some items are missing or damaged, it must be brought up at the closing. This is the time to negotiate with the seller (or the seller's attorney or broker, if the seller is not at the closing) for remuneration. You and the seller should agree to a settlement before you close.

7. Title problems. Sometimes last-minute title problems creep up. A long-lost relative turns up, or the title company discovers the real estate taxes haven't been paid. A contractor may have filed a mechanic's lien. You should insist that these title issues are resolved before you'll close on the home. You don't want to inherit someone else's problems.

8. Someone dies. It doesn't happen too often, but you should know what can happen if either you or the seller dies after the contract is signed and before closing. If the seller dies after signing the contract, the estate must go through with the sale. However, it may be difficult to close on time, particularly if the seller dies close to the day of closing, or if the estate is in probate court. If the buyer dies, the seller may be able to force the estate to continue with the sale, although in the real world, sellers may not force the issue. Check with an attorney for further details about your rights in your state.

9. Catastrophe strikes. In the days (or should I say, nights) before closing, nearly every first-time buyer has a nightmare about his or her new home being destroyed before the paperwork is finalized. Fire, flood, earthquake, lightning—you name it. What happens if a fire actually consumes the home you're supposed to purchase tomorrow? In most cases, depending on what the contract says, you wouldn't have to close if something major happened to the home. Or you can elect to close and take the insurance proceeds (after the seller's lender has been paid off—if the home is underinsured, that could mean little or nothing for you). If you have already taken possession of the home when disaster strikes, you may lose the right to terminate the purchase and be forced to close. Again, have your attorney advise you of your rights.

10. Seller's deal falls through. Usually, sellers take the money from the sale of their home and use it to pay for another home. Your seller is likely to do the same. But if the seller's deal (for any number of reasons) falls through, he or she may have no place to go and might have second thoughts about the closing. In other words, the seller might refuse to vacate the home. If this happens, you have three options: (1) don't close until he or she moves out; (2) close and force the seller out, which is emotionally, physically, and legally difficult; or (3) hold back money from the closing to ensure that the seller gets out by a certain time, and attach a stiff daily penalty for every day he or she remains in the home. And make that incentive *very* stiff, so the seller will want to move rather than stay. The daily penalty should be so stiff that it would be cheaper for the seller to put all of his or her belongings in storage and go to a hotel.

Timing the Closing

How long should the closing last? As we discussed earlier, most closings take less than an hour. One attorney estimates that 10 percent of his closings take less than a half hour. An additional 50 percent take less than an hour. Another 30 percent take less than an hour and a half. Ten percent take less than two hours. So 90 percent of all closings happen in less than two hours. And the final 10 percent? Well, it could take 10 hours, or 10 days, or never happen at all. But most closings happen. And when it's over, and the last fire has been put out, you'll own your very own home.

Congratulations!

WHAT SHOULD I GET FROM THE SELLERS AT CLOSING?

You've signed your name so often your arm is about to drop off. You've tallied up the numbers, made fast and furious calls to your office to reassure them you're still living and breathing, and are wired from cup after cup of stale coffee. The last thing to do is to get the keys to your new home from the seller.

Keys are pretty important, and they require a bit of good faith. After all, when the seller hands you the keys at closing, you don't know if they work or not. You won't find out until much later, perhaps even next spring, that the seller forgot to give you the keys (or combination) to the toolshed lock. Or the combination on the bicycle room. Or the key to your storage locker.

If you're purchasing new construction, you may not get your keys at closing. The developer, or the developer's representative, will give you a letter indicating where keys can be picked up. Usually, the broker for the development will have the keys.

The seller is supposed to turn over all keys to the home at closing. This includes keys to the front- and back-door locks, any deadbolt locks, window locks, interior door locks, shed or storage room locks, or locks on any part of the property. The seller should also give you any combinations you need to open any locks on the property. Finally, mailbox keys and garage-door openers are supposed to be included.

And If They Don't Work?

Just in case your seller doesn't have any good faith left at the end of closing, the brokers (if you used one) can be marshaled in to help the situation. If the brokers have participated, it's likely that they have a set of working keys. They should give you those keys to the home, which you can then use to check against the keys the seller has given you. If the seller refuses to turn over the keys, perhaps your first call should be to the local locksmith.

> Have your attorney or broker make sure the seller has brought all of his or her keys to the closing.

Sam once had a closing where the sellers had moved out of state several months earlier. The seller broker had the condo keys, and the sellers left their mailbox key with a neighbor. On the day of closing, the buyer refused to close until the mailbox key had been delivered. The sellers, reached by telephone during the closing, told the buyer to call the neighbor. The buyer did call, but the neighbor wasn't there. After hemming and hawing for the better part of a day and a half, the buyer finally decided to have a locksmith come and make a new key for the mailbox. Fine. But he wanted the sellers to pay for the locksmith. The sellers refused. He closed anyway.

HOW DOES MY DEED GET RECORDED?

What is a deed? A deed is the physical manifestation of the title to your home. Holding title is an amorphous concept—it's not like holding a handful of dirt and saying, "I own this land." To give you something to show for your money and efforts, our legal system (based on the English system of real estate law) has sanctioned deeds, or pieces of paper, that say you own a specific piece of property at a specific address.

Part of the process to formalize your ownership is to record the deed. This gives legal recognition—in other words, puts the world on notice—of your ownership of the property. Anyone can go to the office of the recorder of deeds and find out that you own your home. The deed becomes part of the public record. And your ownership becomes part of the property's chain of title. If a title company looked up your property now, after the closing and after the deed has been recorded, your name would come up as the official owner.

Recording Your Deed

How does a deed get recorded? If you're closing at a title company, the title company may record the deed. Or the title company will deliver the deed to you, and you will have to take it to your local recorder of deeds office. It's as simple as that. But you want to make sure that the deed is recorded properly, and that your correct name, address, and other information are listed. When real estate tax bills are sent out, they are sent to the name and address listed at the recorder's or assessor's office. If there's a problem with your home or with your tax bill, a notice will be sent to the address listed at the recorder's or assessor's office. If the address, or your name, is incorrectly listed, you may never get your property tax bill or any notices, and you could lose your property.

Make sure your deed is recorded correctly and the information is listed correctly. Verify that the proper authorities have your correct address for tax bills. Mark down the days you're supposed to receive your tax bill (you should find this out at the closing). If you don't receive it, call the recorder's (or real estate tax bill collector's) office to find out why. Nonpayment of property taxes is an easy (and quick) way to lose your property. Make sure it doesn't happen to you.

My Story

In the preface to this book, I invite readers to contact me. Here's my e-mail address (ilyce@thinkglink.com), my website address (www.thinkglink. com), and my post office box (P.O. Box 366, Glencoe, Illinois 60022).

Years ago, when I first got this post office box, I used to receive tax bills for someone else's property. I normally receive a bucketful of mail (the post office employees laugh when I come to pick up my mail), so I sometimes just slit open every piece of mail first, and then look at it. That's how I accidentally came to open one of these real estate tax bills.

The property was located on the south side of Chicago. The address for the tax bill was listed as my box (under someone else's name).

Every six months, another tax bill would come. These I would return, unopened, since I now knew to look for that particular shape. One day, a different sort of letter came to the box. It was a notice from the assessor's office that the property was being auctioned for unpaid property taxes. A few months later, another notice came notifying the owner that the property had been sold.

In the last few years, I haven't received any notices for this property. Nor have I ever heard from the original owner. I have often wondered whether he thought about his property and what happened to it, or whether he simply lost track and forgot about it. I'll never know.

If you move out of your home, but keep it as an investment property, make sure to (1) change the address of your tax bill, and (2) keep paying your taxes. Otherwise, you could lose your home.

HOW SHOULD I PREPARE FOR THE MOVE TO MY NEW HOME?

QUESTION
100

If you feel as if you're the only family moving to a new house, maybe you don't know the right people. Nearly one out of every five families moves each year (this includes both owners and renters). Forty-five percent of these moves happen during the summer, according to the American Movers Conference (AMC), the interstate moving industry's national trade association, which represents some 1,200 moving companies worldwide. (It just *seems* as though everyone is moving on the same day as you are.) These pamphlets can help you plan a successful move:

There are dozens of details to think about when you move, even if your new house is across town. It pays to plan and be organized. Several free, or inexpensive (about 50 cents to $1 each), consumer publications about moving are available.

- *Guide to a Satisfying Move* and *Moving with Pets and Plants* are published by the American Movers Conference. Log on to Moving.org for more information.

- *Helpful Tips in Planning Your Interstate Move* is published by the Interstate Commerce Commission, as is *When You Move: Your Rights and Responsibilities*. Regulated household-goods movers are required to furnish a copy of *When You Move* to prospective customers. You can find links to this information at ThinkGlink.com.

Planning Your Move

Here are some things to think about when planning a move:

1. Don't take everything with you. Sort through, throw out, give away, or sell things you don't need anymore. When you've gotten to the bare minimum, start packing.

2. Save those old newspapers. As soon as you get your mortgage, start saving your old newspapers for wrapping delicate objects like china and glassware. You may want to double- or triple-wrap each piece, so stack away about three times as much newspaper as you think you'll need. If you don't want to rewash the plates after you move, buy packages of plain newsprint or tissue paper for the initial wrap and then put newsprint over that. Or you can buy an extra-large size plastic wrap and do the initial wrap in that, followed by newsprint.

3. The interim move. Will your new home be ready on time? Do you need an interim move? Will you be storing your furniture? If you're moving across state lines, it's best to store your belongings near your new home, not your old one. That way, if you need something, you should be able to get it quickly and easily.

4. Schedule repair or renovation work ahead of time. If you need repair, decorating, or renovation work done on your new house, and have the extra float time, get busy scheduling the work four to six weeks before you move. If you're planning to paint or decorate, you may want to have that work done before you've unpacked most things and settled into your new home.

5. Get your new utility accounts. Three weeks before the move, you'll want to contact your local utility companies (telephone, electricity, cable, gas, water) and inform them of your move. Arrange to have these services cut off at the end of moving day (if you're moving in the afternoon, it would be nice to be able to drink water and use the bathroom, not to mention the telephone). Don't forget to arrange the hookup of utilities to your new home.

6. Reserve the elevators. If you're moving to a condominium or a co-op, you'll need to schedule your move-in day with the building's management. Generally, large condos (those with an elevator) require you to "reserve" the freight elevator for your move. Do this way ahead of time, or the day on which you'd like to move may already be booked. There may even be a fee for having the building maintenance workers "oversee" your move. Ask your new building personnel about moving-in rules, and don't be surprised if you're asked to pay for the privilege.

7. Discontinue delivery services. Two weeks before your move, set a date to discontinue your delivery services for newspapers, milk, dry cleaning, or laundry. If you're moving to a new state, your broker may be able to offer a little advice on employing these services in your new town.

8. Change-of-address cards. About two weeks before your move, fill out and mail your change-of-address cards. Your local post office can give you some cards to fill out, or you may want to have change-of-address cards preprinted. If you receive Federal Express or UPS packages for your home-based business, you'll want to inform these companies of your change of address as well.

9. Moving with pets. If you're moving with pets, you may need to take some special precautions, according to the AMC. Pets cannot be shipped on moving vans. They should travel with you and wear special identification tags with your name, address, telephone number, and the name of an alternative relative in case you can't be located. If you decide to ship your pet by air, make the arrangements ahead of time. If you move across state lines, nearly every state has laws on the entry of animals. Write to the State Veterinarian, State Department of Animal Husbandry, or other state agency for information. Most states require up-to-date rabies shots for dogs and cats. If you're moving to Hawaii with your pet, you'll have to quarantine the animal for 120 days. Some pets must have an entry permit issued by the destination state's regulatory agency. Finally, your new town (or condo or co-op) may have restrictions on the number of dogs or cats that can live at one residence. If this might be a problem for you, check with your new city or village council.

10. Moving with plants. You generally won't have a problem if you're moving houseplants, but some states do require you to have them inspected by an authorized state department of agriculture inspector. Plants are susceptible to shock when moving, and it may be dangerous to move a plant if the temperature is below 35°F or above 95°F to 100°F for more than an hour. The AMC says plants can tolerate darkness for up to a week, but it's best not to store them. Cuttings of your favorite houseplants, while convenient, will not last as long or as well as potted plants.

Finding the Moving Company

As many as eight weeks before moving day, you'll probably need to find a moving company. Shop around and compare prices. Try to use a licensed, insured, and bonded mover. Be careful of overcharges, and if you're moving across state lines, find out how much the company charges per mile. It's better to get a flat fee, if that's possible.

Movers are required to prepare an *order for service* for each customer. Keep a copy of this document, as it shows the terms of the initial agreement with the mover. Next, the mover must issue a *bill of lading*, which is the legal contract between the customer and the mover. It is very important, so keep it handy during the move. The Interstate Commerce Commission warns "not to sign the bill of lading until comparing it with the order of service to be sure that all services ordered are correctly shown."

Rogue movers are fly-by-night operators who use the Internet and the local Yellow Pages to reel in their next victim. Beware using any mover who you have not checked out at movingscam.org or the Better Business Bureau (bbbonline.org). Just checking with those two websites can help you avoid some serious problems, including having your goods held "hostage" until you pay the mover the "ransom." For details and more websites, go to thinkglink.com and type "moving" into the search browser.

A *binding estimate* requires the mover to bill only at the price agreed to for the specific services needed. If you make any changes or increase the amount that is being moved, it may void the estimate, which should be in writing and attached to the bill of lading. With a binding estimate, you must pay the mover with cash, a certified check, or a money order, unless you have prearranged to use a credit card. In a *nonbinding estimate*, the final price for the move will not be known until everything has been weighed and transportation charges have been calculated. In advance of the move, request a copy of the mover's policy on inconvenience or delay (in case the truckers get lost).

Make sure you and the mover understand when your household furniture is supposed to be picked up and when it is supposed to be delivered. Do not accept a promise like, "We'll be there as soon as possible." Get definitive dates, and make sure they are in writing. If the mover cannot meet the pickup or delivery dates, he or she is required to notify you by telephone or telegram or in writing. If you're going across country, be sure to ask the mover to notify you of the charges for the move.

If you have a large or complicated move, it's best to purchase some additional insurance over and above the minimum tagged for your order. Also, invite the mover to inspect the contents of your house. The mover's representative should know how long the move will take, what it will cost, and how big a truck you'll need. You can also negotiate the price of the move with the mover. Ask them, for example, to throw in the wardrobes (large boxes in which you hang your hanging clothes instead of folding and packing them) for free. You'll also want to purchase your own packing tape for 50 cents a roll instead of using the mover's tape at $2 per roll. (You won't believe how many rolls your movers will go through, even if you already have everything all boxed up.) If possible, hand-carry all valuables like cash and jewelry. If you have delicate objects, such as artwork, glasswork, china, or crystal, the movers may not insure it unless they pack it themselves (which is an additional charge). Finally, know where each box should be placed in your new home. The movers can put everything in the basement, but the unpacking will go a heck of a lot more quickly if they put each box in the room in which it is needed.

Licensed movers are responsible for loss or damage to your property. You should have a list of all the items being moved. Number your boxes, and make a list of the contents of each box. Label them clearly with your name and new address and telephone number. You and the mover should agree about the contents being shipped, and make sure the inventory list reflects your mutual understanding. At the time of delivery, note any items that are damaged or missing, and ask the mover for a liability claims form. Finally, you and the mover should agree on the amount of liability the mover will assume for loss or damage to your property.

The mover's liability is limited to 60 cents per pound, so it's wise to add extra insurance if your goods are particularly valuable. The mover can provide you with added coverage, but be sure you understand what's protected and for how much. You must declare the value of your goods with the mover before the move. Otherwise, the mover is required to value them at a lump-sum equivalent to $1.25 times the weight of the shipment. So if your goods weigh 4,000 pounds, the mover is only required to value them at $5,000. Check with your homeowner's or renter's policy to see what other sort of coverage you may have for your move.

12

Happily Ever After

You'd like to think that you'll live happily ever after in your new home. But that's not always the case. Here is some information on what to do if something should prove amiss with your home after you close and move in, and on how to lower your property tax bill. Finally, I've added a few thoughts on how to recognize when it might be time to sell your home and buy another.

Discovering Problems After You Close

The first thing to consider is the problem itself. What happened? Did the boiler blow up? Is a pipe burst? Did the electrical system catch on fire? Is there asbestos in the home? Did you fall through the floor? Did the roof leak? Did the dishwasher break? Did the ceiling paint crack? Is something missing in your new home?

Martha recently bought a home in Washington. She wrote into the contract that the wood-burning stove was supposed to stay in the house. When she moved in, she found the stove was gone. The seller offered her $100, but when she priced out the stove, she found it would cost her $1,200 to replace it. When the seller refused to pay what Martha felt was fair compensation, she sued the seller.

If you've bought a brand-new home, I think you have a right to believe everything will work beautifully for a long time. But if something goes wrong, you'll be happy if your attorney negotiated for a new homeowner's warranty, which covers various items in the home for different periods of time. For example, if your new dishwasher breaks within the first year, the warranty will cover that. If the roof leaks in five years, it may cover that, too.

If you've bought an older or used home, you have to realize some things are going to break. Other items may work, but not well. Each home is different. Each building has its own rhythms. If something goes wrong, you'll have to fix it, unless your seller or the seller broker purchased a homeowner's warranty plan for your older home. (If you live in California, more than 85 percent of the homes are sold with a home warranty plan.) If you have a warranty, then you'll be able to have your problem fixed (for the first year), and all you'll be responsible for is the deductible.

The next question you have to ask is: Did the seller or seller broker know about the problem and simply "forgot" to tell you about it? Or is it possible they simply didn't know there was a problem? Is it a case of puffery, where the broker may have said, "This house is perfect! You'll love it."

Common sense should tell you that when the broker says, "This house is perfect," he or she doesn't mean everything in the home is in perfect working order. (Or maybe that is what they meant, but you'd be foolish to take that claim seriously.) But if the seller and the seller broker told you the furnace was new and a week after moving into the home you discover it's old, covered with asbestos, and just had a paint job, that could be a problem. If you were told the house was freshly painted, and you find out it wasn't, that could be a problem. If you were told the house's roof did not leak, and a day after the first rain your living room looks like a swimming pool, that could be a problem.

Disclosure laws vary from state to state, but most sellers are required to tell you about "known, material defects" that could affect the value of the home. (I put "known, material defects" in quotes because, typically, the legal standard you need to prove is that the seller knew there were material, or serious, defects in the property that were not disclosed to you.) In some states, homeowners have successfully sued their sellers for not disclosing that someone was murdered in their home, or a former owner died of AIDS. In some states, not disclosing that your house is haunted could be a real problem for the seller. (Nope, I'm not making that up.)

The bottom line is, if you feel you've been wronged, or lied to, in the purchase of your new home, you'll need to consult an attorney to learn about the legal rights and remedies you have in your state.

But if you have outsized expectations that everything will work perfectly in your home forever, you're setting yourself up for a series of disappointments that may erode your enjoyment of your new home.

How to Lighten Your Property Tax Load

As a new homeowner, you've probably realized that real estate taxes are about as inevitable as death. You'll eventually get to the end of your mortgage payments, but you'll pay property taxes as long as you own the house.

The good news is, you can do a few things to keep your property taxes as low as possible. According to tax professionals, county and township governments often make loads of mistakes when assessing property. The nonprofit National Taxpayers Union (NTU), a taxpayers' advocacy group based in Washington, DC, indicates that approximately 60 percent of all homeowners are overassessed; in other words, in every group of 100 angry taxpayers who think their taxes are too high, 60 are overpaying. Of those, says the NTU, only 2 percent appeal their real estate taxes. But, of the 2 percent who do appeal, *50 to 80 percent* (the figures vary based on the source) receive some reduction in their property taxes. Those are good odds.

(More recent studies seem to indicate that more people are filing appeals of their tax assessments. The anecdotal evidence appears to prove this true: In 1999, property tax bills in Cook County were delayed by several weeks because so many homeowners filed appeals. In 2004, as this book went to press, property taxes in Illinois were considered so outrageous that the state legislature passed a property tax cap. It remains to be seen which homeowners are actually helped by the tax cap.)

Appealing your property taxes is not a difficult process, but it does require a bit of ingenuity, perseverance, and organization. And the reward—a lower tax bill—is eminently worthwhile.

How worthwhile? That depends on each house. Jim Siudut, an accountant and real estate tax specialist who has produced a video called "Fight Higher Real Estate Taxes and Win," says he saved himself $1,500 in one year. The next year he saved himself an even greater amount because the rise in his property taxes was keyed to a lower assessed valuation. (See the glossary at the end of this section for definitions of relevant tax terms.)

The key to a successful reduction of your property taxes is solid evidence, presented clearly and concisely. Siudut says all homeowners should make sure they're being correctly assessed, especially if their property taxes are high or if they have received steep increases in the last few years.

The time to appeal is when you get your assessment notice—not your tax bill. Not acting in time is the biggest mistake homeowners make when appealing their property taxes.

The assessment notice details your home's current and past assessed valuation and its current estimated market value. It should also list your property's physical characteristics. In other words, if you have four bedrooms and two bathrooms and an attached two-car garage, the notice should say that.

The estimated market value is the price the assessor's office attaches to your property based on surveys and studies of neighboring properties. The assessment is a percentage (usually set by law) of the estimated market value.

It's important to remember that once you receive your assessment notice, you have a limited time to file an appeal—usually 30 to 60 days, depending on the county. If you are not satisfied with your judgment, you may appeal all the way up to your state's supreme court.

In North Carolina, for example, any taxpayer dissatisfied with the assessment made by the county assessor should arrange immediately for an informal meeting with the assessor to explain why he or she thinks the assessment is excessive. If a satisfactory conclusion cannot be reached, the taxpayer can file an appeal with the County Board of Equalization and Review (Board of County Commissioners) and request a hearing. A taxpayer dissatisfied with the decision of the county board may file an appeal with the State Property Tax Commission within 30 days of the mailing of the decision by the county board. That decision may be appealed to the court of appeals and ultimately the North Carolina Supreme Court.

To effectively appeal your assessment, you'll need the current and the prior year's tax bills (for new homeowners, this should be available at your local tax assessor's office), the current assessment notice, the current property survey, the purchase contract or closing statements (if you purchased your home within the last five years), a copy of any building plans, and an itemized account of expenses (for any improvements made to the property), and any recent appraisals.

To analyze your assessment, you'll need the following data: your property record card, a list of comparable homes ("comps"), and their property record cards, sale dates, and prices. Experts recommend that you check with a local real estate agent or broker for some of this information. Agents and brokers should be happy to oblige because it's a good opportunity for them to market their services to potential customers.

The first step is to go to your county assessor's office and take a look at your property record card. Identify it by matching the parcel number or permanent real estate index number with the number on your tax bill. The card lists the physical characteristics of your property, including the number of bedrooms, bathrooms, and fireplaces; garage size; square footage; and lot size.

Many overassessments result from factual errors. That is, the assessor's office may say that your house has four bedrooms when it actually has only three. So check the facts. Factual errors are the easiest to document and to appeal. If you do find a factual error, you'll need either blueprints or a property survey to "prove" your claim. Your evidence should include recent color photographs of the inside and outside of your house. Or you can also ask the assessor's office to come out and reexamine your house.

In addition to factual errors, Siudut uses four tests to determine whether property has been overassessed: (1) an assessment ratio test, (2) an equity test, (3) a market test, and (4) an environmental factors test. Gary Whalen, a real estate broker and tax consultant who has written a book called *Digging for Gold in Your Own Backyard: The Complete Homeowner's Guide to Lowering Your Real Estate Taxes*, refers to property overassessments due to factors other than factual errors as "judgmental errors."

Assessment Ratio Test

"In any county, the assessment is based on the home's market value. The assessment ratio is a percentage of market value. What you want to do is determine whether or not your assessment ratio is in line with that of comparable homes in your neighborhood," Siudut says.

Gathering comparable data is the most time-consuming part of appealing your property taxes. Siudut and Whalen recommend that you check for properties that have sold within the last two years and are similar to yours in size and amenities. Armed with the exact addresses of these comps, ask the assessor's office for the properties' record cards. Compare the assessed valuation of each comp with its sale price to see whether the assessor comes close in determining the correct market value. Did the homes sell for less money than their market value? What percentage did the assessor use to determine the assessed valuation (before the multiplier was applied)? Compare this with the percentage used on your property.

Experts say homeowners' biggest misconception is that they think they can use only market value as a basis. The key test to fairness is uniformity, not market value.

Market and Equity Tests

The law of uniformity also helps homeowners construct appeals based on market and equity tests. Homes in the same neighborhood should be assessed at the same rate, proportionate to their size and amenities.

Siudut's market test compares the assessment per square foot with those of comps in the same neighborhood. To gain an accurate square footage account, measure from your house's exterior walls. Next, find 8 to 10 comps; you should then end up with at least four that have lower assessments per square foot. To find out the assessment per square foot, simply divide the assessed value by the number of square feet in the property.

Like the market test, the equity test compares the value of other homes similar in age and amenities. Again, the idea is to find comps that have been assessed at a lower rate than yours.

Level out the value of the homes by adding and subtracting the value of amenities one house might be missing but another home has. For example, if your house doesn't have a fireplace, but your comps do, subtract $1,500 from your assessed valuation. A local real estate agent can help you determine the appropriate value for each amenity.

Environmental Factors Test

Did the state recently build a nuclear power plant in your backyard? Did the railroad just add a new switching station down the street? Are a large number of people in your neighborhood out of work because a plant closed down? Is a new garbage dump being planned within a couple of miles of your home?

These are environmental factors that could lower your property's market value. (As a new home buyer, you remembered the broker's maxim, "location, location, location," and would never buy a house next to a garbage dump.) If you put these factors to work for you, Siudut says, you might be able to lower your assessment. Document these changes and how they might work against property values in the neighborhood. Use articles and editorials from your local newspapers and include evidence of any television and radio reports. Clip these together to give added weight to your appeal.

Whalen and Siudut recommend combining any errors—both judgmental and factual—to get the biggest reduction.

"If you're organized and present a clear case, it does not substantially increase the assessor's workload," Siudut says. "The more organized and focused you are, the easier you make their job, and the easier it is to get that reduction."

When researching your case, don't be afraid to ask the person behind the desk for help. Homeowners should also apply for all the exceptions to which they're legally entitled: senior citizens, homestead, homestead improvement, disabled, or disabled veterans. The assessor can reduce your equalized assessed valuation anywhere from $2,000 to $50,000, depending on which benefits you're entitled to.

Property Tax Reduction Tools

The best thing you can do is put your case in writing, with photos. Use a camera (here's where that digital camera will prove its use again) to shoot the exteriors of homes that you want to compare with yours. Be sure to get the property address in the photo when you shoot the exterior.

Next, make sure your information is neatly typed under each photo. If you want, use a separate sheet for each house. Bind it neatly together. Your goal is to make the job easy for the person at the assessor's office who is going to help you. The easier it is for him or her to peruse your information, and understand it, the easier it will be for him or her to recommend that your property taxes be reduced.

A Glossary of Tax Terms

Here are a few tax terms you should know.

Assessed Valuation   The value placed on property for tax purposes and used as a basis for division of the tax burden. It's a percentage of the amount that is deemed the home's fair market value.

Assessment Ratio   The percentage of your home's fair market value that an assessor uses to determine the property's assessed valuation. The ratio can vary from county to county.

Notice of Revision   A notice mailed to the property owner after a property has been reassessed.

State Multiplier   Also known as the **state equalization factor,** this is a number the state assigns to each county, depending on the assessment ratio the county uses to calculate assessed valuation, but it is not used in many counties. The multiplier either raises or lowers the assessed valuation to the state-mandated level of 33.33 percent of market value. The multiplier ensures that taxpayers in each of the state's counties pay the same amount proportionately in property taxes.

Tax Rate   The rate at which property is taxed, usually shown per hundred dollars of the property's value.

Uniformity   The legal principle that governs property tax assessments. It states that all property in a given area must be assessed at the same level. That is, you should not be assessed at a higher rate than your next-door neighbor. The principle of uniformity is the basis for many successful assessment appeals.

Special Help for Seniors

Many communities freeze property taxes for seniors who reach a certain age (usually 62 or 65) and have a lower income. Talk to your local county assessor's office or your local village or city hall to find out if your community offers special tax relief for seniors.

The Next House: Knowing When It's Time to Move On

Although you may think you'll live in your first home forever, odds are you'll be looking for another home within five to seven years.

Why do people move? There are dozens of reasons. They may marry, have children, have an aging parent or relative come live with them, change jobs, care for grandchildren, divorce, get sick, or simply decide they want to live somewhere else.

How will *you* know when it's time to move on? You may start to feel cramped, confined, and tight on space. Your house may seem frayed at the edges. Your child may need special services available only in another school district.

Typically, you'll become aware that a subtle dissatisfaction comes over you whenever you walk into your home. If you can't fix the dissatisfaction by remodeling the interior or exterior of your home, adding on, or redoing the landscaping, it might be time to move on.

If that's the case, start creating a new wish list and reality check. Your list may be quite different from the one you compiled when you moved into your home. Creating a new wish list and reality check is the only way to objectively identify what it is you now feel you need and want in a home.

Once you've identified what you want and need, you can go about fixing up your current home to sell. For more information on how to make the most of your sale, check out my books *100 Questions Every Home Seller Should Ask* and *50 Simple Steps You Can Take to Sell Your Home Faster and for More Money in Any Market.*

Feel free to check out my website, thinkglink.com, for news, updates, and further information. And don't forget to sign up for my free weekly newsletter.

APPENDIX I

The Top 10 Mistakes
First-Time Buyers Make

Borrowing a little from one of my favorite performers, David Letterman, I've created a top 10 list of things first-time buyers tend to do when they are searching for a home. Brokers call them "mistakes." These are not egregious errors, but if, for example, timing problems are not worked out or the wrong size home is purchased, these mistakes make the process of home buying a little more time-consuming and heart-wrenching. At worst, they can cause problems down the line, when it comes time to sell the home.

I can't tell you how many times I've heard first-time buyers exclaim "Not me!" when faced with the possibility of having made mistakes. Reading about them in this appendix—presumably after you've read the whole book, but before you've shopped for a home—might help you head 'em off at the pass. You may not see yourself doing everything on this list, but brokers agree that the average first-time buyer makes at least one of the following mistakes.

   1. Incorrectly Timing Your Move. As a first-time buyer, you've probably been renting until now. If so, the best time to close on a house is when your current lease ends. Don't sign another year-long lease if you expect to buy a home before that lease period expires— otherwise you'll end up with a dent in your pocketbook from writing rent and mortgage checks. If you can't time your closing correctly, approach your landlord about a shorter lease—say, three to six months— or, alternatively, a month-to-month lease. Another option is to ask your landlord to include an escape clause in your new lease that will allow you to get out of your lease with 30 or 60 days' notice.

2. Looking at Homes You Can't Afford. First-time buyers often hear that they can buy a home up to two and a half times their combined income. If interest rates stay in the 6 to 7 percent range, you might actually be able to push that number to three or three and a half times your combined income. If they fall below 6 percent, as they did in 2002–2003, you may be able to push that to three and a half to four times your combined gross annual income. Still, you have to factor in your debts, property taxes, insurance premiums, private mortgage insurance (PMI), and the down payment. If you look at homes you can't afford, you'll get spoiled. When you finally come to your senses and start looking at homes in your price range, they will probably disappoint you. For example, if you've been looking at four-bedroom homes with attached garages in plush suburbs, a three-bedroom home in a so-so neighborhood with street parking is going to seem, well, not quite nice enough. To save yourself the heartache, get prequalified through a local lender. There's no cost or obligation, and the lender will tell you exactly how much house you can afford to buy.

3. Buying the Wrong Size Home. Many first-time buyers, especially those who are single and in their late 20s and early 30s, purchase one-bedroom condominiums. What they don't realize is how likely it is they will meet someone, fall madly in love, and marry. Unless you marry a next-door neighbor who has a condo that can be combined with yours, that one-bedroom, one-bath condo will soon seem too small. For nearly the same price, and possibly even the same location, your dollars might buy a two-bedroom, two-bath condo, which would give you additional flexibility. When you buy property, think about how long you intend to live there. Is this a five-year home? A 10-year home? Or is this the home you intend to die in? The average American family changes residences every five to seven years. If you're in your 20s, anticipate significant changes in your lifestyle within five to seven years. Buy smart by planning for those changes ahead of time.

4. Buying in a Neighborhood You Know Nothing About. Sometimes first-time buyers fall in love with a house in a neighborhood that is inappropriate for them. While shopping for a home, never forget that you'll have to travel through the neighborhood to get to and from your home. Is it a nice neighborhood? Is there graffiti on every wall? Are there gangs? Is there a neighborhood crime watch group? Are the neighbors your age? Are there families around the same age as yours? Is it a transient neighborhood, or do families stay there forever? To avoid making this mistake, spend a lot of time in the neighborhood before you buy. Drive to and from the house. Sit in your car and watch your future neighbors come home from work. Listen to how loudly their children play their favorite rock music. Walk to the local bar, restaurant, grocery store, and cleaners. Think about whether you'll be as happy in this neighborhood as you might be in the house.

5. Operating on a First-House-Is-Best Theory. Coming from a cramped, one-bedroom rental, almost any home will look good. Try to avoid jumping at the first home you see. Look at 5, 10, or even 20 houses to see what's on the market within your spending range. Season your eyes by inspecting different types of homes: condos, town houses, duplexes, and single-family houses. When you've narrowed down your choices to three or four, visit them again. By this time, some form of objectivity should have returned, and you'll be able to make a sensible choice. Completely impulsive decisions do not usually work out, and you could wind up paying dearly for your impulsiveness.

6. Buying a Property That's Difficult to Resell. Although you say you don't mind that the house backs up to the local railroad, you will when it comes time to sell the home. It's unlikely you'll be able to easily convince another buyer just how quiet and peaceful life is there. When buying a home, try not to buy one that will be difficult to resell because even though you think you'll be there forever, you probably won't. Most first-time buyers sell within five to seven years. *Before you buy a home, think about how difficult it will be to resell the property in the future.* Walk yourself through and point out all the negatives. Say them out loud. Then ask your agent or broker how long it would take him or her to sell it. Keep in mind that homes that are difficult to resell tend to appreciate at a slower rate than homes without significant issues for buyers to overcome.

7. Overextending Your Budget. The lender who prequalifies you for a loan may tell you that you're able to afford a $100,000 home, but keep in mind that buying in that price range may stretch your budget beyond your comfort zone. To avoid feeling pinched, or losing ground financially, it's important to understand how you spend *all* of your money. You may be comfortable spending 35 percent of your take-home pay on rent, or you may prefer to spend less—say, 25 percent. Write down every amount that you spend (down to that last piece of bubble gum) for two months. Can you live without buying your favorite group's latest CD? Would you feel uncomfortable knowing you can go out to dinner only once a month? Or that you must eliminate your yearly vacation, or your children's summer camp or piano lessons? As a homeowner, you'll have additional expenses besides your mortgage payment. There will be the maintenance and upkeep of the home, plus property taxes. If you live in a condo, you will have assessments. Buying a less expensive home will give you greater peace of mind, allow for savings, and permit a few extras.

8. Being Indecisive. When you're searching for the right house, you should take all the time you need. Don't let your broker bully you into making a decision before you're ready to do it. Ask to see 5, 10, 20, or 50 homes, if you haven't found one you like enough to bid on. Indecisiveness kicks in, however, when you've found a home you would like to live in but you're afraid of making the commitment. First-time buyers often lose two or three homes because they can't bring themselves to actually make an offer. Or they might find two wonderful properties and face a tough choice. If you're afraid, admit that fear and conquer it by talking with your broker. You're not the only first-time buyer who has had trouble making up his or her mind.

9. Choosing the Wrong Mortgage. Many first-time buyers have heard from their parents that the only mortgage to get is a 30-year fixed-interest-rate loan. That's because the generation ahead of you didn't have the tailor-made financial options buyers have today. Consider choosing an adjustable-rate mortgage (ARM) to take advantage of super-low interest rates. Or pick a 10- or 15-year fixed-interest-rate loan to maximize your mortgage interest deduction *and* save you hundreds of thousands of dollars in interest. You might want to look into a two-step mortgage, which combines a little of the risk of an ARM with the dependability of a fixed-rate loan. Explore all the options. Have your lender show you on paper how much each option will cost and how they compare with one another.

10. Underinsuring the Property. First-time buyers know they have to buy home insurance to cover their mortgage. Sometimes they forget to increase the coverage of that insurance as the neighborhood improves and the home appreciates in value. Sometimes they forget to insure the contents of the house. Think about how much it would cost you to replace your furniture, clothing, books, CDs, artwork, and pots and pans. Add up everything and then tack on the cost of actually re-building the home (a single family or town house) if it were to burn to the ground. Add on your mortgage, which would still have to be paid. That's how much insurance you should buy.